WALLACE W. ABBEY

RAILROADS PAST & PRESENT

GEORGE M. SMERK & H. ROGER GRANT, EDITORS

INDIANA UNIVERSITY PRESS

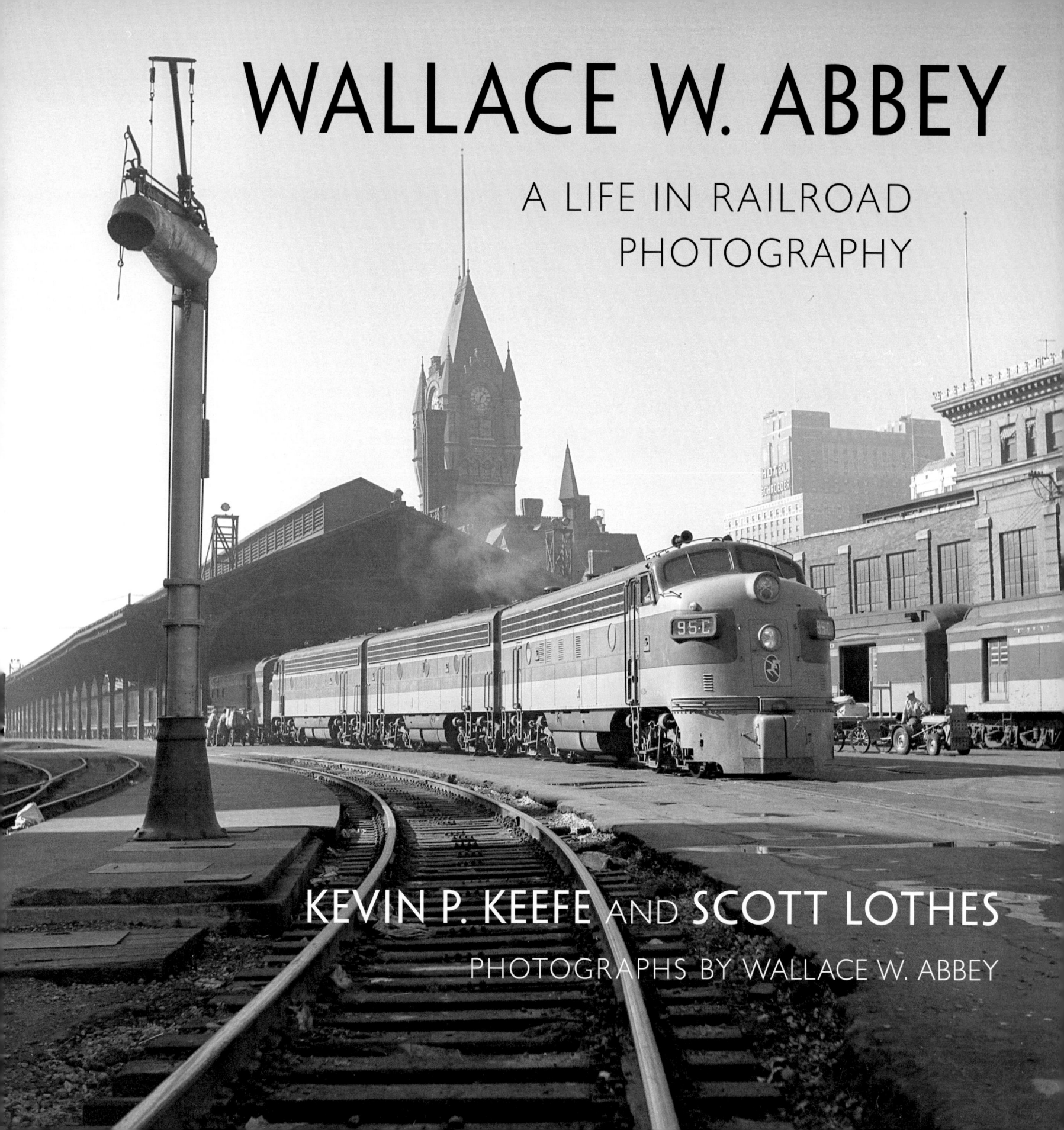

This book is a publication of

Indiana University Press
Office of Scholarly Publishing
Herman B Wells Library 350
1320 East 10th Street
Bloomington, Indiana 47405 USA

iupress.indiana.edu

© 2018 by Center for Railroad Photography and Art

All rights reserved

No part of this book may be reproduced or utilized in any form or by any means, electronic or mechanical, including photocopying and recording, or by any information storage and retrieval system, without permission in writing from the publisher.

The paper used in this publication meets the minimum requirements of the American National Standard for Information Sciences—Permanence of Paper for Printed Library Materials, ANSI Z39.48–1992.

Manufactured in the United States of America

Cataloging information is available from the Library of Congress.

978-0-253-03224-9 (cloth)
978-0-253-03225-6 (ebook)

1 2 3 4 5   23 22 21 20 19 18

Contents

Introduction 3

1 Along the Santa Fe 33

2 The *Trains* Magazine Years 63

3 Soo Line Storyteller 95

4 Chicago at Its Zenith 127

5 Class by Itself 157

6 Fighting for the Milwaukee Road 171

Epilogue 201

Acknowledgments 203

Index 207

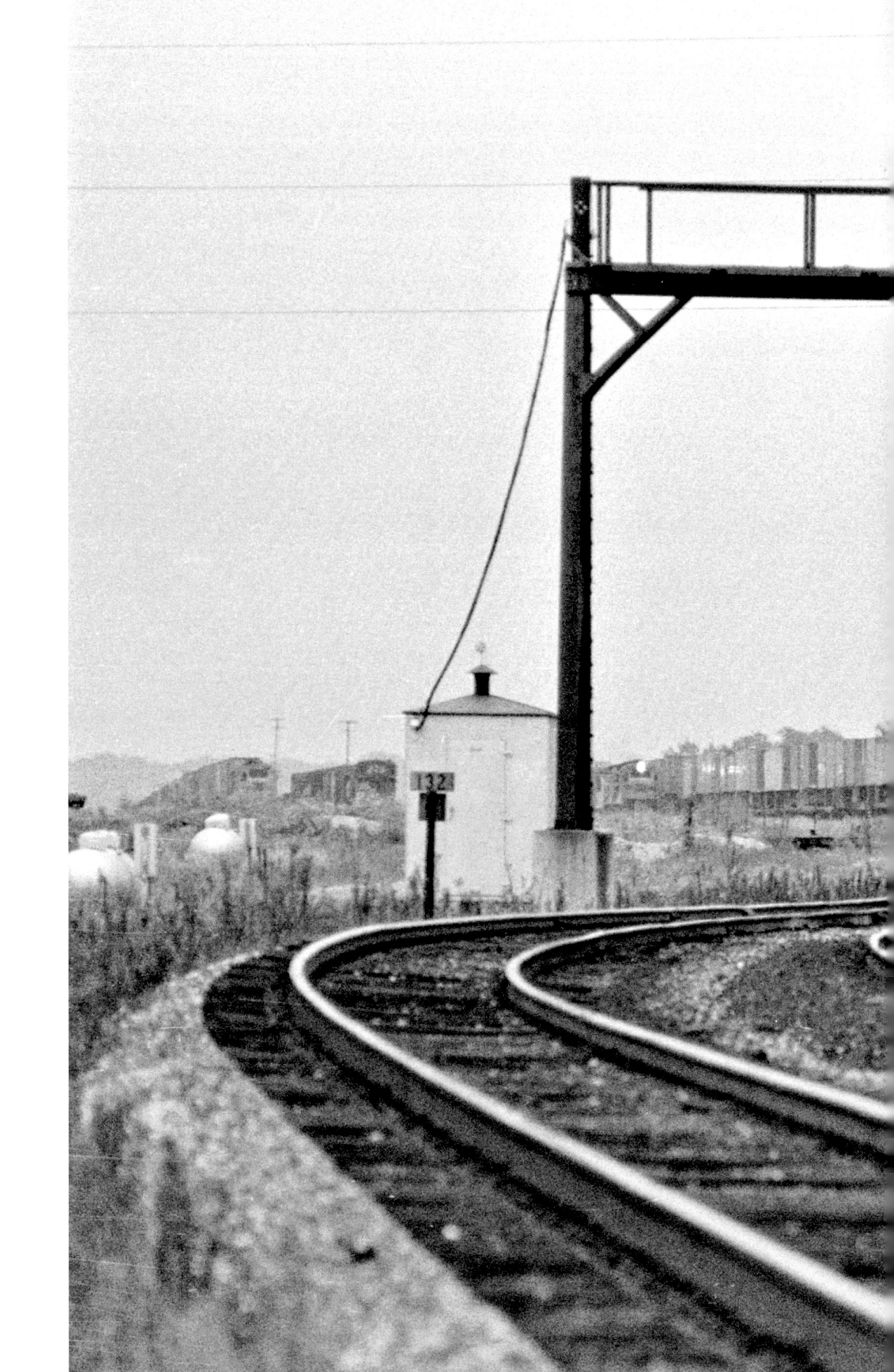

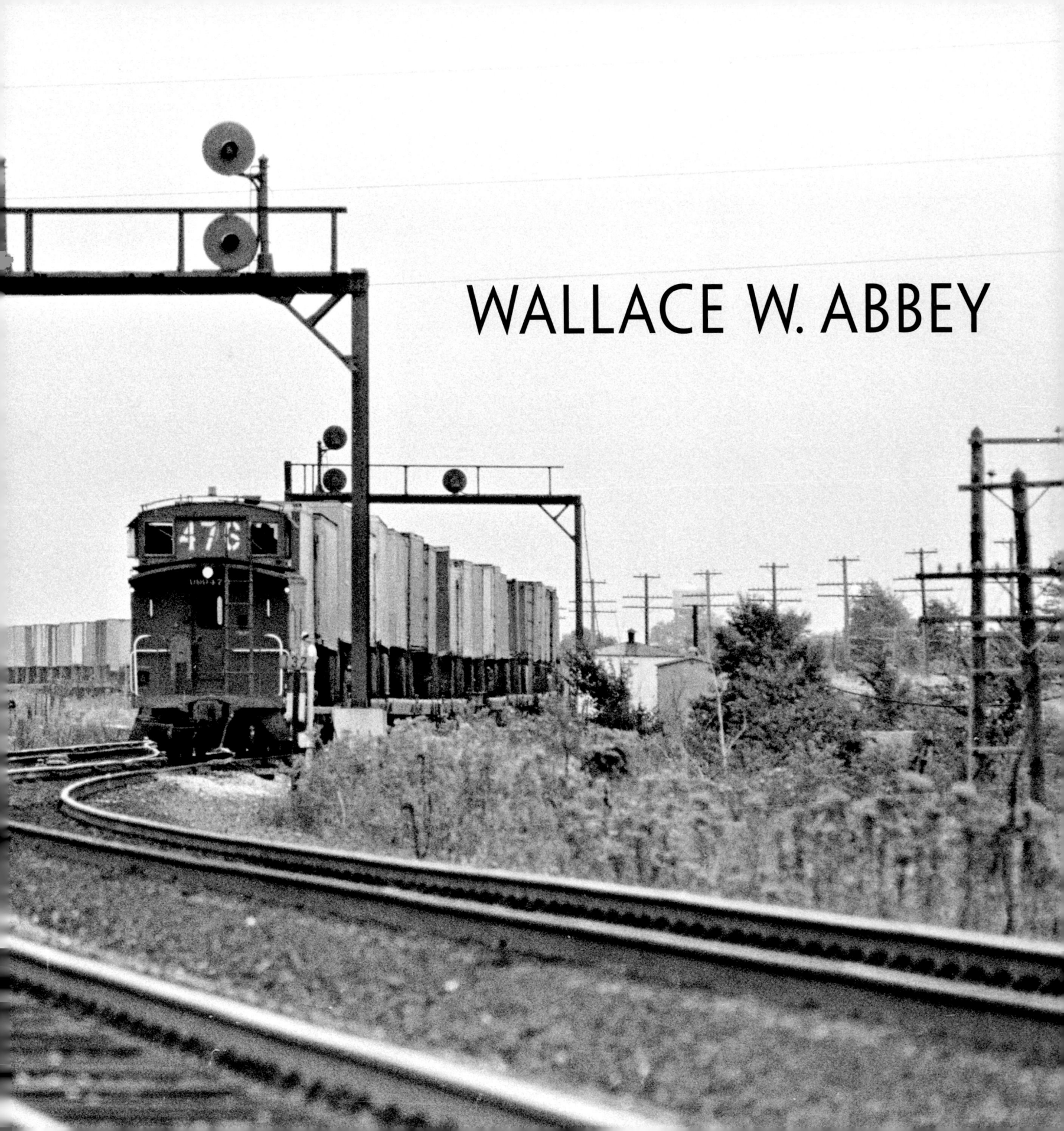
WALLACE W. ABBEY

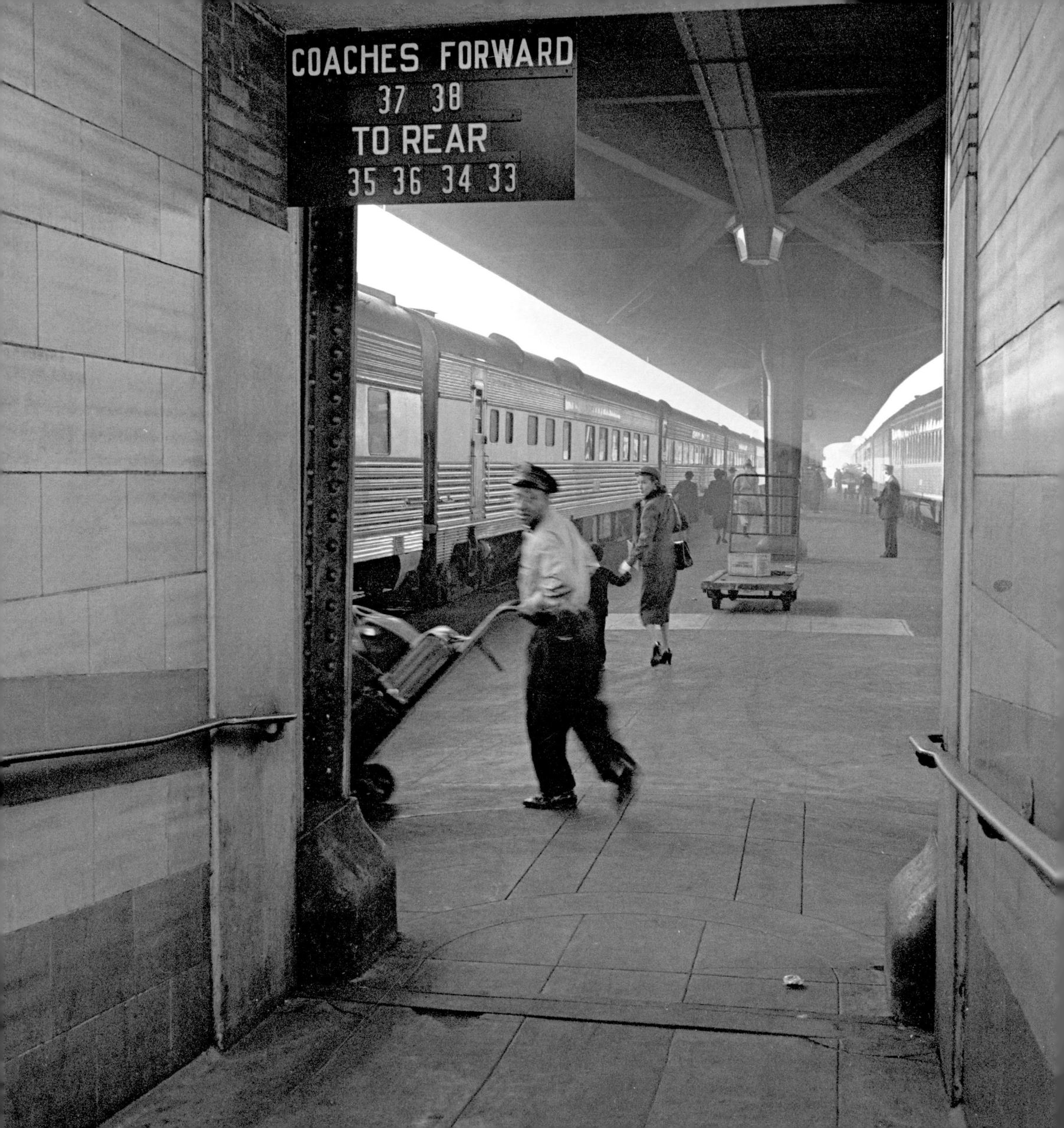

INTRODUCTION

THE IMAGE IS AT ONCE PROSAIC AND DEEPLY MYSTERIOUS. THE photographer has placed you in the portal of a doorway leading to the Track 4 platform at Cincinnati Union Terminal. Before you is a scene of urgency and commotion. Passengers scramble to board the westbound *James Whitcomb Riley*, the New York Central's morning streamliner to Chicago, and a redcap hurries with a handcart loaded with suitcases. It is 1952, still the high tide of the American passenger train, and everything you see is commonplace.

And yet, in this tiny moment, the photographer has created something magical. Light shimmers over the top of the train, almost blindingly, overexposed in order to bring out detail in the foreground, a ghostly proscenium arch for the stage below. The redcap appears to glance at the photographer, but only for an instant, his uniformed body creating a slight blur. Just beyond him, an elegantly dressed woman also turns to the camera, almost hauntingly.

The image is a masterpiece, and just one of tens of thousands created by Wallace W. Abbey III, an influential force in the world of railroad photography. From the late 1940s onward, Wally Abbey created a body of work that is a rare combination of journalistic and artistic vision. His success was the product of a diverse career that took him from newspaper newsrooms to magazine editorial offices to the corporate suites of major railroad companies, seasoned with countless experiences in locomotive cabs, cabooses, and junction towers. A camera was with him almost every step of the way.

Viewed through a doorway leading to the Track 4 platform at Cincinnati Union Terminal, a redcap hurries a handcart loaded with suitcases toward New York Central's *James Whitcomb Riley* as passengers hustle to board the Chicago-bound streamliner. Making just a handful of stops en route, the *Riley* had the fastest schedule of NYC's several trains between Cincinnati and Chicago, covering the 300 miles in just five and a half hours. For its strong composition and great human interest, *Trains* magazine selected this photograph among its "100 Greatest Railroad Photos" in 2008.

Abbey's ascendance as a photographer coincided with the rise of the first golden age of railroad photography, a genre driven in part by railroad enthusiast magazines and the emergence of several gifted practitioners. Together they revolutionized a durable old hobby, veering from traditional and often static "train pictures" to deeper, more meaningful portrayals of the entire railroad environment.

In the most fertile period of his photography, the late 1940s through the 1960s, Wally Abbey's work was comparable to that of any of the emerging new talents. His composition was imaginative, sometimes even daring. He had mastered the photographic technology of the moment. He knew railroad operations and technology cold. Most of all, he had the instincts of a skilled journalist, and the necessary reflexes to react.

FROM EVANSTON TO KANSAS

Wally Abbey was born October 30, 1927, in Evanston, a leafy old suburb along Lake Michigan on the north edge of Chicago, and also the home of Northwestern University. His parents were Wallace William Abbey II, a career newspaperman with the *Chicago Tribune*, and Margaret Peal Squier Abbey, herself an occasional editor and writer. The young Wally spent his entire childhood and youth there, graduating from Evanston Township High School in 1945.

Abbey wrote warmly of his Evanston roots, recalling Fourth of July parades, swimming in Lake Michigan ("no further than the nearest sandbar"), Sundays at Northminster Presbyterian Church, and, of course, frequent visits to the Chicago & North Western Railway depot on Davis Street. "By the time I got to high school, I'd developed interests in three areas far removed from more conventional pursuits: certain off-brands of music [Abbey loved old-time country and Western swing], photography, and railroads—particularly railroads."

Abbey's attachment to trains was forged in the 1930s during family trips to Falls City, Nebraska, his father's hometown, and Cherryvale, Kansas, where his mother grew up. In fact, one specific incident when he was four or five was a catalyst. "I'd always been told that when I was a very little child, I disappeared one day while we were visiting in WaKeeney, Kansas, and I was found at the Union Pacific depot." Abbey's frightened parents notwithstanding, he was probably having a fine time.

Although Abbey's father was not especially interested in railroads, trains were a ubiquitous presence in most people's lives, and his father was knowledgeable. "Dad couldn't be called a card-carrying railfan by any means," Abbey recalled, "but I know that I developed some of my interest from him. Almost every summer we used to drive west to Falls City, using U.S. 34 across most of southern Iowa. In those days the highway wandered back and forth across the railroad many times, and each time Dad would say 'Once again we cross the main line of the Burlington!'"

Years later, on a vacation with his grandmother, Abbey rode the Pennsylvania Railroad's *General* to Philadelphia. He was mesmerized to learn about one of the Pennsylvania's great rituals. "I remember the ticket agent making a point of telling me that in the middle of the night, at Paoli, the steam locomotive would be taken off and an electric locomotive put on." Next morning, in the wee hours, Abbey almost certainly raised the window shade on his lower berth to see.

Abbey's most resonant childhood railroad experiences came in Cherryvale, home of his maternal grandparents, Samuel Webner Squier and his wife, Luella Russell Squier. Located in the southeast part of Kansas, Cherryvale sat astride the Tulsa Subdivision of the Atchison, Topeka & Santa Fe, the railroad Abbey later claimed as his favorite. It wasn't Santa Fe's principal main line, but the Tulsa Sub offered plenty of diversions, including two trains Abbey often rode, the *Oil Flyer* and the *Tulsan*.

Abbey's grandfather ran Squier's Drugstore on Main Street and was a scion of the community. The young Abbey enjoyed hanging out in the drugstore, partly because of the soda fountain, partly because the store was only a few hundred feet from the AT&SF tracks. And if the Santa Fe action was slow, there were other trains to see on the St. Louis–San Francisco Railroad's Wichita–Joplin (Missouri) line, which crossed the Santa Fe just a few blocks north of the drugstore. The Frisco was a less glamorous railroad, but its vintage steam locomotives and friendly crews added to Cherryvale's appeal.

It was on one of those trips to Kansas that Abbey passed a station newsstand and encountered *Railroad Magazine*, at the time the only nationally distributed consumer title about railroads. "Up to the moment I didn't know that there was any sort of publication about railroads," Abbey recalled. "But soon I found myself trying to obtain everything I could read." And while photography was not one of *Railroad*'s strong suits, Abbey was impressed to see pictures of trains made simply for their own sake.

As a teenager, Abbey was fortunate to find five like-minded high-school friends. His pals—Chic Kerrigan, Tom Harley, Dave Wallace, Vint Harkness, and Bob McElroy—accompanied him on modest railfan jaunts around Chicago, and Abbey was comforted to discover the hobby needn't be a lone pursuit. He learned from his friends. "If anyone introduced me to what might be called a fan trip, it was Harley and Wallace. They had found that Roosevelt Road in Chicago extended over the track of many railroads and made an excellent point to watch trains from."

THE PULL OF JOURNALISM

The first thing to know about Wally Abbey the photographer is that he was first and foremost a journalist, even if he didn't always describe himself that way. From his first job as a cub reporter on a small-town daily to his last as the public relations director for a major research center, Abbey brought formidable skills as writer, reporter, and historian. These gifts informed his photography.

Abbey came by his interest in journalism honestly. His father, Wallace W. Abbey II, graduated in 1923 from Northwestern's Medill School of Journalism, then moved on to a forty-four-year career with the *Chicago Tribune*. As a sportswriter at the paper, he was credited with coming up with the nickname "Wildcats" for Northwestern's sports teams. The senior Abbey was news editor of the *Tribune* when Wally was born, and by the time he retired in 1966 was assistant managing editor of the entire newsroom.

When it came time for college, Abbey decided against staying in Evanston and instead headed for the University of Kansas and its William Allen White School of Journalism. There he immersed himself in the work of the *University Daily Kansan*, the school's newspaper and the eighth-largest daily in the state. Abbey worked as picture editor, city editor, and, finally, managing editor, supervising the work of fifty student reporters, a telegraph editor, and incoming wire news from United Press.

It was at KU that Abbey met fellow student Martha Jewett, who lived right in Lawrence. The pair hit it off—she was a journalist, too, active on the publishing front at KU, and also a watercolorist—and they were married November 6, 1949, to start a successful sixty-year marriage. Martha's father was Dr. J. M. Jewett, a geologist for the State Geological Survey of Kansas, based at KU, and her mother was Mavis Laizure Jewett. Wally and Martha Abbey went on to have two daughters, Mary, born in 1951, and Martha, in 1954.

After graduating in 1949, Abbey got his first break in time-honored fashion: he went to work for a small-town paper, joining the *Chanute Daily Tribune*. Chanute is 29 miles north of Cherryvale and was a division point on the Santa Fe. At the *Daily Tribune*, Abbey was thrown into all the classic jobs of a rookie reporter, including writing general assignment stories, covering schools and sports, taking news photos, and working in the photo lab.

Then came Abbey's short but all-important tenure at *Trains* magazine, the Milwaukee-based monthly launched in November 1940. By 1945 it was the bible of the faithful. Abbey was hired in 1950 as an associate editor and worked his way up to managing editor by the time he left in December 1953. At *Trains* he joined forces with the soon-to-be-legendary David P. Morgan, who became editor in chief in 1953 and stayed there for thirty-three years. From the perspective of sixty years, it's amazing to ponder that these two giants were on the same staff at the same time.

Their arrival at *Trains* was opportune. It was a critical time for the magazine, as significant numbers of readers were drifting away with the relentless passing of the steam locomotive from the American railroad scene. The onrushing diesel held much less interest, at least at first. Publisher Al Kalmbach even briefly changed the magazine's name to *Trains & Travel* in an effort to gather in a larger audience. It's no exaggeration to say that the future of *Trains* depended on Morgan and Abbey.

Although Abbey was involved in editorial production of all kinds, from editing freelancers' stories to working with the art department to policing deadlines, his most lasting contribution was as a feature writer. The magazine frequently sent him out on the road to write long-form articles, reporting from the front lines of main-line railroading, illustrated with his own photographs. He had a gift for getting the corporate perspective from management, then mixing it with what he learned in the field, often from working railroaders.

Those early feature stories had a lasting influence. They also helped inspire careers. One is that of Fred W. Frailey, former editor of *Kiplinger's Personal Finance* magazine and a longtime contributor to *Trains* as a feature writer and columnist. Frailey also went to KU's journalism school, although you get the feeling he learned more from mentors such as Abbey than he ever did in class. Frailey recalled Abbey in a 2017 interview:

> Before I knew there was a David P. Morgan, I knew there was a Wallace W. Abbey. To me, not yet a teenager, Wally had the world's best job. Every month he would take his notebook and his camera somewhere into America and return with a fascinating feature story. It might be a profile of railroads I'd scarcely heard of, such as the Western Maryland or Litchfield & Madison, or a day in the life of a Baltimore & Ohio train dispatcher in Deshler, Ohio. "Super Railroad!" in the January 1954 issue opened my young eyes to the great empire my grandfather had devoted his entire working life to, the Santa Fe.

A fine stylist himself, Frailey admired Abbey's prose, which was direct, animated, always loaded with telling details. "The tale I returned to time after time was 'Look Out Texas—Here Comes The Comet,' his account of the Katy's crack freight train between St. Louis and Fort Worth. I'll never erase from my mind his description of that trip through Missouri, Kansas, and Oklahoma, of being 'lulled to sleep at some undetermined point in the night' aboard the caboose and being awakened 'with the deftness of a Pullman porter' as the Comet approached Parsons. Wally, you purposed my life with your stories, infecting me with your love of railroads in a manner that could never be cured."

NEVER WITHOUT A CAMERA

Abbey professed that he couldn't remember when he got started in railroad photography, but it was early in life, to be sure. He did recall that as a young child he acquired a small, green fixed-focus camera of unknown manufacturer, probably in the 127 format, which he used to take photographs around the house or on picnics to Harms Woods, a forest preserve near Glenview, not far from Evanston.

By the time Abbey was in high school he was using a 620-format Brownie Bullet camera, which got him started with train pictures. He recalled discussing the Brownie's suitability for railroad photography with Axel Jensen, who ran a photo store in downtown Evanston. Abbey soon made another improvement by acquiring a 35mm Argus camera before moving on to a Kodak 3A in the 122 format, a folding contraption that could manage a maximum 1/100 shutter speed, fast enough for action photography.

Abbey soon traded up again. With the help of his dad, he acquired from the *Tribune* a used 4 × 5 Speed Graphic, the standard news camera of the era. The huge device was ponderous, but its lens was super sharp, and soon young Abbey was lugging it everywhere. He also gradually learned the craft of printing, using a cramped darkroom he cobbled together under the basement stairs of his house. "Time passed, and in due course I could develop film safely and even make nice big prints. I'd taught myself how to select a subject and compose a picture of it."

Once in college, Abbey began taking his camera on jaunts into eastern rural Kansas. He was drawn to Olathe Hill, where the Santa Fe climbed up the valley of Mill Creek to get out of the lowlands of the Kaw Valley. It was a 12.5-mile bottleneck, even with the centralized traffic control put in before World War II, so the action was thick. Double crossovers at Holliday and Olathe allowed trains to operate in either direction on either track, and the resulting choreography appealed to Abbey's love of operations. "Doing some walking to find a likely spot along the track for a photo was a lot more fun than was going to classes," he said.

Abbey's increased devotion to railroad photography was timely. Whether he fully realized it or not, his work paralleled that of numerous other practitioners who were drawn to trackside in the postwar years. Improved highways, better automobiles, and the explosion of roadside culture in the late 1940s had made it easier for railfans to launch railroad safaris. Each month, their work was beginning to show up in *Trains*. The popular regular feature called Photo Section was the place to be.

WITNESS TO HISTORY

Something else was afoot. By the late 1940s, railroads were fully engaged in the historic transition from steam locomotives to diesel, a process that would be completed in merely a decade. It was more than a simple evolution in technology—it was a cultural sea change. Steam railroading was rooted in the American psyche for more than a century, with its romantic notions of brave engineers and steam whistles in the night. Steam had a profound impact on the landscape, with its dependence on a sprawling infrastructure of water tanks, coaling towers, roundhouses, and 100-mile crew districts. Visually and aurally, the steam locomotive was uniquely compelling.

In its place came a technology that was coldly efficient, aided by lessons learned in the mass-production automobile industry. In the railroad enthusiast community, the diesel was sometimes portrayed as an evil invader. But its advantages to the railroad industry were obvious, and an epic battle played itself out on main lines across the country. Division by division, railroad by railroad, the steam locomotive surrendered to the sleek, often colorfully painted invader. The drama was irresistible to photographers.

In the postwar years, the market for serious railroad photography basically came down to *Trains* magazine. Publisher Al Kalmbach was himself a skilled photographer, and in the very first issue had pledged his magazine would have "the unending curiosity of *National Geographic*." In 1947, the magazine's format was enlarged, providing an even bigger showcase for emerging talents. The images were credited to scores of new names, especially the work of three young lions: Philip R. Hastings, Richard Steinheimer, and Jim Shaughnessy.

Abbey was surely paying attention to all this, having moved beyond *Railroad Magazine* to embrace *Trains*. Although he never explicitly credited other photographers with influencing him, his work began to exhibit a deepening insight and maturity. Getting into *Trains* became a goal, and he earned his first credit line in the June 1949 issue, a two-page photo story headlined "Diesel Display on the C&NW," showing action photos of various passenger diesels rolling through his hometown of Evanston.

Abbey's photography exploded onto the scene when he joined the *Trains* staff in 1950 and his advantages as a double threat came to the fore. Not only could he write and report a compelling article, he could illustrate it himself, using the new 120-format f/3.5 Automatic Rolleiflex he acquired via Kalmbach payroll deductions. He had already mastered the basics of photography in college and in Chanute, where the demands of daily newspapering forced him to think on his feet.

Morgan sanctified Abbey's growing reputation in the November 1955 issue, in which the editor set aside an unprecedented fifteen pages for a single favorite photograph from an all-star lineup. The rest of the group included most of the luminaries shaking up readers each month: Hastings, Shaughnessy, and Steinheimer, of course, but also William D. Middleton, James A. LaVake, J. Parker Lamb, Robert Hale, Henry R. Griffiths, H. Reid, Don Sims, and Morgan's art director, Bill Akin.

The introduction to the article was a sort of mission statement for *Trains*' approach to photography. "The circulation and longevity of the magazine have been due in no mean measure to the photographers who've hauled their gear to trackside, there to record the ever-changing mode of the flanged wheel," Morgan wrote. "In a demanding yet specialized field of illustration the standards have been high and the material rewards necessarily meager."

Abbey's contribution was telling. It was the only one in which a train wasn't the central subject. Framed by the vine-covered stucco arch of the Santa Fe depot in Albuquerque, New Mexico, a woman with a suitcase strolls past the gleaming flank of a coach on the *El Capitan*. It's a timeless image of railroading as the average person experienced it. Commenting on the picture, Abbey wrote: "[This] contains something no railroad can be without—and I maintain few railroad photos should be without—the well-known human element."

A full generation after that big appearance in *Trains*, Abbey's work remained influential to yet another new wave of photographers. One of them was Blair Kooistra, a daring shooter who, like Abbey, melded a professional journalism background with

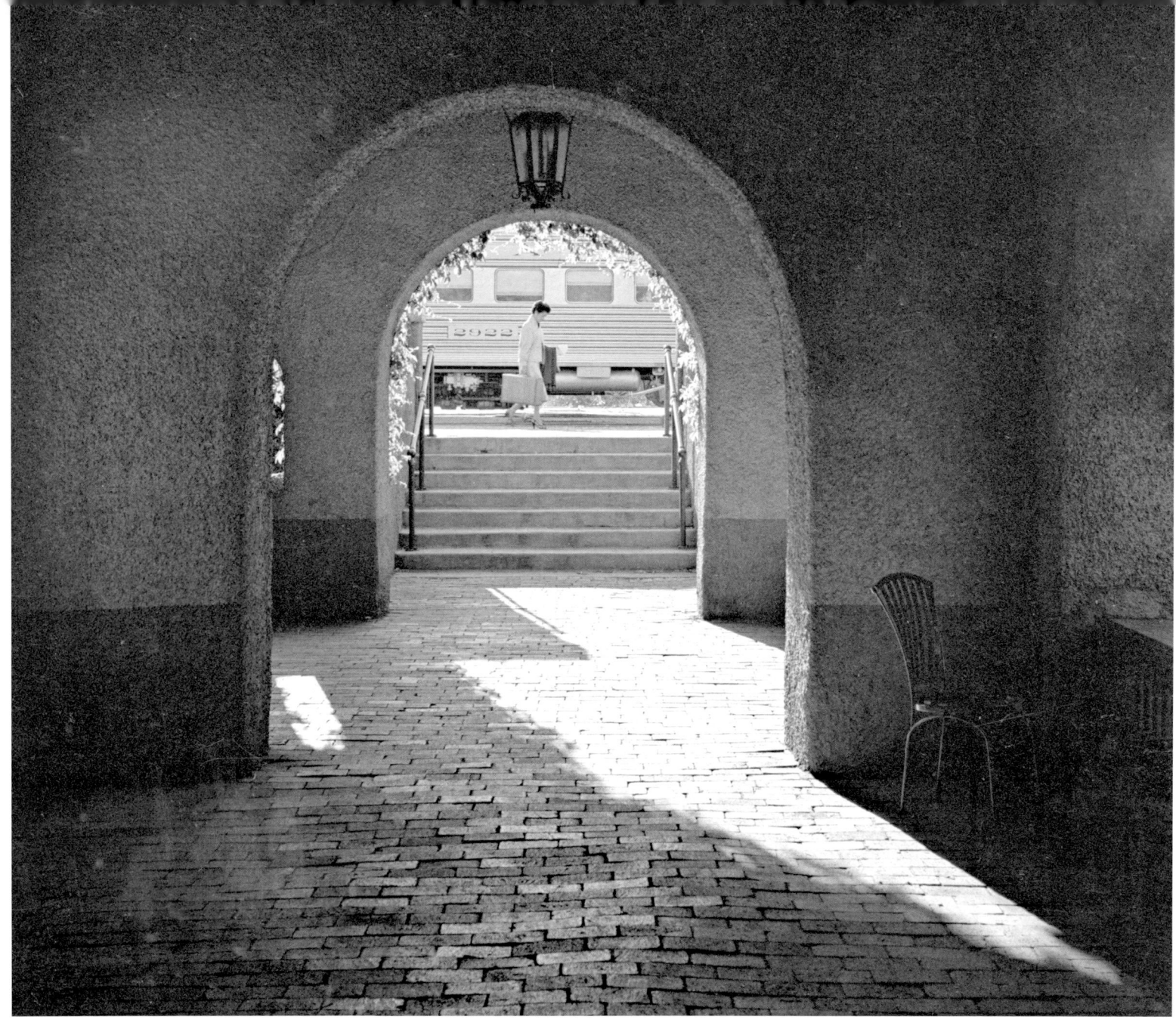

Having just alighted from Santa Fe's *El Capitan* passenger train, a young woman walks past one of the graceful arches of the station at Albuquerque, New Mexico, on January 4, 1953. The station complex included a lunchroom, shops, a museum, and the Alvarado Hotel—among the grandest of the many grand hotels that the Fred Harvey Company operated along the Santa Fe. While some have been preserved, the Alvarado was demolished in 1970. Late in life, when Abbey assembled an album of his twenty-five favorite railroad photographs, he selected this one for its cover.

an artist's sensibility. Kooistra began to make his own big splash in *Trains* in the late 1970s. "Wally was a modern thinker when it came to railroads, evident in his published work," says Kooistra. "This wasn't stodgy of-the-era words and pictures, but progressive, cutting-edge stuff that followed the trends of the big picture magazines like *LIFE*," said Kooistra in a 2017 interview.

PROUD TO BE A RAILROADER

Abbey was an innovative railroad photographer, but he also had an advantage over most of his brethren: among those anointed by Morgan in that 1955 picture salon, Abbey was the lone professional railroader. He knew the business from the inside, courtesy of an astonishingly wide-ranging career.

Abbey's apprenticeship in railroading began in college with a succession of three summer jobs, all in Chicago. In the summer of 1944, he worked as a diesel locomotive repairman's helper at the Santa Fe shop on 21st Street, learning the intricacies of 16-cylinder prime movers and traction motors. The following year he landed a position as a filing clerk in the freight claim department of the Chicago, Burlington & Quincy's general offices at 547 West Jackson, a job he found boring but instructive.

Then came two pivotal summers—1947 and 1948—when he worked as a leverman, or operator, for the Chicago & North Western, working in various towers at important junctions around the northwest side of the city. The key requirement was simple: learn the ins and outs of train operations. It was a difficult challenge, given the dizzying complexities of signal indications and train orders, but it was an aspect of railroading Abbey came to love.

When his stint at *Trains* ended in late 1953, Abbey returned to the industry, first as the assistant to the director of public relations for the Association of Western Railways based in Chicago. For two years, Abbey tackled such issues as labor relations and state and federal regulation. He followed up that job with three years as western editor of *Railway Age*, the industry's dominant trade magazine.

Abbey's work at *Railway Age* led to his next job, and one he treasured. He had covered a complicated grain rate case involving the Soo Line, an upper Midwestern railroad, and one of the company's vice presidents was so impressed he recruited Abbey to become the railroad's director of public relations, a position Abbey held from 1959 to 1970.

At the Soo, Abbey was able to flex all the professional muscles he had acquired so far, improving the company's relationship with the local and national press, upgrading its publications, representing management in countless public meetings and legislative hearings, even taking the lead role in creating the company's bold new paint scheme of 1962. As a photographer, now working in the 35mm format, he also had the resources and access to create a comprehensive visual record of the era, much of it revealed in *The Little Jewel*, a rollicking memoir of his Soo Line years, published in 1984.

In 1970, Abbey launched his own public relations shop in Minneapolis and for a time was quite busy with work for Soo Line; Burlington Northern; and Detroit, Toledo & Ironton; along with such nonrailroad clients as Dayton-Hudson and 3M. He consulted for railroads on the repeal of antiquated "full crew" laws in Wisconsin and Arkansas, and helped make the public case for Chicago's Regional Transportation Authority. But after five years, the rigors of running a one-man show were wearing on him.

Abbey's next job could scarcely have been more challenging. In 1975, the fabled Milwaukee Road was careening toward financial insolvency, a fate it shared with a number of American railroads, aggravated by its own problematic history. Abbey jumped right into the war zone, first as the Milwaukee's director of corporate communications reporting to the president and, after 1977, as right-hand man to a succession of two bankruptcy trustees.

When Abbey first arrived back in Chicago at the Milwaukee Road offices, he confronted a challenge similar to the one he had encountered sixteen years before at the Soo. "They handed me an old, unprofessional operation the roots of which were deep in passenger-train advertising, even though the passenger trains were long gone," he recalled. He did his best to professionalize the office, but soon the company's financial problems overwhelmed everything, crowding Abbey's schedule with trips to House and Senate offices and long hours writing testimony for congressional hearings.

Abbey kept his camera close, notably for a bittersweet inspection trip to the Milwaukee Road's fabled but doomed Pacific Extension. Throughout the chaos, he stayed true to his favorite tenet of good public relations: "If our concern is the reputation of the Milwaukee Road, that reputation is created not in the public relations department but as the sum total of every encounter between and among thinking persons that in any way involves our company."

Abbey left the shuddering Milwaukee Road in 1980, battle-scarred but eager to continue his career. Up next was Chicago-based Trailer Train Company, a leading firm in the intermodal logistics business, known for the use of "piggyback" truck trailers carried on trains. Abbey was the first communications professional in the company's twenty-five-year history. He followed that up in 1982 with a move west to Pueblo, Colorado, site of the Association of American Railroads' Transportation Technology Center, a vast proving ground inherited from the US Department of Transportation. Abbey reveled in this last chapter of his regular career, which included trying new approaches to photographing technology.

After the test center, Abbey embarked on a rewarding retirement. He and Martha remained in Pueblo, and Abbey returned to writing, authoring numerous articles for magazines and historical organizations. He became a regular on the railroad speakers' circuit, delivering speeches and photo presentations with the same brand of wit and candor that distinguished his industry career.

Wallace W. Abbey III died at age eighty-six on January 3, 2014, in Minneapolis, where he had lived with his beloved wife Martha for several years, near their youngest daughter, Mary (Maggie) Abbey. His wife, Martha Abbey, had died on October 10, 2010, at age eighty-four. Together they are interred in the Abbey family plot in lovely Steele Cemetery, on the Nebraska prairie just west of Falls City.

"Ansel Adams I'm not," Abbey once said, a bit too dismissively. Regardless, Abbey came to recognize the lasting value of his archive. He certainly knew that in countless moments he had been in the right place at the right time, making photographs no one else could make, summoning in a fraction of a second all that experience as a railroader and a storyteller.

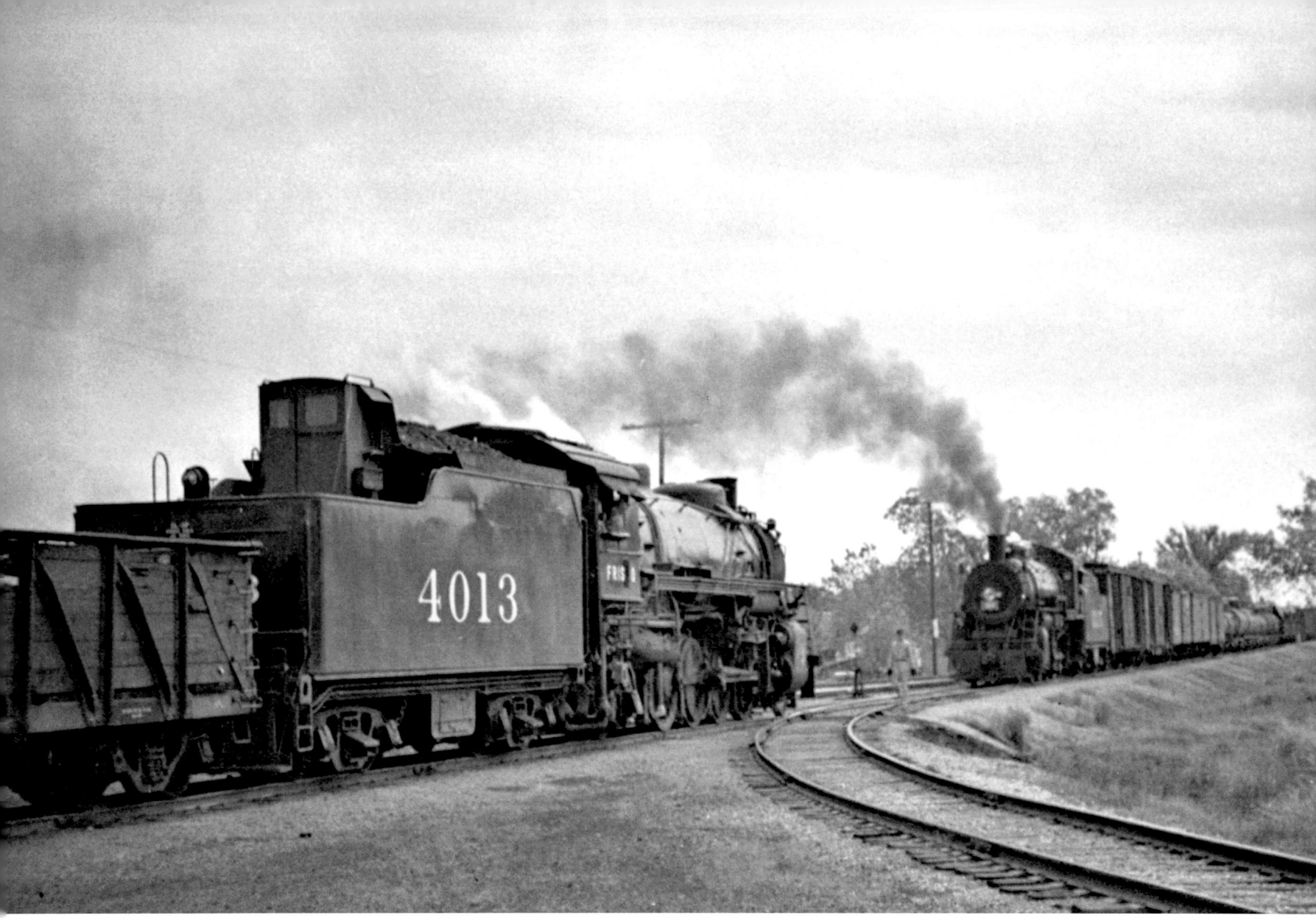

In one of Abbey's earliest railroad photographs, Frisco Lines freight trains meet at Cherryvale, Kansas, in 1940. Located in the southeastern corner of the state, Cherryvale, with a population just above 3,000 at the time, loomed large in Abbey's early photography. His maternal grandparents lived there, and Abbey visited often with his family. Two Frisco routes met and crossed the Santa Fe at the north end of town, a place where Abbey spent many carefree hours of his youth, camera in hand.

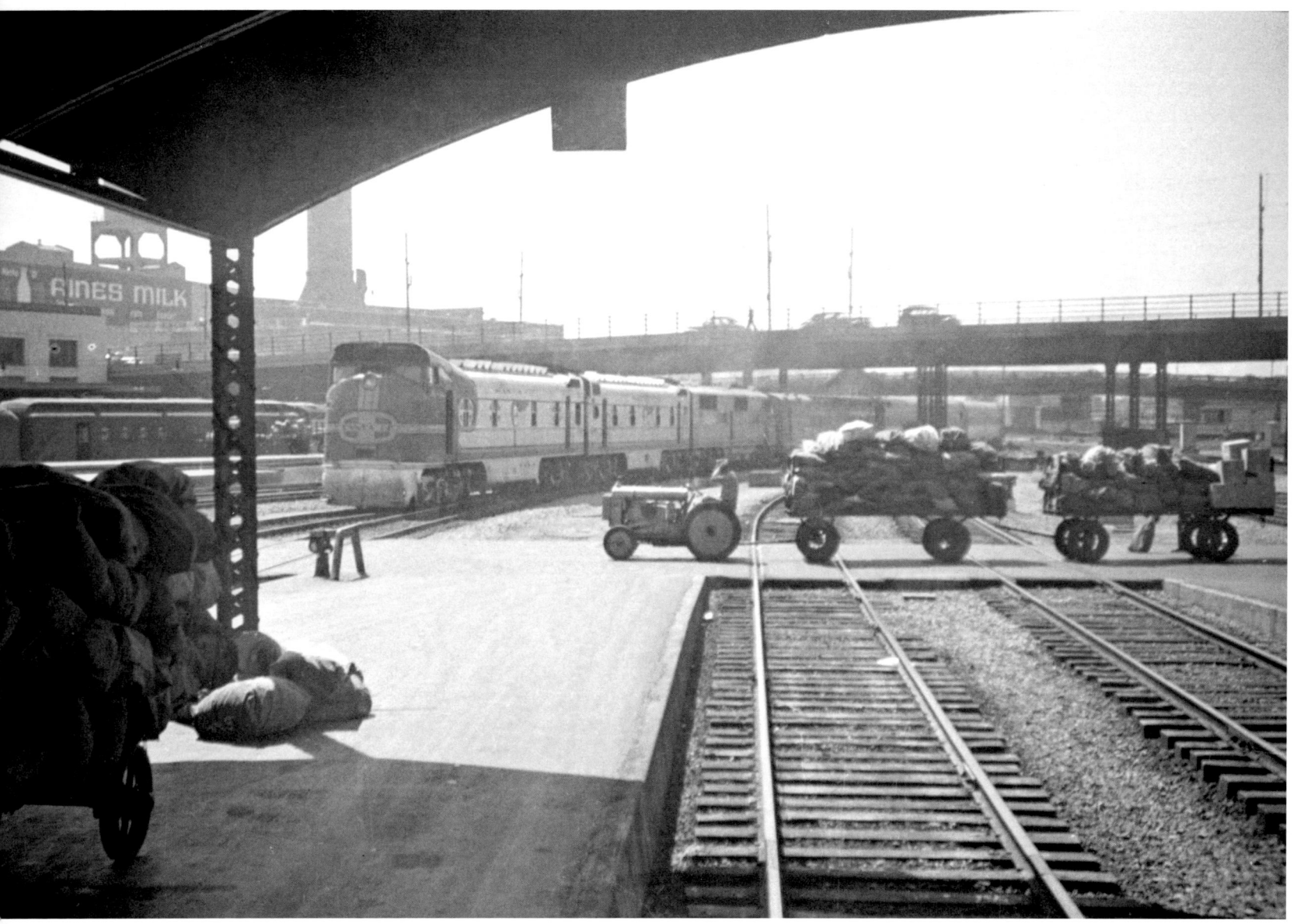

Above: Santa Fe train no. 12, the eastbound *Chicagoan*, arriving at Kansas City Union Station in 1940 as a worker on a tractor pulls two carts of mail onto the platform. Leading the train are unique "boxcab" diesel-electric locomotives nos. 1 and 1A, built by the Electro-Motive Corporation in 1935. Already showing a strong sense for composition, thirteen-year-old Abbey made the photograph from the observation car of train no. 212, the *Tulsan*, which he and his family would have caught that morning in Cherryvale, Kansas. The family was likely continuing to Chicago aboard no. 12.

Facing: Union Pacific 4-12-2 steam locomotive no. 9046 leading an eastbound freight train near Lawrence, Kansas, in 1946. UP was the only railroad in the world to use the 4-12-2 wheel arrangement—it owned a total of eighty-eight, built by the American Locomotive Company between 1926 and 1930. Weighing in at 355 tons each, they were among the most successful 3-cylinder locomotives of all time. While attending journalism school at the University of Kansas in Lawrence, Abbey frequently went out photographing in the surrounding area.

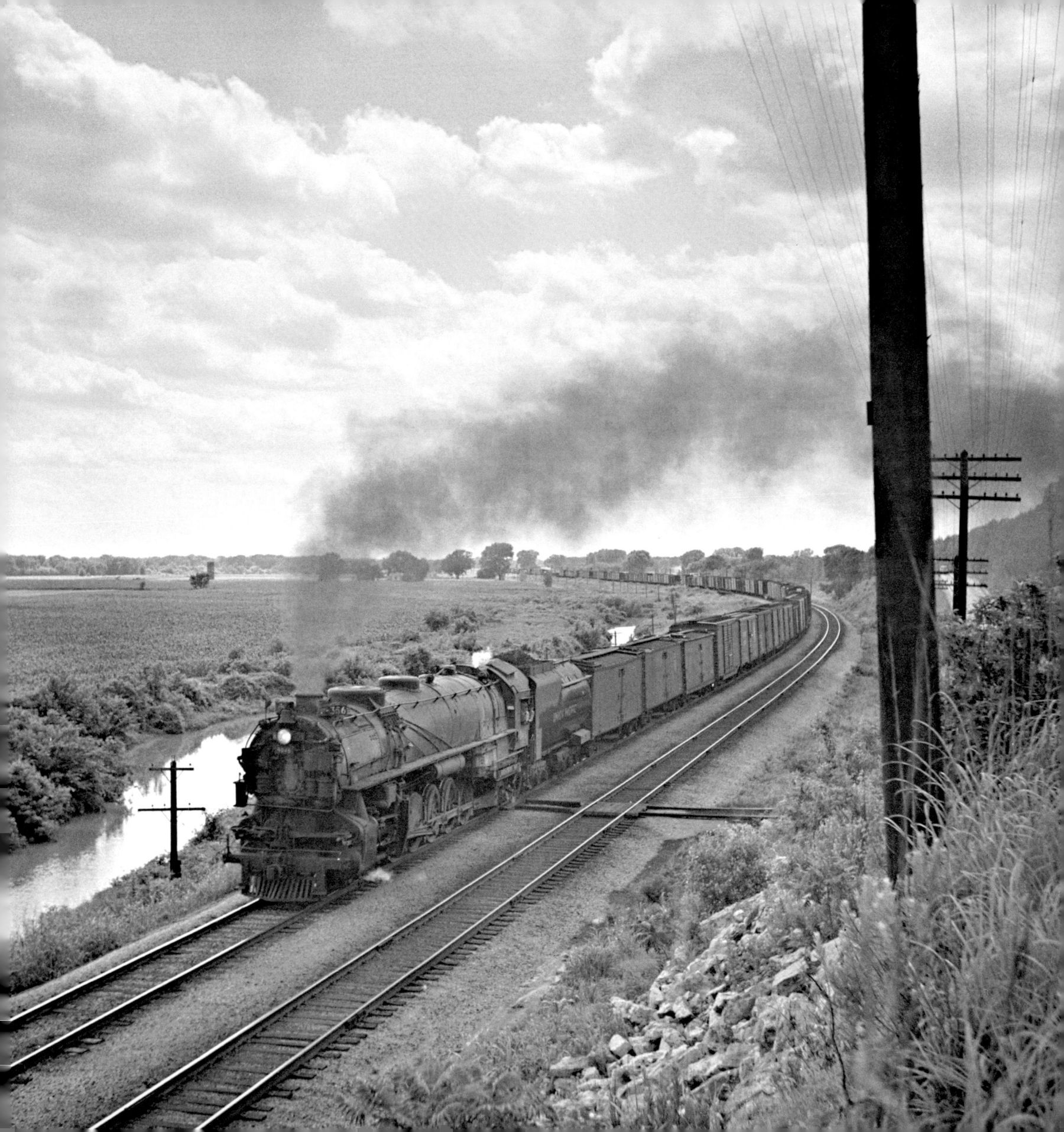

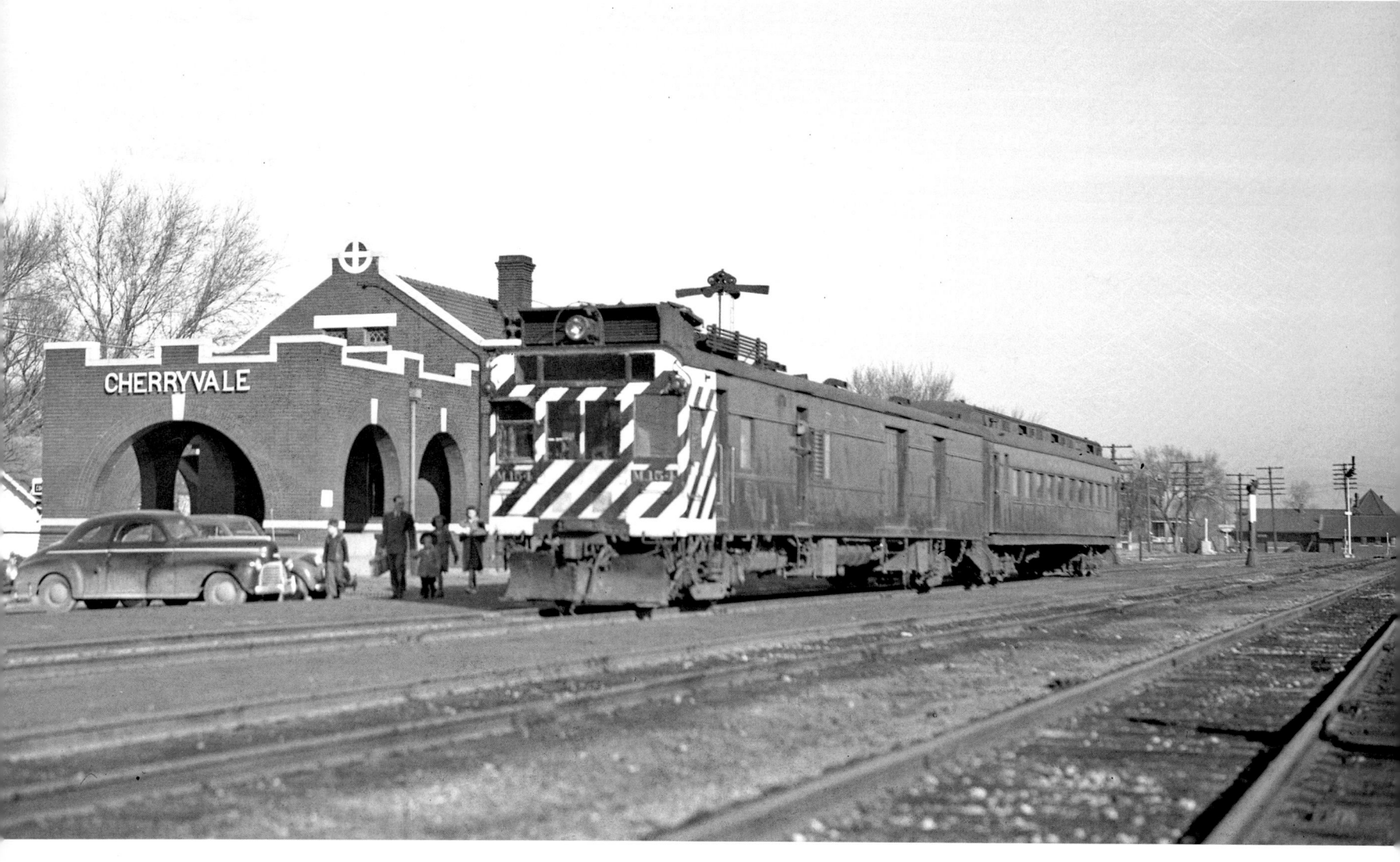

Above: Santa Fe M.154, a gas-electric "doodlebug" at the depot in Cherryvale, Kansas, on November 9, 1946. It ran on the railroad's branch line to Coffeyville and also west to Winfield. Developed in the early twentieth century, motorized railcars like this one gave railroads a more economical way of providing passenger service on lightly traveled routes. The Santa Fe used them extensively on its branch lines in the Great Plains and the Southwest.

Facing: As a child, Abbey frequently visited his maternal grandparents in Cherryvale, Kansas, and the Frisco depot there became one of his favorite train-watching haunts. The depot sat at the southwest corner of a crossing with the Santa Fe. Abbey recorded this view in 1950, which looks east and takes in a riot of since-vanished details of the railroad landscape, from train order semaphore signals to the water tower, telegraph poles, and smash boards protecting the crossing.

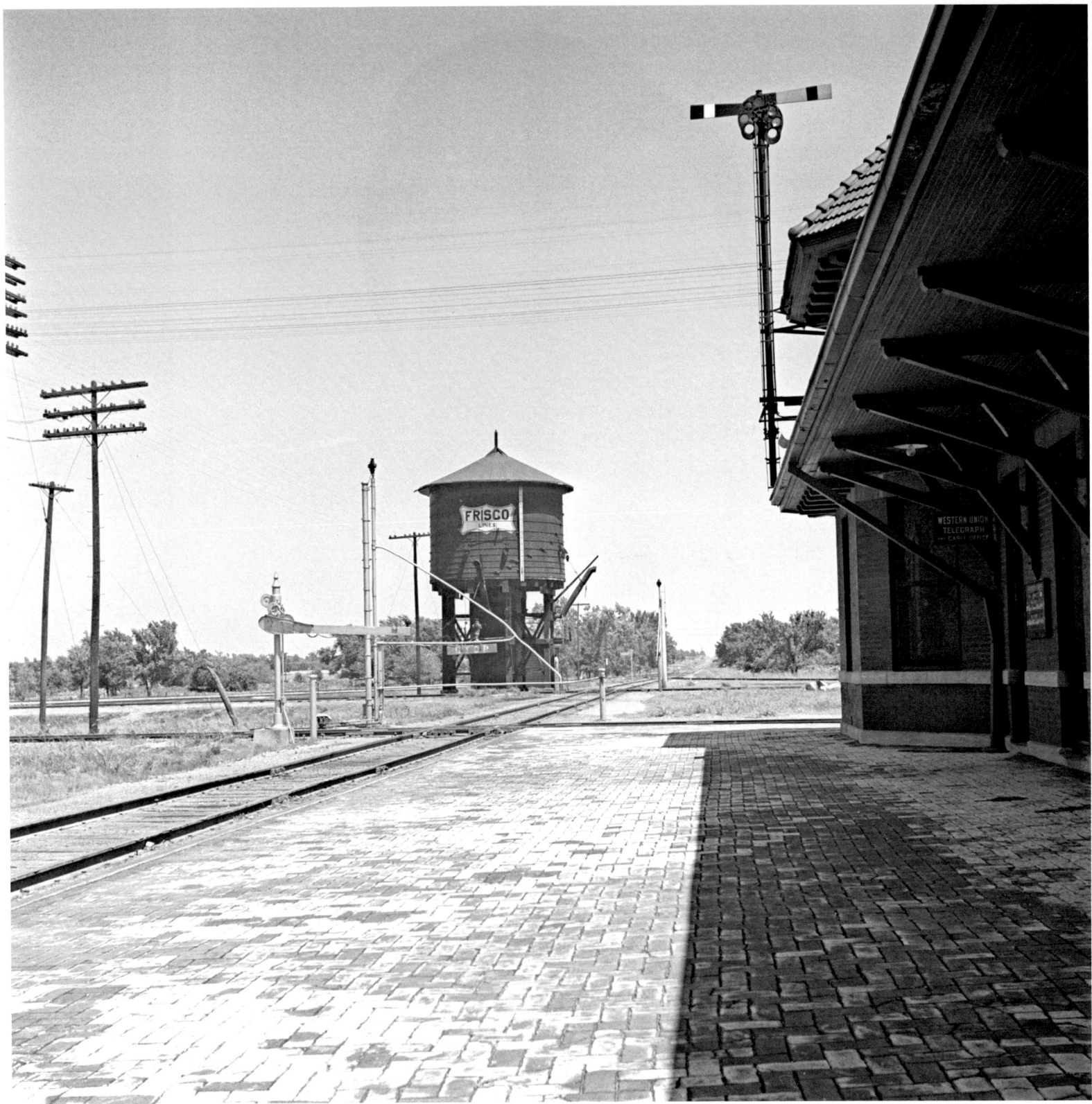

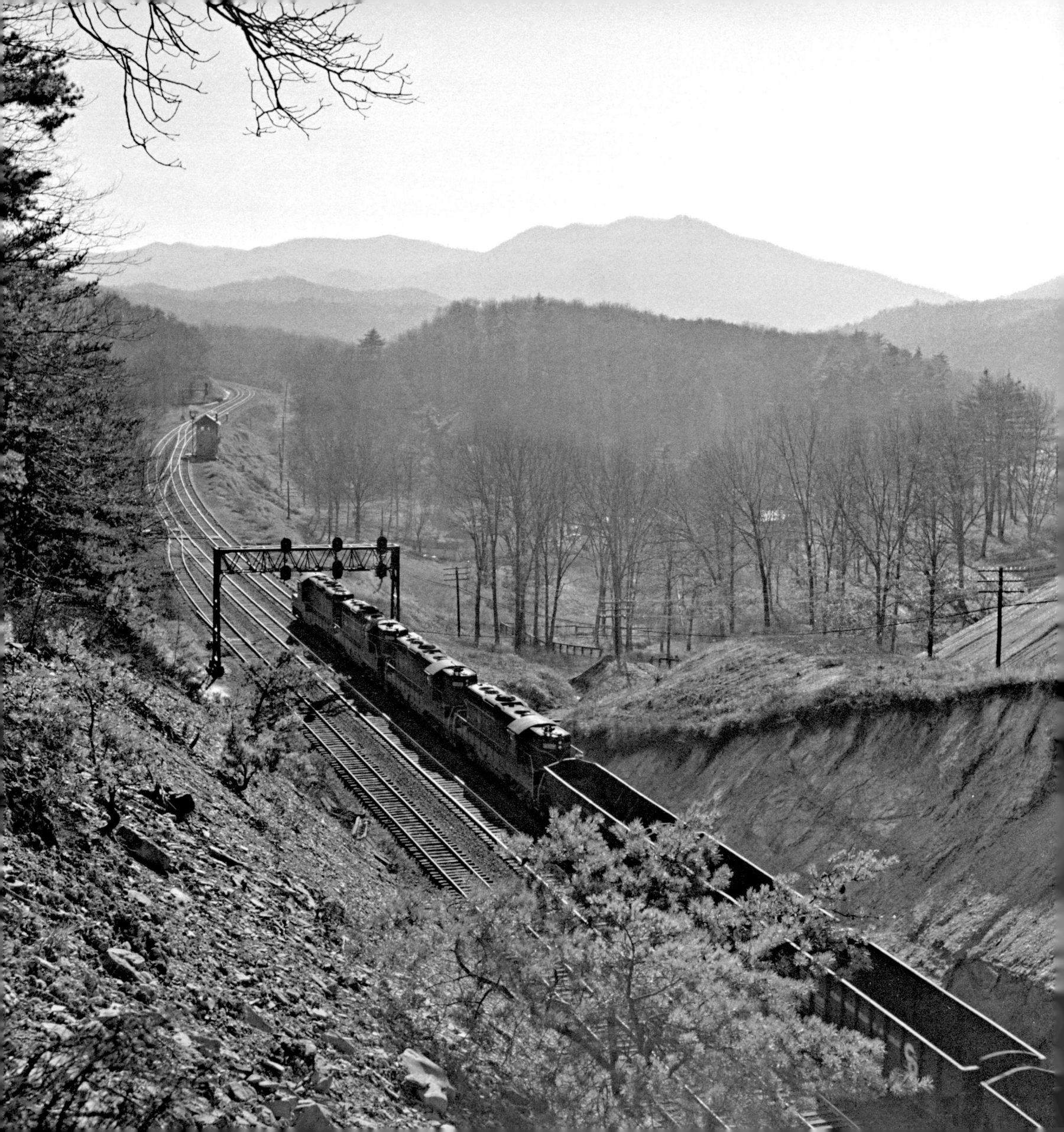

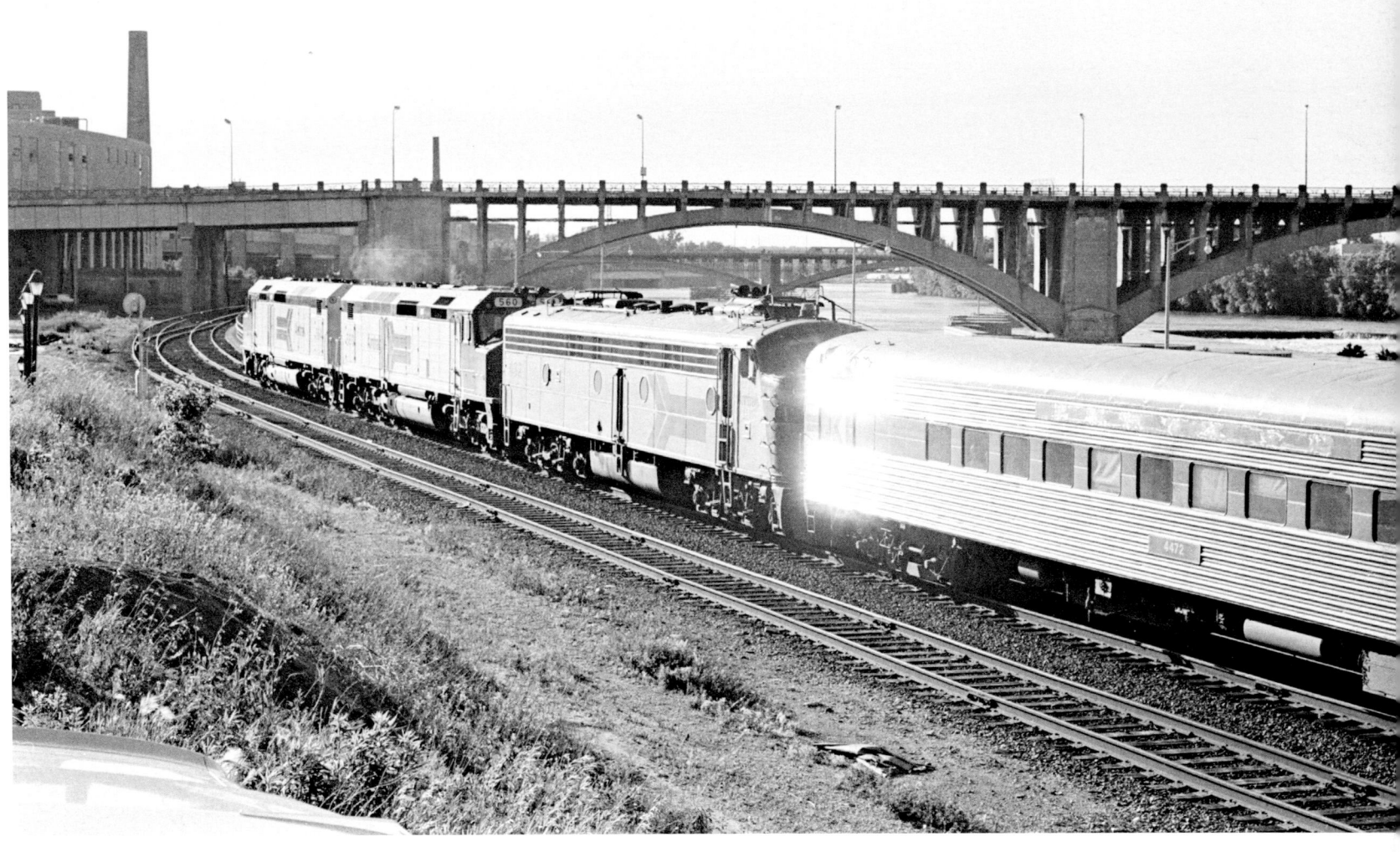

Facing: Four Chesapeake & Ohio GP9s lead a westbound empty hopper train downgrade through the Allegheny Mountains at White Sulphur Springs, West Virginia, on March 9, 1957. Abbey was attending an industry conference at the Greenbrier, a luxurious resort hotel built by the C&O in 1913. He made time to photograph several trains, but this view, looking almost directly into the late winter sun, is emblematic of the railroad and the region.

Above: Amtrak's *Empire Builder* heads west along the Mississippi River in Minneapolis on a summer evening in the late 1970s. The arch spans of the Third Avenue and Hennepin bridges stand behind the locomotives; barely visible beyond them is the Great Northern's Nicollet Island Bridge. Amtrak took over most of the nation's remaining intercity passenger trains in 1971. Its first new locomotives were 150 SDP40Fs built by Electro-Motive in 1973 and 1974; two of them lead a venerable E-unit on this train.

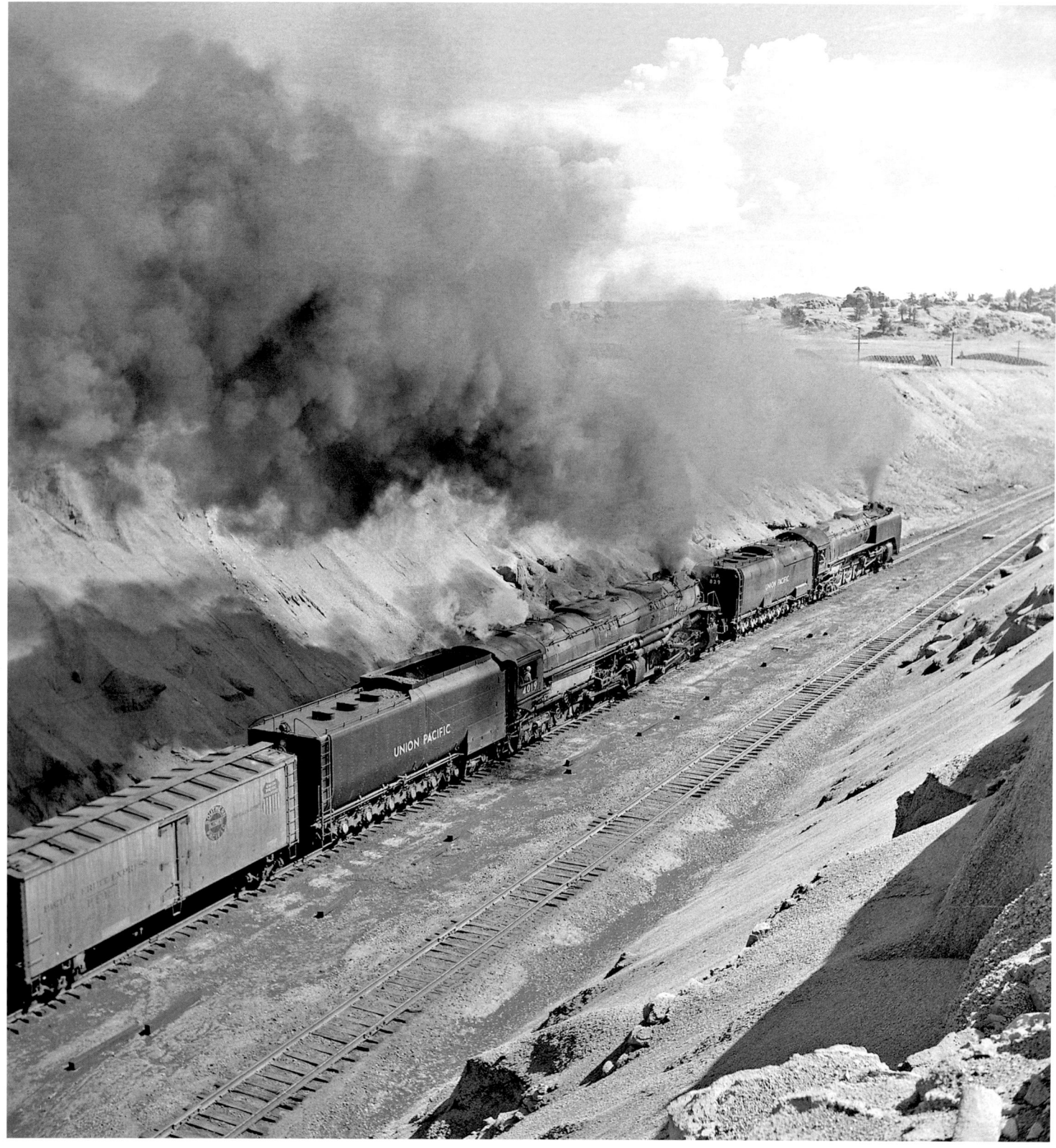

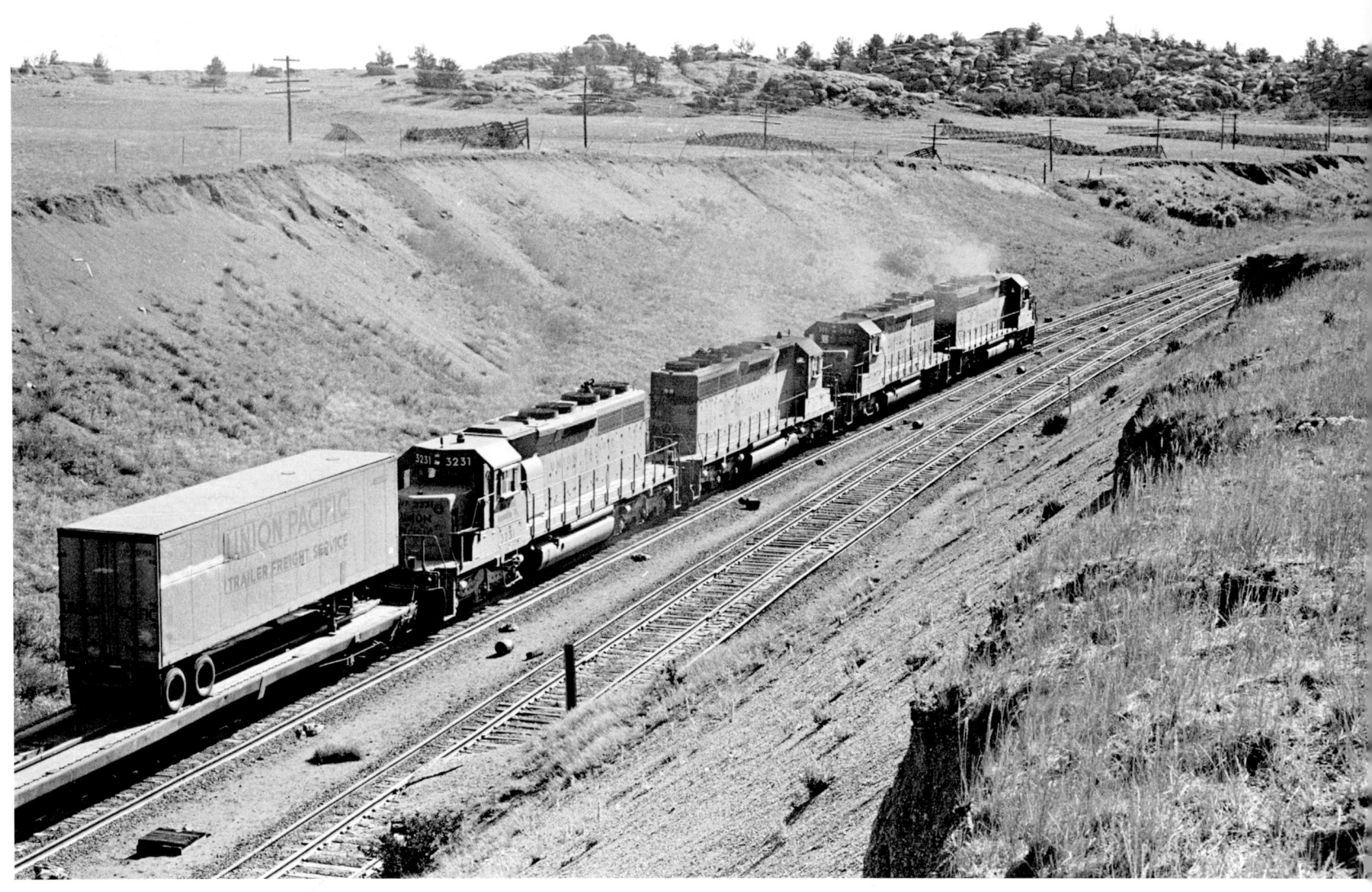

Facing: The summer of 1957 was the last great showing of steam power on Union Pacific's Sherman Hill in Wyoming. A traffic surge brought several recently stored steam locomotives back into service on the railroad's main line. Abbey was one of many railroad photographers to make the pilgrimage to Wyoming that summer. On August 17, he recorded this evocative view of two UP behemoths—4-8-4 no. 829 and Big Boy no. 4019—powering a westbound freight out of Hermosa Tunnel (out of view to left).

Above: Around 1980, Abbey revisited the Hermosa Tunnel on Union Pacific's Sherman Hill in Wyoming. He had been there once before, in 1957, to photograph the end of steam operations on this crucial main line. The setting remains largely the same, and the railroad is still busy. Four 3,000-horsepower SD40-2s have replaced the 4-8-4 and Big Boy from Abbey's previous view, while solid trains of truck trailers now vie for space with traditional manifest freights.

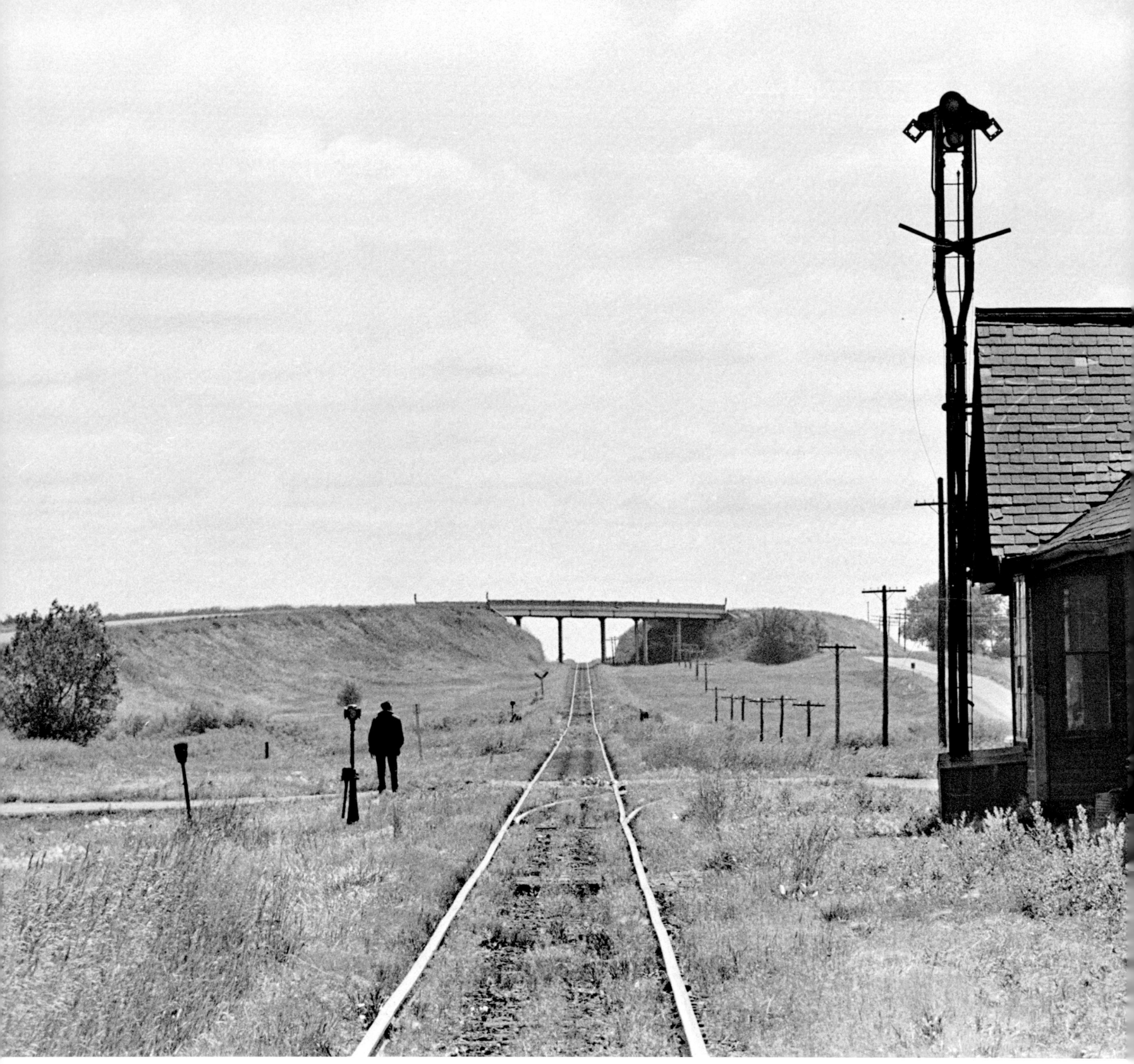

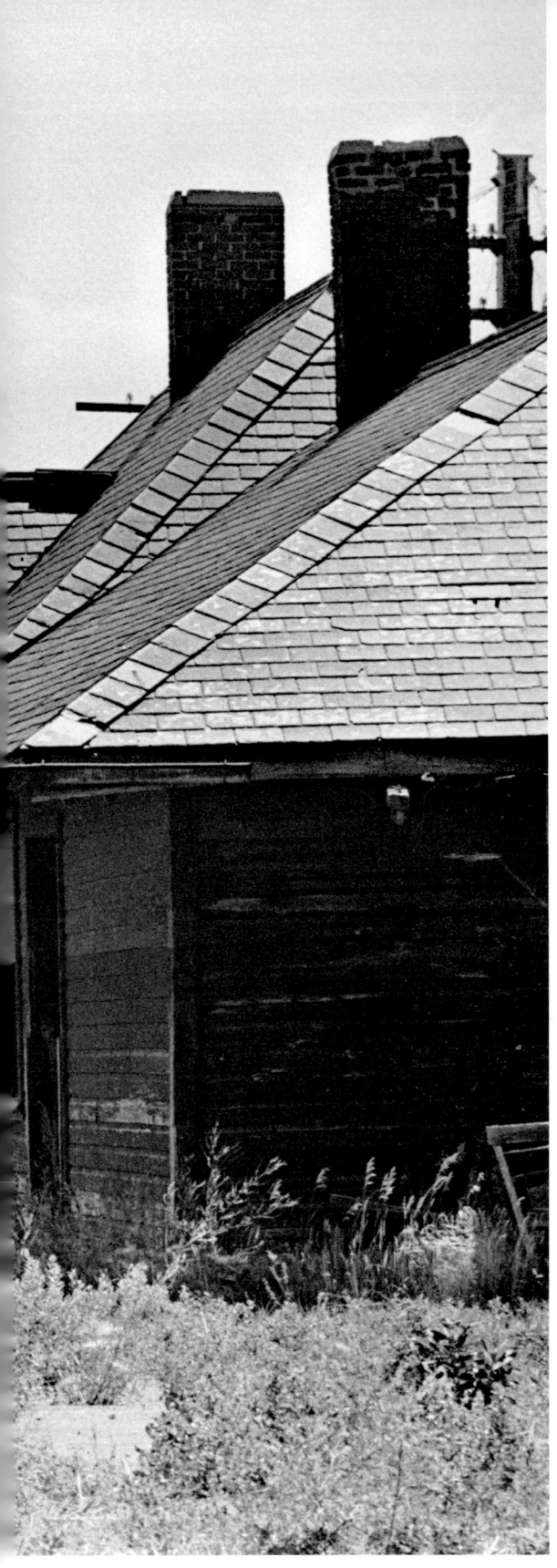

A lone figure ponders the weed-grown Chicago & North Western line past the dilapidated depot in Iroquois, South Dakota, around 1980. From its zenith as the nation's backbone during World War II, much of the railroad industry had fallen far and fast over the ensuing three and a half decades. Abbey had seen and photographed much of it. You would never know it from this scene, but a railroad renaissance was beginning. Abbey would see it take shape, although he would largely leave its visual documentation to a new generation of photographers.

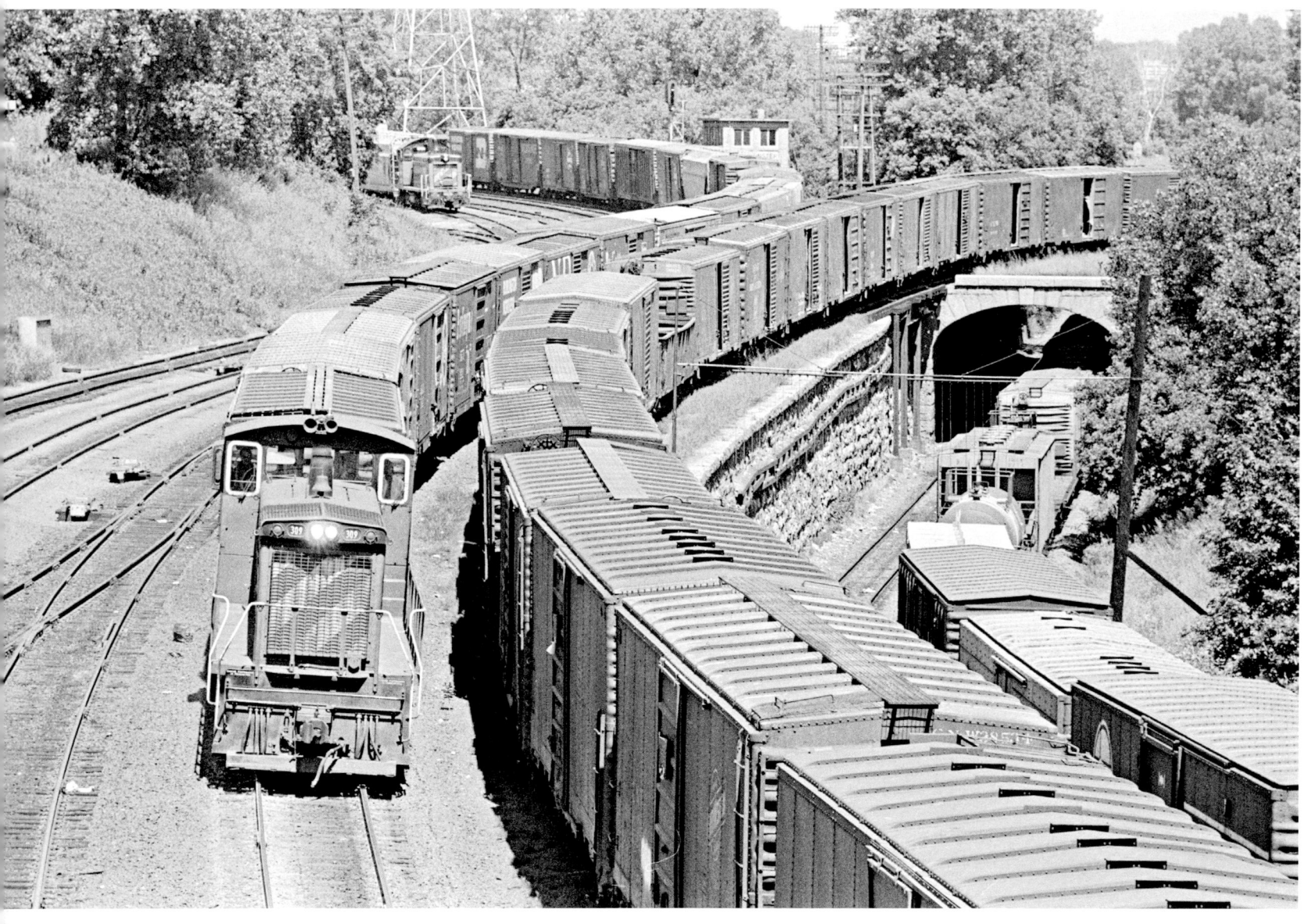

Above: Two Burlington Northern switchers shuffle freight cars at Westminster in St. Paul, Minnesota, as two trains pass on the tracks at right. The Burlington Northern merger of 1970 combined the Great Northern; Northern Pacific; Burlington Route; and Spokane, Portland & Seattle into a massive system that sprawled across the northern half of the country from Chicago to the Pacific. The consolidating power of successful mergers was one of many factors fueling the railroad renaissance that was taking shape by the end of Abbey's career.

Facing: Soo and Great Northern freight trains meet at the Minneapolis suburb of Crystal, Minnesota, on April 10, 1961. Abbey was at Crystal Tower to document the Soo Line's installation of new centralized traffic control equipment. While this type of photograph would not necessarily have been part of his assignment, he knew an opportunity when he saw one, using wheels and couplers of the passing Soo train to frame the waiting GN F-unit in the distance.

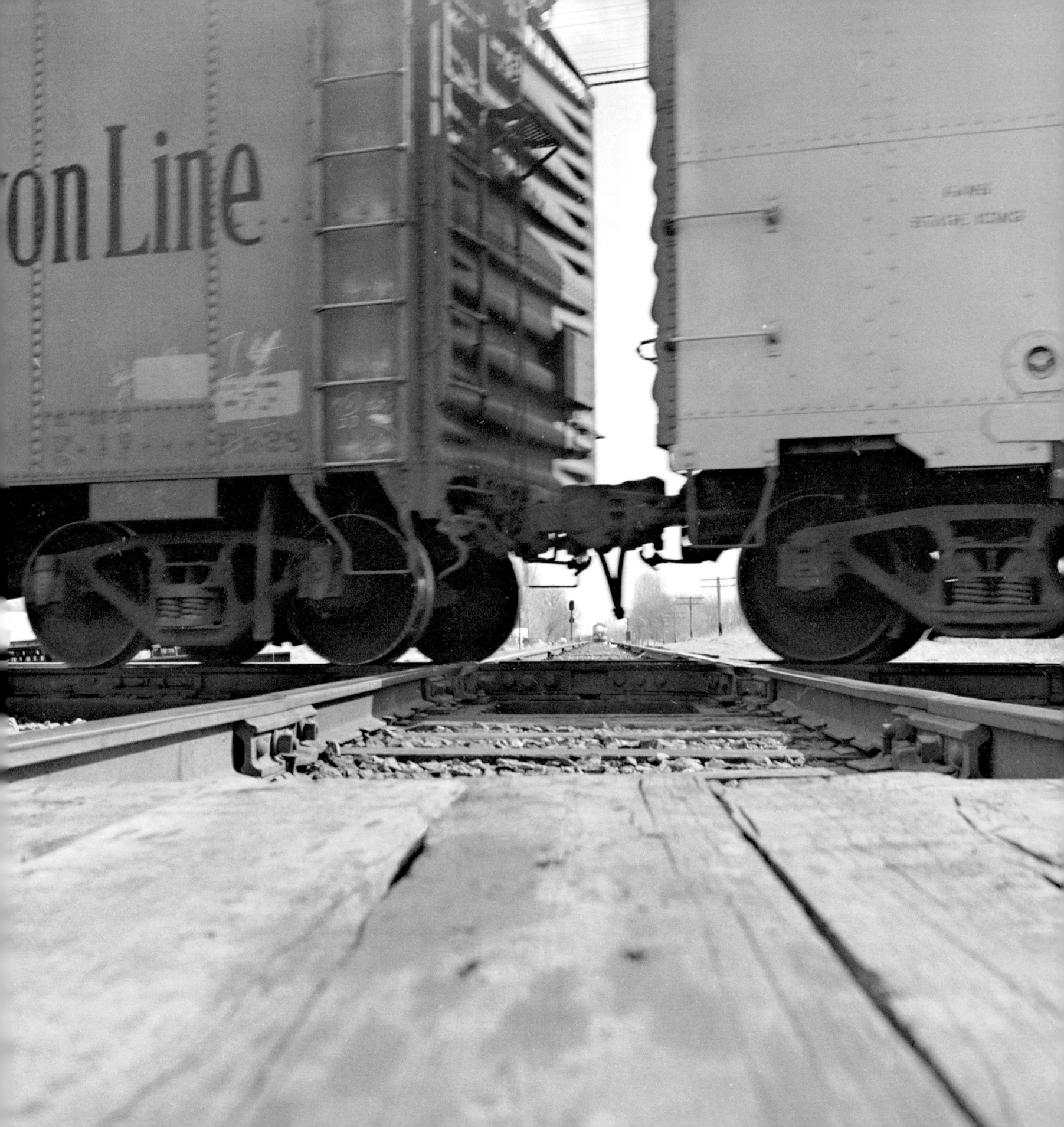

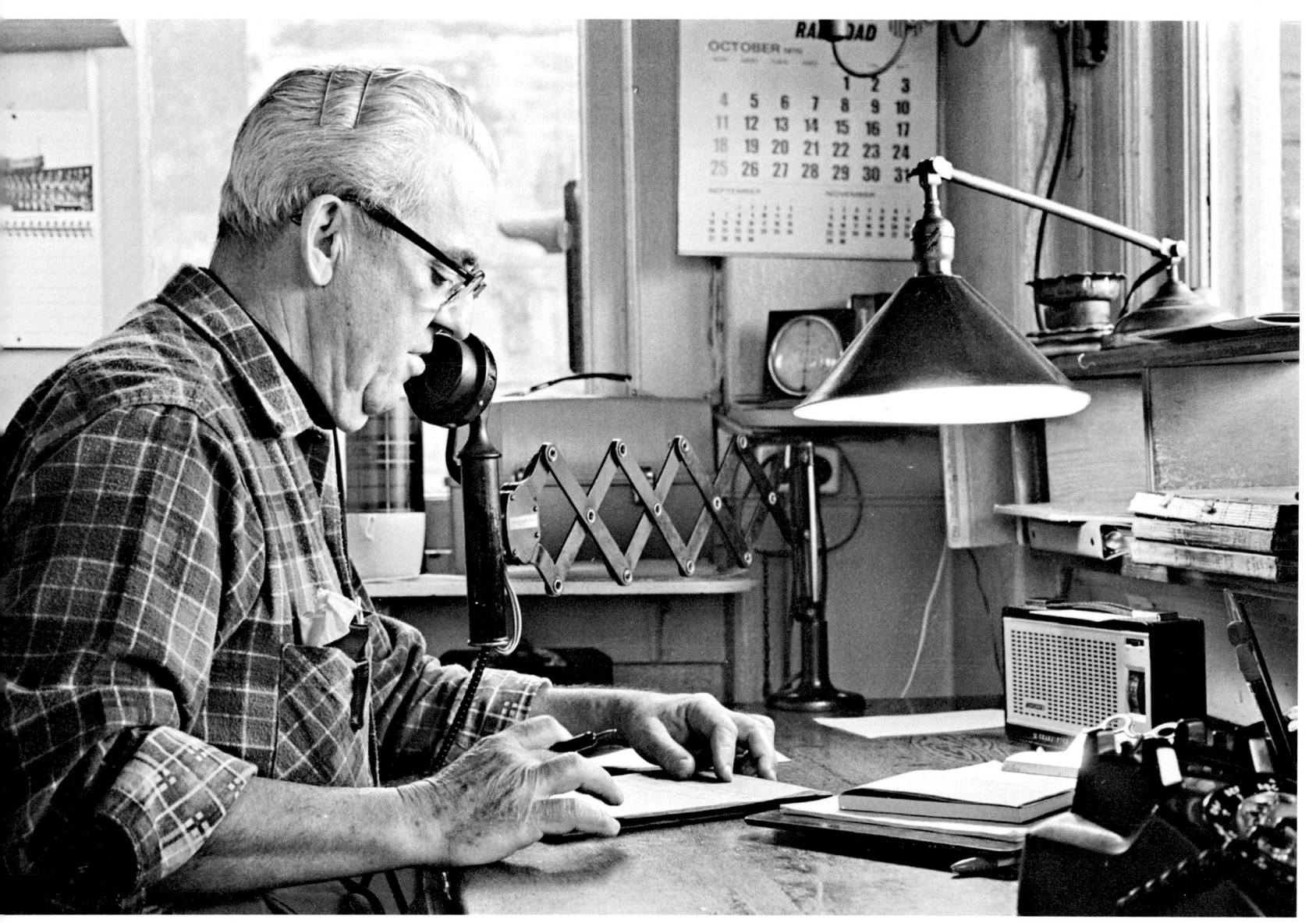

Grover O'Dell copies train orders by hand at East Portland Tower in Portland, Oregon, in October of 1970. The tower lacked a typewriter and was rarely used for orders until Union Pacific eliminated its telegrapher job at Portland Union Station at the beginning of the year. O'Dell was the regular night shift operator and is likely taking down orders for train no. 18, the eastbound *Portland Rose*, which departed just before the end of his shift.

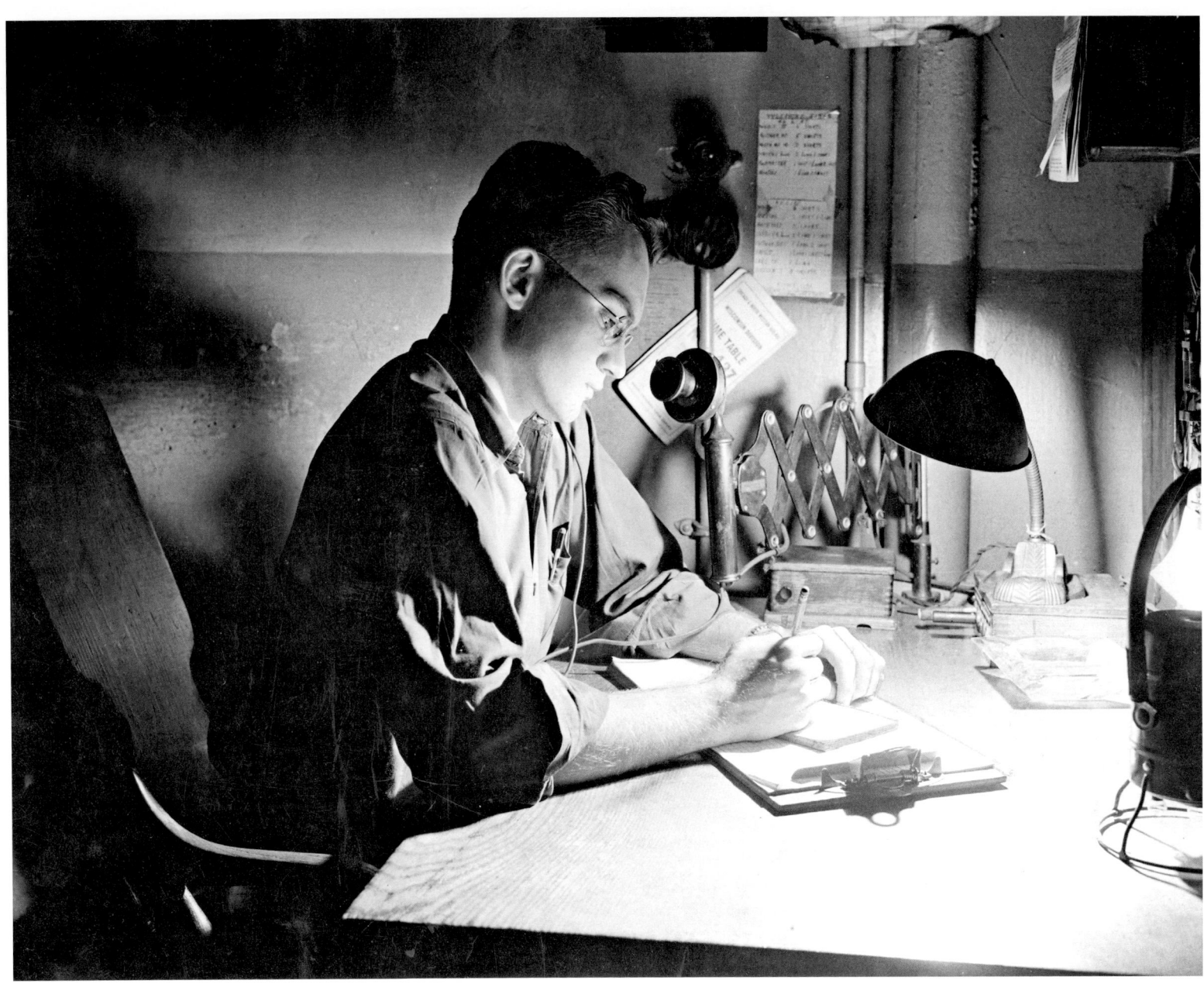

As a college student in the late 1940s, Abbey spent two summers working as an operator for the Chicago & North Western at several towers in and around Chicago. From these jobs he learned the operations side of railroading from the ground level, and the familiarity he gained with the work as well as these interior spaces informed his photography throughout the rest of his life. *Courtesy of the Abbey family.*

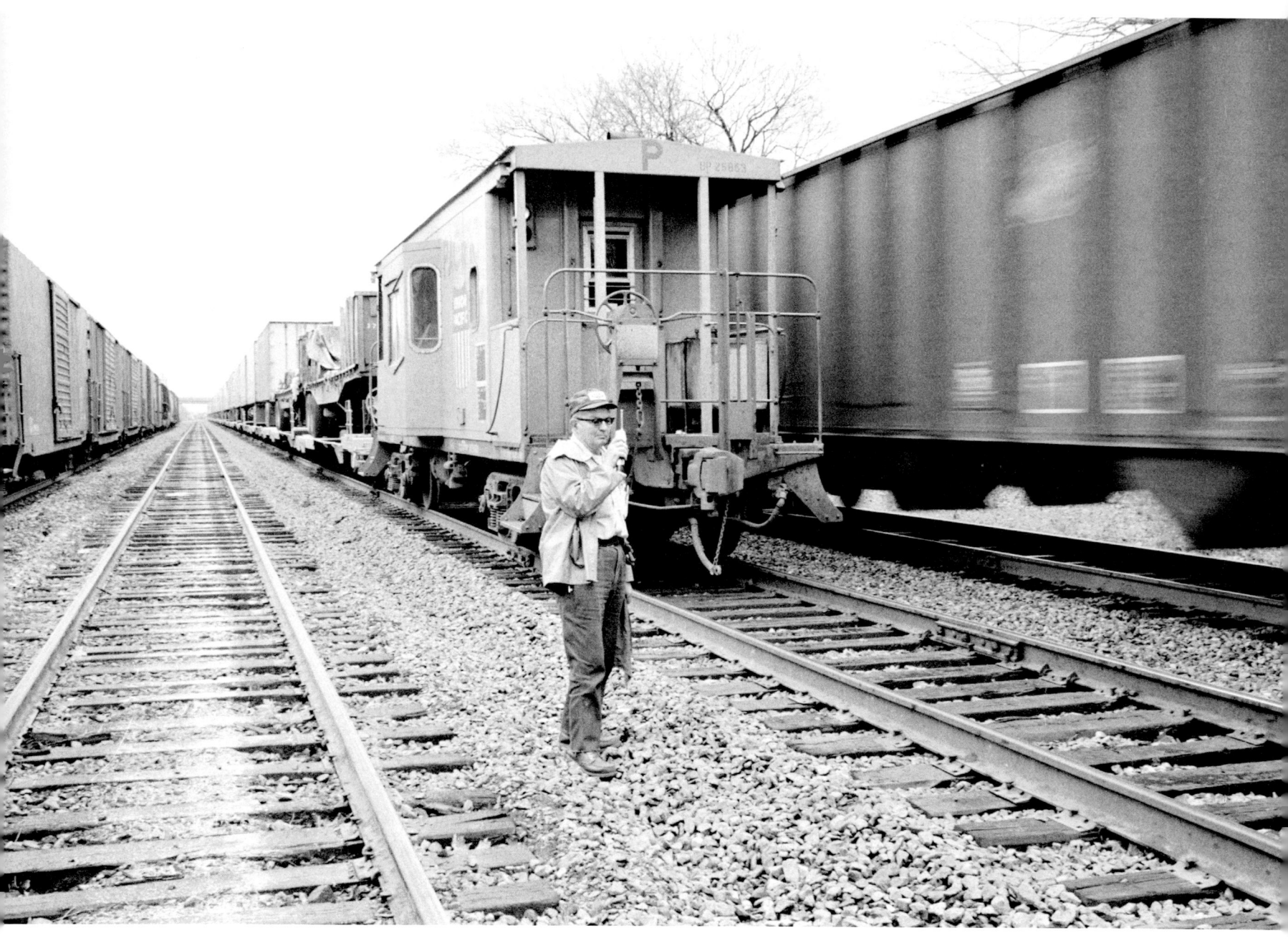

Above: The conductor of a Union Pacific piggyback train watches, radio in hand to report any problems, as a coal train sails by on an adjacent track. A "manifest" freight train stands on the track at far left, representing the traditional model of freight railroading. The two trains at right represent recent innovation and some of the biggest sources for rail traffic growth in the late twentieth century.

Facing: Self-portrait from 1950, the year Abbey joined the staff of *Trains* magazine, with his new Rolleiflex. Abbey used the 120-format camera—which took square negatives with a fixed, 80mm, f3.5 lens—for the majority of his photography from 1950 into the early 1960s, when he shifted to a smaller 35mm Pentax system with interchangeable lenses. *Courtesy of the Abbey family.*

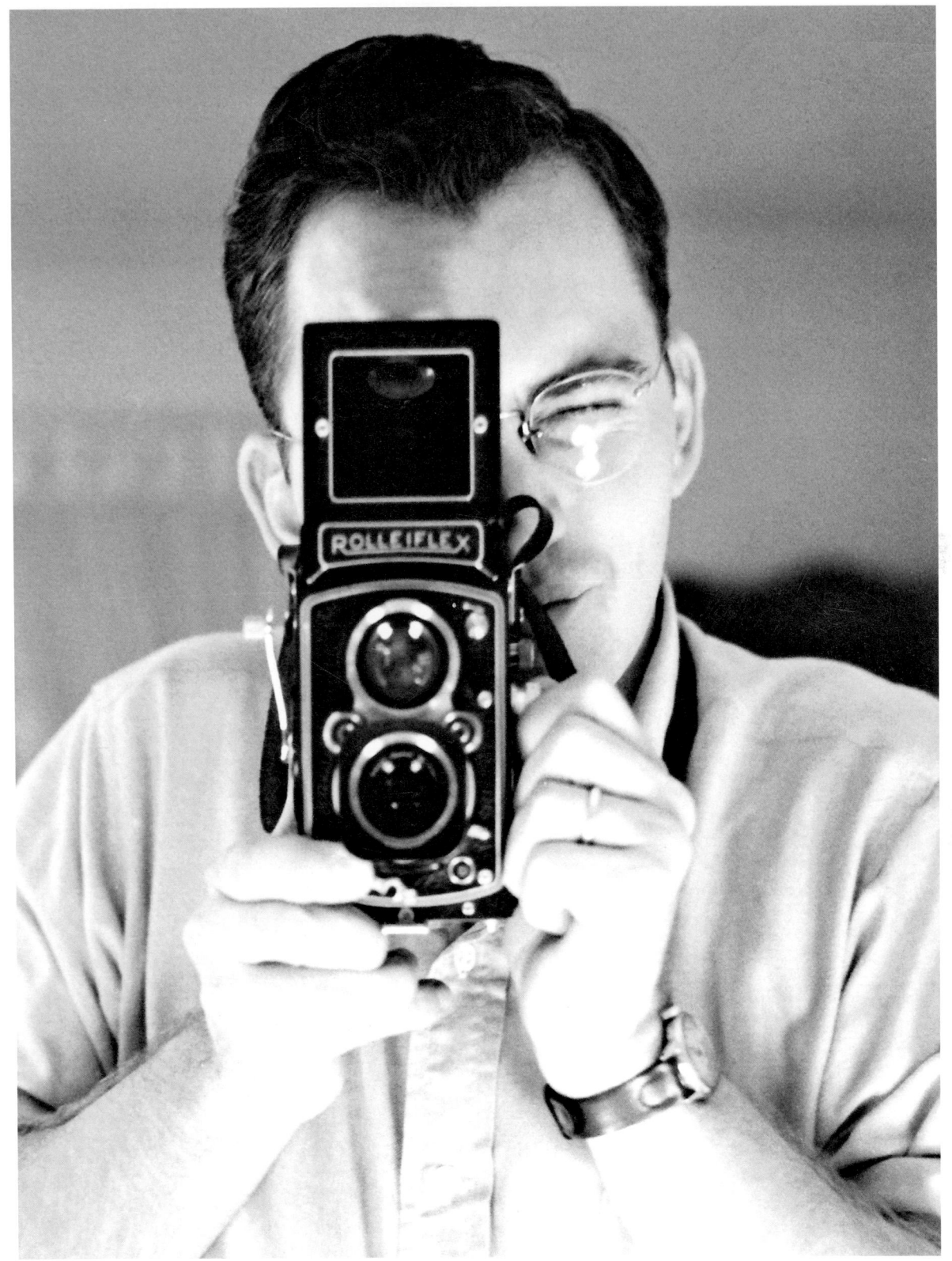

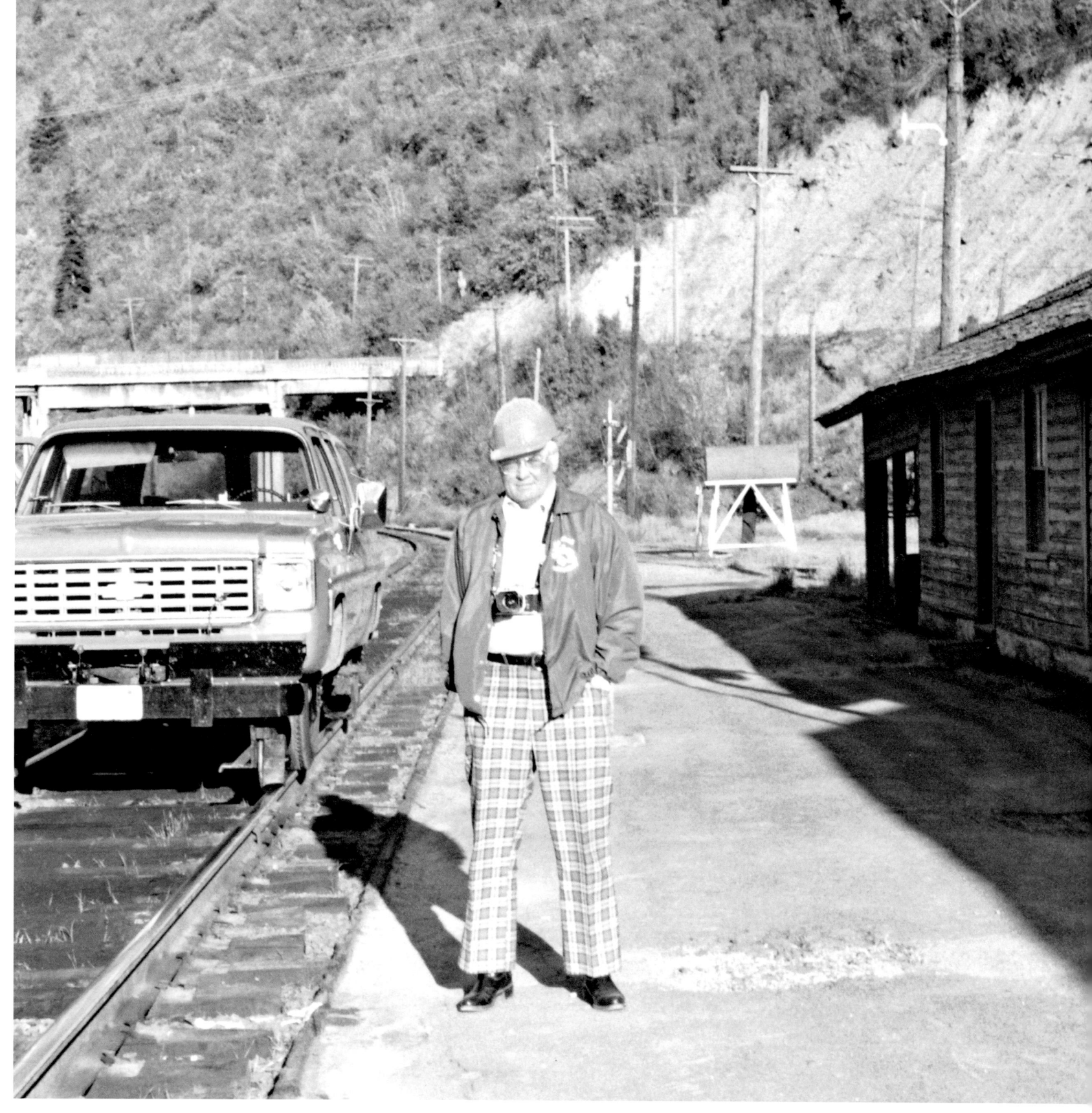

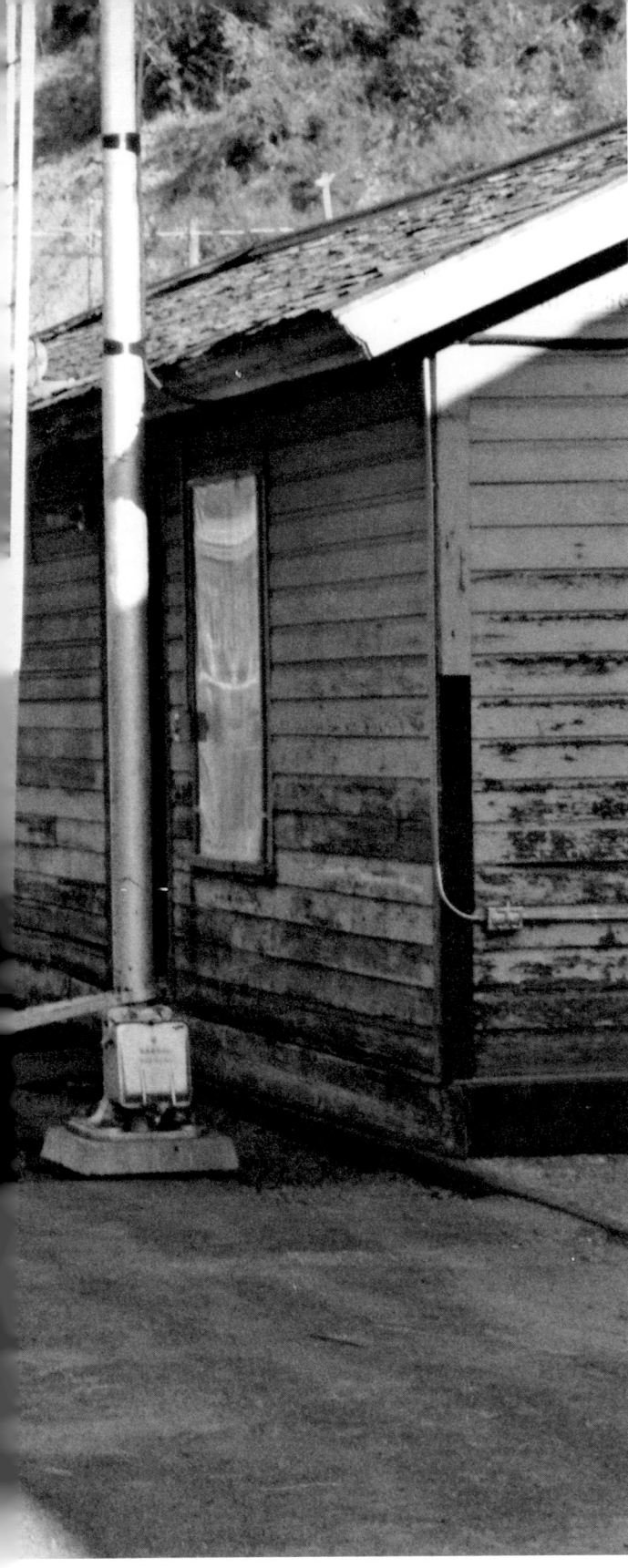

Abbey poses with the hi-rail-equipped Chevy Suburban used to make his 1979 inspection trip of the Milwaukee Road's Pacific extension with bankruptcy trustee Richard Ogilvie. *Courtesy of the Abbey family.*

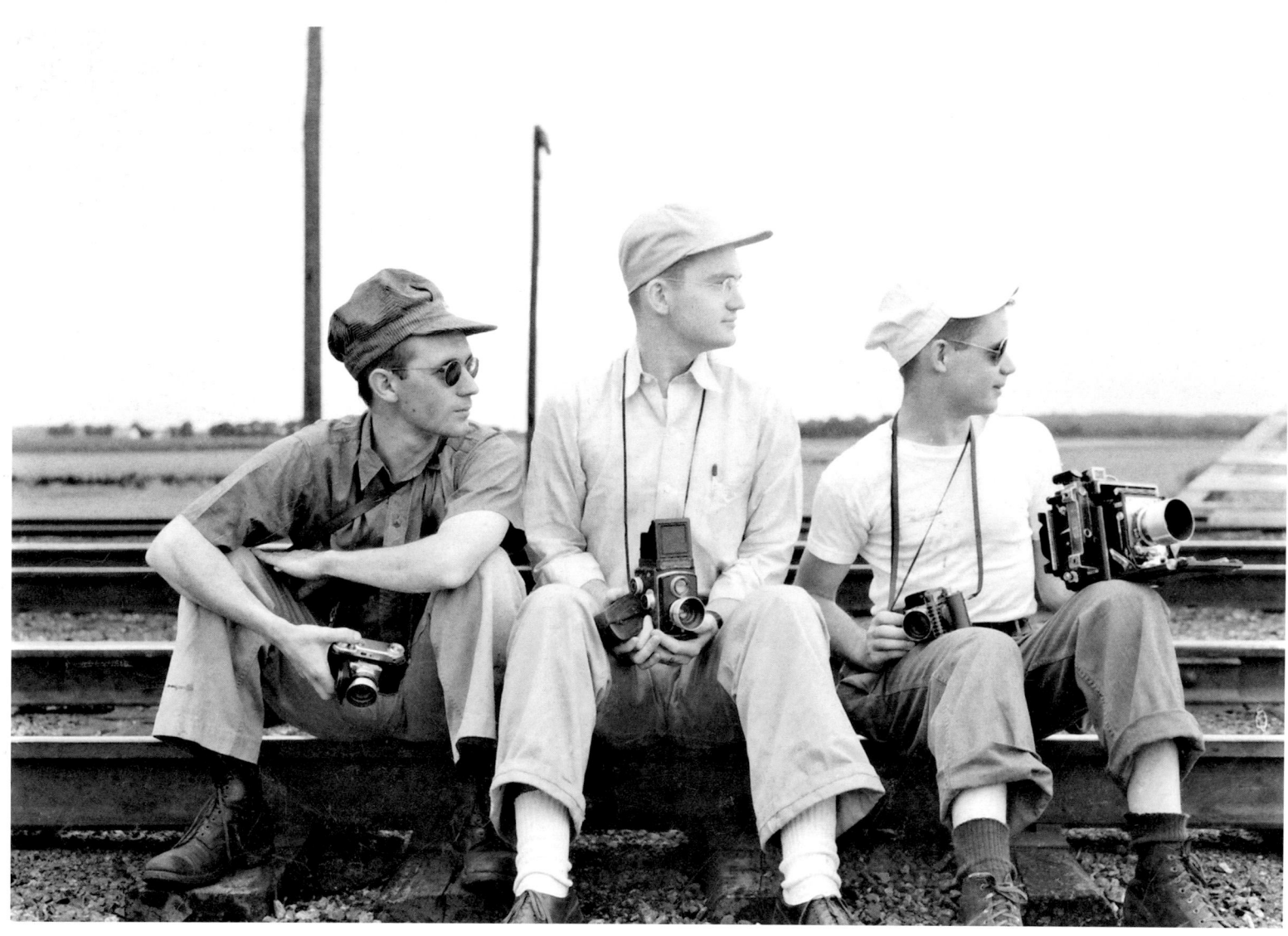

Above: Abbey, center, with railroad photographer friends Ted Cole and Chic Kerrigan somewhere near Chicago in the late 1940s. *Courtesy of the Abbey family.*

Facing: Abbey, standing in center, with other *Trains* magazine staff members in Kalmbach Publishing Co.'s Milwaukee offices on February 28, 1952. David P. Morgan sits at his desk, with associate editor Rosemary Entringer to the left of Abbey and Katie McMullen, editorial secretary (and soon to become editor of Kalmbach's *Better Camping* magazine), in the background at right.

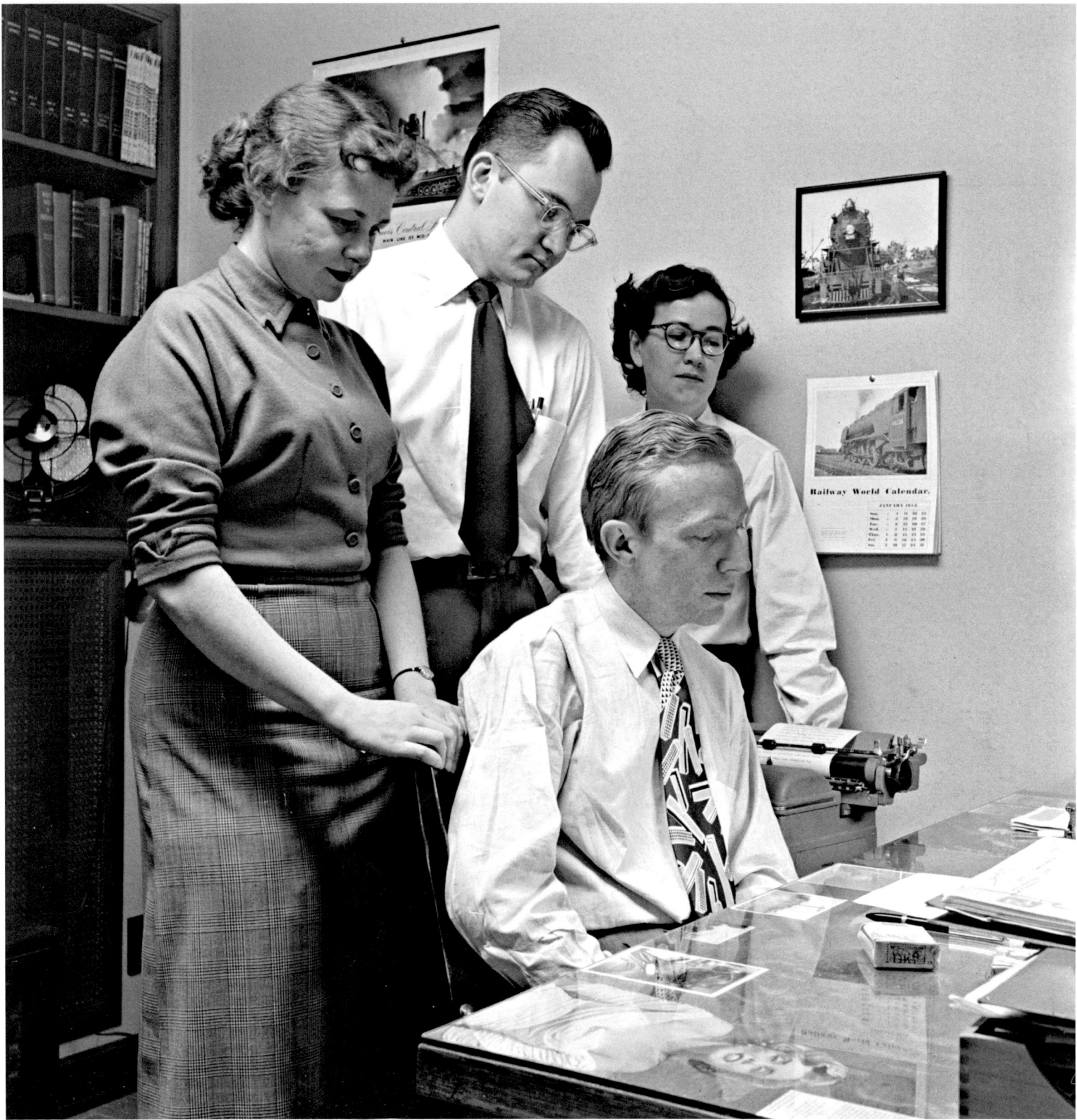

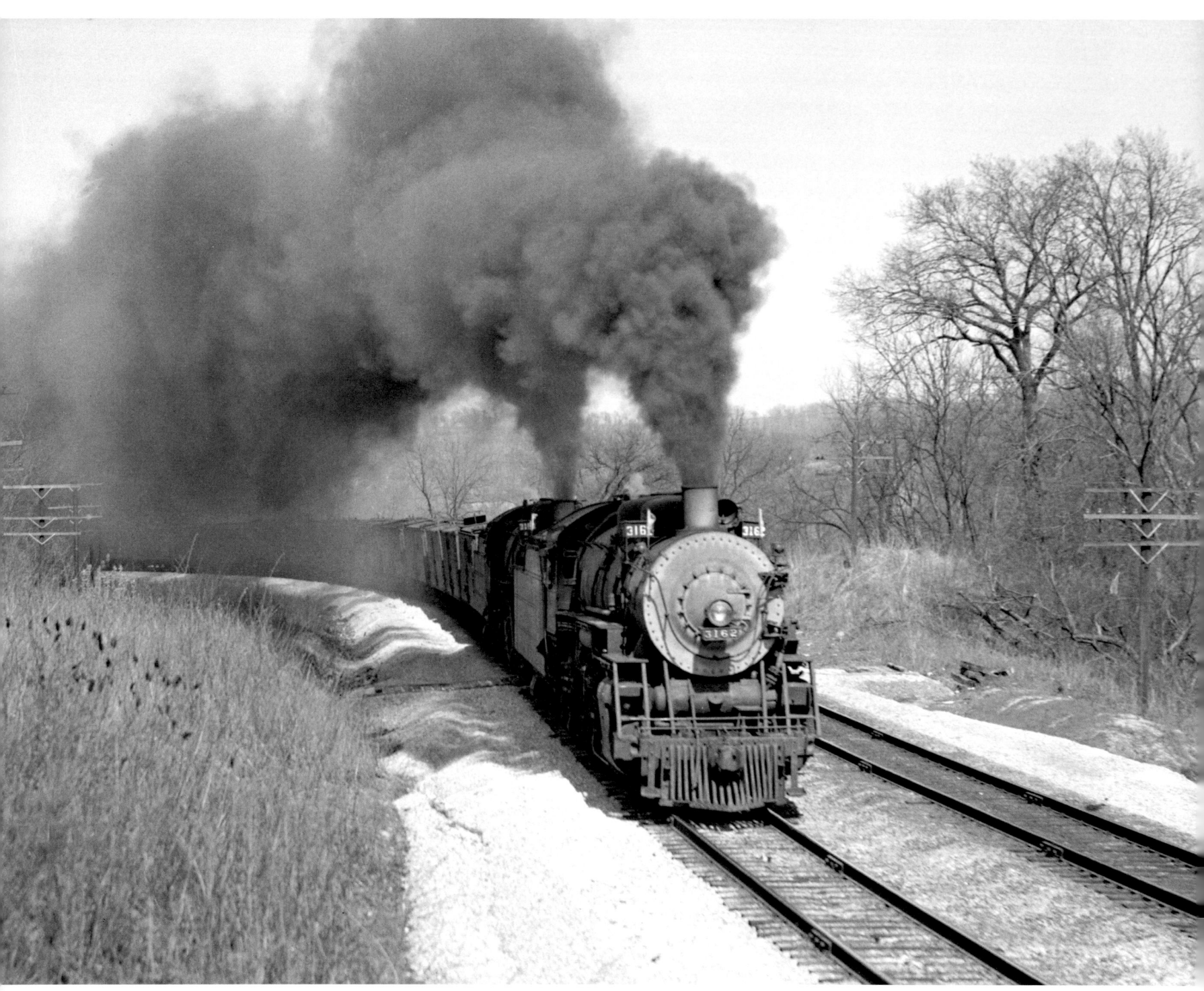

ONE

ALONG THE SANTA FE

DID WALLY ABBEY HAVE A FAVORITE RAILROAD? HE NEVER explicitly said. But it would come as no surprise to learn that, if pressed, he answered "Santa Fe."

For a schoolboy living in one of Chicago's north shore suburbs, the Atchison, Topeka & Santa Fe might as well have been a thousand miles away. The Santa Fe operated out of Dearborn Station, way across the Loop from Abbey's more familiar North Western Terminal on Canal Street. And when the *Chief* and all the other famous AT&SF trains pulled away from Dearborn's gates, they immediately headed in a southwesterly direction, away from Abbey's childhood Evanston turf.

But family often trumps geography, and for that reason some of Abbey's earliest encounters with trains came 607 railroad miles west of Chicago, in little Cherryvale, Kansas, home of his maternal grandparents, Samuel and Luella Squier. From as early as he could remember, Abbey took family trips to visit "the folks," usually by train. And once he got to Cherryvale, there was plenty to see.

Cherryvale is in southeast Kansas, on what once was Santa Fe's Tulsa Subdivision linking Kansas City with Oklahoma's second-largest city. It wasn't one of the railroad's premier main lines, but the Tulsa Sub saw its share of business, including some passenger trains that made strong impressions on the boy from Chicago. "The Santa Fe figured in my early travel rather strongly, because of those frequent trips to Cherryvale," Abbey recalled. "I have no idea what year it would have been, but I can distinctly

Two Santa Fe 2-8-2 steam locomotives, nos. 3262 and 3160, lead a westbound extra freight train up Olathe Hill west of Zarah, Kansas, on March 31, 1946. The Olathe grade brought the railroad out of the Kansas River Valley, and the Santa Fe later rebuilt this part of its main line to reduce or eliminate many curves. Today dozens of BNSF Railway freight trains run over the rebuilt route every day, while suburban housing developments from nearby Kansas City now stand on the surrounding hills.

remember riding in the observation of what must have been the *Oil Flyer*, northbound out of Cherryvale in the afternoon."

The *Oil Flyer* wasn't the only name train running through town. In the prewar years, Abbey also saw the *Tulsan*, an early streamliner, as well as the daily M.154 gas-electric doodlebug to Coffeyville and Winfield, the latter via Santa Fe's branch to Wichita. And if he ever got tired of watching the Santa Fe (not likely), there was always the St. Louis–San Francisco depot a few blocks to the north, where the Santa Fe crossed the Frisco's Wichita–Joplin line.

Cherryvale's Santa Fe depot was a great place for a boy to get started with trains. Built in 1910, it was a sizable brick affair, with broad eaves, arched windows, stylized Santa Fe logos, and a handsome porte cochere on the street side of the building. Today it appears to be in pristine condition, serving as the local offices of the South Kansas & Oklahoma Railroad, a regional line owned by the Watco interests. In the late 1930s, it must have been the perfect hangout for a budding young photographer.

As Abbey got older, he continued to be drawn to the Santa Fe. When he graduated from high school, he chose the University of Kansas, certainly in part for its great journalism school, but also because the campus was only a mile from the AT&SF main line.

Like many college students in those days, Abbey tried his hand at hitchhiking, and his frequent destination was 25 miles or so eastward to photograph trains on Olathe Hill, an especially difficult grade between Holliday and Olathe, Kansas, where, as Abbey wrote, "Santa Fe found a reasonably graceful way to climb out of the Kaw River lowlands." There he photographed FT freight diesels, 4-8-4s on passenger trains, double-headed 2-8-2s, and just about anything else on the railroad's roster.

When Abbey graduated from KU in August 1949, the Santa Fe was still tugging at him, and he took his first journalism job in Chanute, Kansas, just 29 miles up the road from Cherryvale. There he reported for duty as a reporter and photographer for the *Chanute Tribune*, a daily newspaper with a circulation of approximately 3,500. Between chasing police cars and attending school board meetings, Abbey could hang out around the city's grand station, which included division offices and a Harvey House hotel.

Abbey left the *Tribune* after only a year to join *Trains* magazine in Milwaukee. It was there that Abbey's love of the Santa Fe was crystallized in January 1954, when the magazine published his eighteen-page, 10,000-word cover story simply titled "Super Railroad." The article kicked off what editor David P. Morgan said would be a series of comprehensive system stories on several major railroads. For the magazine, a lot was riding on the series, and the Santa Fe, with its glamorous reputation as a passenger carrier, was the perfect place to start.

To accomplish the assignment, Abbey got the support he needed from Morgan: nearly fourteen months to prepare for the story, and arrangements to ride approximately 6,300 miles of the Santa Fe system, much of it in the cabs of steam and diesel locomotives.

Abbey's reporting and photography was comprehensive. He visited yard towers and dispatchers' offices; spent time in the offices of officials across the system, including at the railroad's Michigan Avenue headquarters in Chicago; inspected the new retarder yard at Argentine, Kansas, and the locomotive shops in Albuquerque; enjoyed a Fred Harvey lunch in the station at Gallup; and relished the view of New Mexico's Wagon Mound from the dome of the *Super Chief*.

It was great magazine writing, full of facts and figures and expert analysis, but always delivered with Abbey's characteristic exuberance: "Santa Fe is making a liar out of whoever it was who said the railroad industry is not modern. Indeed, John Santa Fe runs probably the most progressive railroad in the country. Its operations set the standard for modernity; its thinking is fresh and relatively unfettered by tradition. It dwells not, principally, in the criticisms of declining patronage, government regulation and subsidized competition which typify many roads old enough to know better, but looks forward to extending itself with new trains, new territories, new ways to greater efficiency." If Abbey's copy sounds a bit like a public relations man's dream, then that might say something about the career direction the author was headed. In fact, "Super Railroad" was very nearly Abbey's swan song at *Trains*. The February 1954 issue one month later would be the last with his name on the masthead. But not before he had the chance to make good for his favorite railroad.

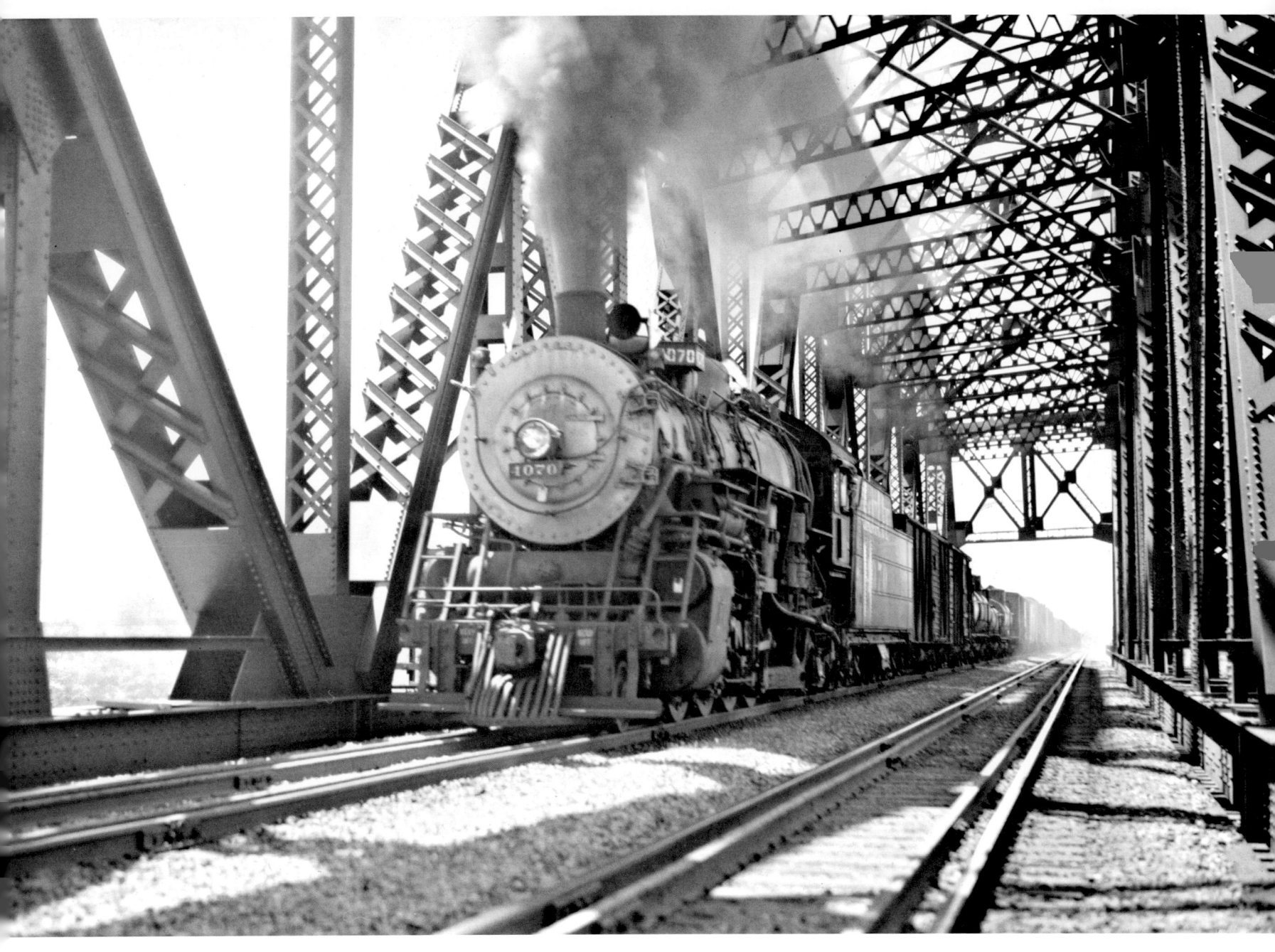

Santa Fe 2-8-2 steam locomotive no. 4070 charges through the trusses of the railroad's Illinois River bridge at Chillicothe, Illinois, with an eastbound freight train sometime in the late 1940s. The 2-8-2 wheel arrangement was among the most common for freight-hauling steam locomotives in North America; Santa Fe owned more than 300 of them. All had been scrapped by 1955, except for two that were lost in a flood in 1952 and sunk in the Kansas River at Topeka, where they remain to this day.

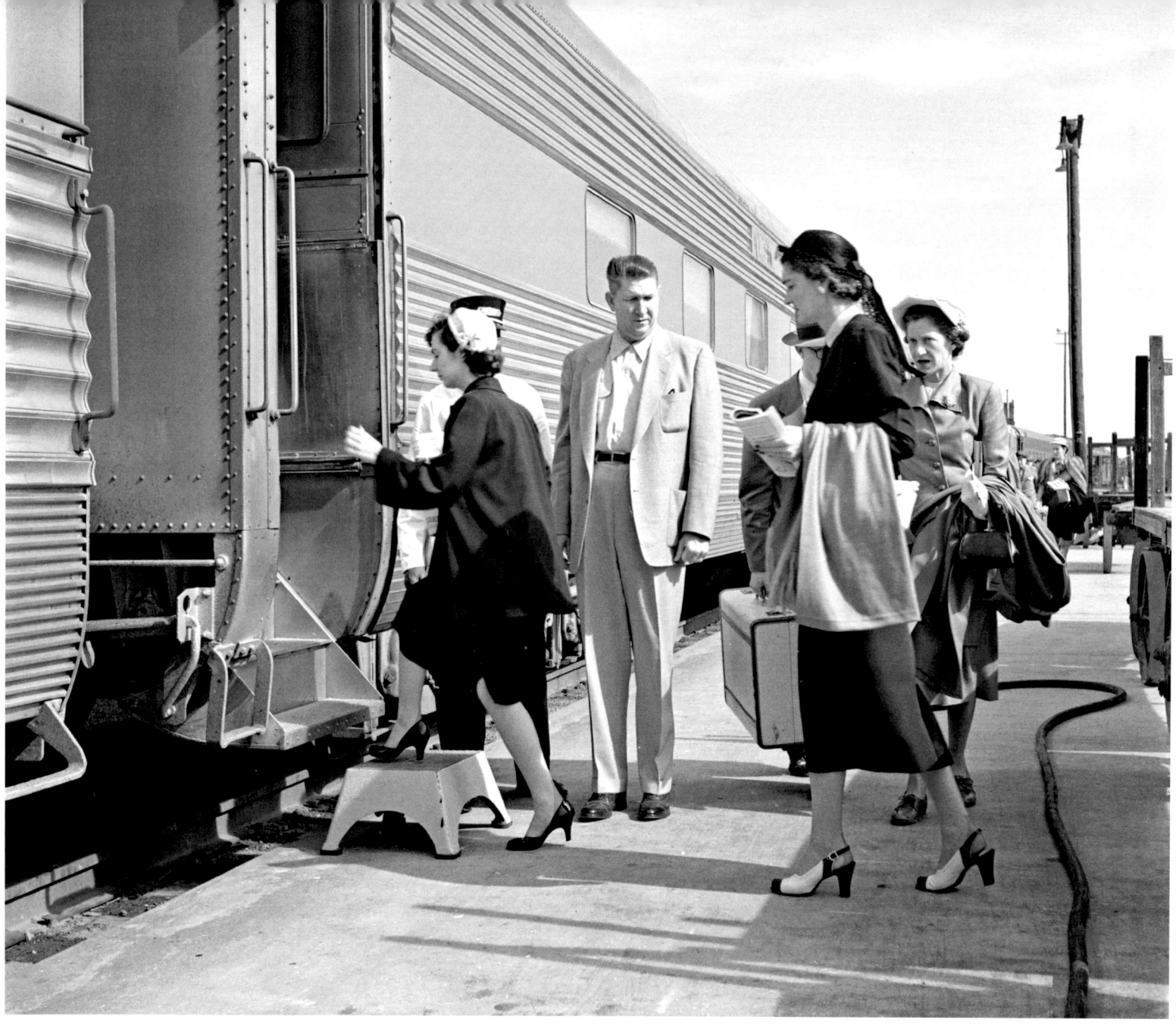

Above: Well-dressed passengers board the streamlined *Texas Chief* at Oklahoma City as the low sun casts long shadows on a spring day in 1953. Connecting Chicago with the largest cities in Texas, the train split in Gainesville, with separate sections serving Dallas and Houston/Galveston.

Facing: Despite being the first major adopter of diesel power, as late as April of 1953 Santa Fe was still performing major work on its steam fleet. This view from inside the Albuquerque back shop shows at least nine big locomotives, including 4-8-4s nos. 2926, 3754, and 2902, as well as 2-10-4 no. 5003. Three years later, the railroad donated no. 2926 to the City of Albuquerque. Today it is being restored to operating condition by the New Mexico Steam Locomotive and Railroad Historical Society.

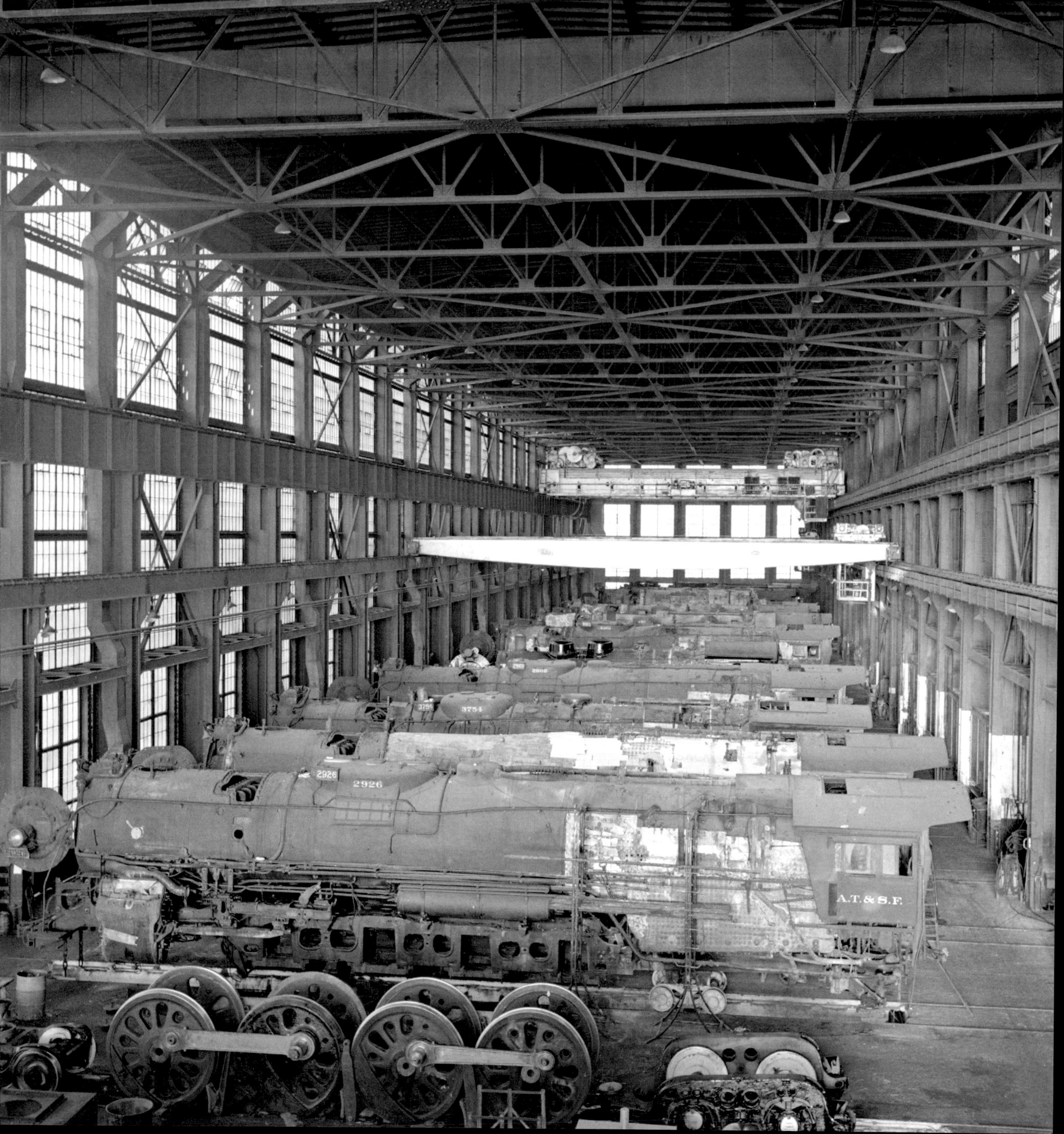

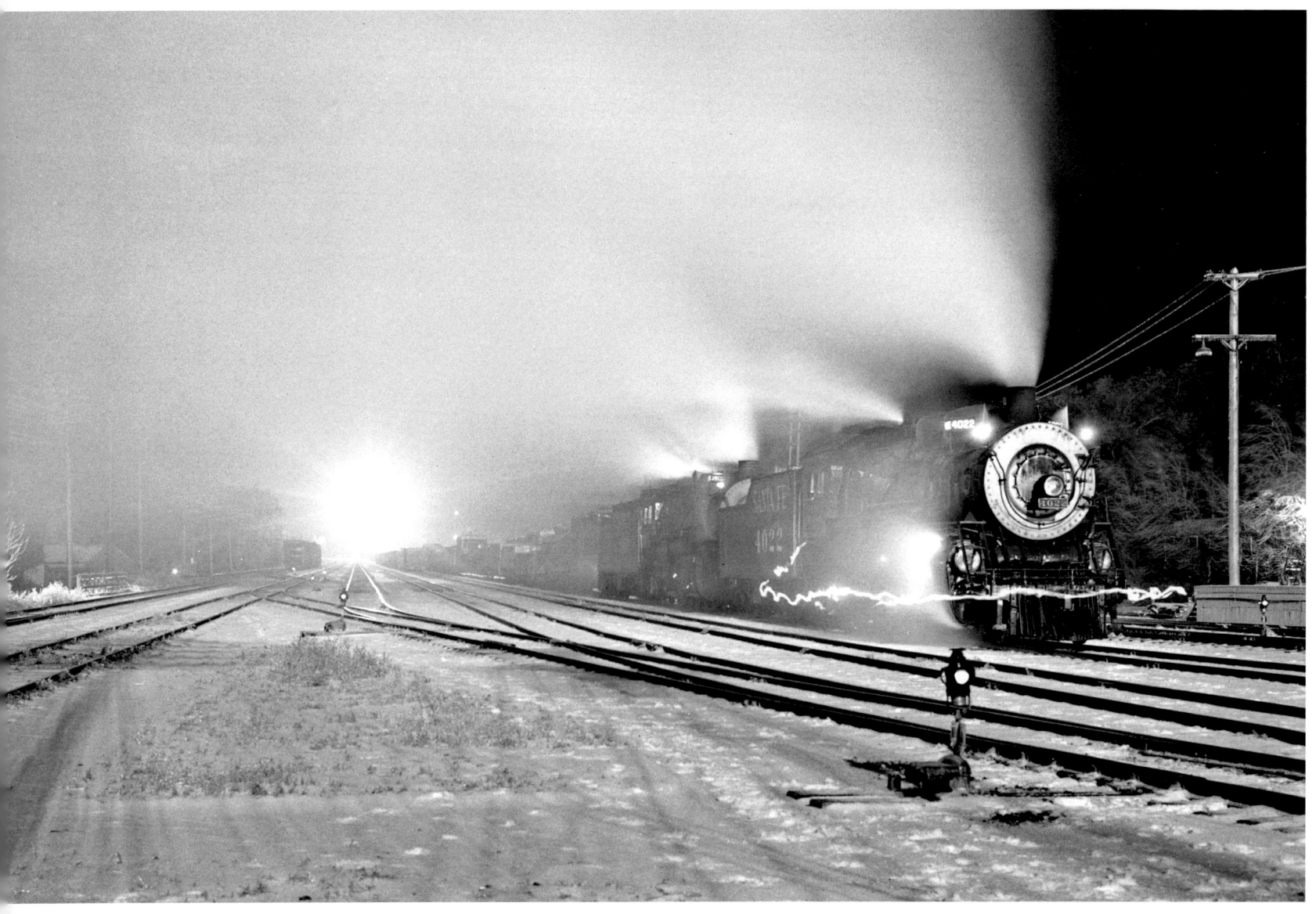

Above: Santa Fe eastbound freight train no. 86 standing in the yard at Chanute, Kansas, on the night of December 21, 1949. Locomotives nos. 4022 and 3803, a 2-8-2 and a 2-10-2, lead the train. Instead of flashes, Abbey used ambient light and a long exposure time to make the photograph. While the shutter was open, a crewmember carried a lantern between the cab and the front of the lead locomotive, leaving a trail of light on the negative.

Facing: E3 diesel no. 11, an A-B pair built in 1939, leads a passenger train out of Chicago's Dearborn Station in the winter gloom of February 2, 1952. The switchman has come out of his shanty to inspect the train as it passes. In the background at right, one of Santa Fe's Alco diesel switchers shuffles passenger cars while a Grand Trunk Western 4-8-4 steam locomotive gets another passenger train moving.

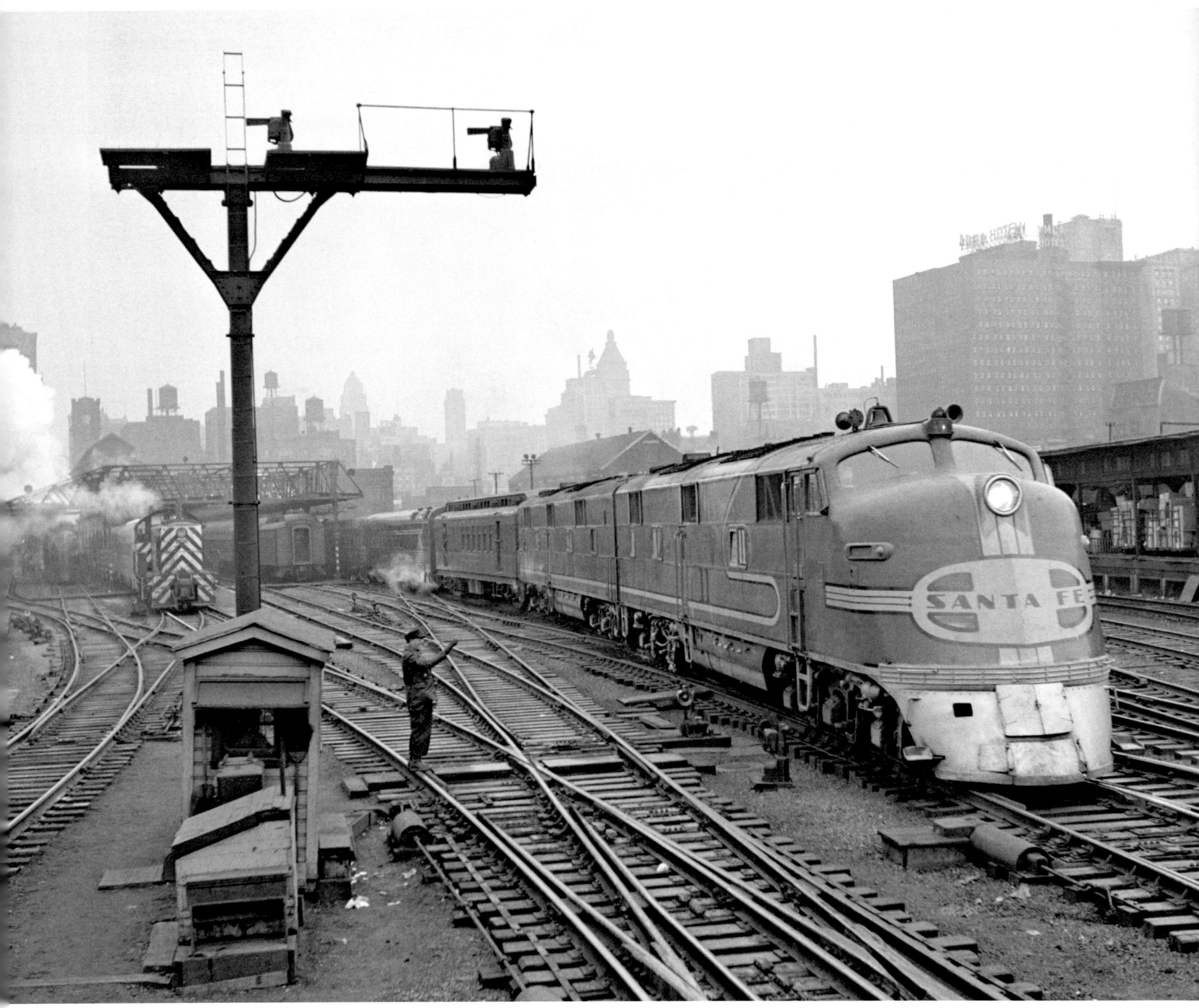

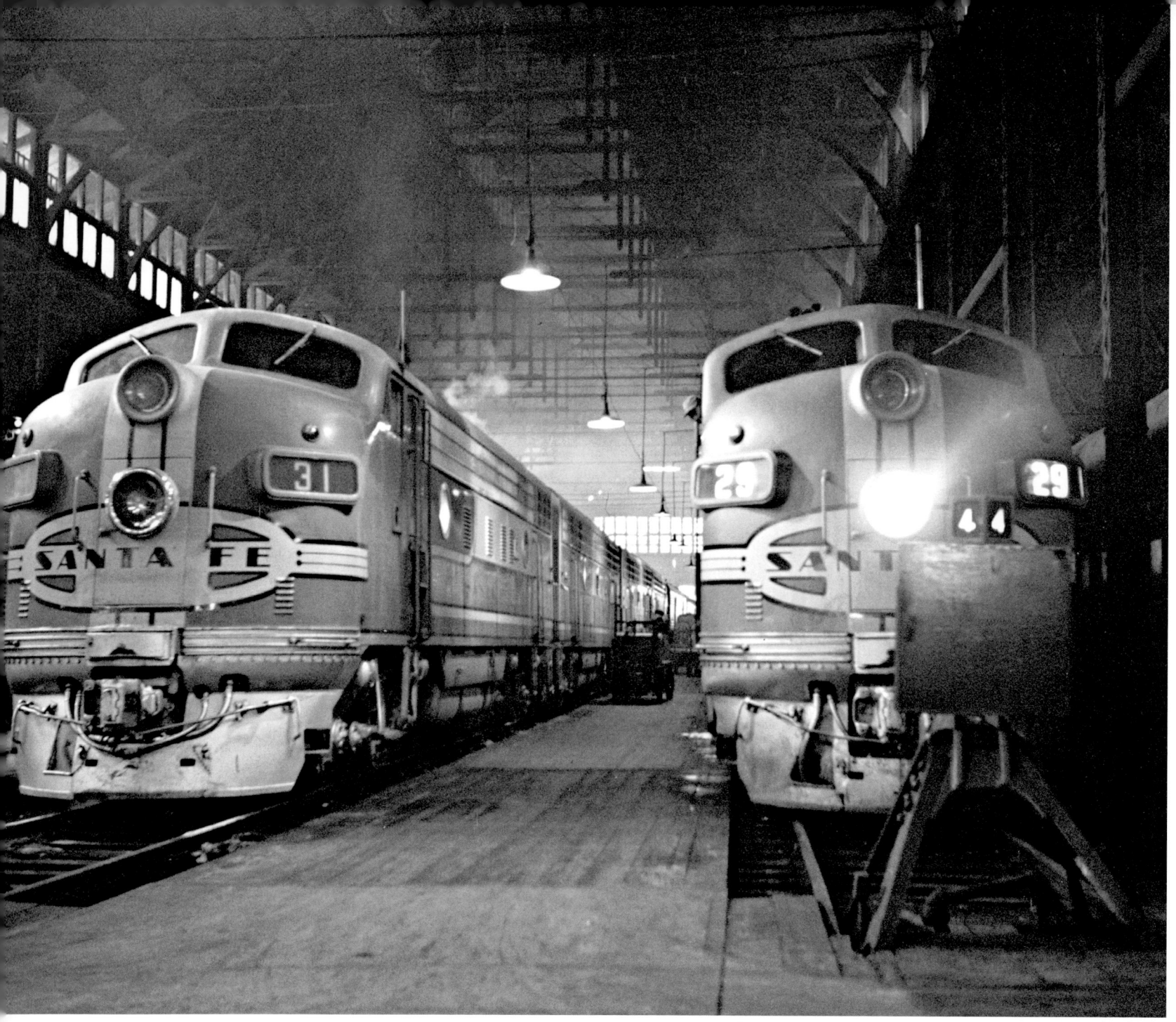

Two streamliners rest at the bumping posts under the shed at Dearborn Station in downtown Chicago on February 2, 1952. Leading both trains are F7A diesels built by the Electro-Motive Division of General Motors. At the time, Santa Fe ran no fewer than eight long-distance passenger trains in and out of Dearborn each day.

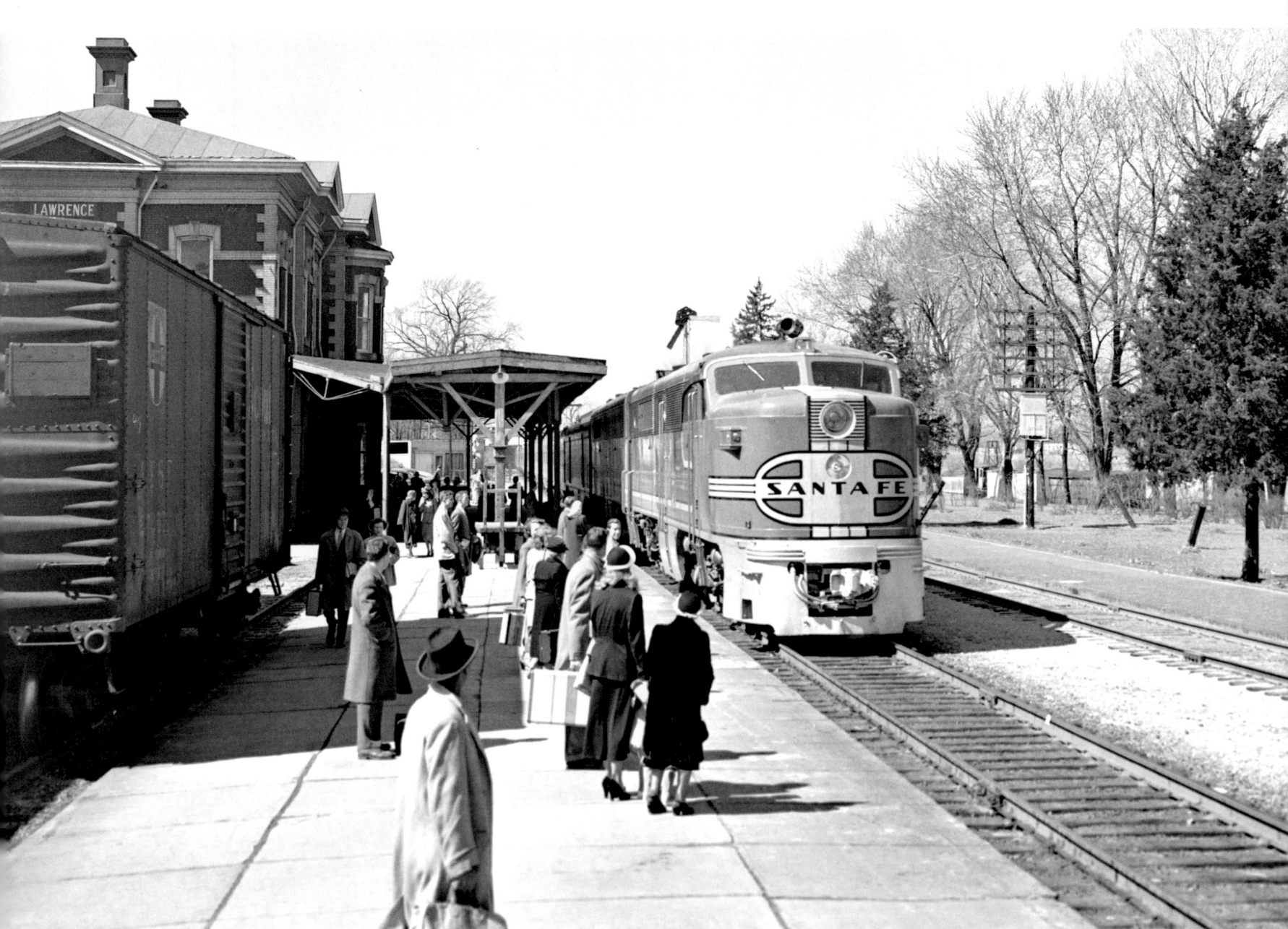

Santa Fe eastbound passenger train no. 12, the *Chicagoan*, pulls into the depot at Lawrence, Kansas, behind PA1 locomotive no. 71 on March 19, 1949. The *Chicagoan* and westbound counterpart no. 11, the *Kansas Cityan*, made daytime trips with streamlined equipment between Chicago and Oklahoma City. When *Trains* magazine was briefly renamed *Trains & Travel*, this photograph made the cover of the inaugural issue of the renamed publication.

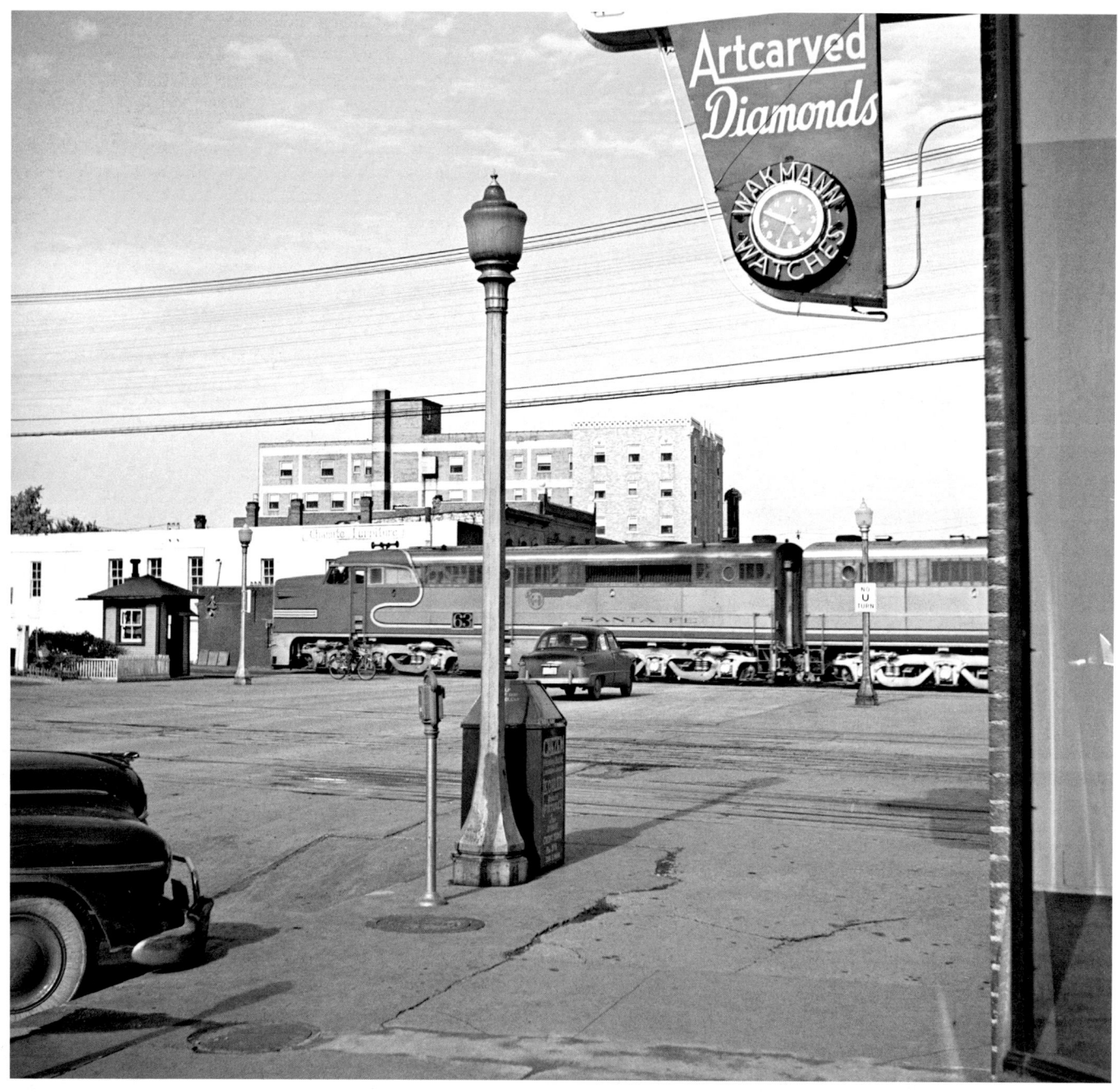

Above: In a wonderfully evocative sidewalk scene from downtown Chanute, Kansas, in 1950, Santa Fe's eastbound *Oil Flyer* passenger train arrives five minutes early according to the jewelry-store clock. The train made an evening run from Tulsa, Oklahoma, to Kansas City, Missouri. A timely connection with the eastbound *California Limited* in Kansas City enabled travelers to be in Chicago the next morning.

Facing: A three-unit set of Alco's handsome PA locomotives leads Santa Fe train no. 19, the westbound *Chief*, across the Des Plaines River in Lemont, Illinois, on a June afternoon in 1952. A couple at water's edge appears unimpressed by the passage of the stainless-steel train. The unused piers carried an older Santa Fe bridge across the river.

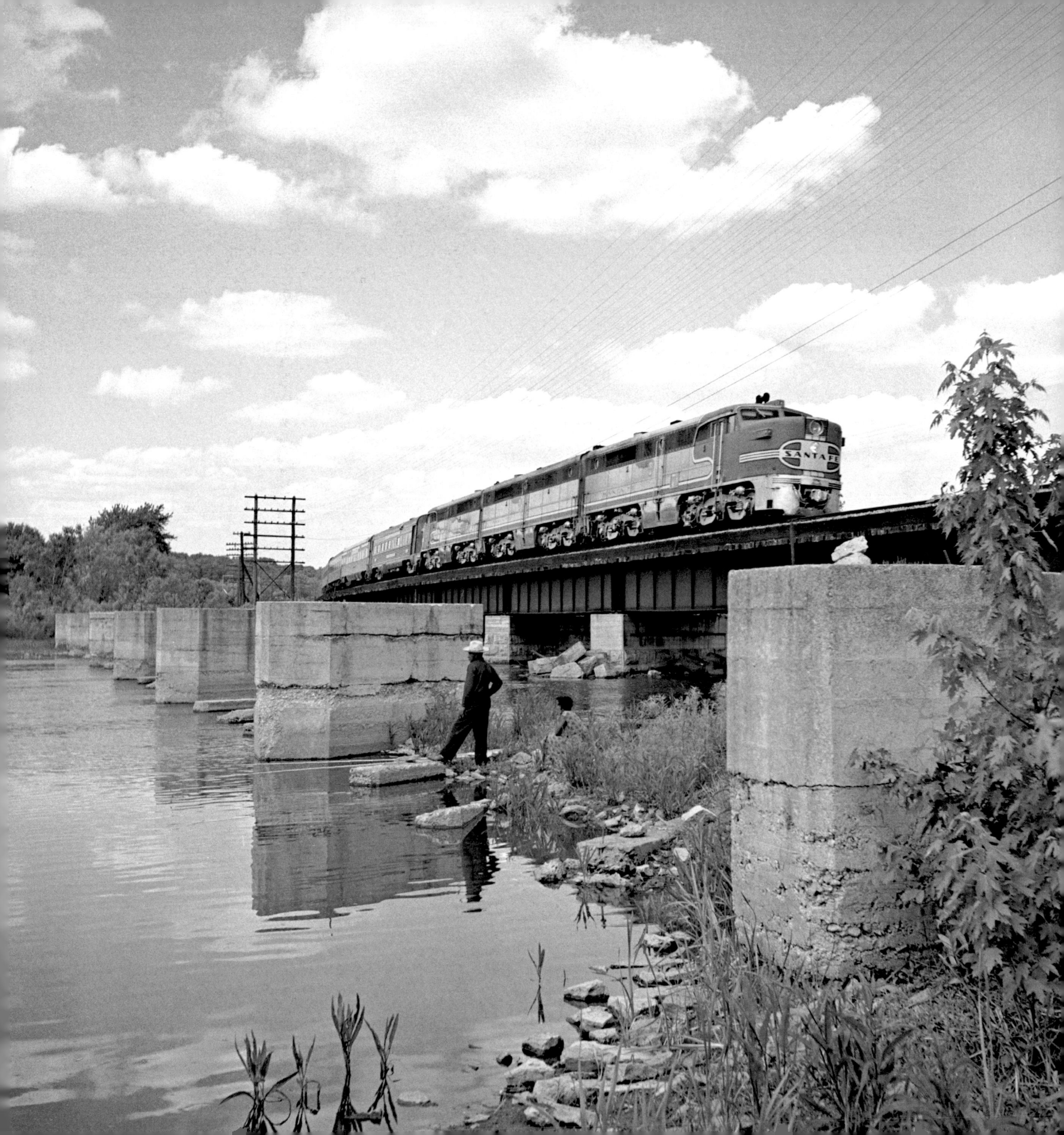

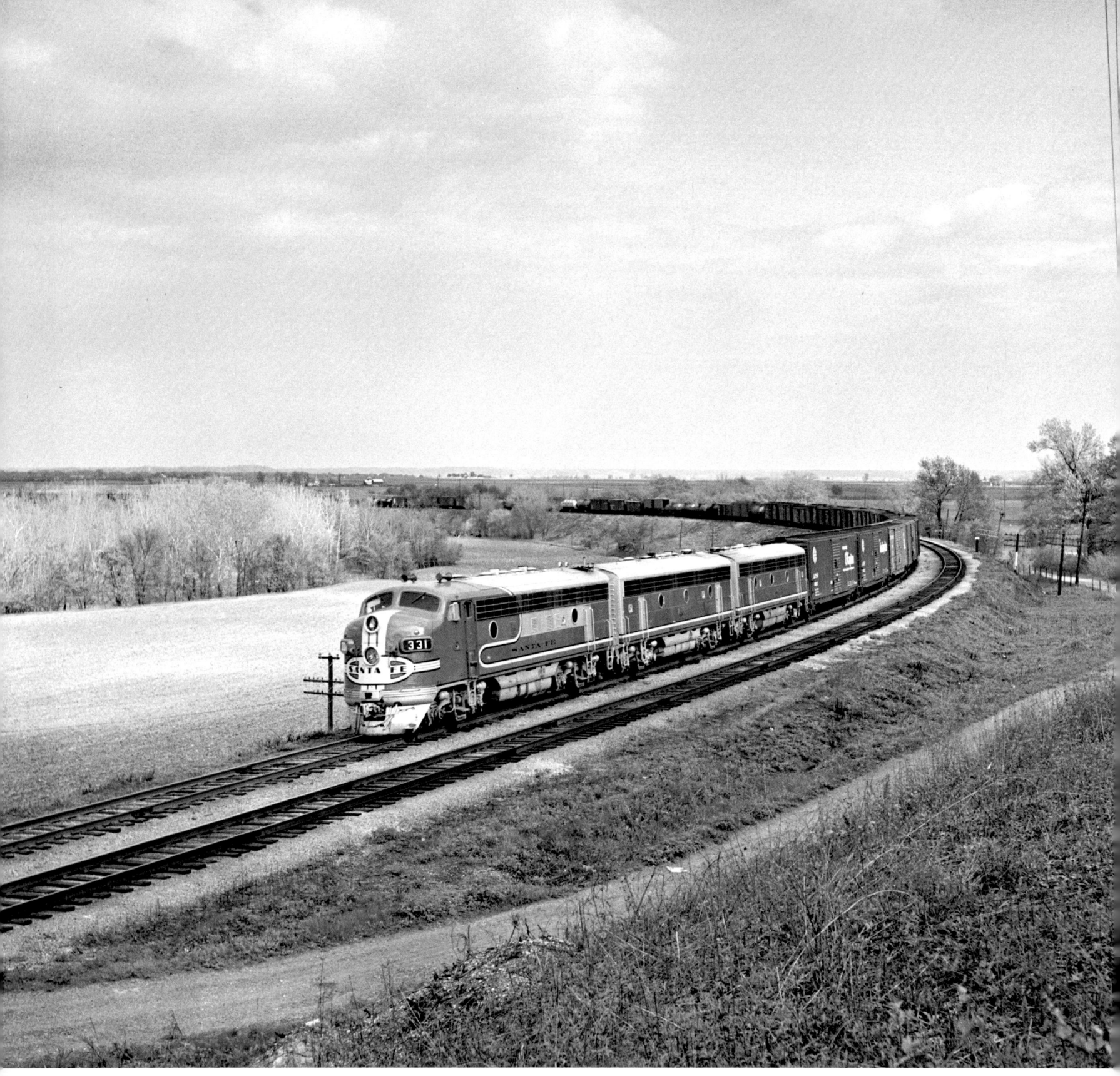

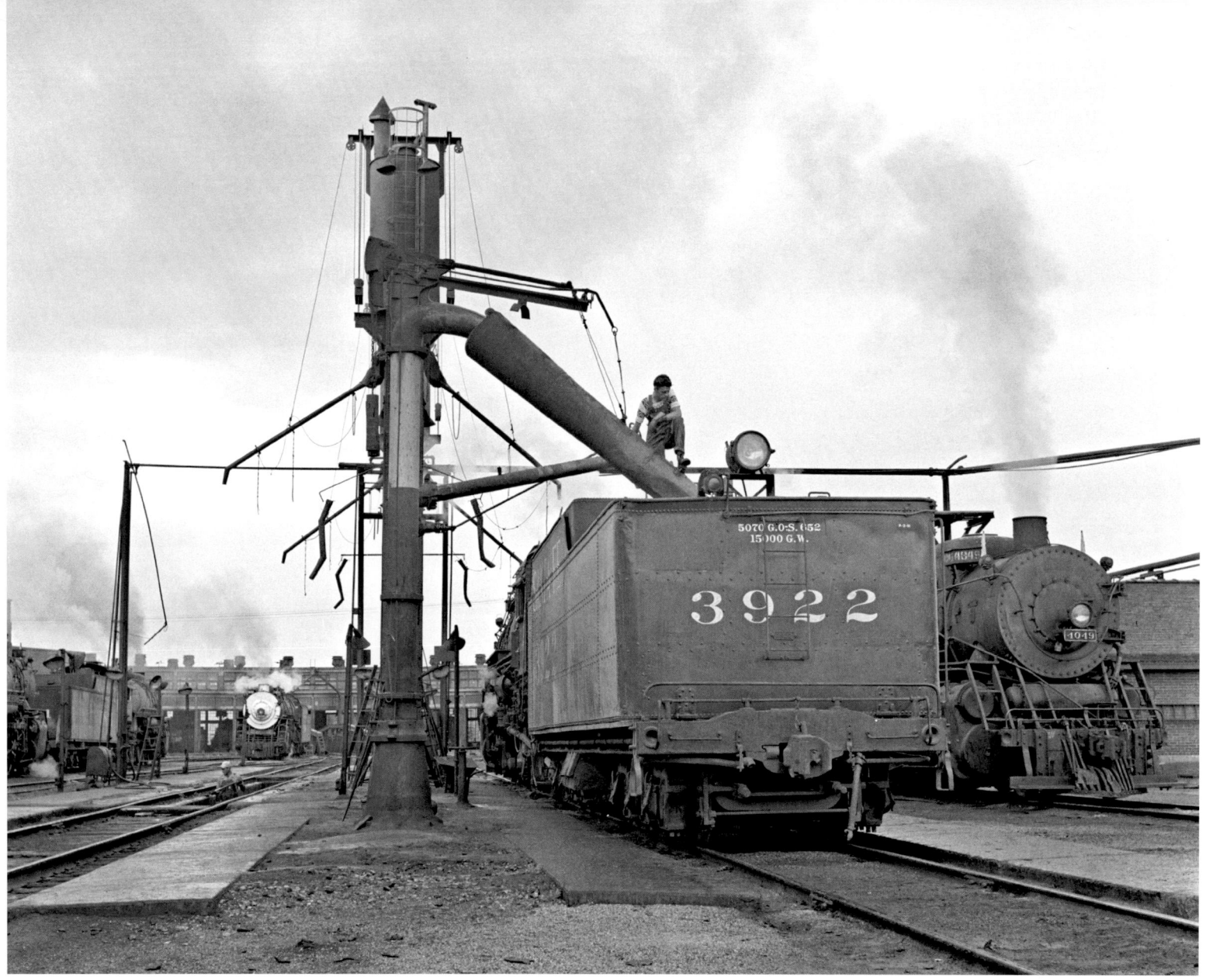

Facing: An A-B-B set of F7 locomotives in Santa Fe's classic "Warbonnet" paint leads a westbound freight train up Edelstein Hill west of Chillicothe, Illinois, on May 1, 1953. The short but substantial hill brought the Santa Fe out of the Illinois River valley, which it crossed at Chillicothe. The grade required most freight trains to use helper locomotives during the steam era.

Above: Santa Fe 2-10-2 no. 3922 takes water at the roundhouse in Emporia, Kansas, on July 7, 1952. At least four other steam locomotives are visible, but their time was running out—Abbey photographed newly delivered GP7 diesels on the same day. Emporia was a division point during the steam era where trains changed locomotives, which were then serviced at the thirty-stall roundhouse. Built in 1928, it spanned 200 degrees of a circle, but it soon fell into disuse since diesels required far less maintenance than steam. Santa Fe demolished the Emporia roundhouse in 1984, and almost nothing of the structure remains today.

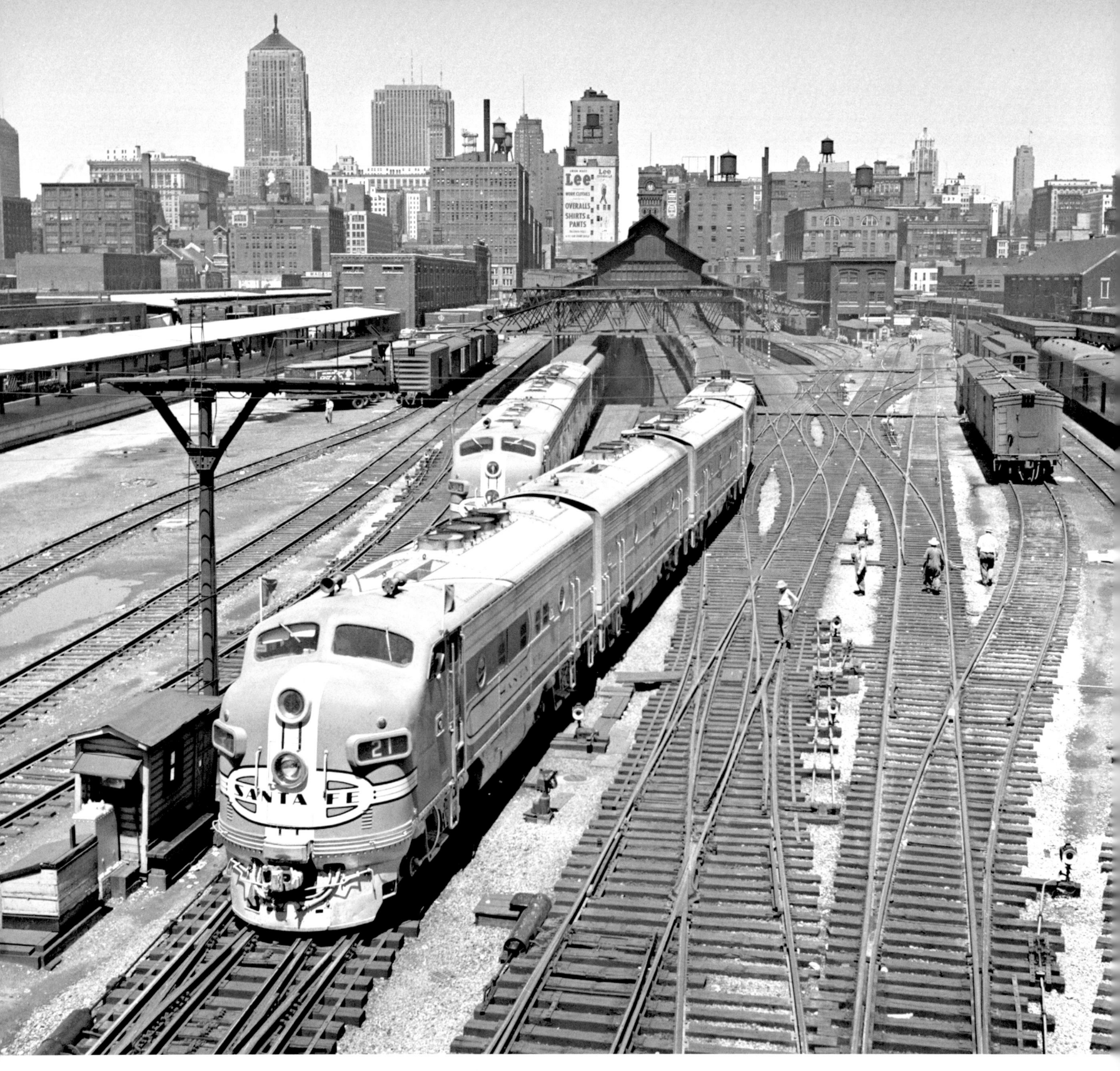

Facing: The first section of Santa Fe train no. 19, the westbound *Chief* for Los Angeles, departs from Chicago's Dearborn Station on July 7, 1952, behind an A-B-B-A set of F-series locomotives in the railroad's iconic "Warbonnet" paint. Lead unit no. 21 is flying green flags, indicating that another section of the train is following. Visible directly behind this one, the second section would depart a few minutes later to maintain a safe distance.

Below: Dispatcher Harry Flottman controls train movements over two sections of the Middle Division from the centralized traffic control (CTC) machine at his desk in Newton, Kansas, in 1952. A schematic diagram of the railroad appears at the top of the panels; the switches below allow him to remotely control track switches and signals along the line. Santa Fe was an early adopter of CTC, which allowed one person to do the work of many while eliminating considerable paperwork and delays.

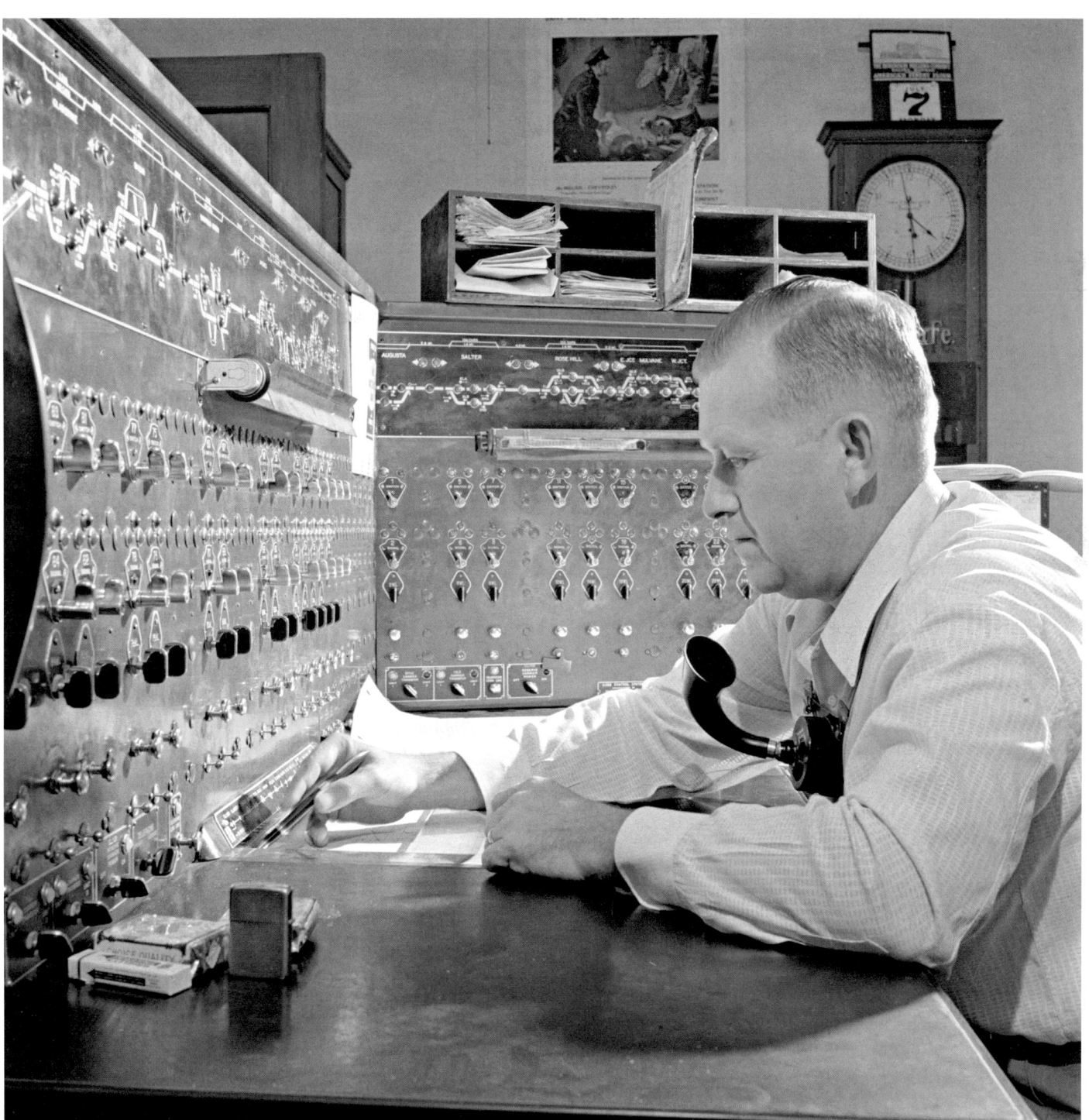

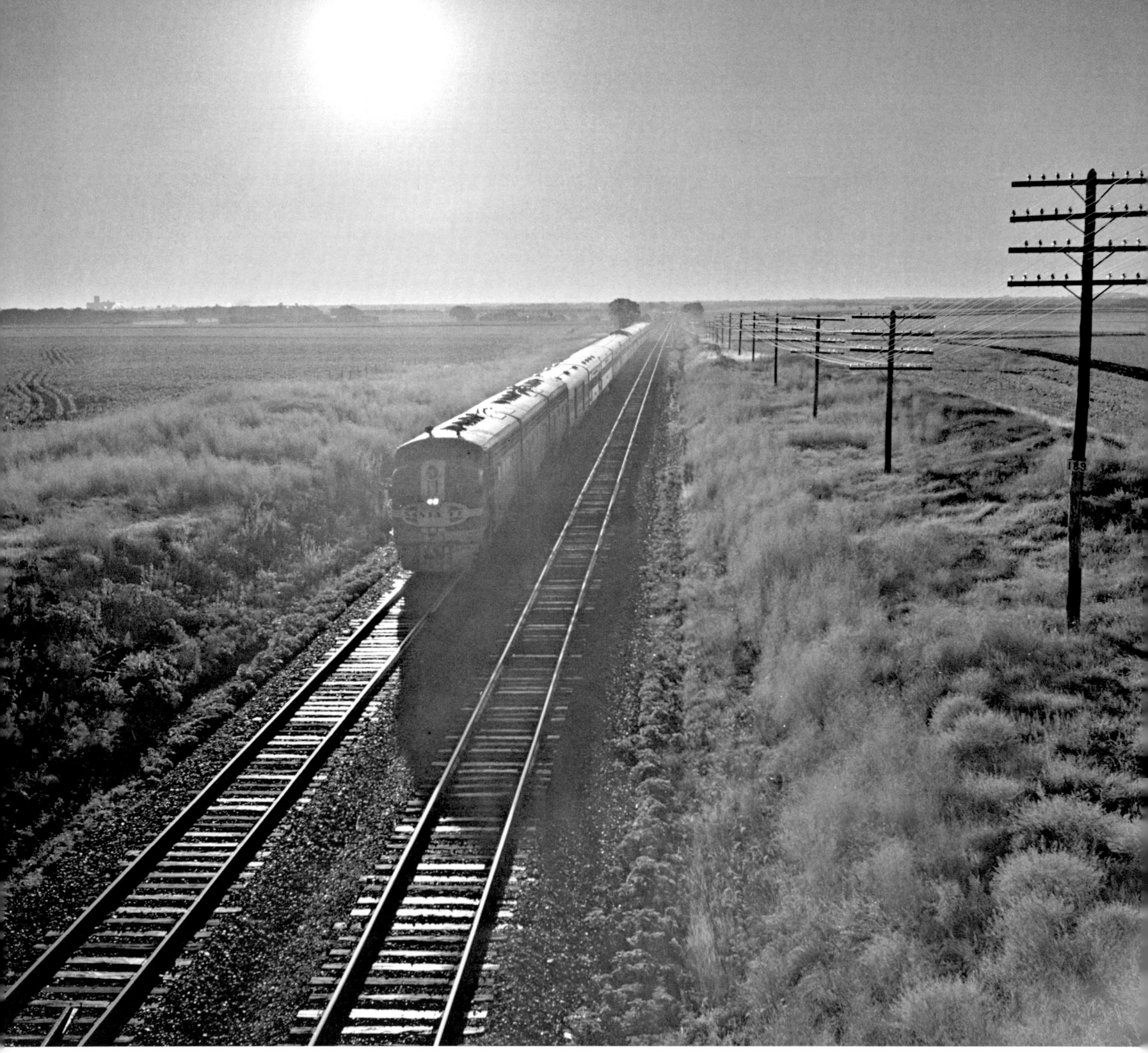

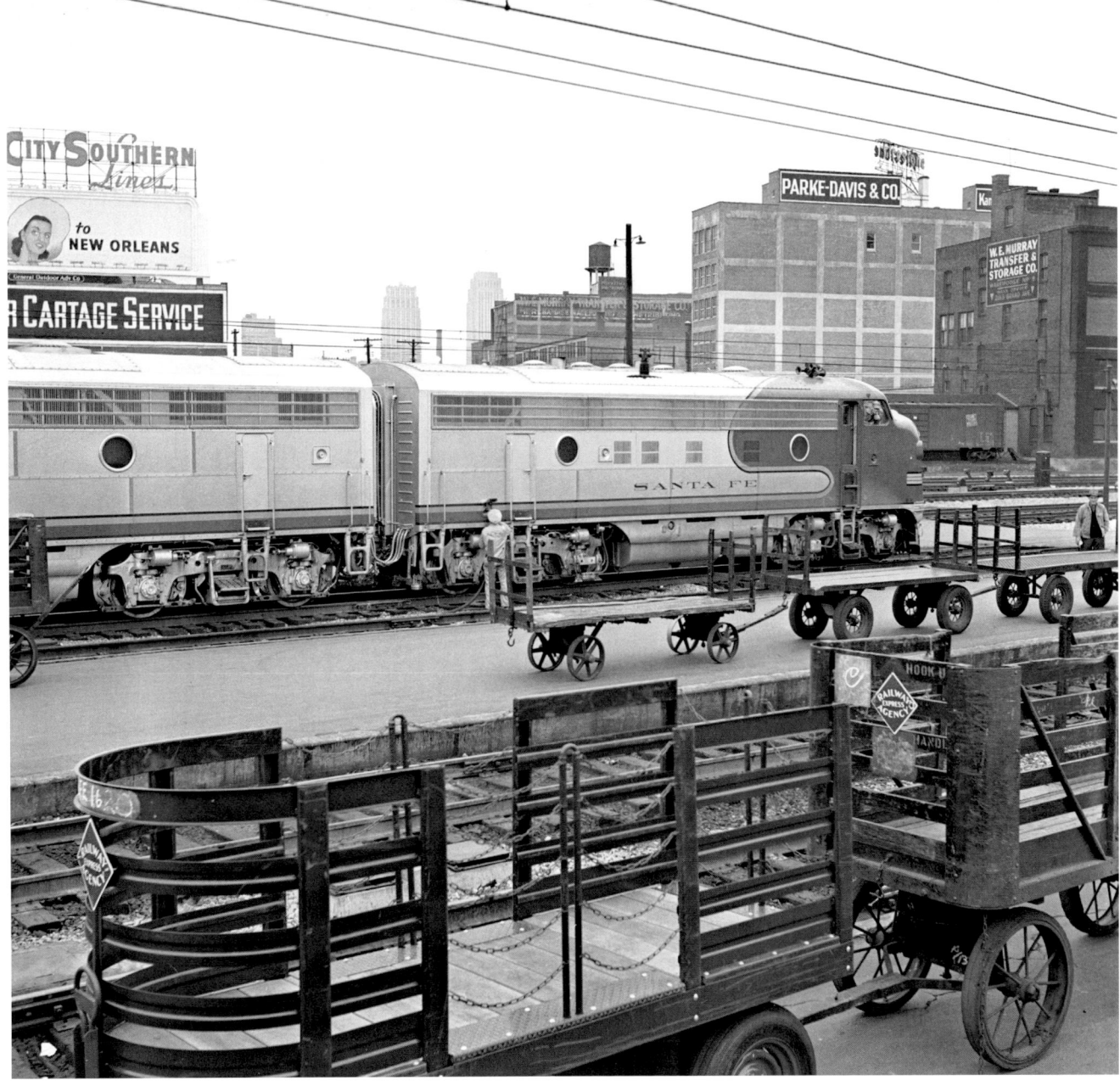

Facing: Train no. 17, the westbound *Super Chief*, comes out of the rising sun as it races across the prairies east of Newton, Kansas, on July 8, 1952. Introduced in 1937 with diesel power from the outset, the *Super Chief* made the Chicago–Los Angeles run in just under forty hours and quickly became Santa Fe's flagship passenger train. The railroad's own promotional literature called it "the train of the stars" due to heavy celebrity patronage in its early years.

Above: Baggage and express carts surround F7 locomotives at Kansas City Union Station in July 1952. Abbey recorded this scene from the cab of eastbound train no. 12, the *Chicagoan*, which he was riding. The locomotives in view likely belong to train no. 212, the *Tulsan*, which would have just arrived from its namesake city to connect with no. 12. Abbey frequently rode trains nos. 212 and 12, as well as their west- and southbound counterparts, nos. 11 and 211, to visit his maternal grandparents in Cherryvale, Kansas.

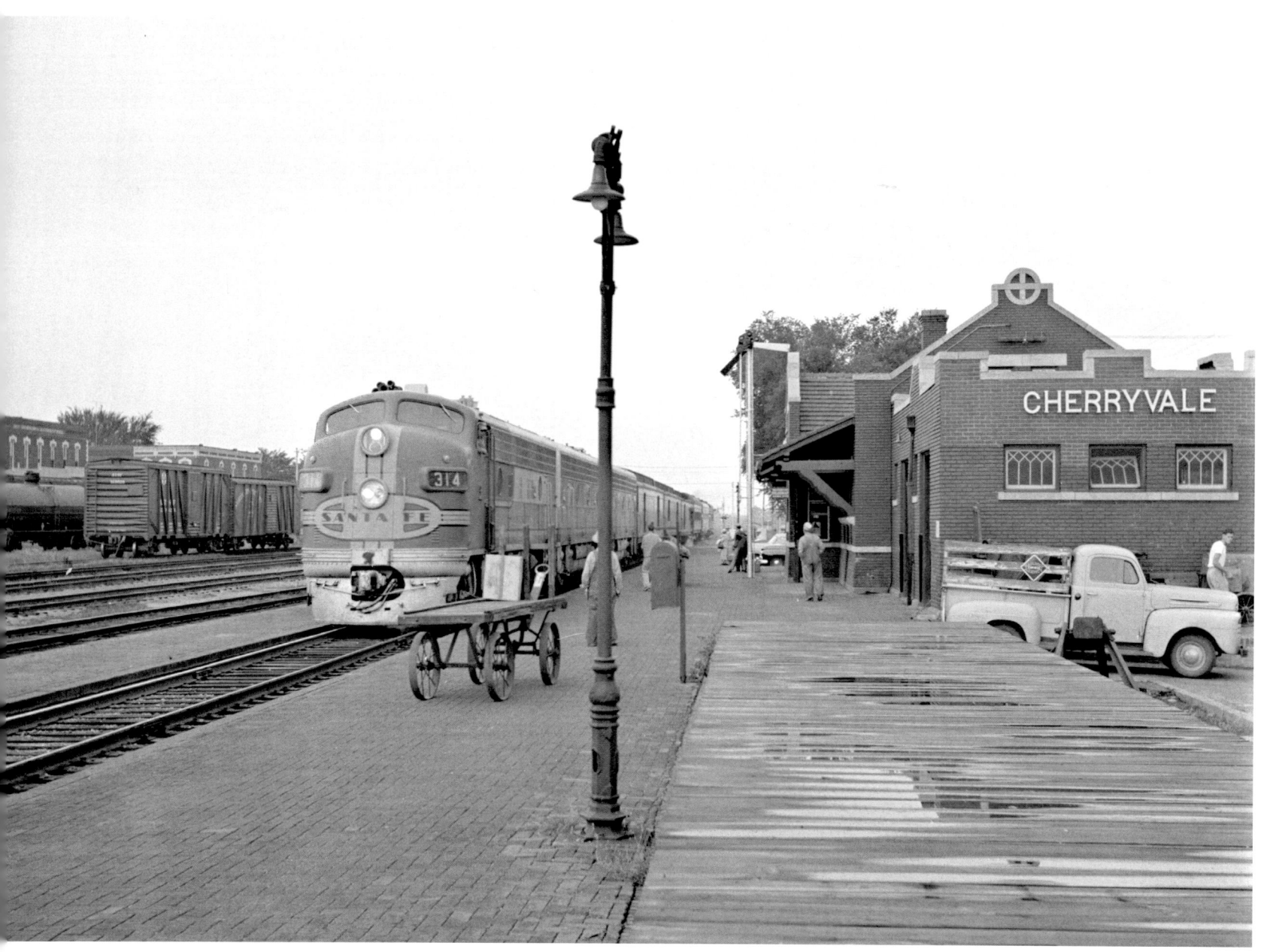

Passenger train no. 48, the northbound *Oil Flyer*, pulls into the depot at Cherryvale, Kansas, on a July evening in 1953. The *Oil Flyer* combined with the *Tulsan* to offer two daily roundtrips between Tulsa, Oklahoma, and Kansas City, Missouri. Note the Railway Express Agency (REA) pickup truck parked at right. A precursor of today's UPS and FedEx, REA provided swift package delivery around the country, facilitated by the nation's passenger trains.

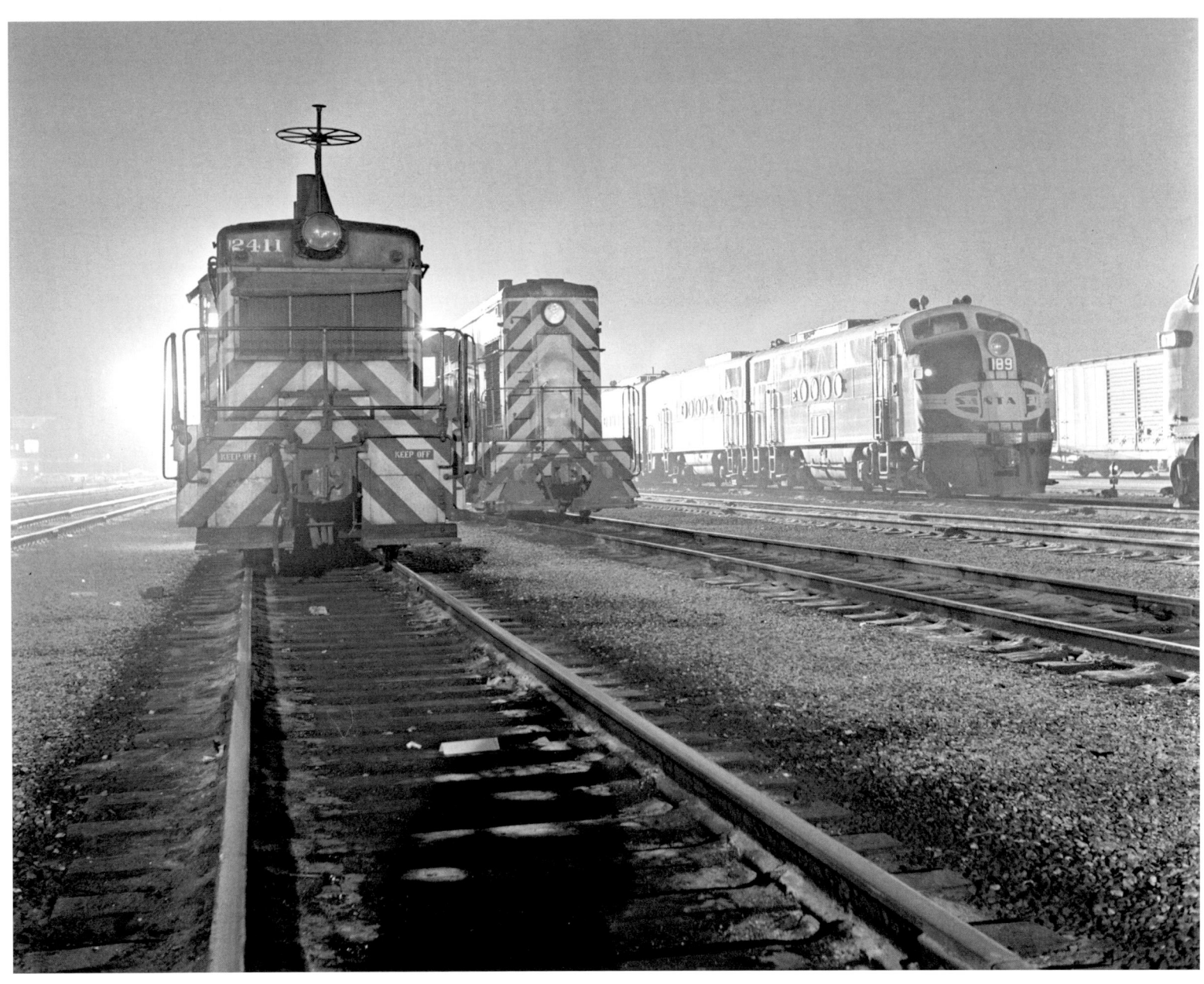

Three models of diesels from two different builders rest at Corwith Yard in Chicago on the night of March 13, 1958. From left to right are switchers from Electro-Motive and Fairbanks Morse, NW2 no. 2411 and H-12-44 no. 522, followed by two sets of Electro-Motive FT units led by nos. 189 and 173. The railroad had just upgraded Corwith as a gravity-powered "hump" yard, the reason for Abbey's visit.

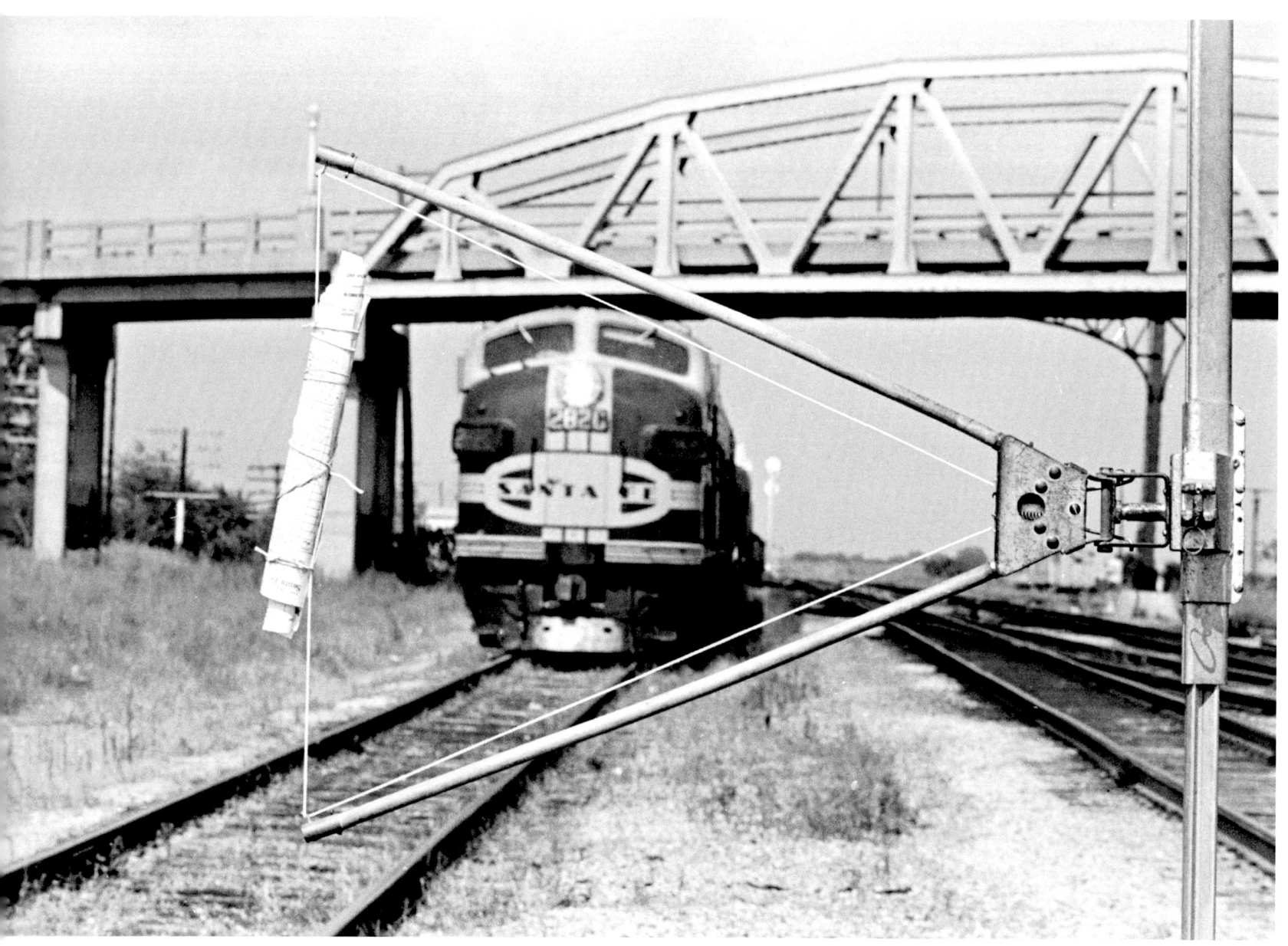

Train orders tied in string await pickup by the crew of a westbound freight train approaching the depot at Ottawa, Kansas, on August 10, 1963. The bridge in the background carries the town's Main Street, which is also US Highway 59, over the Santa Fe's main line to California. Ottawa was an important junction on the railroad between the east–west main line and the north–south Tulsa Subdivision.

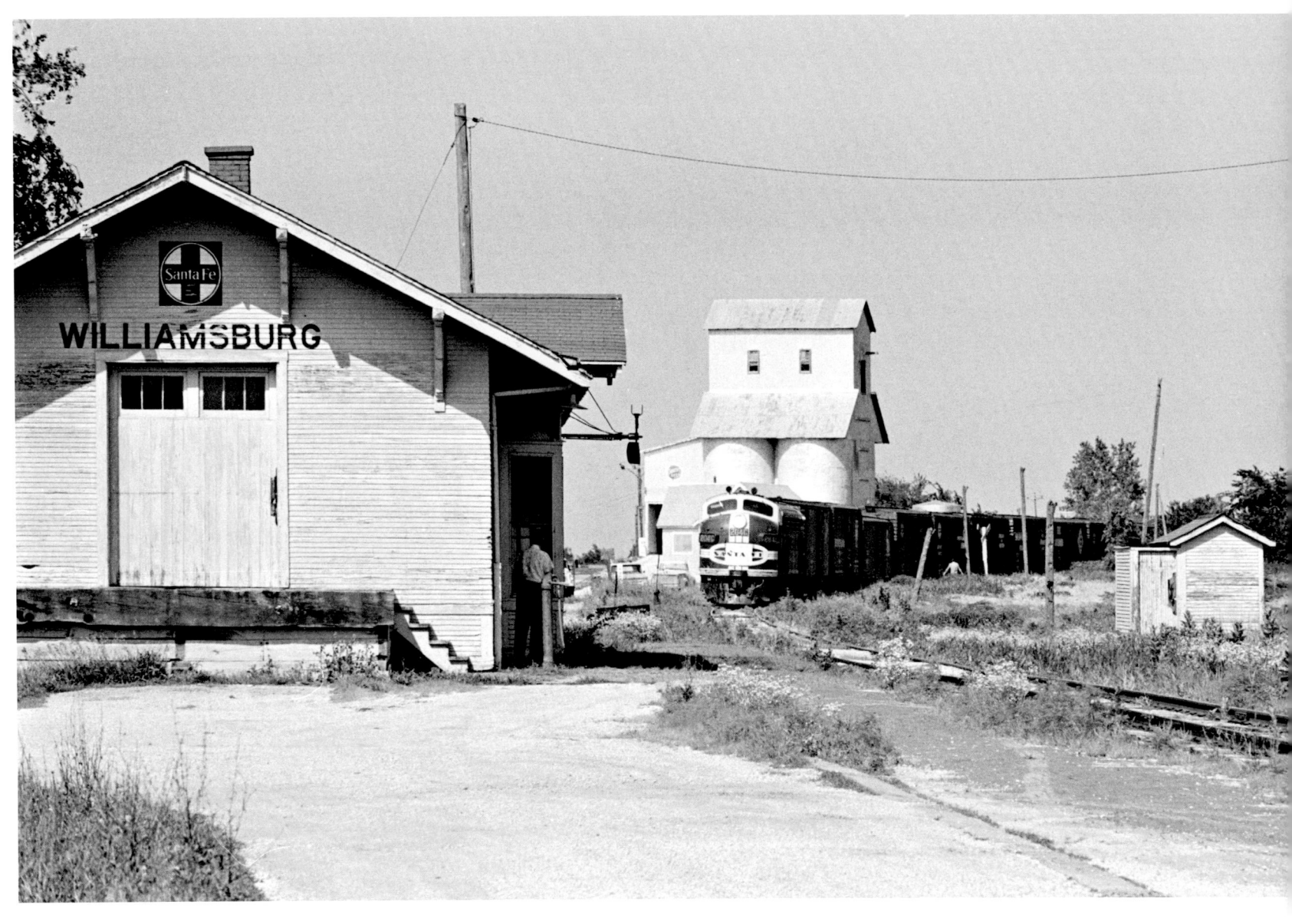

A freight train approaches the wooden depot at Williamsburg, Kansas, on the Santa Fe's branch line from Ottawa to Gridley on June 17, 1965. The Santa Fe once had an extensive network of branch lines in Kansas, but the weed-grown track of this one speaks to the struggles that so many branch lines faced from trucks and a much-improved highway system. The Santa Fe abandoned many of its branches, including this one, while it sold others to short-line operators.

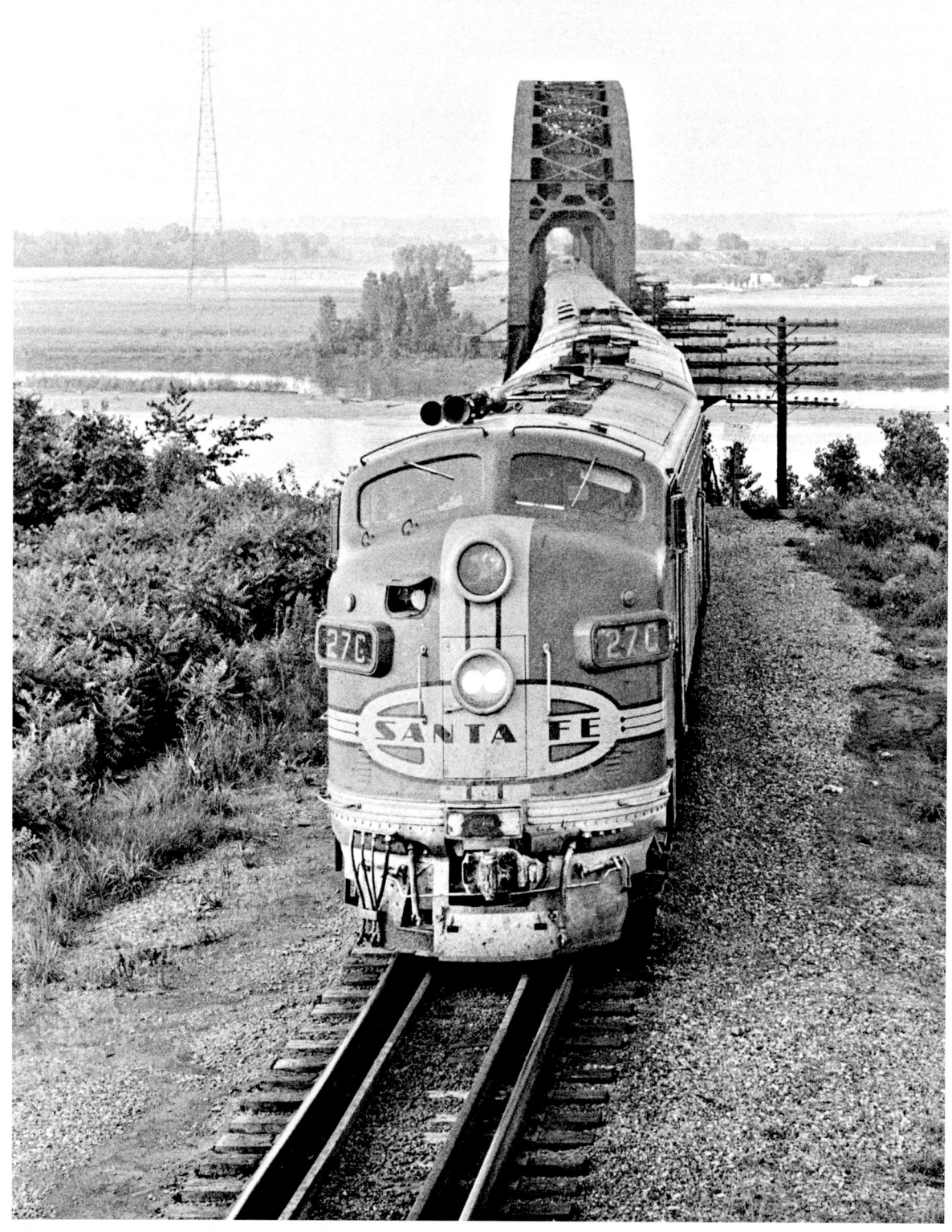

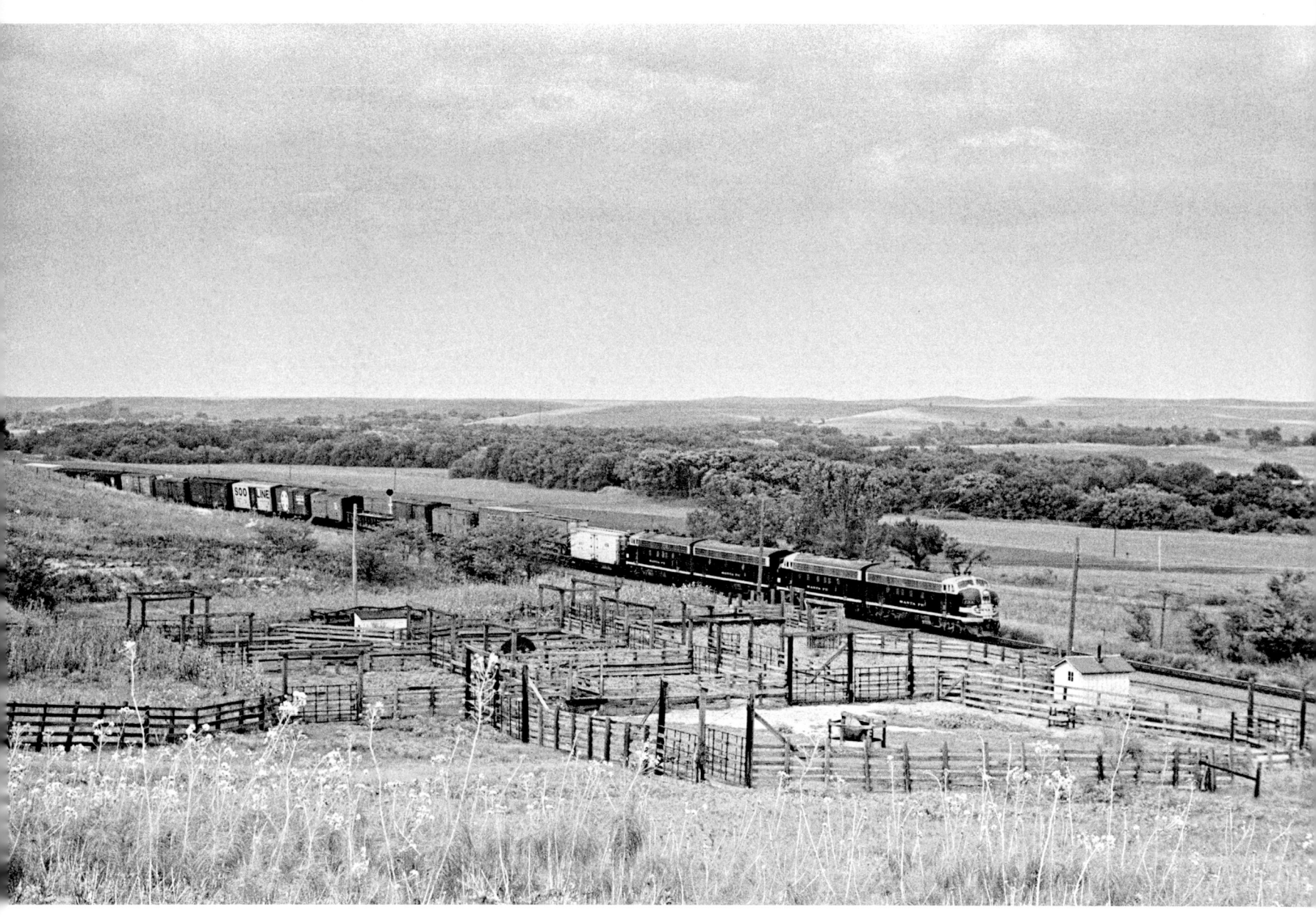

Facing: Train no. 23, the westbound *Grand Canyon*, crossing the Missouri River at Sibley, Missouri, in July 1969. Postwar competition from the automobile and jet airliner had taken quite a toll on the railroad passenger business, and Santa Fe's once-great fleet of passenger trains was much diminished by this date. In less than two years, the Santa Fe and most other US railroads would turn over their passenger operations to the National Railroad Passenger Corporation, better known as Amtrak.

Above: On a late summer day in 1969, four Santa Fe F-units power a freight train past trackside livestock pens in the rolling hills at Matfield Green, Kansas. Shipping livestock by rail was once common; it had been big business on the Santa Fe, which ran dedicated livestock trains and gave them high priority to ensure the animals arrived to meatpackers in optimum condition. The trucking industry began taking over livestock transportation after World War II, and the Santa Fe hauled its last carload just three years after Abbey recorded this scene.

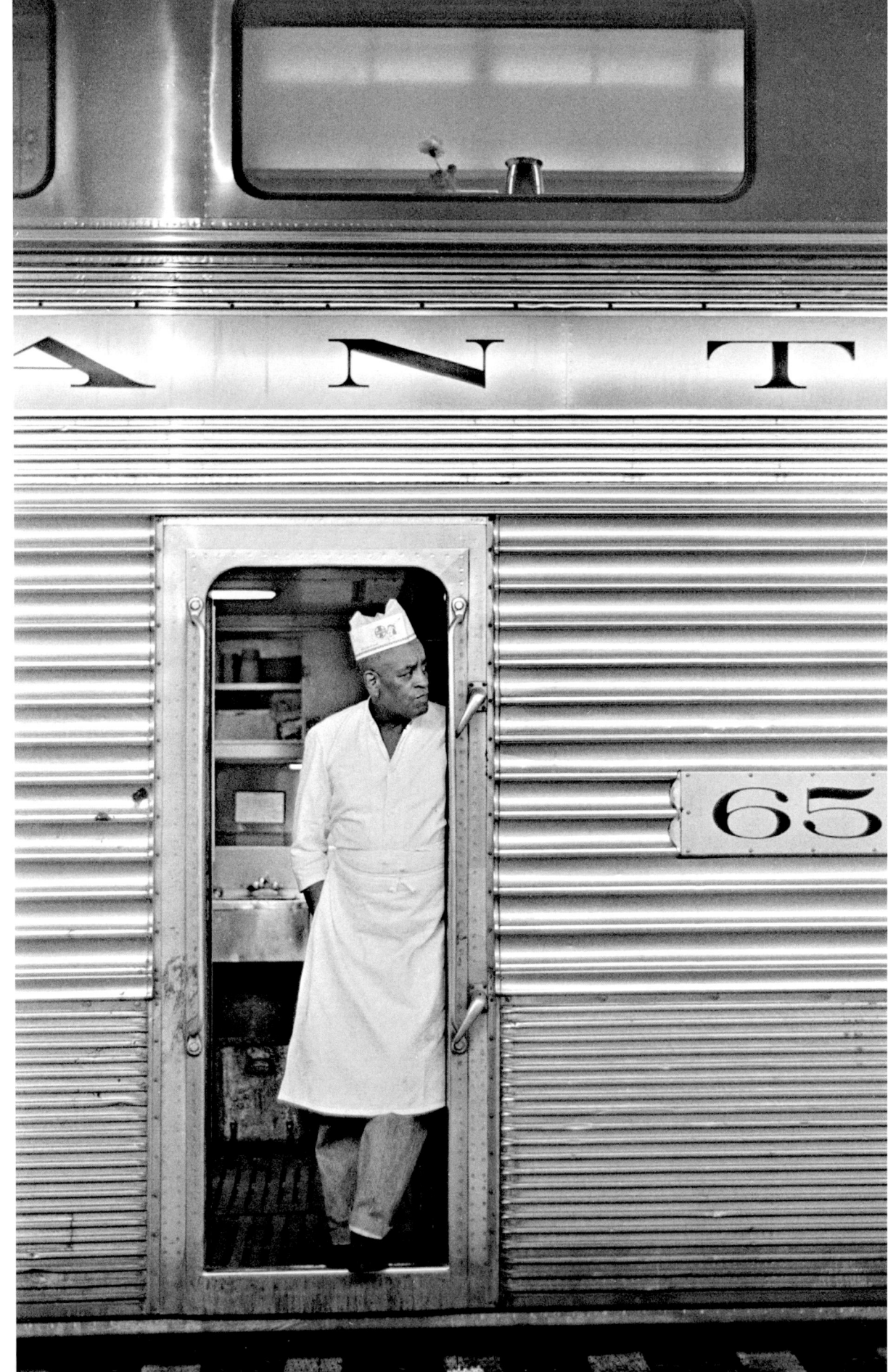

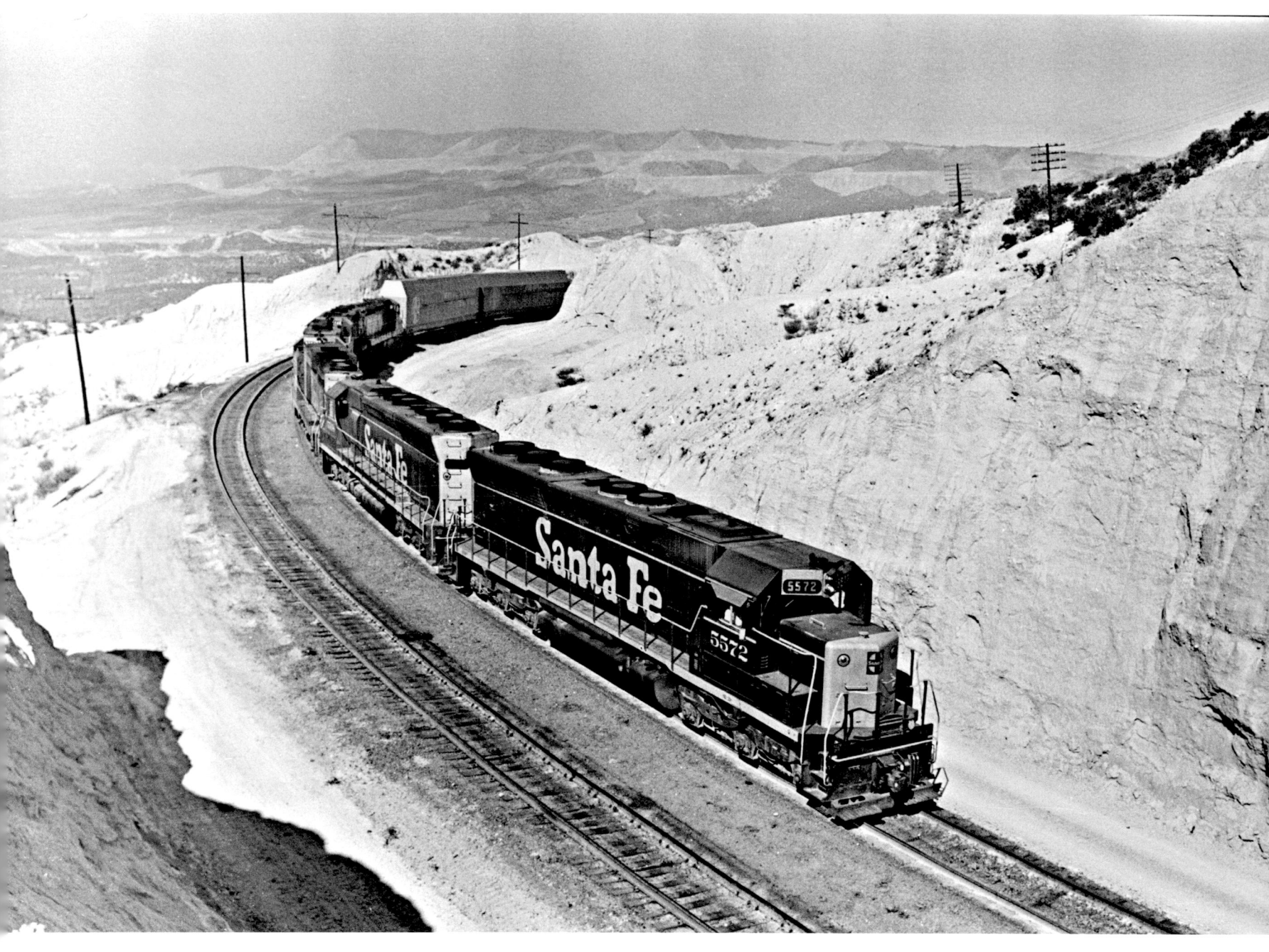

Facing: A Santa Fe dining-car worker contemplates his eastbound run to Chicago and, ultimately, an uncertain future from the door of his Hi-Level car at Los Angeles Union Passenger Terminal in April of 1970. Formerly separate trains, the combined *Super Chief–El Capitan* is one of just two on the railroad still making the LA–Chicago trek. It would be the only one left after Santa Fe joined Amtrak a year later.

Above: SD45 no. 5572 leads a consist of six diesels heading an eastbound freight train at the summit of California's Cajon Pass in 1970. The train has climbed out of the Los Angeles Basin from San Bernardino and will soon be heading across the Mojave Desert for Arizona. Cajon Pass was—and remains—one of the busiest railroad mountain crossings in the country.

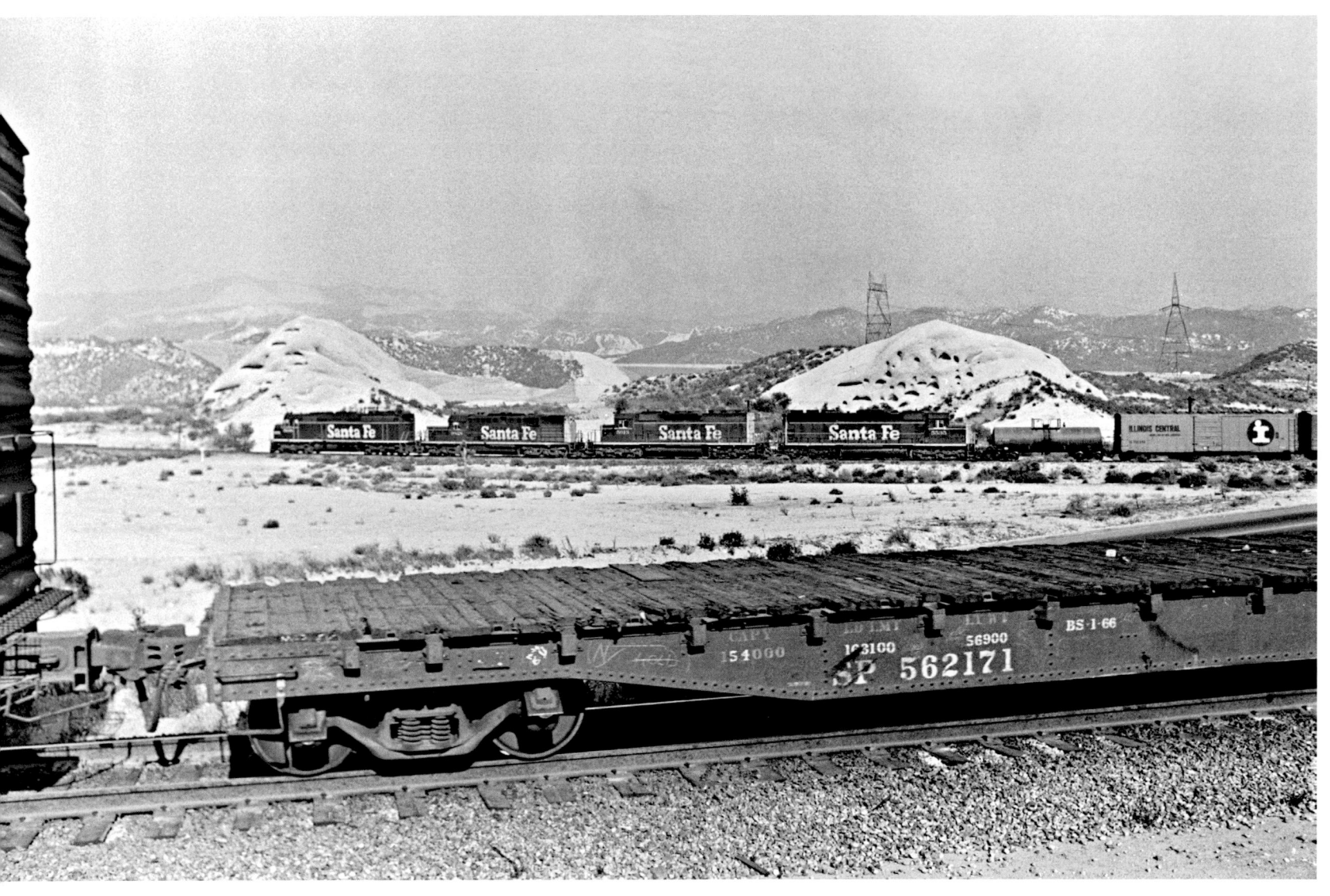

Legendary on the Santa Fe and in southern California, Cajon Pass received only one visit from Abbey, in 1970. Hosting the trains of both Santa Fe and Southern Pacific (today BNSF Railway and Union Pacific), Cajon is one of the busiest mountain crossings in the North American rail network. Abbey got at its essence with this view, using the cars of an eastbound train heading uphill to frame a descending westbound with some of the pass's uniquely eroded rock formations.

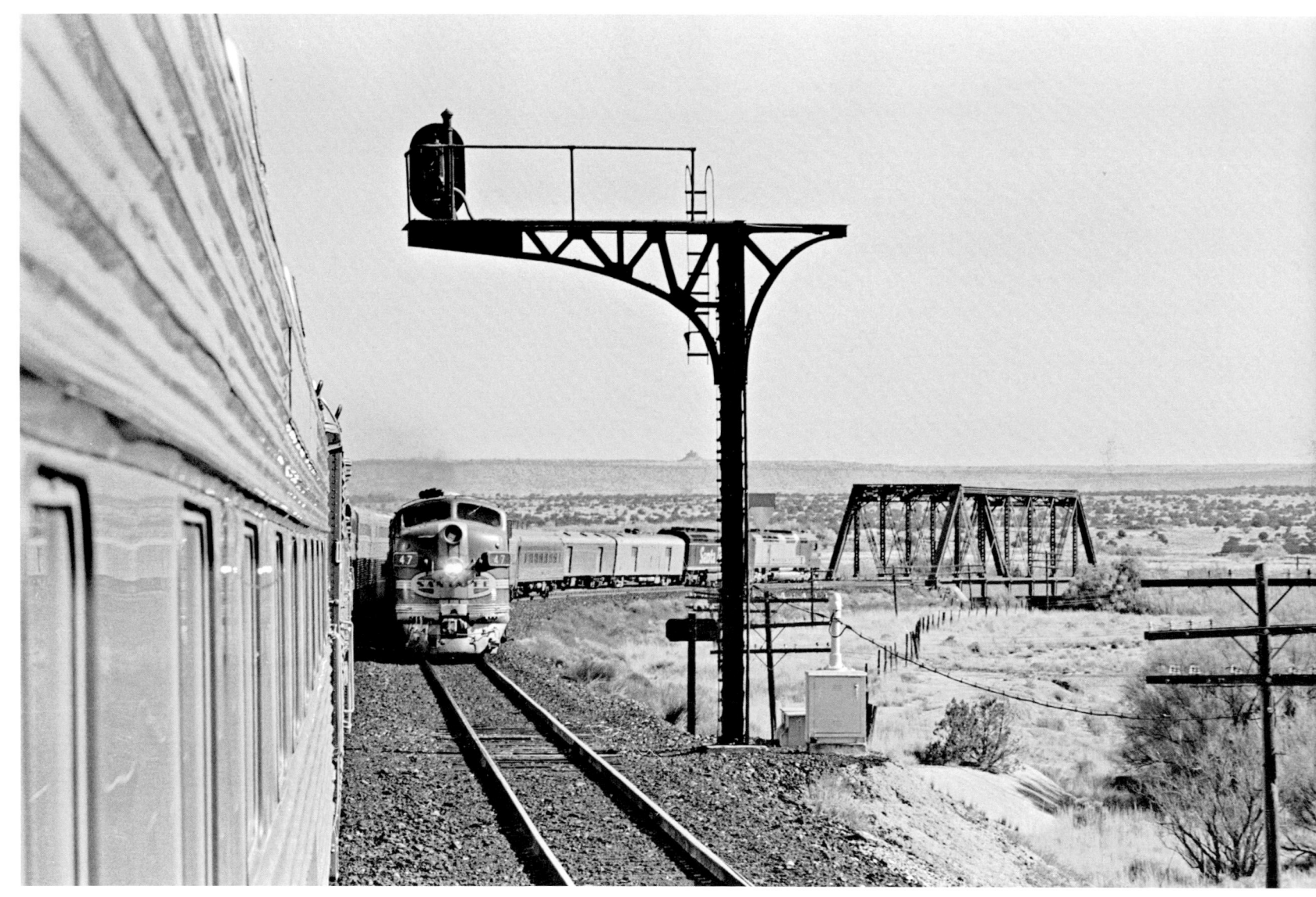

Riding back east on the combined *Super Chief–El Capitan* after a visit to southern California in April of 1970, Abbey captured this iconic view of the final days of the Santa Fe's once-vaunted passenger service. In the high desert country west of Albuquerque, New Mexico, classic passenger power in the form of F7A no. 47 leads westbound train no. 23, the *Grand Canyon*, while a new FP45 and F45 power Abbey's train. Just a year later, the *Grand Canyon* made its final run, and Amtrak took over operation of the *Super Chief–El Capitan*.

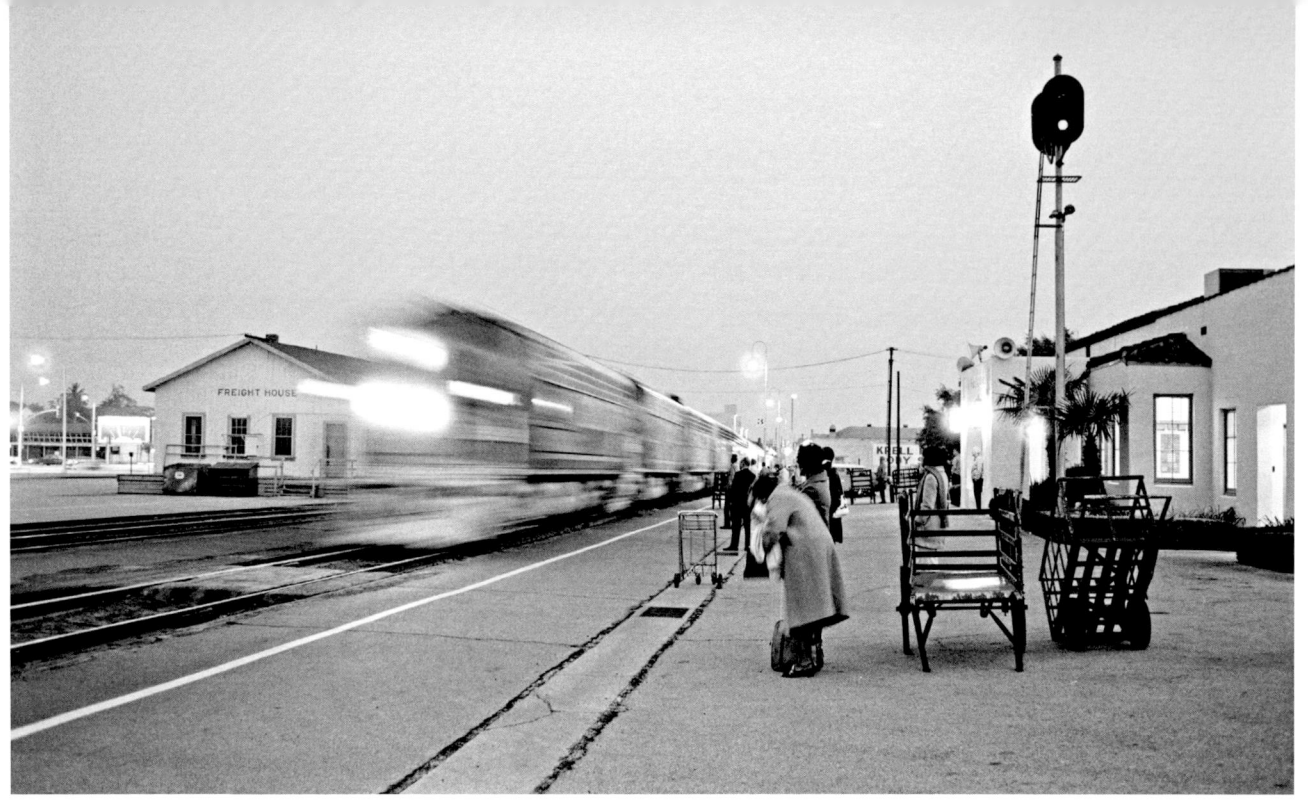
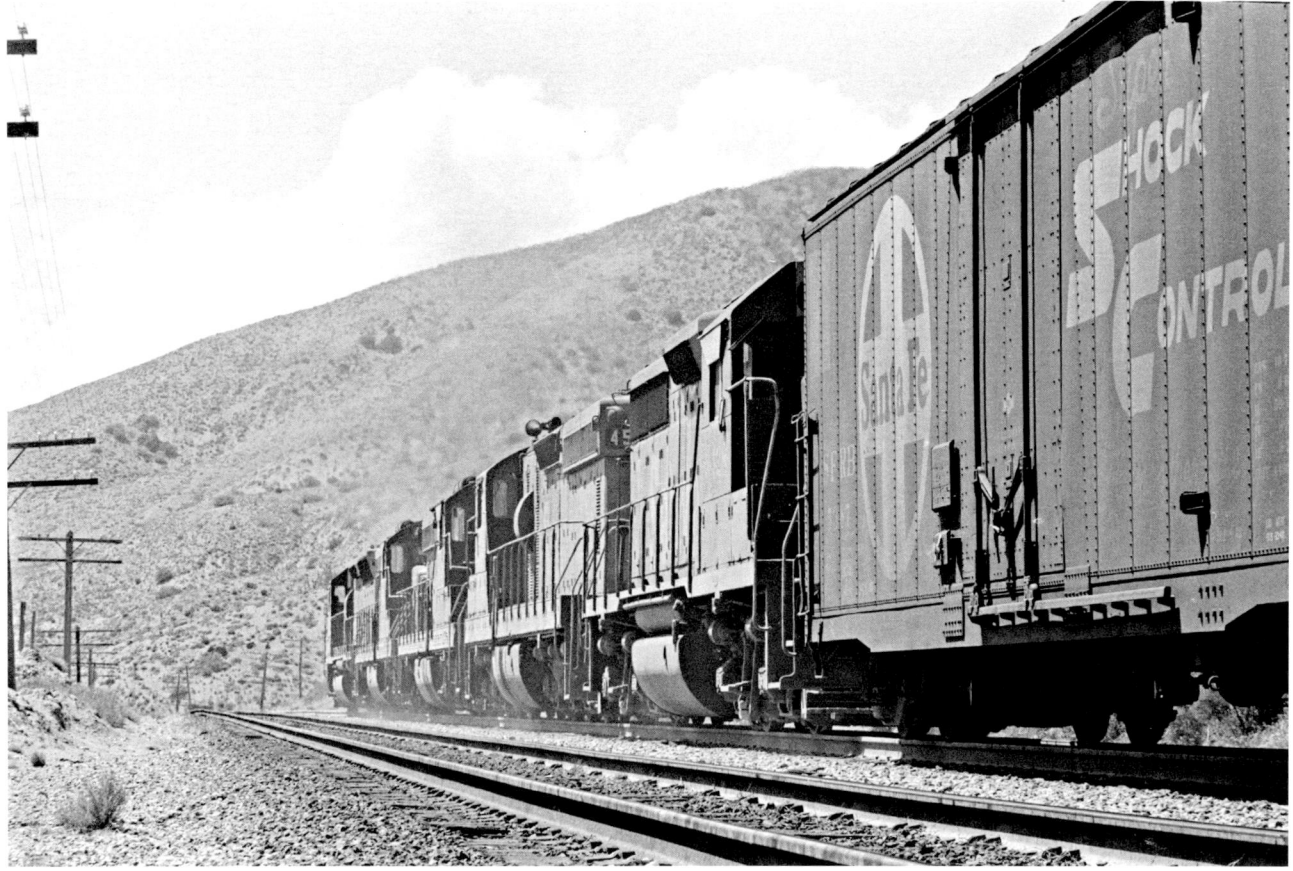

Facing top: Just out of Los Angeles, eastbound train no. 18, the combined *Super Chief–El Capitan*, makes its first station stop at Pasadena, California, on an April evening in 1970. Amtrak would take over most of the nation's passenger trains in a little more than a year. In 1994, Amtrak shifted the route of its successor train, the *Southwest Chief*, to Fullerton, ending more than a century of long-distance passenger train service in Pasadena. Today the depot houses a restaurant.

Facing bottom: To climb out of California's San Joaquin Valley, Santa Fe utilized Southern Pacific's line over Tehachapi Pass. Abbey visited this hallowed piece of mountain railroading only once, in the spring of 1970, when he captured this muscular view of Santa Fe at the dawn of the decade. Five big hood units charge away from the camera, with the railroad's logo in the foreground, stretching from the floor to the ceiling of a "Shock Control" boxcar, while cumulus clouds build over the arid mountains.

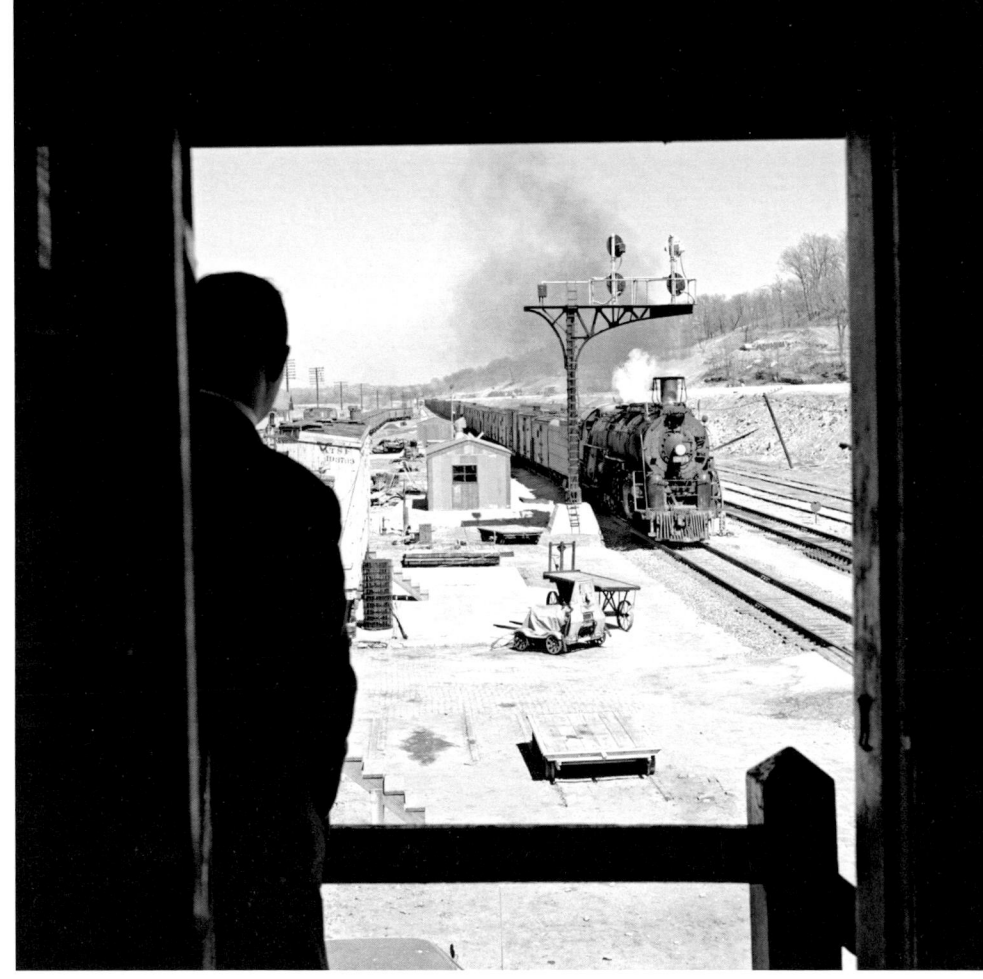

Trains coworker and future editor in chief David P. Morgan watches from the second-story doorway of the signal tower at Holliday, Kansas, as a train approaches in 1953. Locomotive no. 2925, its stack fully extended, leads a long mixed freight, heavy with refrigerator cars. The engine was one of thirty built by Baldwin in 1944, which were the heaviest and among the largest 4-8-4s of all time. Sister no. 2926 is currently being restored in Albuquerque, New Mexico.

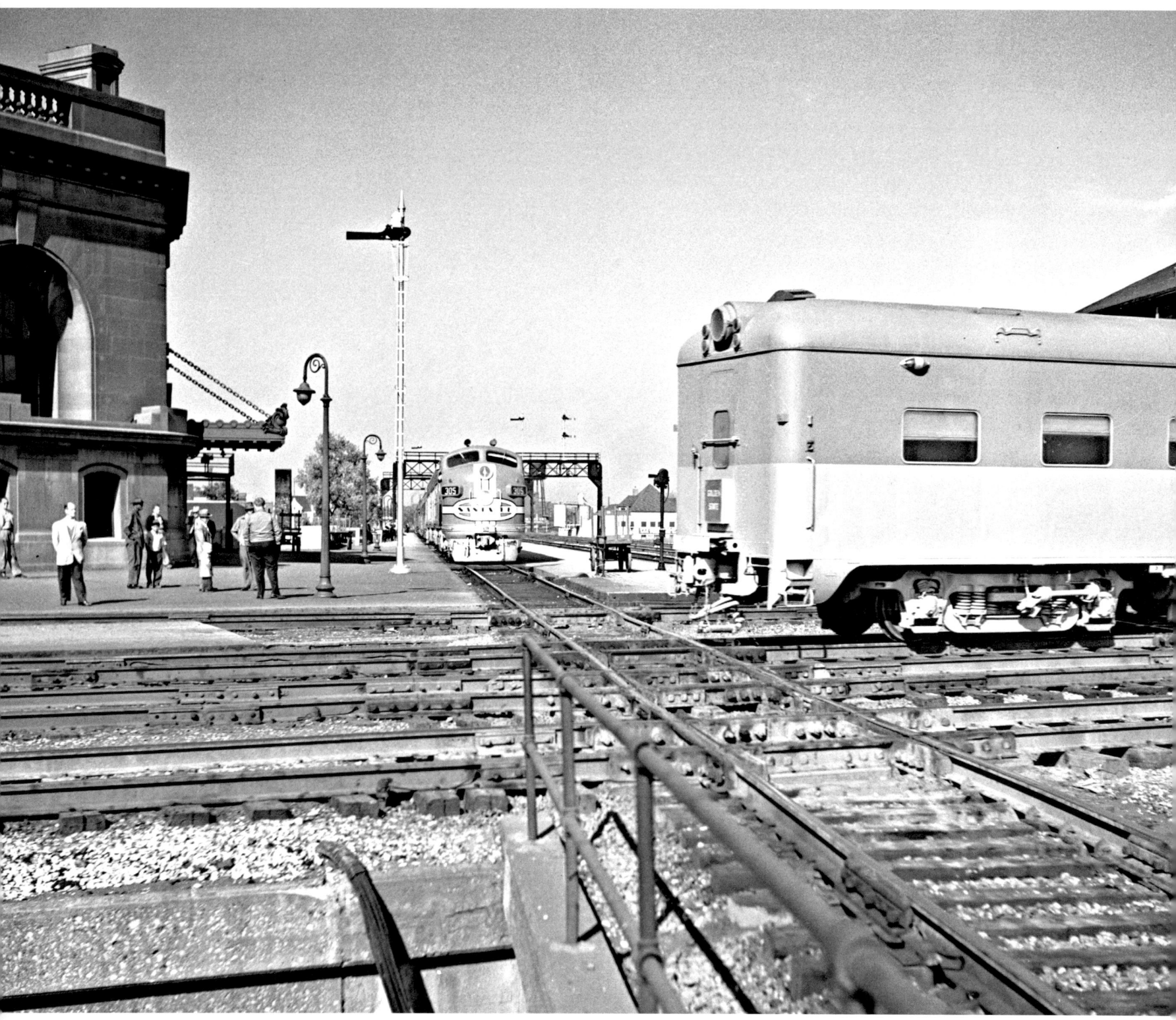

TWO

THE *TRAINS* MAGAZINE YEARS

Chicago–Los Angeles trains meet at Joliet, Illinois, on October 14, 1951. Rock Island eastbound no. 4, the *Golden State Limited*, clears the crossing as Santa Fe westbound no. 23, the *Grand Canyon*, waits at Union Station. At-grade crossings of multiple railroads were among Abbey's favorite photography subjects, and he strove to show more than one train whenever possible.

WALLY ABBEY ARRIVED AT AL KALMBACH'S SMALL BUT GROWING publishing company in the summer of 1950, reporting for work at the firm's stolid old eight-story building on the northwest fringe of downtown Milwaukee. His timing couldn't have been better, both for himself and for the magazine staff he was joining.

By 1950, *Trains* was at a crossroads. Launched by Kalmbach ten years earlier out of sheer passion and contrary to good business advice, the magazine's first few years nonetheless were a sensation. It tapped directly into a market of railroad enthusiasts hungry for something that treated its subject with intelligence and craft. In his first message to readers in November 1940, Al Kalmbach even named *National Geographic* as his standard. *Trains* would be a literate magazine, printed on slick paper and illustrated with the best photographs. In the immediate postwar years, its circulation surged.

But by the end of its first decade, *Trains*' fortunes stalled. The reason was obvious to anyone who came trackside to watch trains: the steam locomotive was disappearing. Always railroading's central object of affection, steam had defined America's romance with the industry for more than a century. By 1950 the barking, hissing, whistling engines of songs and novels and movies were giving way rapidly to mass-produced and decidedly unromantic diesels.

Abbey loved steam, but mostly he loved railroading, in all its forms, and as a professional journalist he was determined to tell good stories, steam engines or no steam engines. It helped that he was coming to a staff loaded with comparable talent. Abbey's name first appeared on the *Trains* masthead in the September 1950 issue, joining David P. Morgan and Rosemary Entringer among the small corps of associate editors working for then editor Willard V. Anderson.

Pairing Abbey with Morgan was pure serendipity. Abbey had already proven himself to be a skilled reporter and photographer, his early freelance work informed by his experiences as a working railroader. In Morgan, he had a colleague that would go on to become a legend, someone blessed with incredible writing chops and a vision of the industry that thrilled readers. That both men found themselves working out of the same shop constituted a dream team long before anyone invented the term.

The challenge for Abbey and Morgan was simple but daunting: make this brave new world of the modern railroad interesting to an audience raised on steam and coal smoke.

Trains' bosses quickly figured out Abbey's role: get out on the road and cover the hell out of what's going on. As a reporter and photographer, he was too good a double threat to keep in the office. His skills with the camera probably had as much to do with it as anything, given the magazine's graphic aspirations. A bonus was Abbey's talent for capturing railroaders at work. "It was understood that photography was part of the job," Abbey told writer John Gruber in the Summer 2010 issue of *Classic Trains* magazine. "While not a direct assignment, there was lots of it, and it was better if we had pictures with people."

So with his camera always in hand, Abbey went on a dizzying variety of assignments. In that very first September 1950 issue, Abbey contributed a brief but highly readable report on how Union Pacific humped its freight cars at the giant yard in North Platte, Nebraska, illustrated with nine photos by Abbey. Abundantly evident was his gift for elegantly weaving together the salient fact, the telling detail, even in this little piece about such a common aspect of the industry.

Then the plum assignments began rolling in: "Night Ride on the El Capitan," in which Abbey rode one of Santa Fe's most famous passenger trains; "Central States Dispatch," an odyssey aboard a unique freight train across seven different eastern railroads; "Route of the Flying Saucers," analyzing the Erie Railroad's hottest freight trains; "The Press Previews the Congressional," showcasing the Pennsylvania Railroad's newest high-profile passenger train; and "Temple of Transportation," an homage to illustrious Cincinnati Union Terminal. His article on the Terminal was especially memorable; legions of talented photographers flocked there in the early 1950s to record the Art Deco passenger-train mecca. But Abbey's photographs were definitive.

The capstone of Abbey's *Trains* years came with the January 1954 issue, featuring his eighteen-page you-are-there analysis of his beloved Santa Fe, called "Super Railroad," an article profusely illustrated with the author's photographs. This unprecedented look at a single railroad showcased all of Abbey's skills: his arresting, vivid photographs, of course, but also his engaging text, a detailed but absorbing exercise in long-form narrative that would stand up today as state-of-the-art magazine journalism.

Abbey's years at *Trains* were a happy chapter of his life. He and his wife, Martha, settled in Cedarburg, a charming little German-heritage town on the northern fringe of the Milwaukee suburbs. With the births of their two daughters, Mary and Martha, they began their family. Wally and his wife enjoyed the social whirl of those early Kalmbach years, making lifelong friends of a number of employees and their families. At work, Abbey embraced the relentless magazine deadlines and enjoyed the healthy competitive pressure that comes with talented colleagues. His career was off to a great start.

But his tenure at *Trains* wouldn't last long. In less than four years, Abbey was ready to move on, his last appearance on the masthead coming in the February 1954 issue. By then he had taken a job at the Association of Western Railways, an industry trade group. Perhaps he was motivated by a rivalry with Dave Morgan, who went on to be the beloved editor in chief of *Trains* for thirty-three years, although Abbey denied that in an interview decades later. In fact, he was quite fond of Morgan. More likely is that Abbey was responding to simple ambition, the kind that could not be rewarded fully at a small magazine for enthusiasts. Instead, he felt the pull of railroading itself.

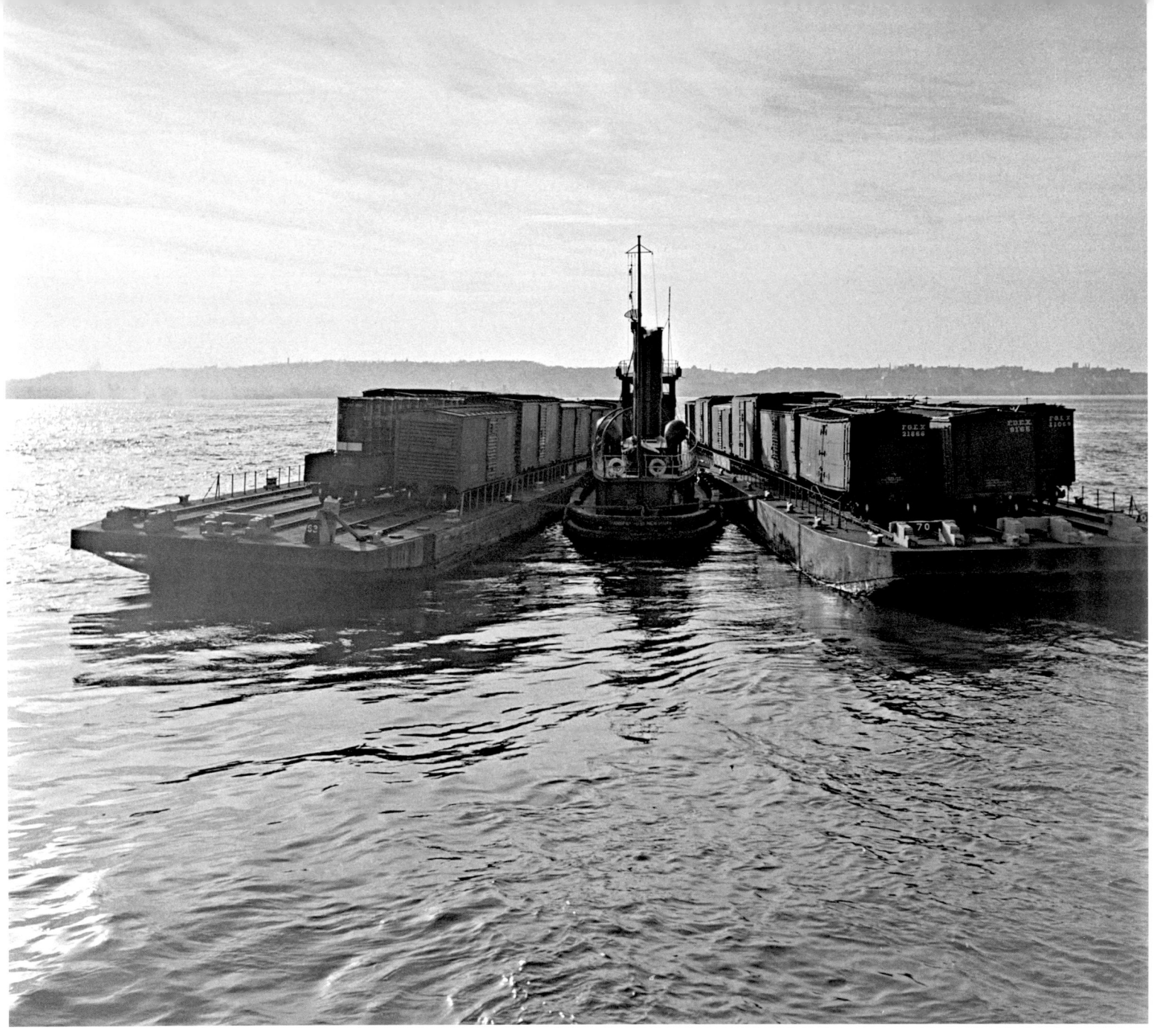

An Erie Railroad tug departs Manhattan with two car floats to take across the Hudson River to New Jersey in January of 1951. Waterborne traffic around New York Harbor was big business for the Erie. In his article about the railroad that ran in the May issue of *Trains* that year, Abbey reported, "The Erie owns 12 tugs, three lighters, 102 barges, 19 refrigerator barges, 14 gas-hoist and two steam-hoist lighters, 74 scows and 26 car floats."

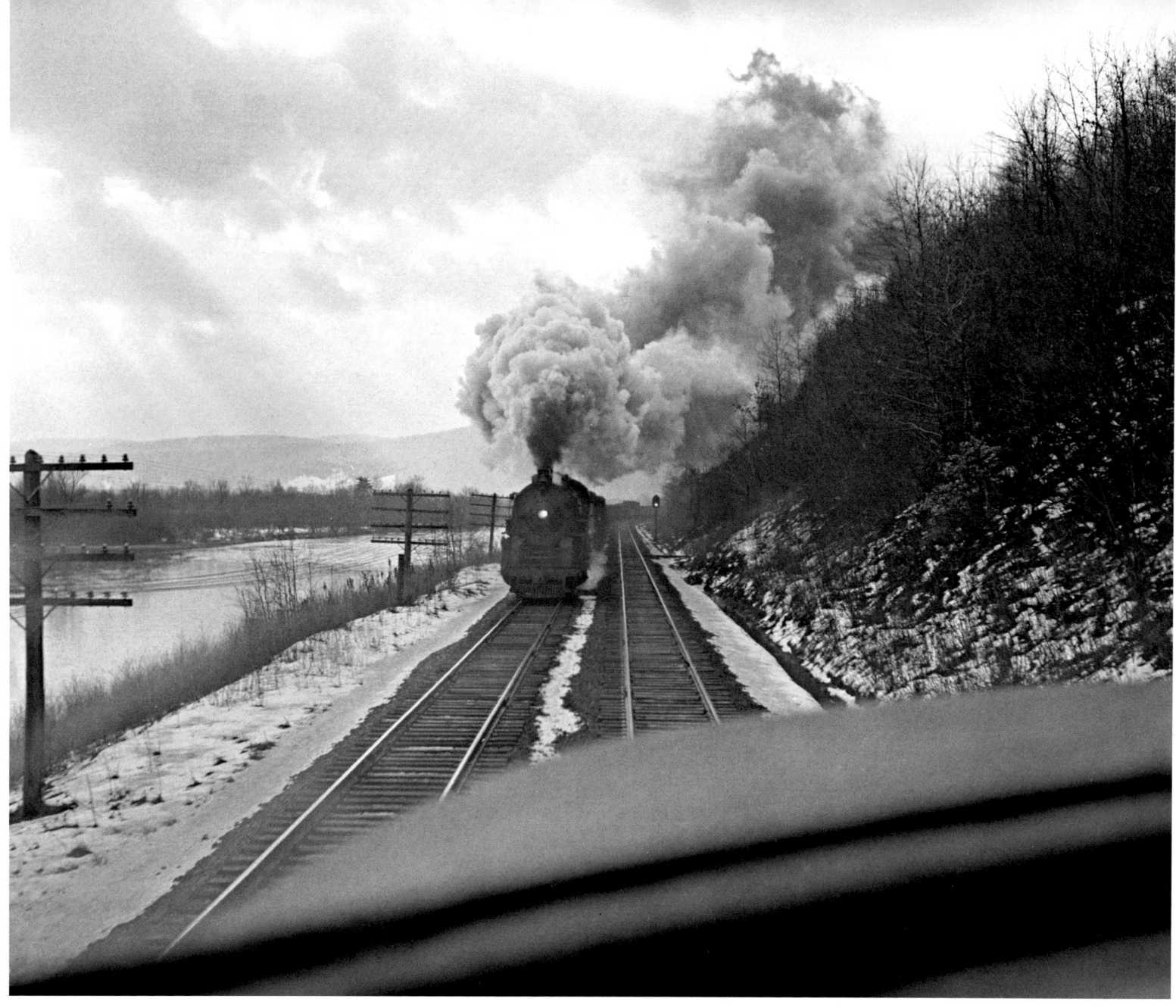

Above: In snow-covered western New York on a January day in 1951, freight trains pass on the Erie Railroad. A steam-powered eastbound bears down on westbound no. 99, the so-called *Flying Saucer*—hottest westbound freight train on a railroad full of hot freights. Named by employees, the *Saucer* forwarded cars from the big yards of Croxton, New Jersey, and Maybrook, New York, all the way across the railroad to western connections in Chicago. Its eastbound counterpart left the Windy City at 8:00 p.m. and arrived in Jersey City just two mornings later.

Facing: A Pennsylvania Railroad passenger train led by one of its iconic GG1 electric locomotives soars over the Erie's Croxton Yard at Secaucus, New Jersey, in 1951. A crane on the Erie is in the process of unloading steel girders—given the date, very likely bridge girders for the New Jersey Turnpike, which opened in 1952. The turnpike now parallels the Pennsy line, which today is part of Amtrak's Northeast Corridor, while Croxton Yard is mostly gone, replaced by extensive commercial, office, retail, and residential development.

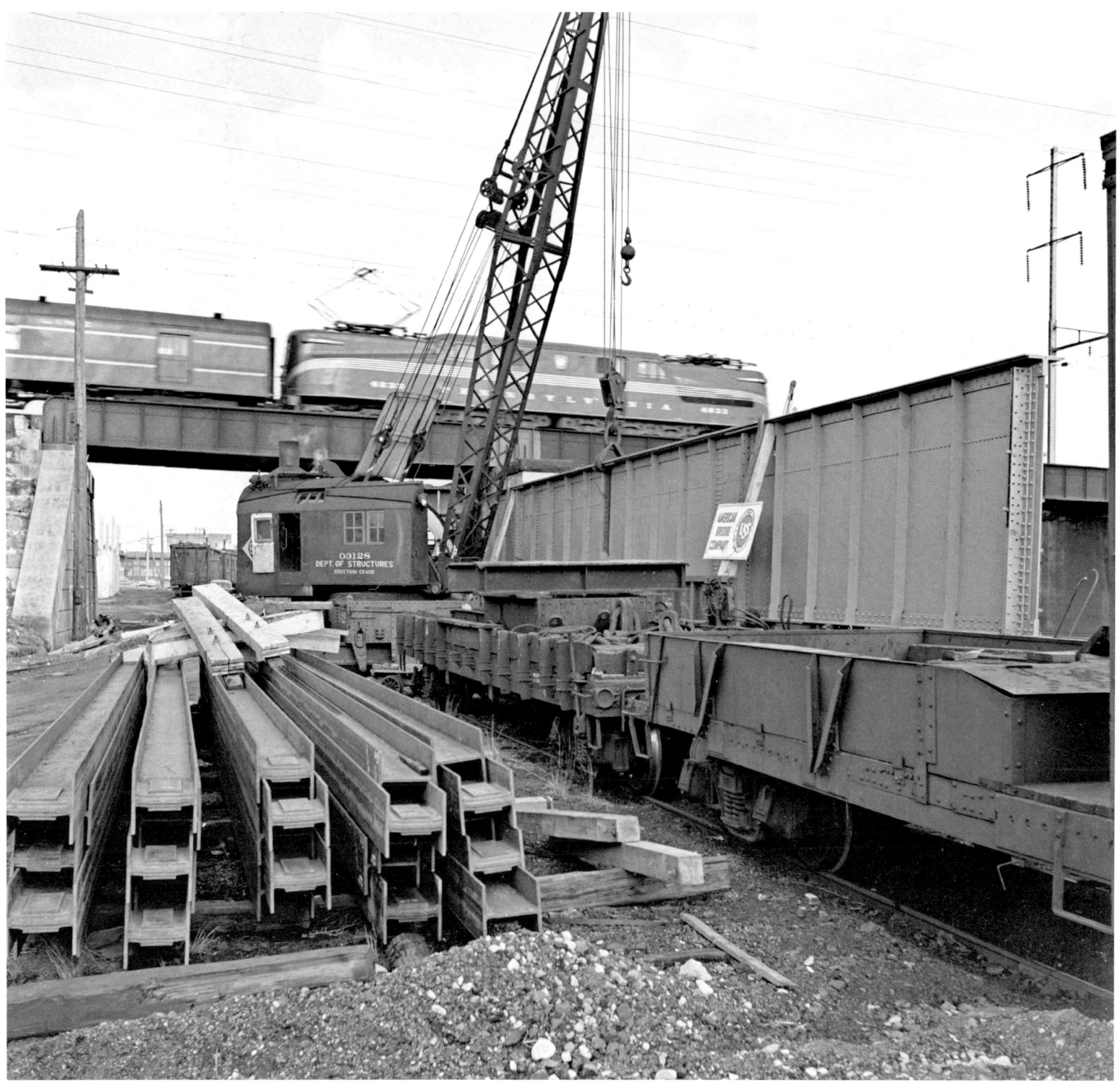

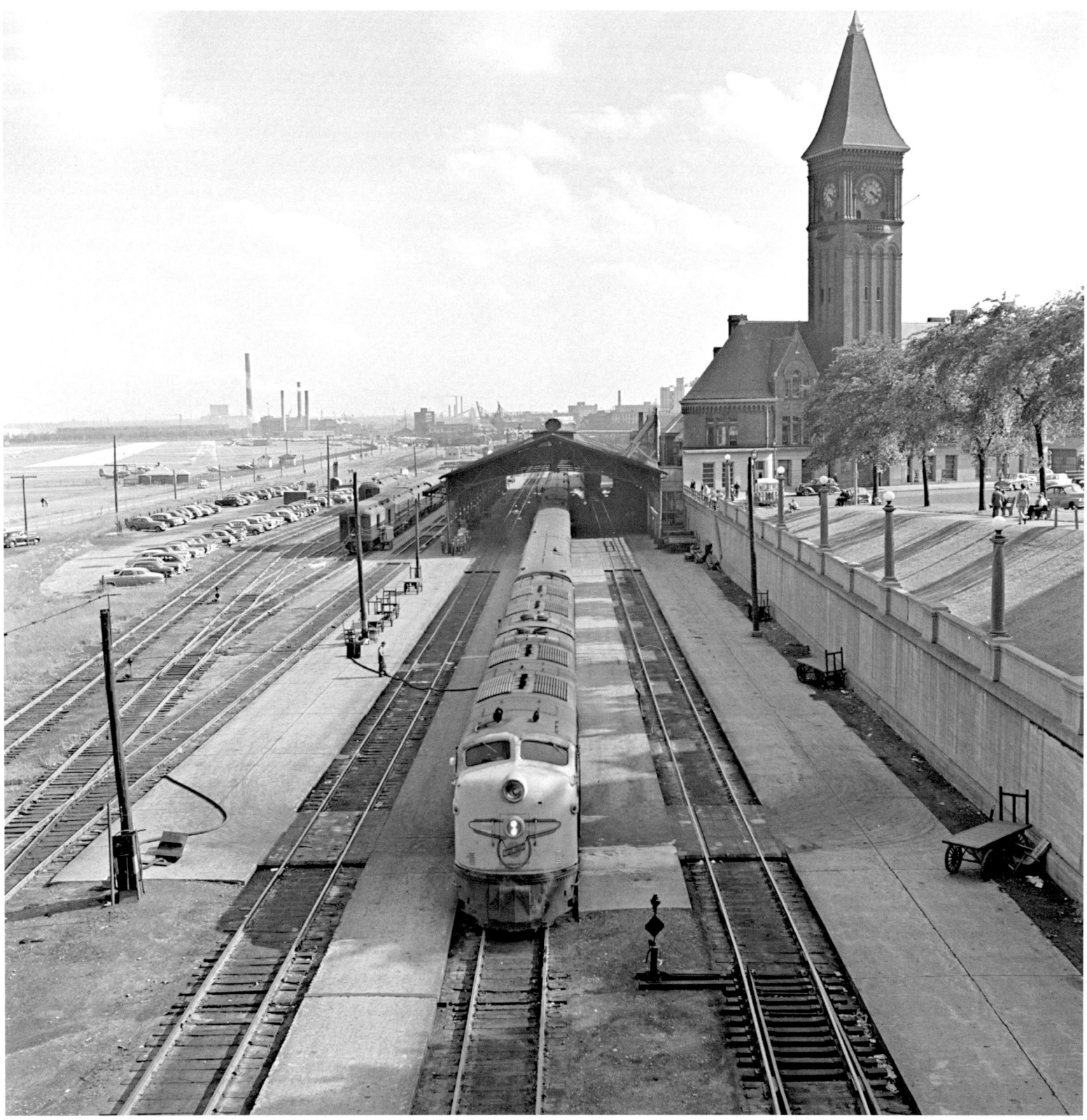

Facing Westbound Chicago & North Western train no. 401, the *Twin Cities 400*, pauses at the road's lakefront depot in Milwaukee, Wisconsin, on June 26, 1951. Introduced in 1935 to compete with the Milwaukee Road and the Burlington Route on the highly competitive Chicago–Minneapolis corridor, the *400* took its name from both the (approximate) number of miles between its terminals and the number of minutes in which it covered them.

Below: The engine crew of Lehigh & Hudson River freight train HO-6 picks up orders from the operator at Andover, New Jersey, where the L&HR crossed a Lackawanna branch line, on June 28, 1951. The train is the *Central States Dispatch*, a high-priority freight that seven railroads teamed up to move from Cumberland, Maryland, to Boston, Massachusetts, on a thirty-three-hour schedule. Abbey was riding on assignment for *Trains & Travel*; his article appeared in the March 1952 issue.

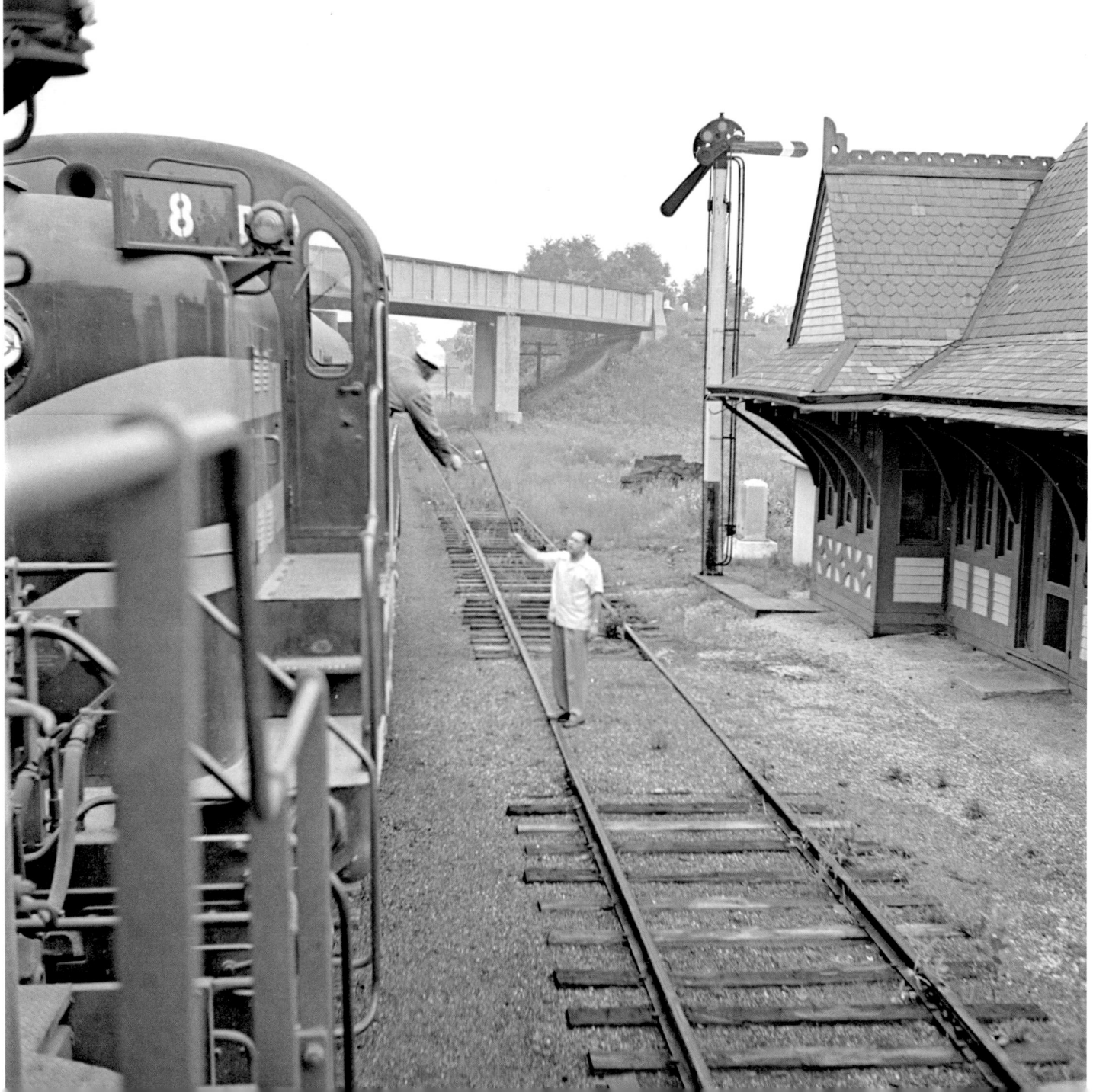

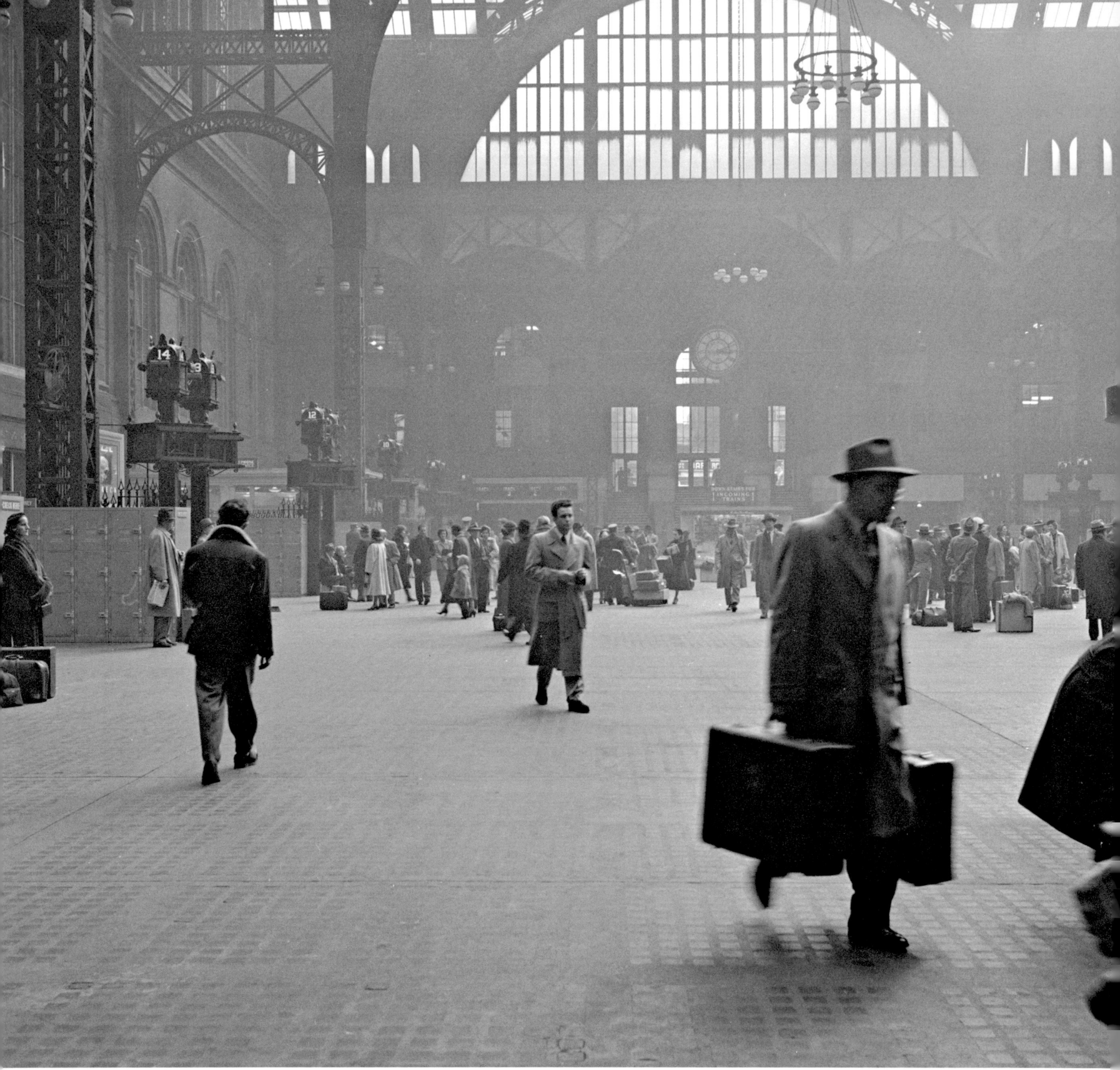

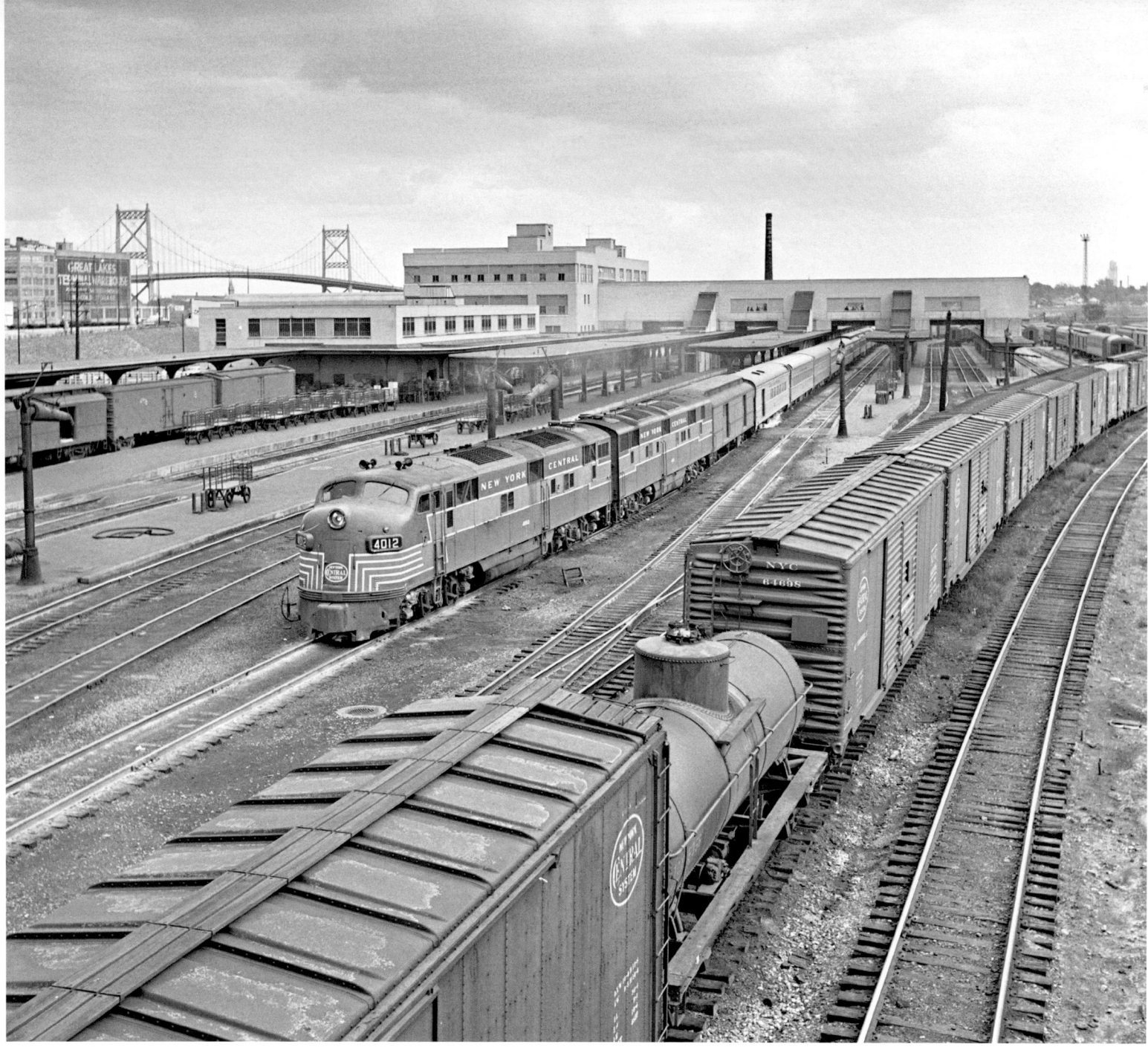

Facing: Travelers hurry through New York City's Pennsylvania Station on a March day in 1952. Unimaginable at the time, this grand space would be demolished in just a little more than a decade to make way for Madison Square Garden and an office tower. The loss of Penn Station catalyzed the modern preservation movement, leading directly to the passage of New York's Landmarks Preservation Act in 1965.

Above: Westbound New York Central passenger train at Central Union Terminal in Toledo, Ohio, in September 1952. The station had opened just two years earlier. Besides the NYC, the twelve-track facility also served the Baltimore & Ohio, Chesapeake & Ohio, and Wabash railroads. Behind the station at left stands the Anthony Wayne Bridge over the Maumee River, also known as the High Level Bridge and completed in 1931.

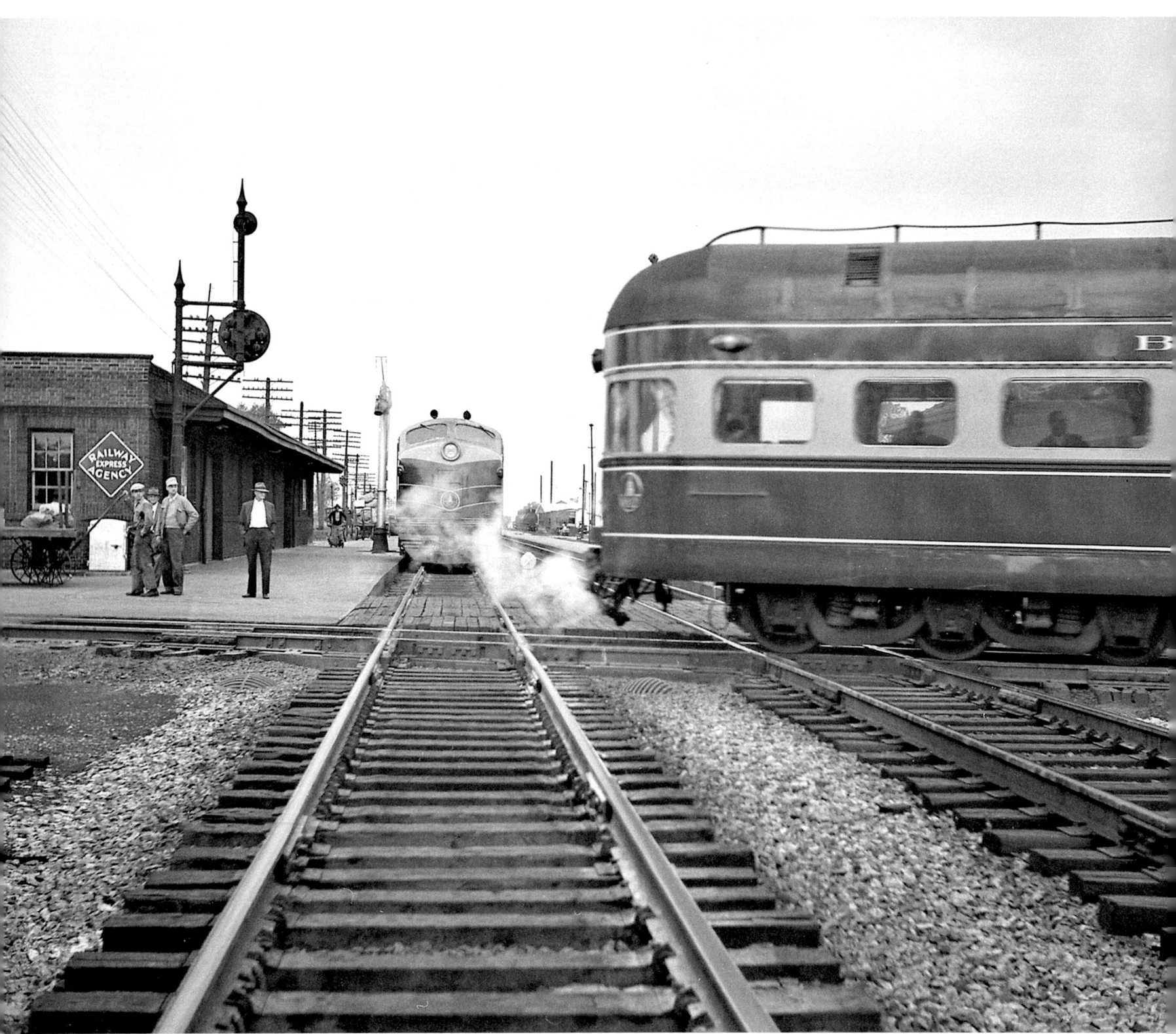

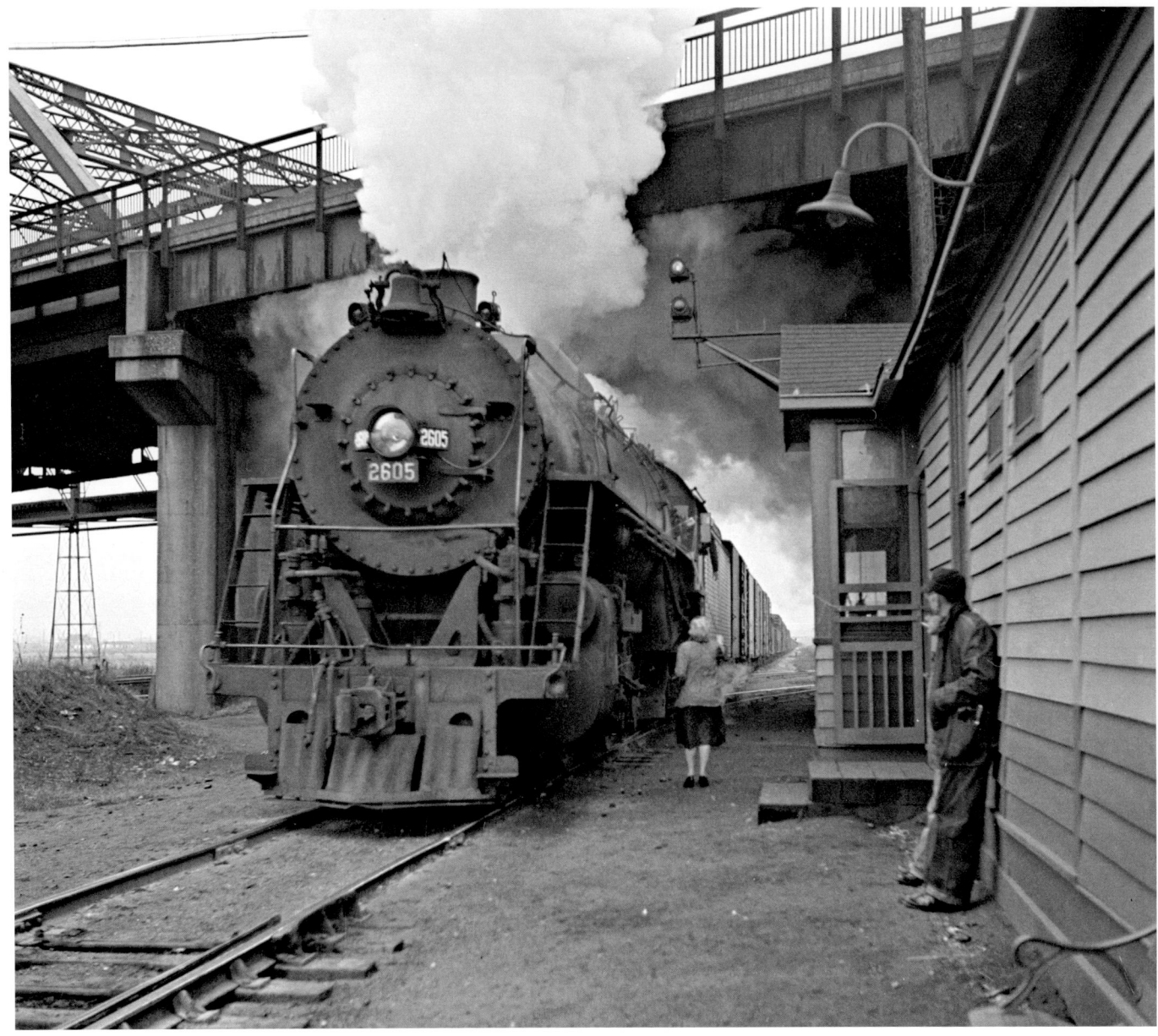

Facing: In Deshler, Ohio, Baltimore & Ohio's main line from the East Coast to Chicago crossed its north–south Toledo Division line between Cincinnati and Toledo. On a September day in 1952, Abbey caught passenger trains on both lines in this view looking west, where an eastbound train waits as the observation car of the northbound *Cincinnatian* clears the crossing. A depot in the northwest quadrant of the crossing, behind the observation car, served trains on both lines.

Above: One of Illinois Central's big Mountain-type 4-8-2 locomotives blasts under the McKinley Bridge while its crew grabs orders from the woman operator at Madison, Illinois, on Halloween, 1951. Abbey had just arrived on a Chicago & North Western freight train from Benld, Illinois, running over the Litchfield & Madison. The bridge carried both Route 66 and the Illinois Terminal Railroad over the Mississippi River to St. Louis, and it was named not for the twenty-fifth president of the United States, but for another William McKinley, who had served as chief executive of the IT when the electric interurban line built the bridge in 1910.

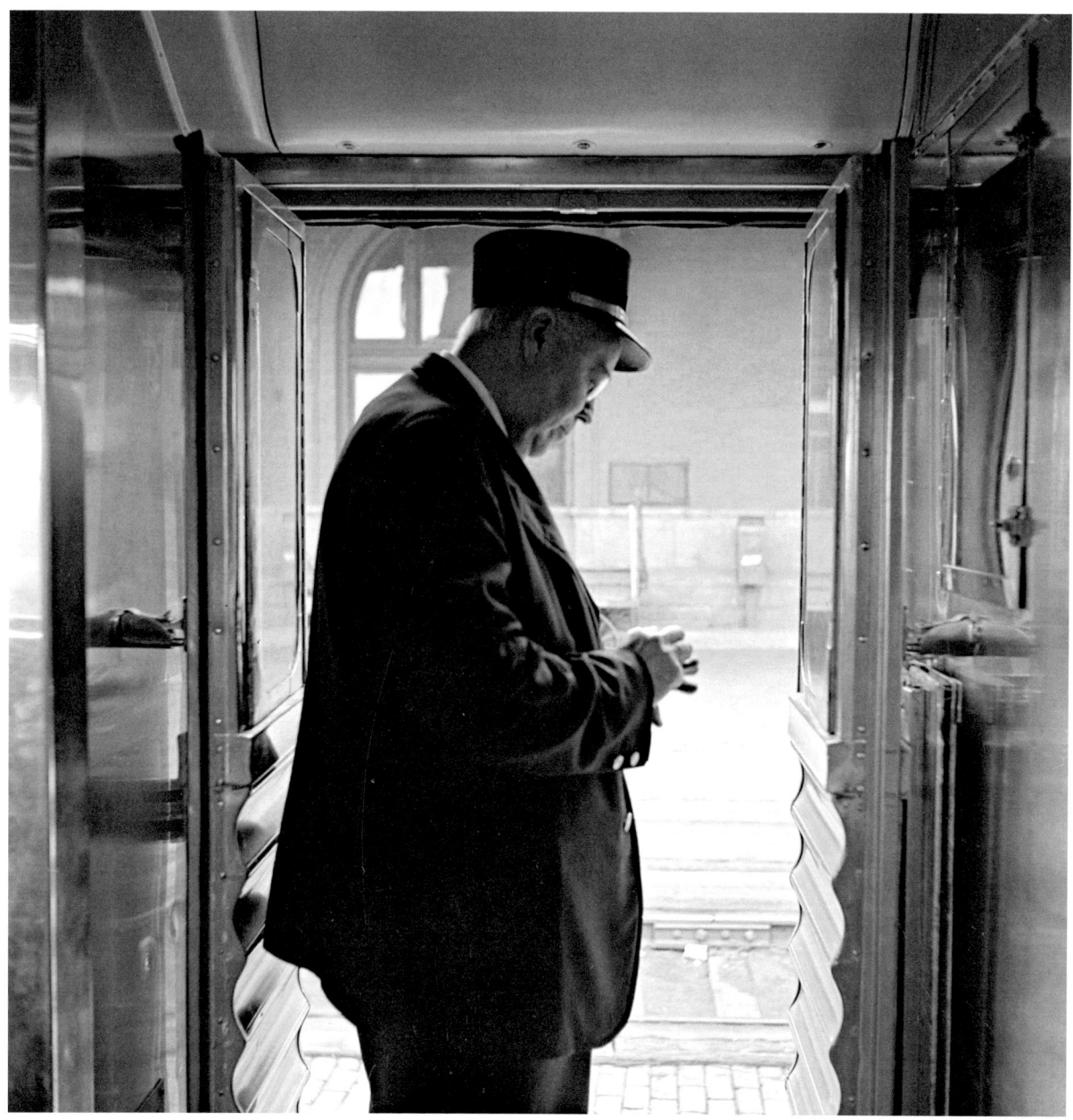

The conductor of the Chicago, Burlington & Quincy's *Pioneer Zephyr* checks his watch as the train arrives in Galesburg, Illinois, on November 1, 1951. The *Pioneer Zephyr* was the original of the Burlington's famous fleet of *Zephyr* trains. Introduced in 1934, it set a speed record on May 26 of that year by making the 1,015-mile trip from Denver to Chicago in thirteen hours and five minutes. It ran all over the Burlington system until its retirement in 1960, whereupon the railroad donated the train to Chicago's Museum of Science and Industry, where it can still be seen today.

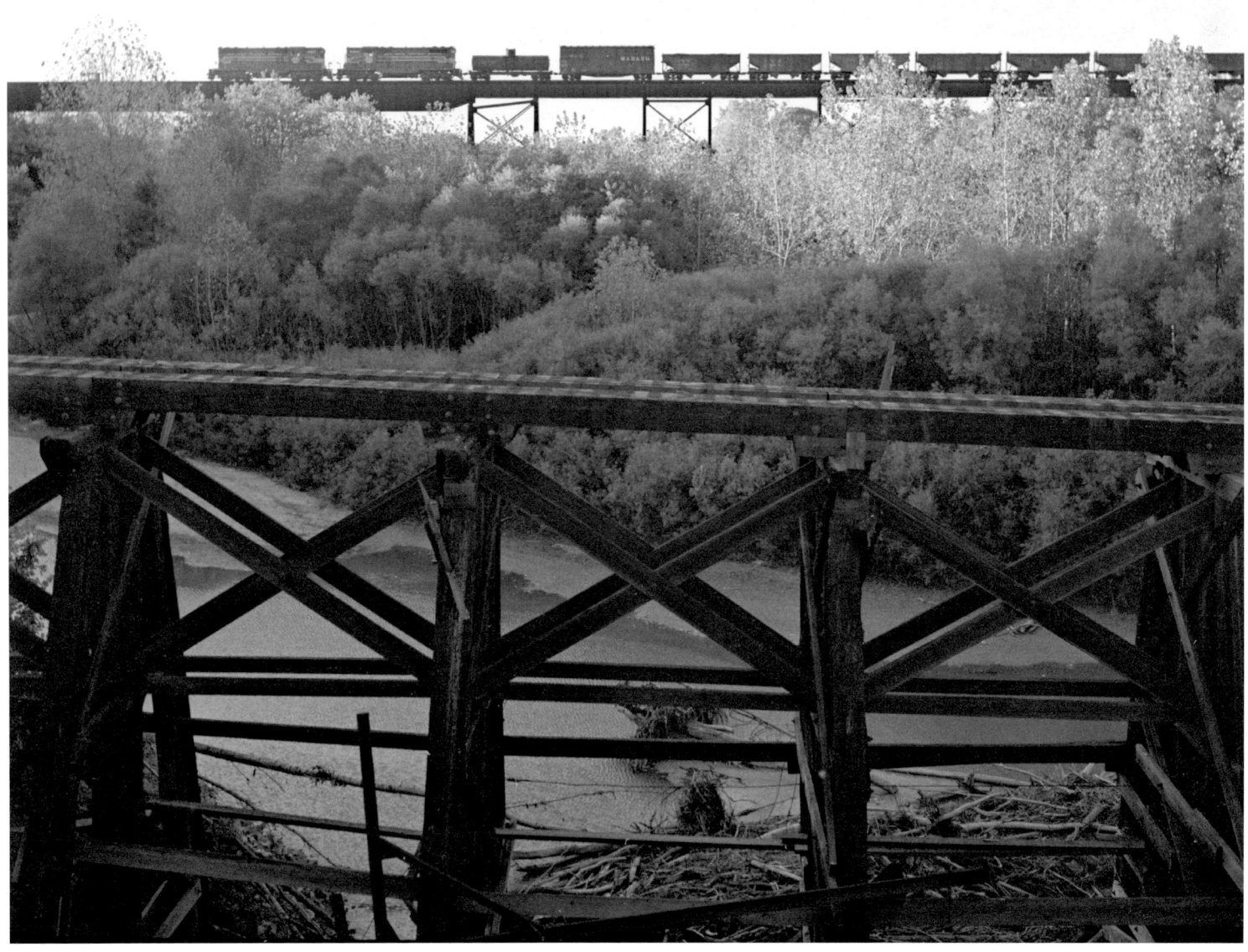

Westbound Peoria & Eastern freight train crossing the Middle Fork of the Vermillion River west of Danville, Illinois, on September 26, 1952. The trestle in the foreground carried a recently abandoned line of interurban Illinois Terminal Railroad, which crossed the river valley with a lower bridge and steeper grades. The last train crossed the bridge exactly five months earlier. Abbey was following the P&E all the way from Indianapolis to Peoria.

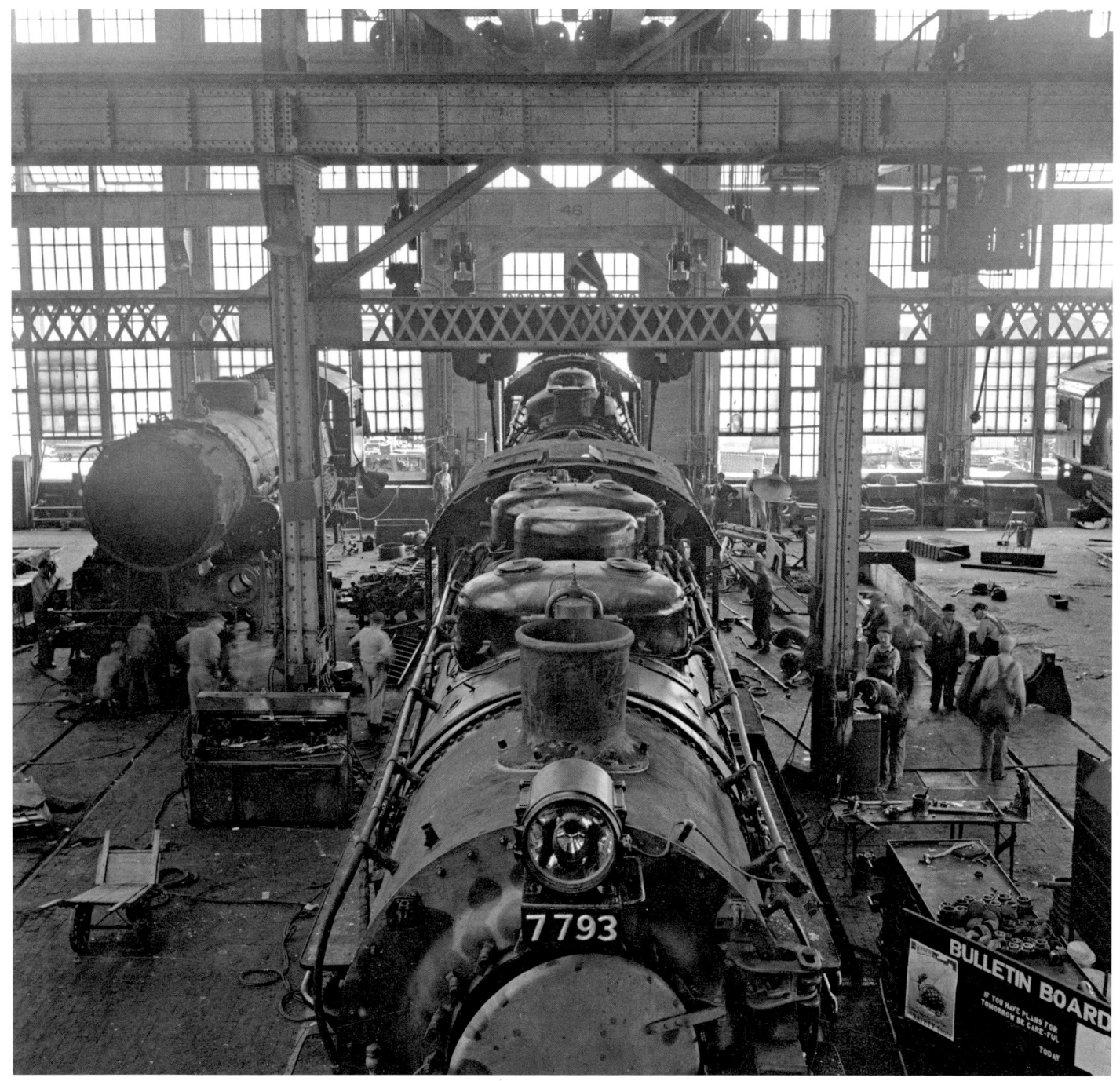

New York Central steam locomotives including 0-8-0 no. 7793 inside the railroad's Beech Grove Shops on August 31, 1953. Beech Grove is in the southeastern quadrant of the Indianapolis metropolitan area. The NYC created the community in 1906 to serve as a railroad shop town. Amtrak operates the shops today.

One of the Baltimore & Ohio's massive EM-1 2-8-8-4 steam locomotives noses into its stall between two other engines in the roundhouse at Cumberland, Maryland, on June 27, 1951. Years later, Abbey included this view in his collection of 25 favorites. He wrote: "Behind the scenes, railroading could be grubby business. . . . Lots of people, railroaders even, deplored the loss the of steam—well, they wanted to keep the romance and glamour of it. But we've noticed that even the romanticists didn't want back everything the steam locomotive took with it!"

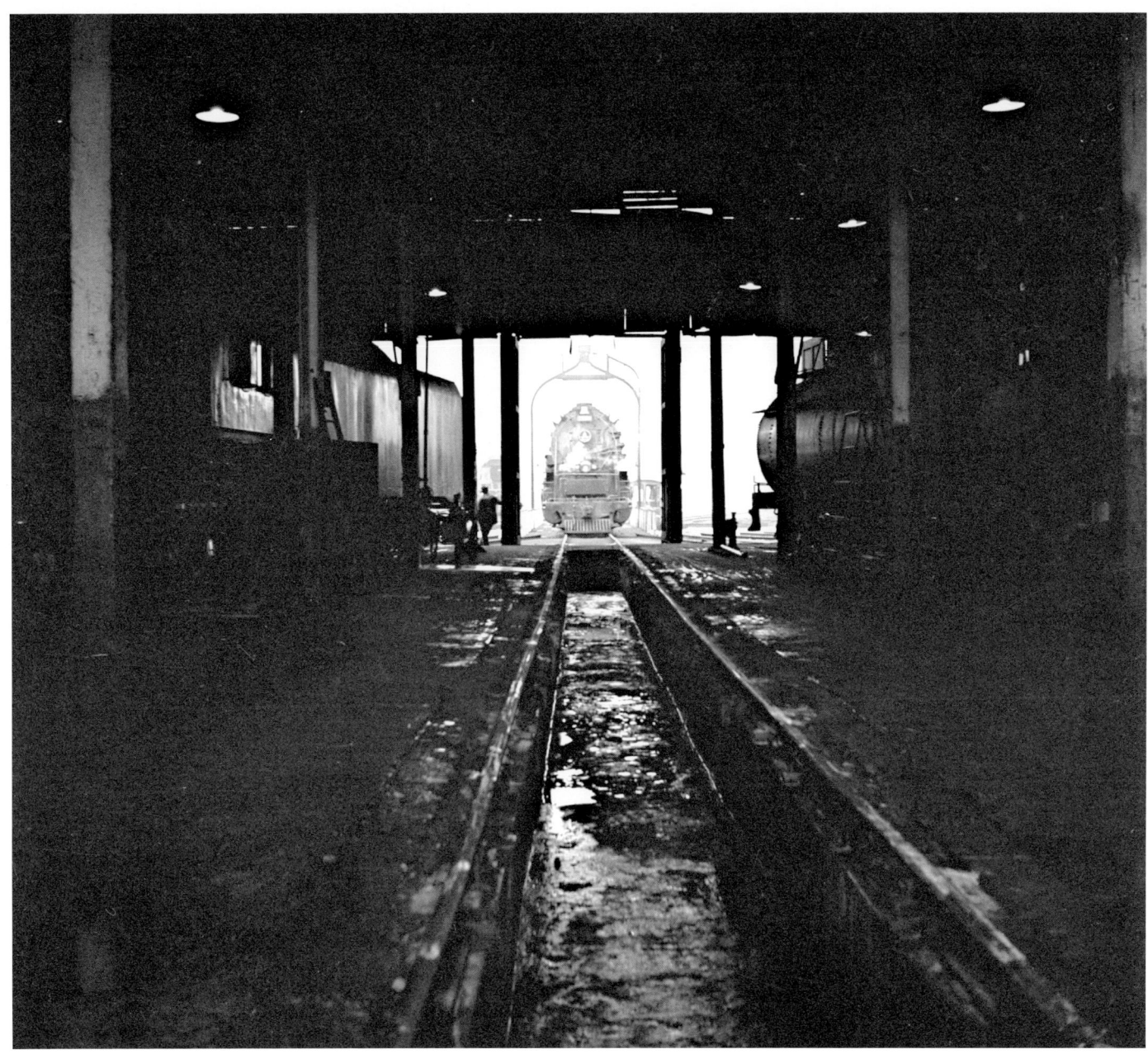

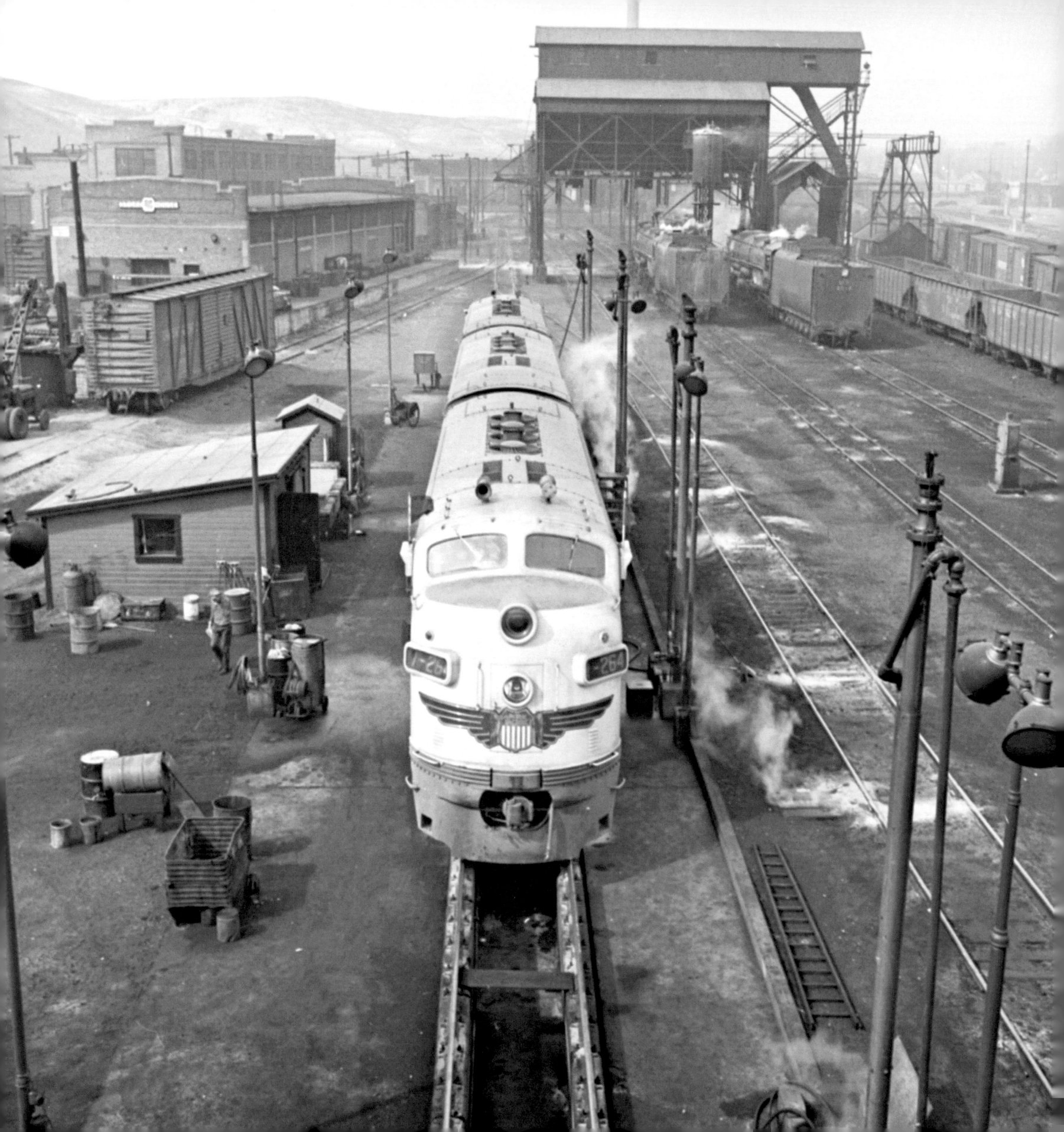

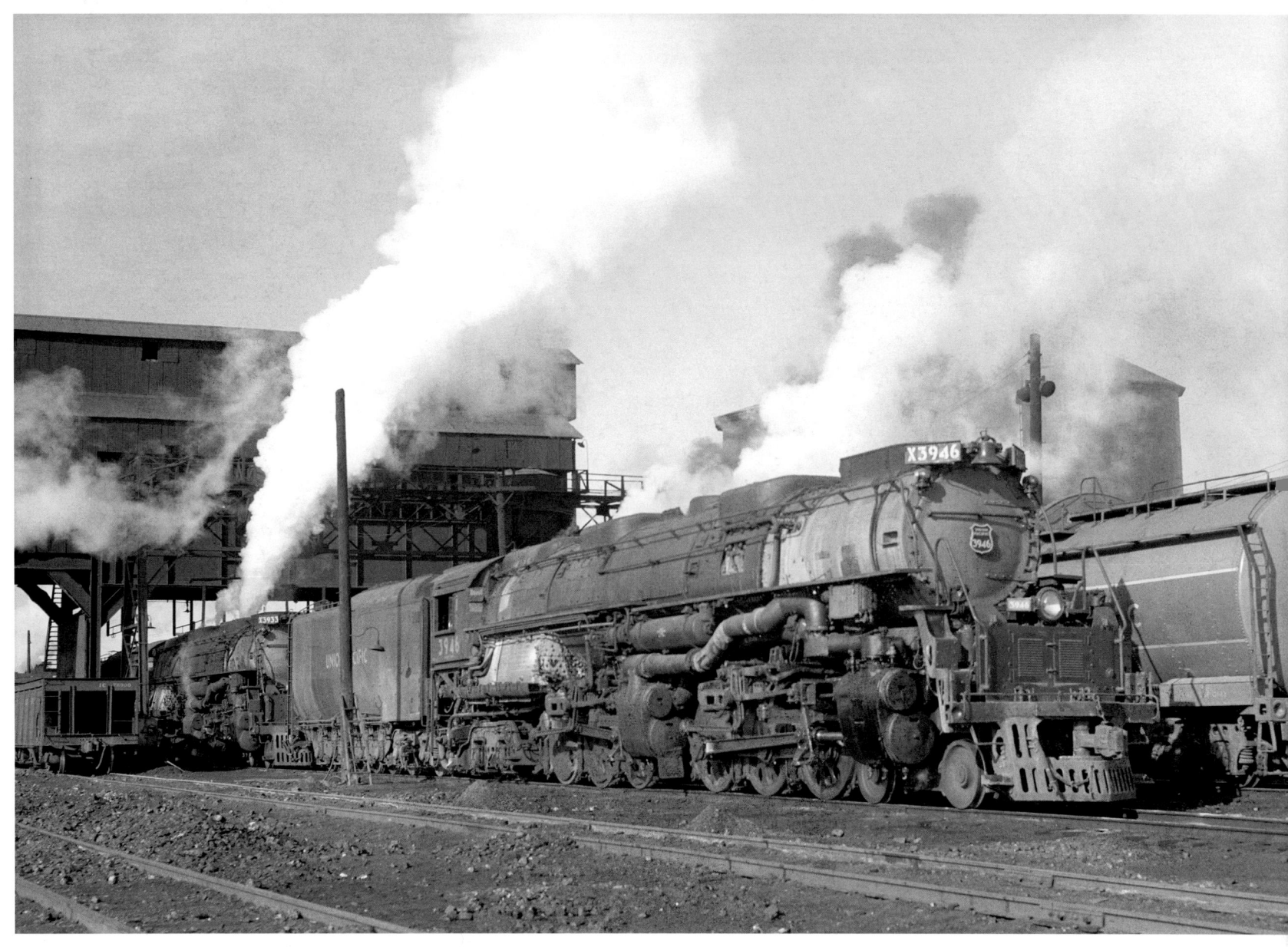

Facing: Union Pacific F-series freight diesels from General Motors at Green River, Wyoming, on February 28, 1953, having just arrived with train no. 264 from Pocatello, Idaho. In the distance at right, two 4-8-8-4 Big Boy steam locomotives stand near the coaling tower. The roundhouse is visible beyond them in the background, while the shop buildings are to the left. Abbey was on assignment to cover UP's unique gas-electric turbine locomotives.

Above: On Thanksgiving Day in 1948, Union Pacific 4-6-6-4 Challenger steam locomotives wait beneath the coaling tower at North Platte, Nebraska, for their next trip west to Cheyenne, Wyoming. Earlier that year, Union Pacific had upgraded North Platte's Bailey Yard to a forty-two-track hump facility. This visit provided Abbey with material for his first feature article in *Trains* magazine, which appeared in the September 1950 issue. Later upgrades have made Bailey the largest classification yard in the world.

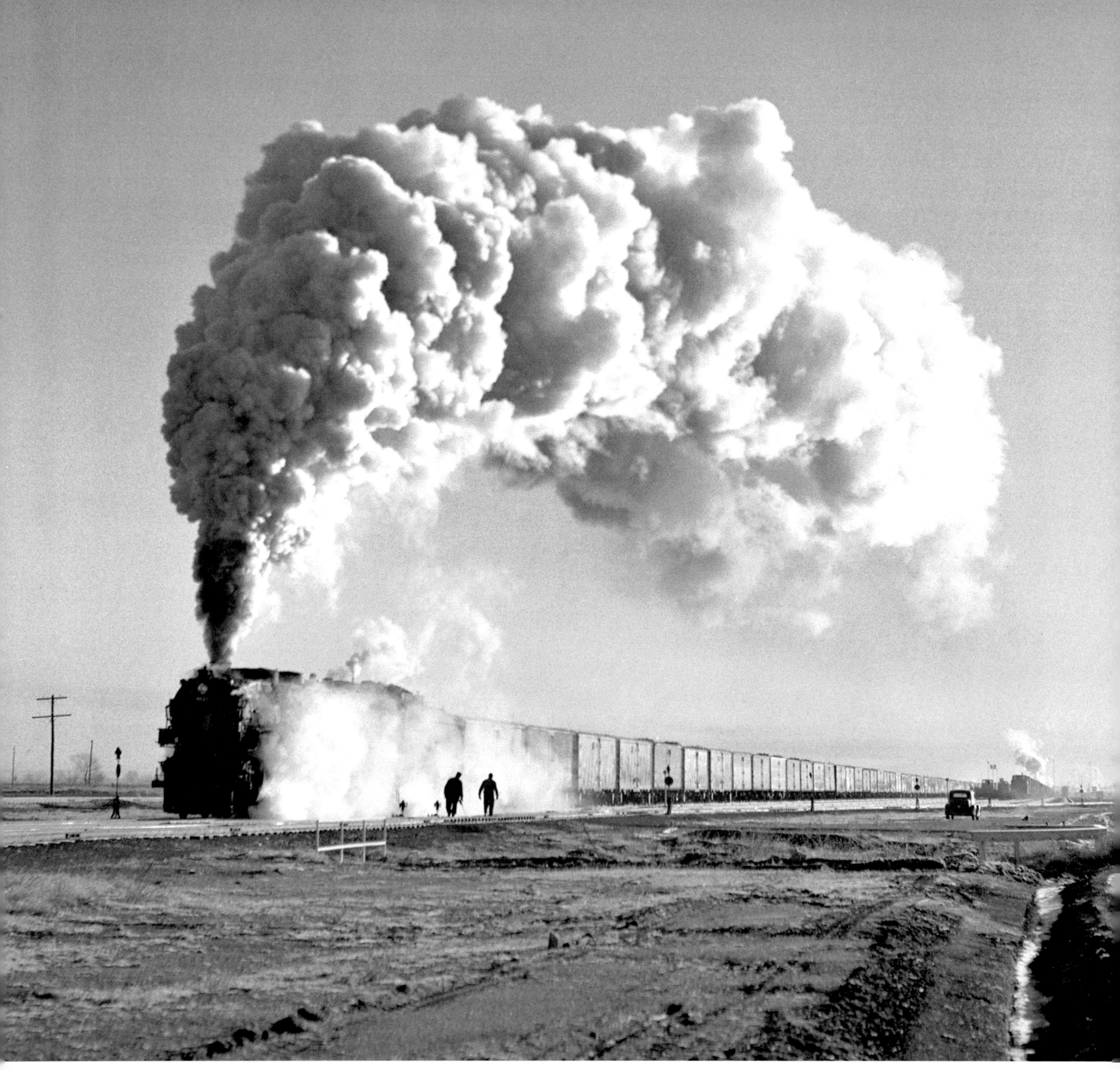

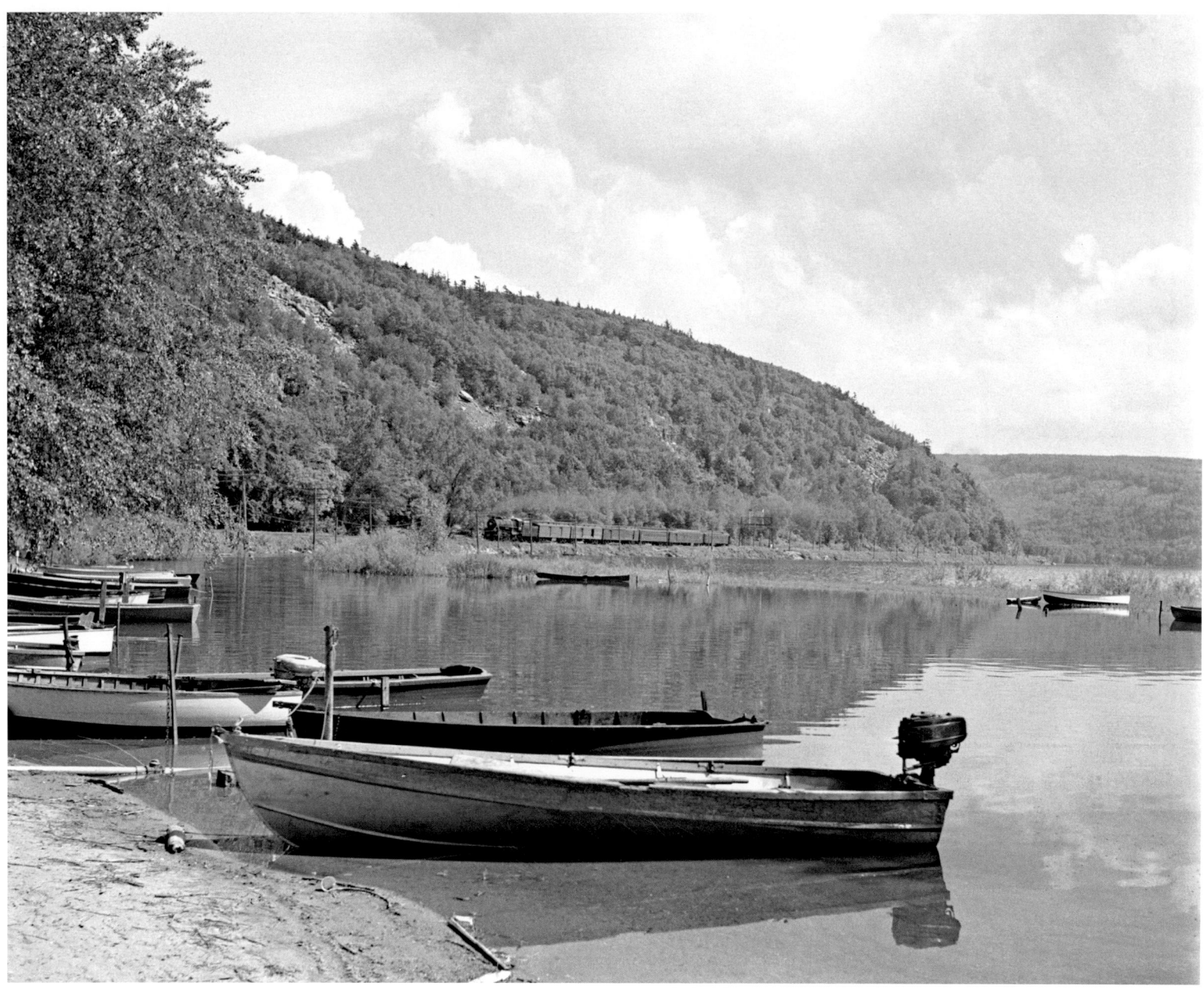

Facing: A westbound Union Pacific drag freight with empty Pacific Fruit Express refrigerator cars for the west coast departs Bailey Yard in North Platte, Nebraska, behind a 4-12-2 locomotive on Thanksgiving Day 1948. North Platte was a hub of operations for the big 4-12-2 freight engines, which worked out of the city in three directions: southeast to Kansas City, east to Council Bluffs, Nebraska, and west to Cheyenne, Wyoming.

Above: Chicago & North Western passenger train no. 501, the westbound *Viking*, steaming along Devil's Lake in south-central Wisconsin on a pleasant June afternoon in 1952. Formed by glacial deposits at the end of the last ice age, today Devil's Lake is the largest state park in the Badger State. Early visitors arrived by train, and the railroad played a major role in establishing tourism at the park.

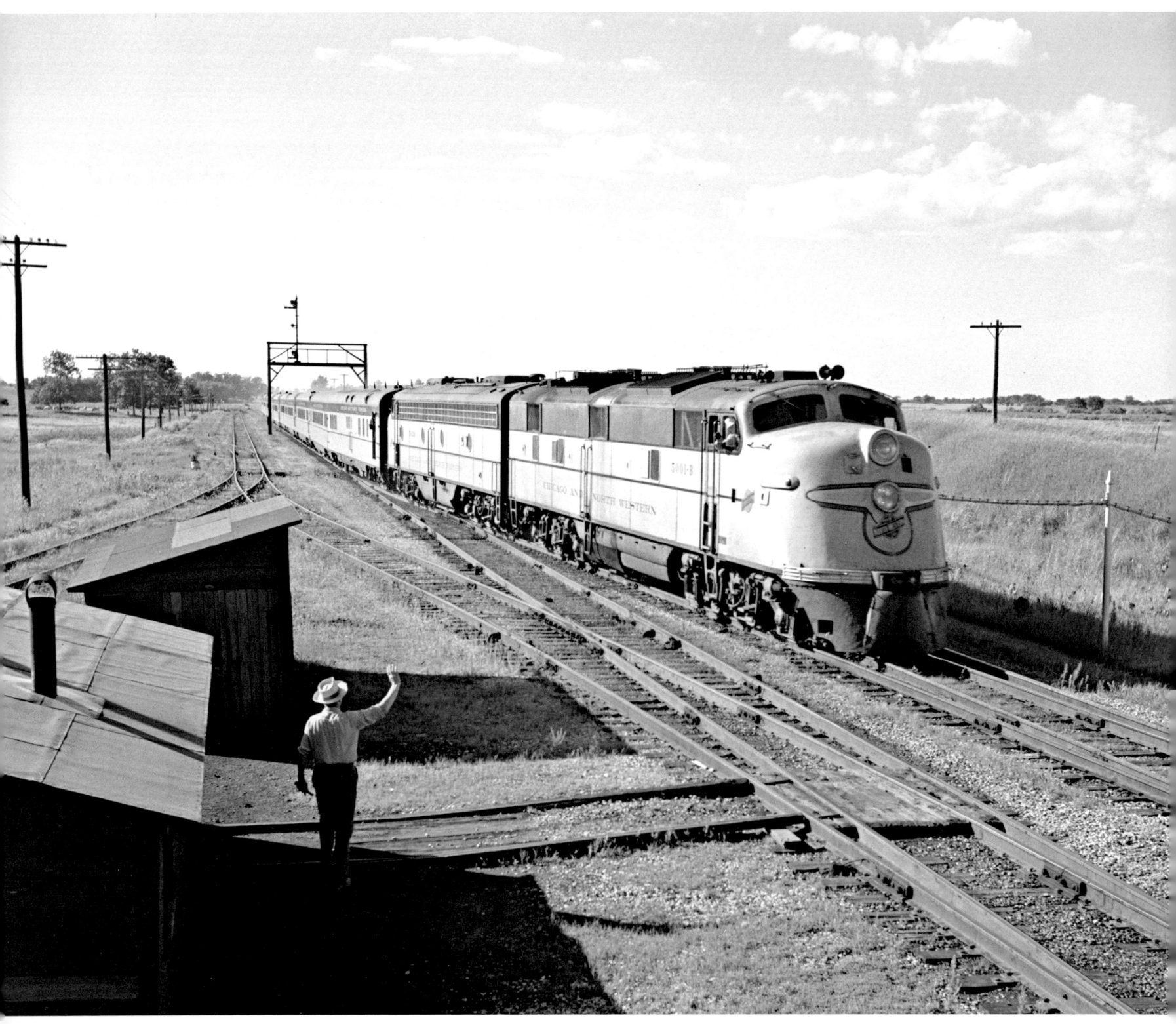

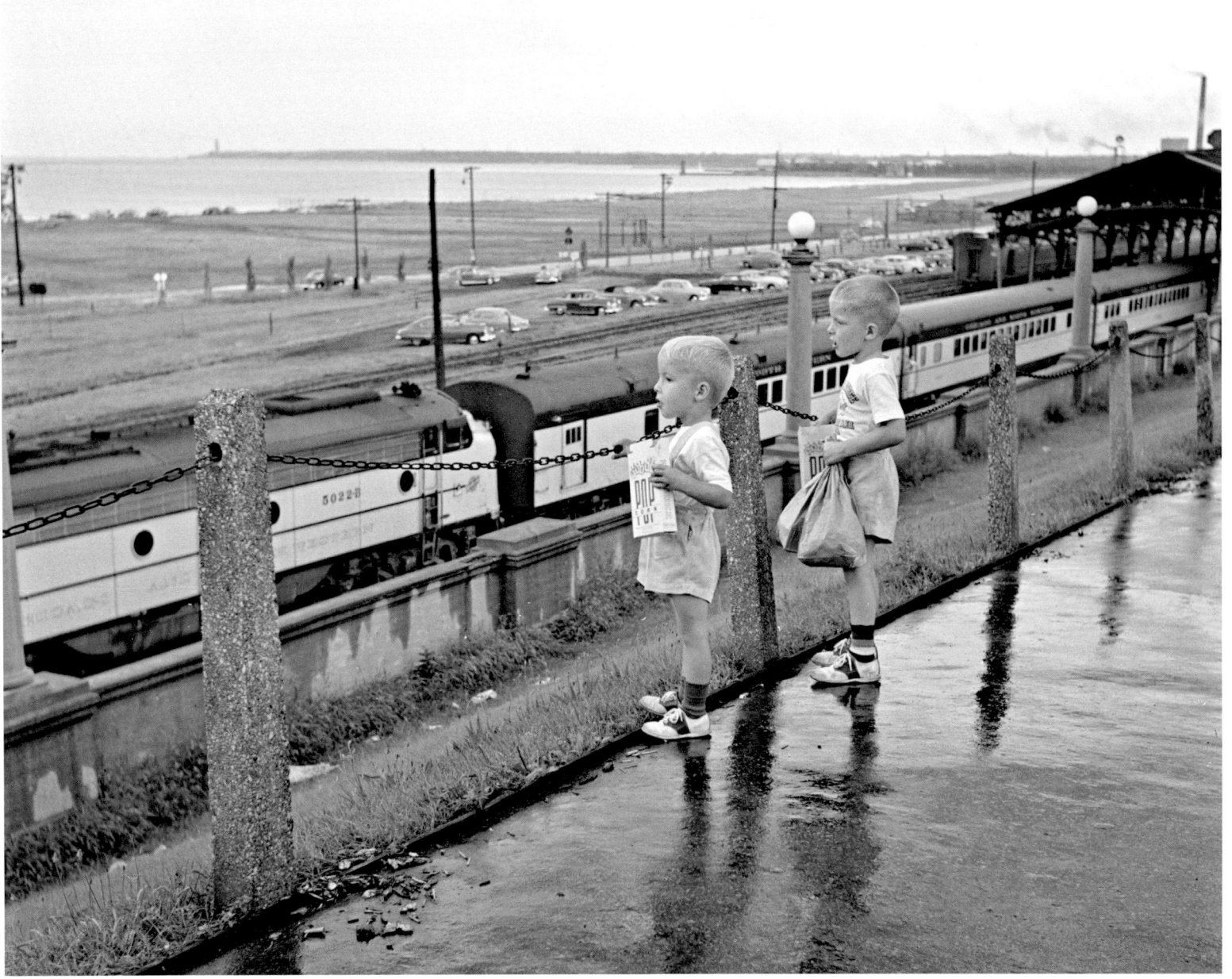

Facing: Chicago & North Western train no. 400, the eastbound *Twin Cities 400*, gets a wave from the operator at Clyman Junction, Wisconsin, as shadows grow long on the evening of July 26, 1952. The C&NW opened this railroad, known as the Adams Line for a town through which it passes, in 1911 as a more direct route for trains traveling between Milwaukee and Minnesota's Twin Cities of Minneapolis and St. Paul.

Above: On a rainy summer day in Milwaukee, Wisconsin, in 1952, two boys watch as the Chicago & North Western's westbound *Twin Cities 400* makes its stop at the city's lakefront depot, near the shore of Lake Michigan. The station opened in 1890 and served nearly one hundred trains a day at its peak, but it would be demolished by the time these children reached adulthood.

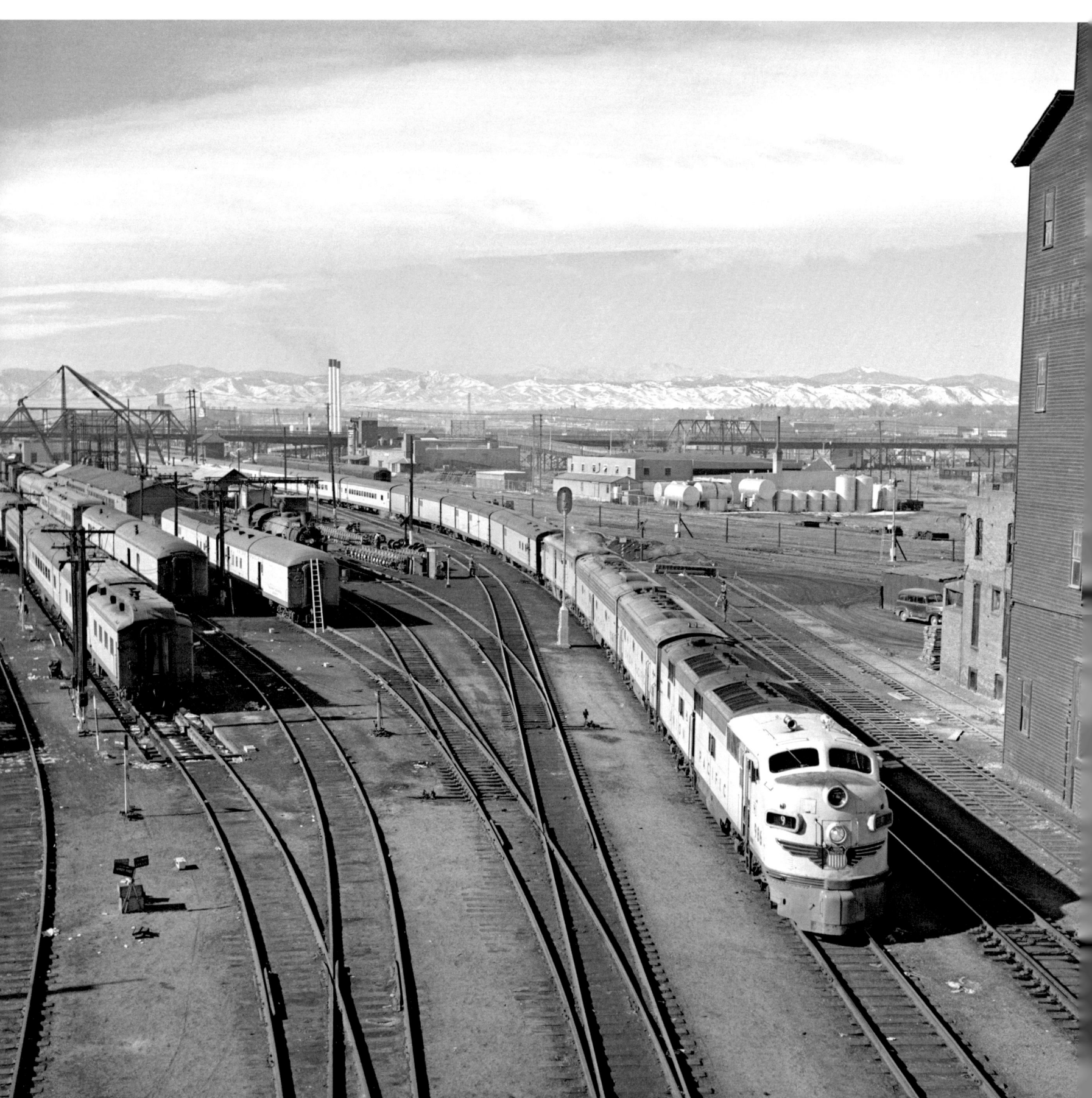

Facing: Union Pacific train no. 9, the westbound *City of St. Louis*, departs Denver Union Station behind four locomotives on the morning of February 26, 1953. The train ran between St. Louis and Los Angeles on a two-day schedule, taking a north–south jog between Denver and Cheyenne, Wyoming. The snow-covered Front Range of the Rocky Mountains stands in the distance.

Below: Passengers confer with a station worker inside the grand concourse of Kansas City Union Station on April 20, 1953. Completed in the Beaux Arts style in 1914, the station served 670,000 passengers in its busiest year, 1945—the end of World War II. Patronage then dropped sharply until the station closed in 1985, but with strong public/private support for its renovation, it reopened in 1999 as a museum center. Train service returned in 2002.

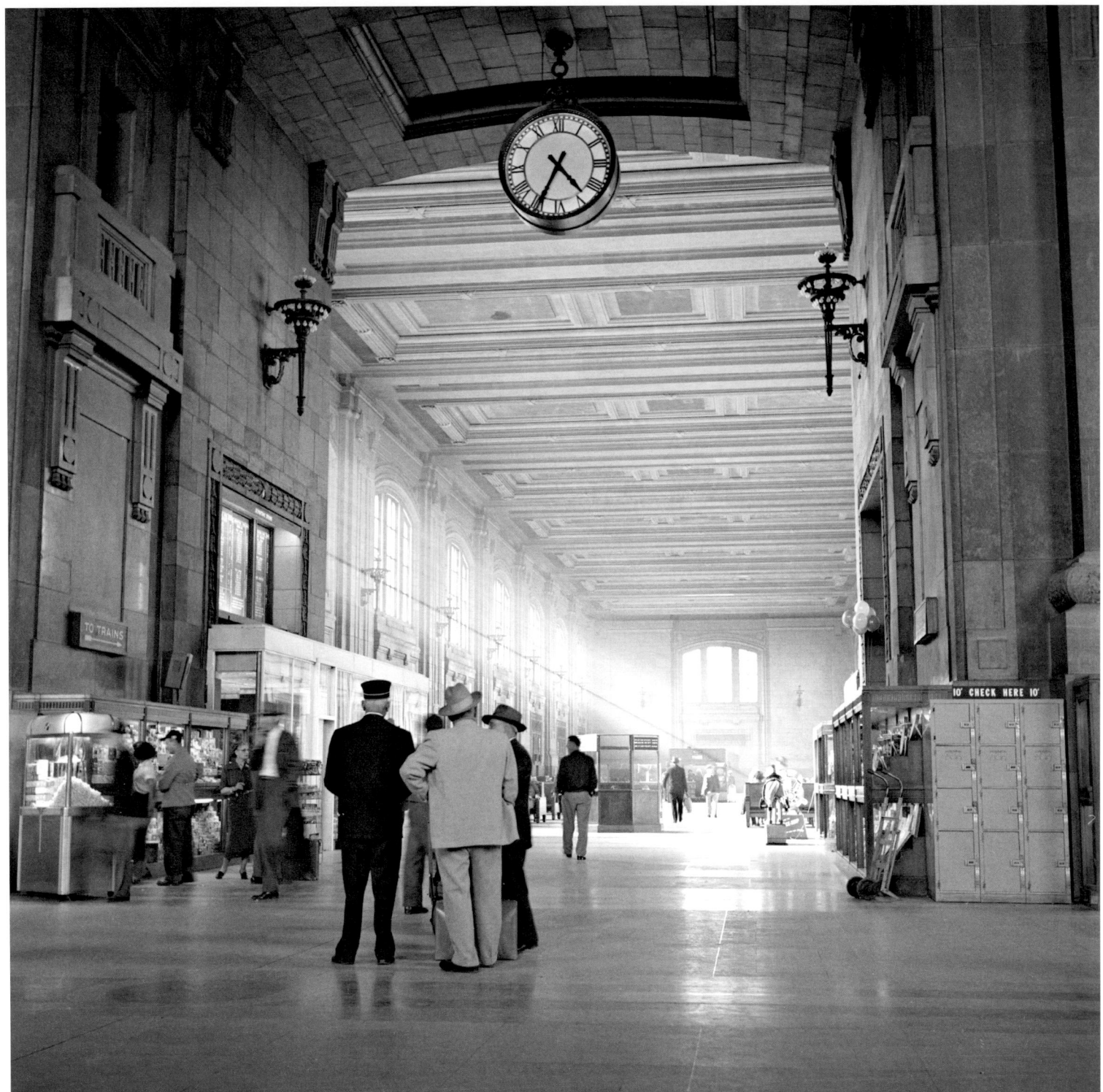

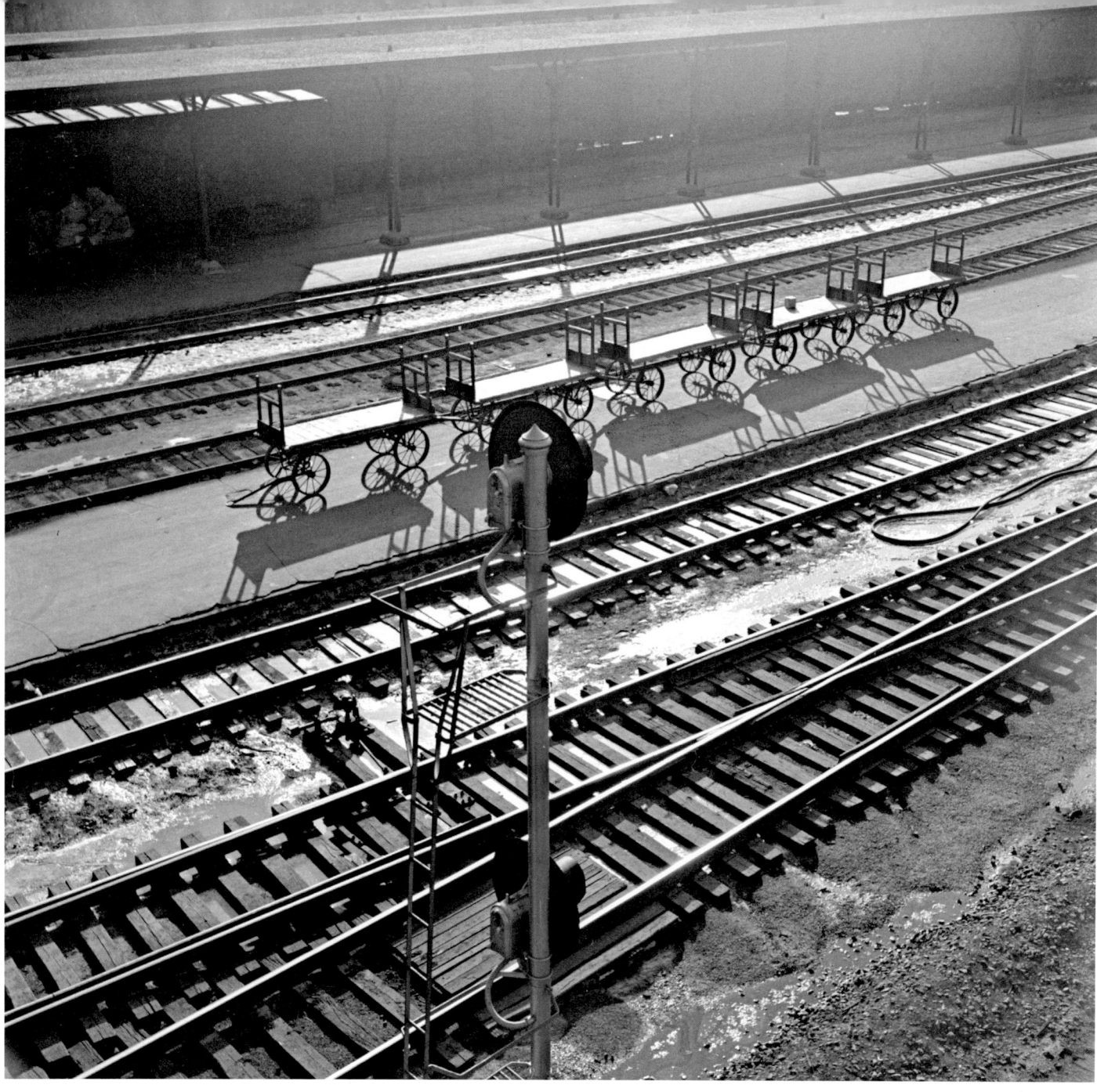

Above: Backlit by low winter sun, baggage carts stand on a platform of Omaha, Nebraska's Union Station in 1957. Opened in 1931, at its peak in the mid-1940s the Art Deco station hosted sixty-four trains and as many as 10,000 passengers each day. Business declined sharply until passenger service ended in 1971. Two years later, Union Pacific donated the station to the city, which soon made it home of the Durham Museum.

Facing: Union Pacific steam locomotives stand inside the roundhouse at Council Bluffs, Iowa, on a February day in 1957. At left is 2-8-2 no. 2242, a 1913 Baldwin product that was scrapped the following year. Thanks to ventilation hoods over every stall, this roundhouse stayed cleaner than earlier ones. Located across the Missouri River from Omaha, Nebraska, Council Bluffs was the eastern terminus of the first transcontinental railroad. Today its Carnegie Library houses the Union Pacific Museum.

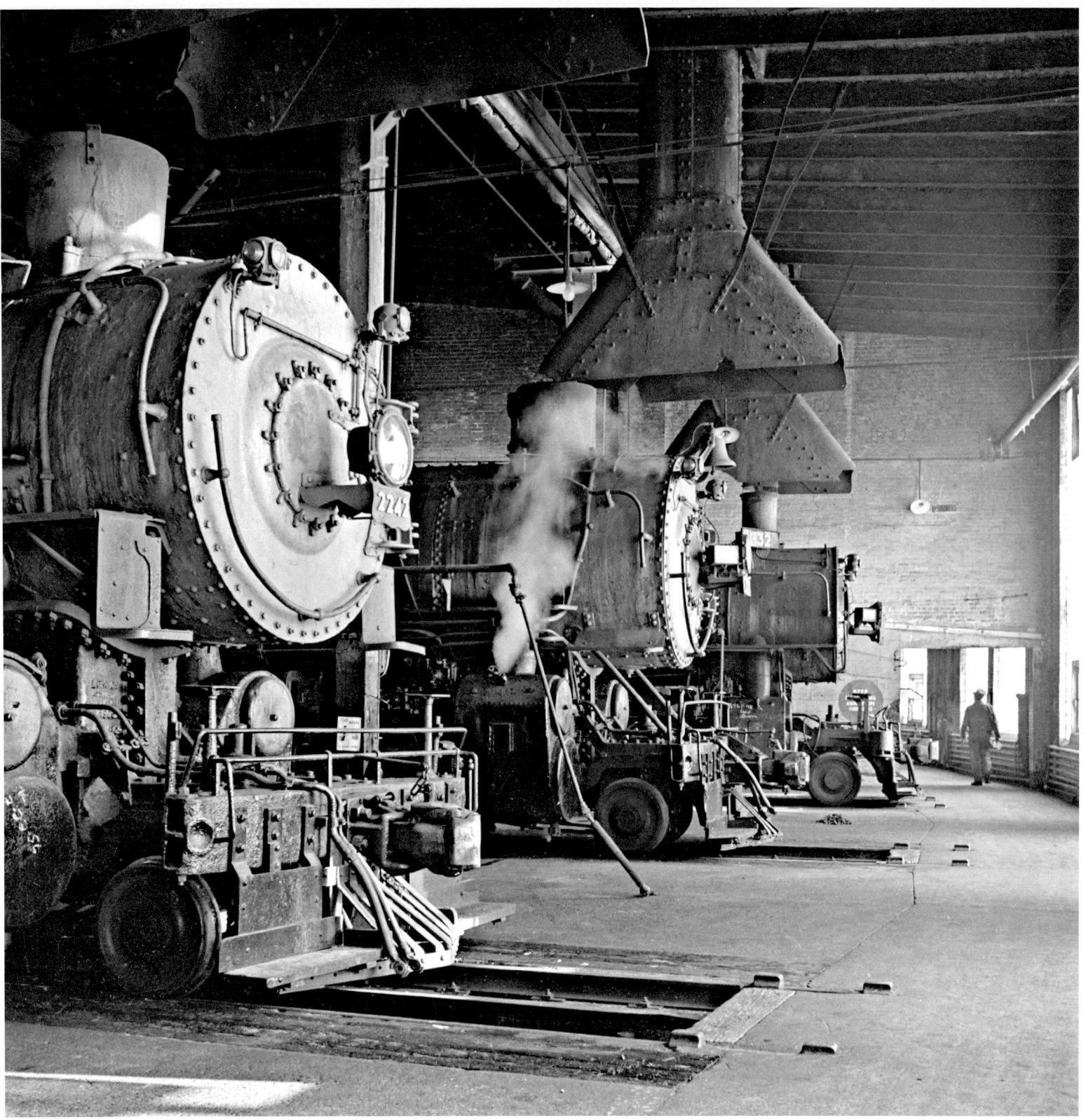

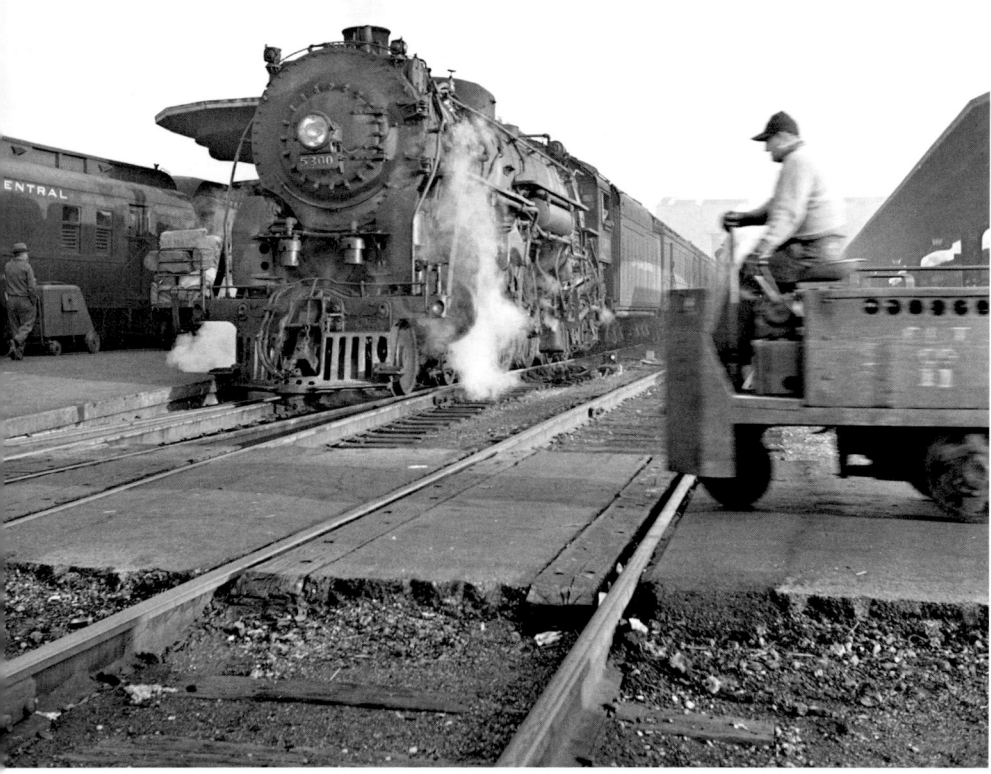

A Cincinnati Union Terminal worker drives a cart in front of New York Central Hudson no. 5300, which had just brought in the *Midnight Special* from Cleveland on the morning of September 24, 1952. The train made a seven-hour overnight run via Columbus, one of several NYC passenger trains that linked Ohio's three major cities at the time.

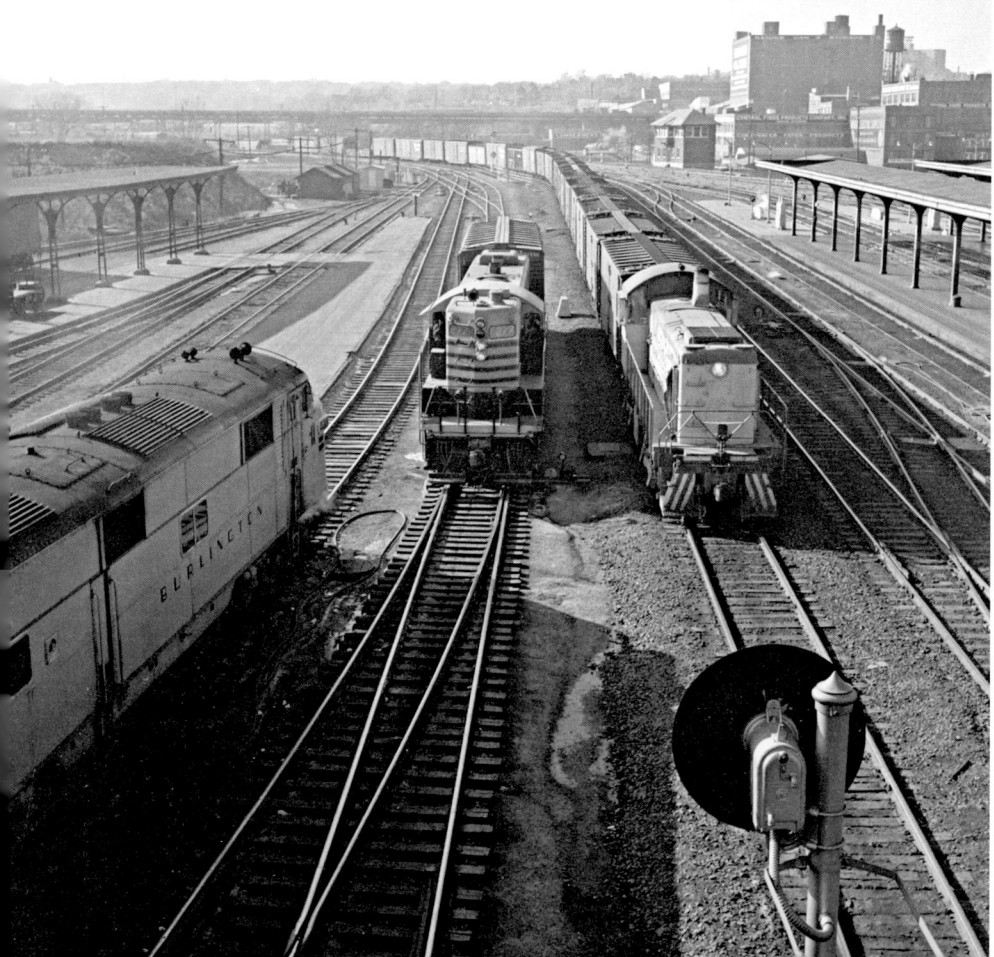

Left: Burlington Route and Union Pacific diesels shuffle freight cars at Omaha Union Station in Nebraska, next to one of the Burlington's streamlined E-units on a Chicago–Denver passenger train. The view looks west from the South 10th Street overpass on the afternoon of February 5, 1957. The station's tracks were still busy with both freight and passenger traffic, but the latter was in decline.

Facing: Crew members of a Baltimore & Ohio passenger train chat on the platform of Cincinnati Union Terminal in September of 1952. Of the seven railroads serving CUT, the B&O was the only one whose trains ran through the terminal; trains of the six other railroads began or ended their journeys in Cincinnati.

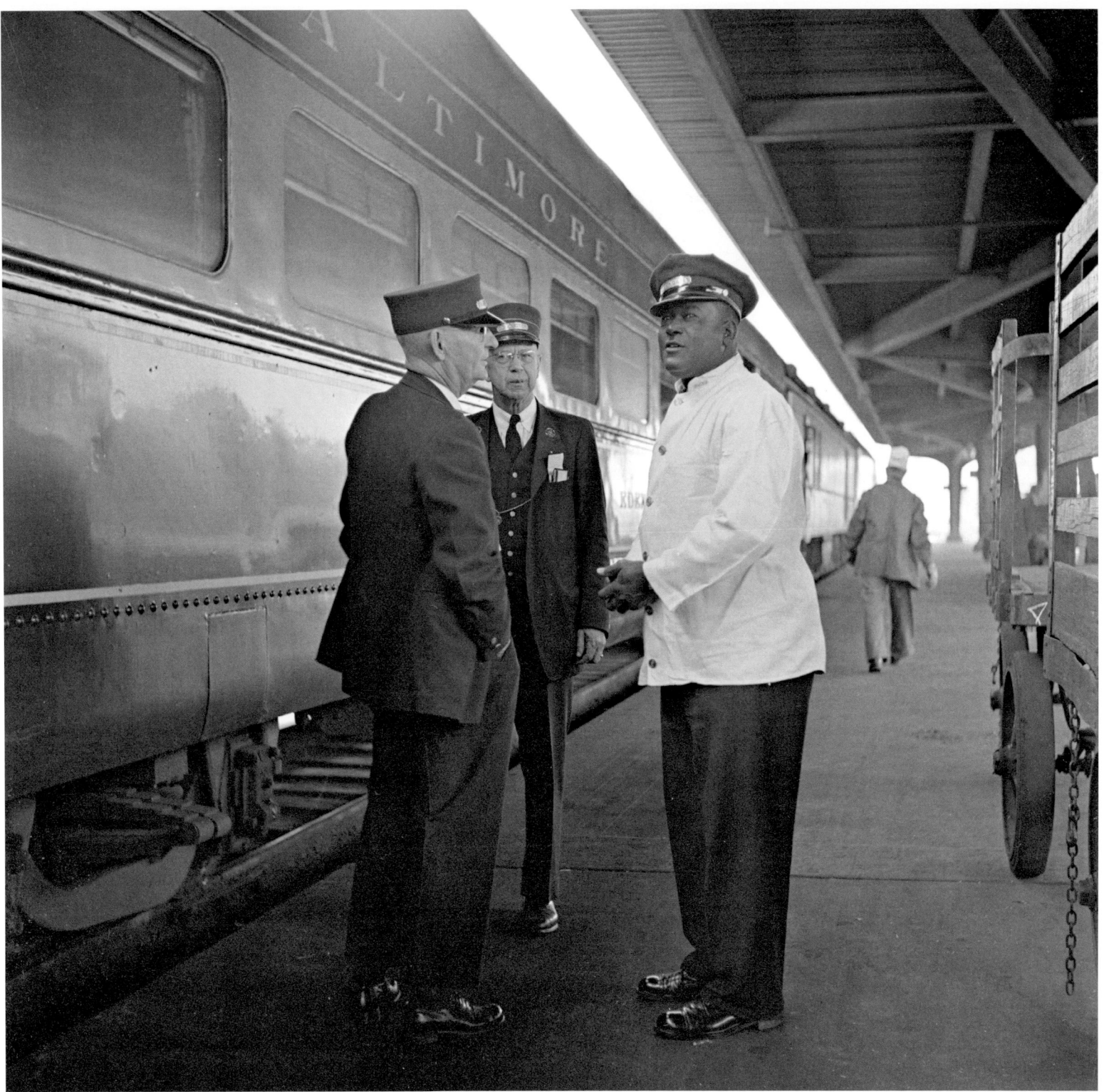

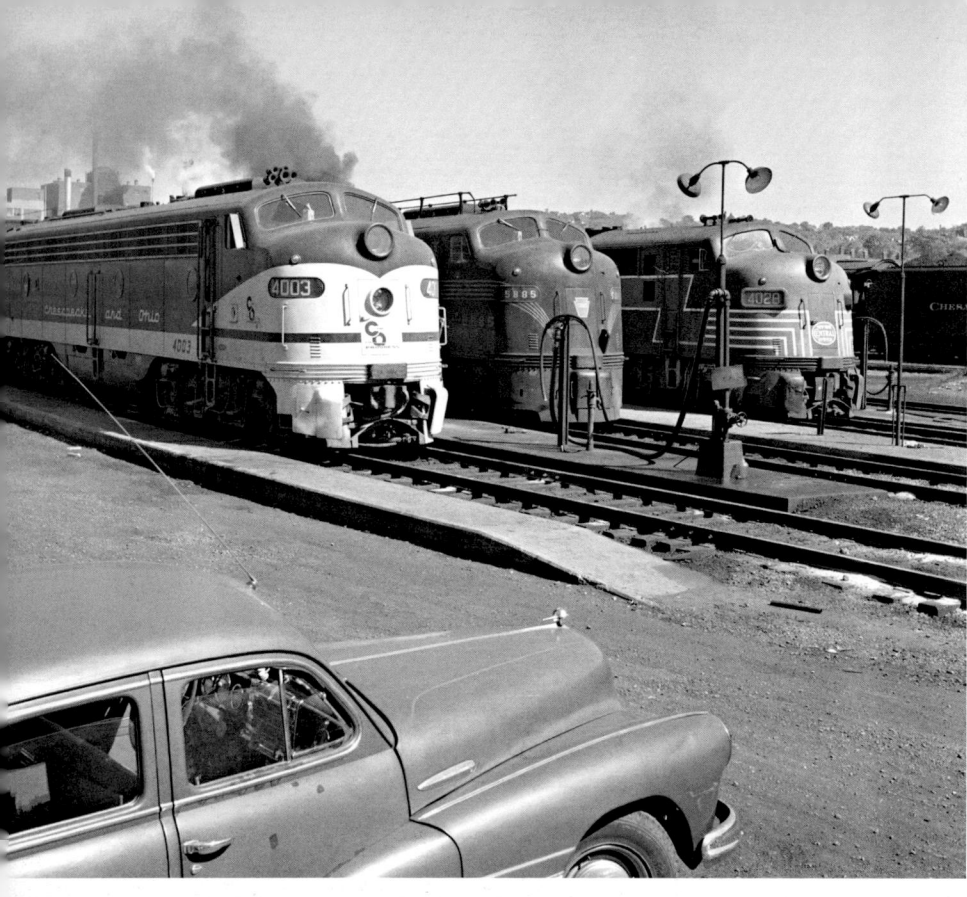

1950s streamliners of the roads and the rails stand together at Cincinnati Union Terminal in September of 1952. Joining the Buick in the foreground are E-units of three of the seven railroads serving CUT: Chesapeake & Ohio E8 no. 4003, Pennsylvania E8 no. 5885, and New York Central E7 no. 4028. Barely visible beyond them is a C&O steam locomotive.

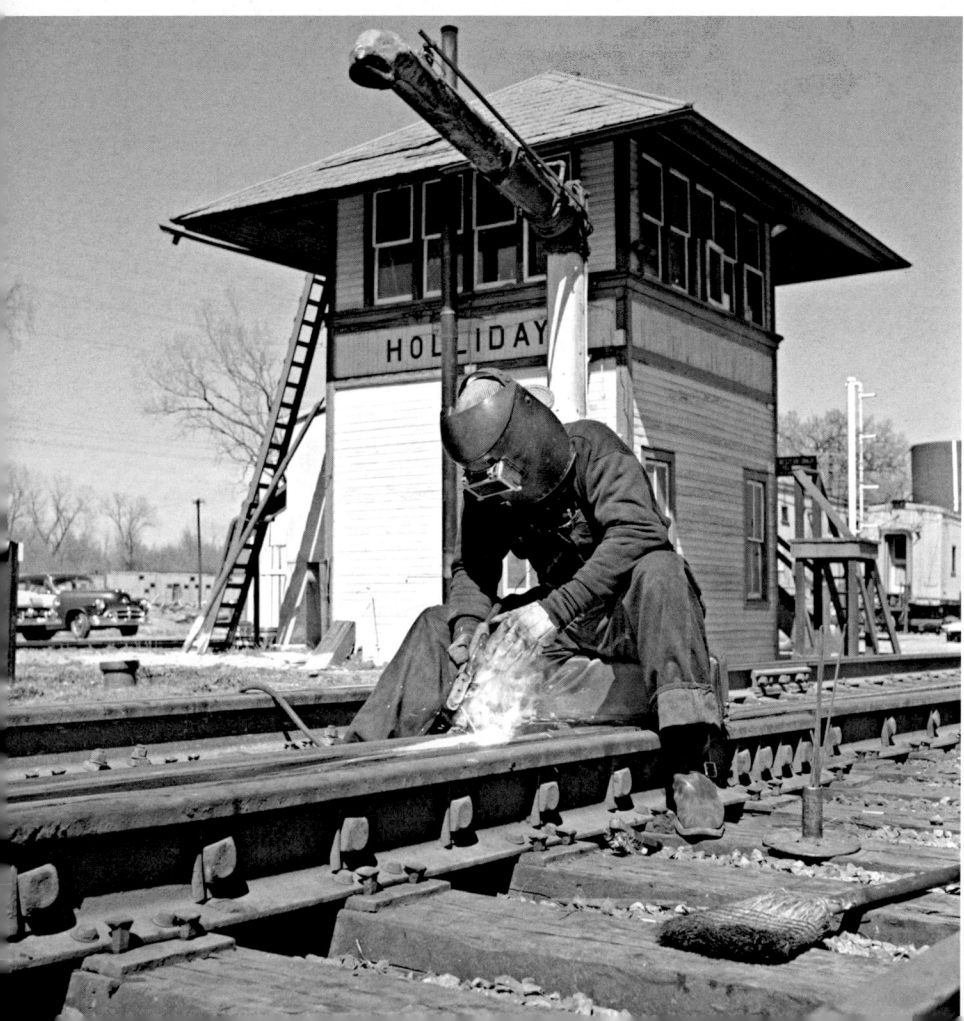

Left: Santa Fe track worker building up worn spots on a "frog," the track component that lets one rail line pass over another, "without spilling trains all over the countryside," in Abbey's words. The location is Holliday, Kansas, 13 miles west of Kansas City, Missouri, on the Santa Fe's main line. The place was named for Cyrus K. Holliday, the entrepreneur who served as the railroad's first president from 1860 to 1863; except for a one-year hiatus, he served on its board of directors until his death in 1900.

Facing: A Baltimore & Ohio Railroad worker washes the streamlined nose of Electro-Motive diesel no. 368 at Cumberland, Maryland, on an overcast September day in 1952. Near the end of his life, Abbey selected this photograph for his collection of twenty-five favorites. Not one to mourn the demise of steam, he wrote, "Now, this proves that railroads are cleaning up their act. More to the point, diesels are doing it for them."

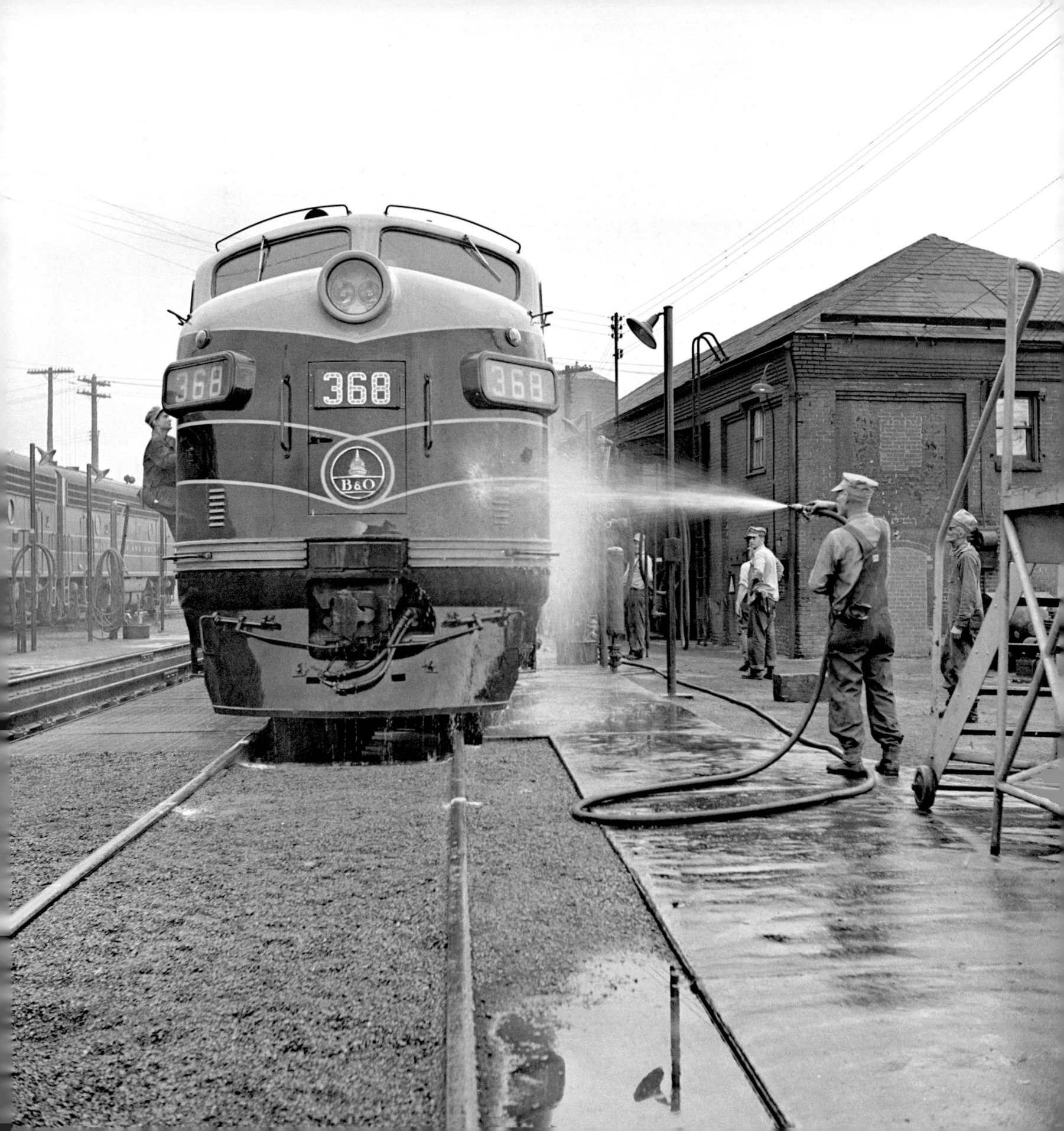

At the Beech Grove Shops of the New York Central near Indianapolis in 1953, a driving wheel from steam locomotive no. 6844, an 0-6-0 switcher, gets a new tire. The tire ring is expanded slightly by a gas flame and is then pounded into place by men with sledge hammers; when the ring cools, it shrinks tightly around the wheel. The NYC created the community in 1906 to serve as a railroad shop town. Amtrak operates the shops today.

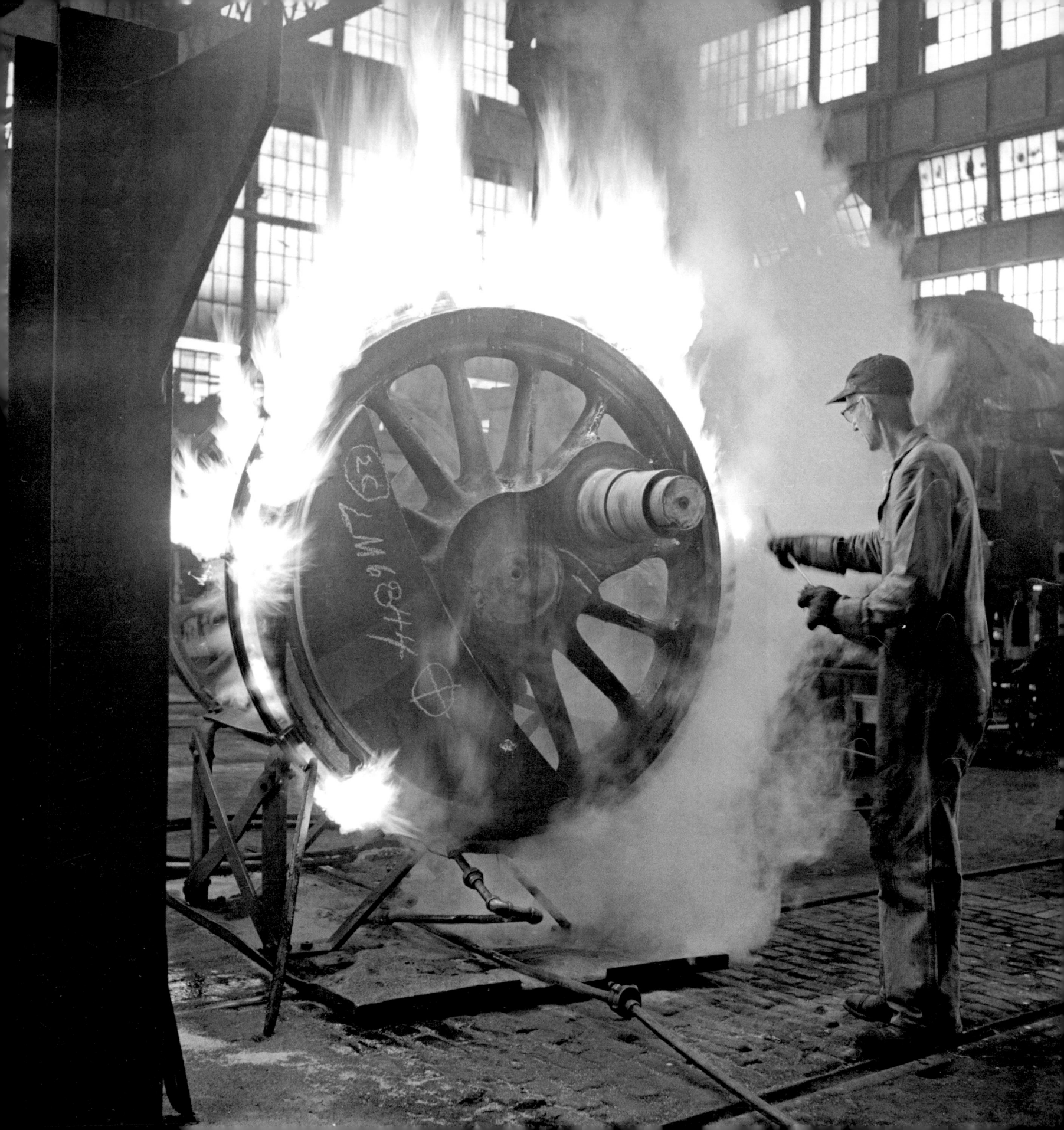

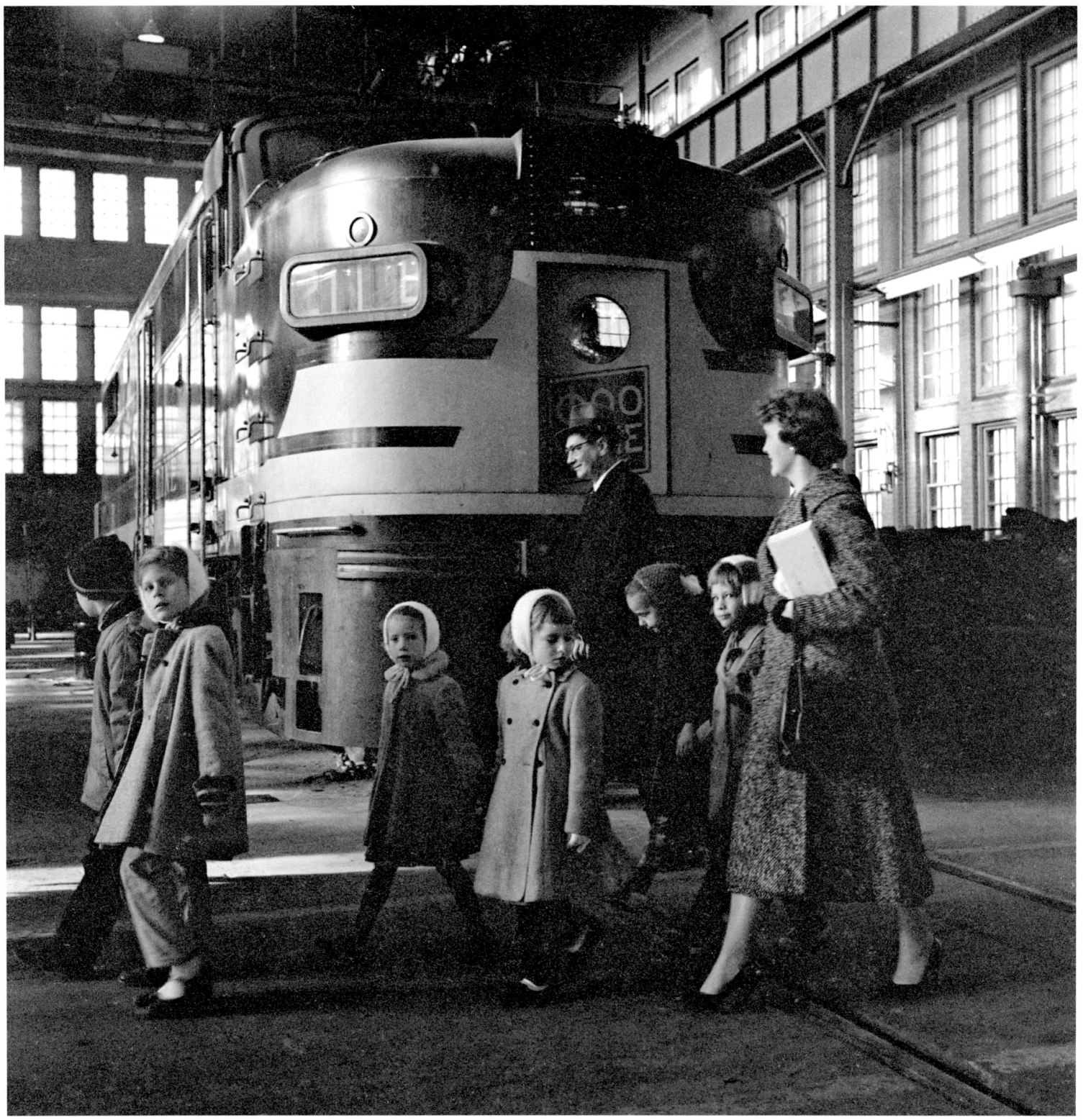

THREE

SOO LINE STORYTELLER

School tours were a staple event for Soo Line public relations during Abbey's tenure with the railroad. This view from 1959 shows an elementary class from Hopkins Public Schools in suburban Minneapolis touring the diesel shop at Shoreham Yard. Maroon and gold FA-1 no. 211B towers behind them. The Soo had acquired the 1,500-horsepower Alco a decade earlier and would retire it in just a little more than three years.

BY 1959, ABBEY WAS READY TO MOVE ON TO SOMETHING NEW. He'd proven himself as a transportation journalist in both the consumer market at *Trains* and the trade arena at *Railway Age*. He'd had success at an industry association. Now he was ready to work in the middle of the action, the executive suite of a major railroad.

His first opportunity was unexpected: an offer from a vice president of the Soo Line, who had admired Abbey's *Railway Age* coverage of a landmark rate case Soo had before the Interstate Commerce Commission. Surprised and perhaps a bit flattered, Abbey embraced the opportunity, taking over as special assistant to the president and director of public relations at the Soo Line Building in Minneapolis.

Abbey's arrival was timely. The old Soo Line, a stalwart carrier in the upper Midwest, was in the throes of becoming the "new Soo" via the 1961 merger of its three key related entities, the Minneapolis, St. Paul & Sault Ste. Marie; Duluth, South Shore & Atlantic; and Wisconsin Central. In truth, it wasn't all that much of a groundbreaking merger. All three properties were wards of the Canadian Pacific, and all shared enough operating practices that, in many ways, they functioned as a single railroad.

But it was an old-fashioned operation, a barely profitable company still stuck in the world of written train orders and loose-car railroading. The Soo owned 5,000 miles of railroad, but too much of the system was light-density branch lines. The railroad was heavily dependent on overhead Canadian traffic. The only salvation lay in the economies of scale available in a merger, a turnaround ultimately fed by new high-horsepower diesels, hundreds of miles of welded rail and centralized traffic control, and intelligent cost cutting.

The Soo Line had never been high on Wally Abbey's list of favorite railroads. He wasn't even aware of the company until high school, when, after church on Sundays, his dad would take the family to a barbecue chicken place near Deerfield, a far northwest suburb of Chicago. "I remember us bouncing across a single-track railroad and me asking Dad, what railroad is this? 'The Soo Line,' he said. 'Goes up into Wisconsin somewhere.'"

Now, suddenly, Abbey was a Soo executive, and what he found wasn't altogether encouraging. Before Abbey, the company appeared to treat modern corporate public relations as an afterthought, leaving it to a clunky three-man department headed up by a vice president whose responsibilities also included personnel and safety. There was only minimal contact with the local news media.

Abbey would change all that. "I found that it wasn't so much that the Soo Line was misunderstood in the world at large but that the Soo was hardly understood at all. I soon began to hear how, should a train be derailed or some other misfortune occur to cause reporters to begin calling (someone) at home, the fellow who should have handled the calls would unplug his phone. Very little in the way of the mechanisms of a public relations operation were in place. There was not even a reliable mailing list."

The company's handling of those derailments gave Abbey an opportunity to school upper management. Rather than wait for the news media to call, Abbey suggested the railroad be proactive and contact the press first. "My superiors didn't think that was an altogether wise move. But sooner or later they grudgingly, but tacitly, agreed that the news reports on the accident were factual and non-inflammatory. And sooner or later they quit arguing with me when I suggested that the only way to not have derailments show up in the newspapers was to not have derailments."

Abbey's efforts began to be appreciated by people across the industry, not least by his successor, John Bergene, whom Abbey hired initially to edit the company magazine. Bergene went on to oversee the Soo's public affairs for many years and recalls Abbey's role as critical in the company's history.

"Wally was the first professional PR type at the Soo," said Bergene in a 2017 interview. "When he came in they had a former passenger agent acting as an advertising manager who also edited an employee publication—both in old-school fashion. In just the short time we worked side-by-side, he was constantly on the phone working with national media and trades to gin up some press about the new Soo. And he was good at it, as the files were full of stories about the 'New Soo.' We were small, but he kept us in the public arena."

The Soo Line's higher public profile also owed something to a new corporate image, largely concocted by Abbey. Convinced that Soo's traditional maroon-and-gold paint scheme was dated, Abbey began experimenting with various new approaches on scale-model plaster locomotives. Soon he came up with a winner. The new paint scheme began appearing on diesels in February 1962: a stunning combination of light-gray flanks and bright red front and rear end, with the word SOO emblazoned in black across the hood in 48-inch-high Venus Bold Extended. It was a clean, stark New Frontier design very much in tune with the times.

Abbey never explicitly said so, but his job at the Soo had a deeply personal benefit because he got to take his camera with him wherever he went. Along the way he created a portfolio of work quite unlike anything seen previously in railroad public relations. Certainly he performed the usual duties: photographing company officers standing stiffly on the running board of the newest diesel, making serviceable images of new yards and buildings, shooting sterile portraits of freight cars and other equipment.

But out on the road, Abbey also found the time and had the necessary access to continue his work as an objective documentarian, even if the intent was unstated. In a word, his portrayal of the 1960s Soo Line was vivid. Far from making just sanitized views to fit corporate purposes, he focused on the railroad as it was, shooting trains on the North Dakota prairie in bad weather, recording the work of diesel mechanics amid the gritty interior of Shoreham Shops, demonstrating that light-gray hood units didn't always look pretty.

Much of this work surfaced in 1984 in the hardcover book *The Little Jewel*, a pithy, irreverent memoir Abbey published

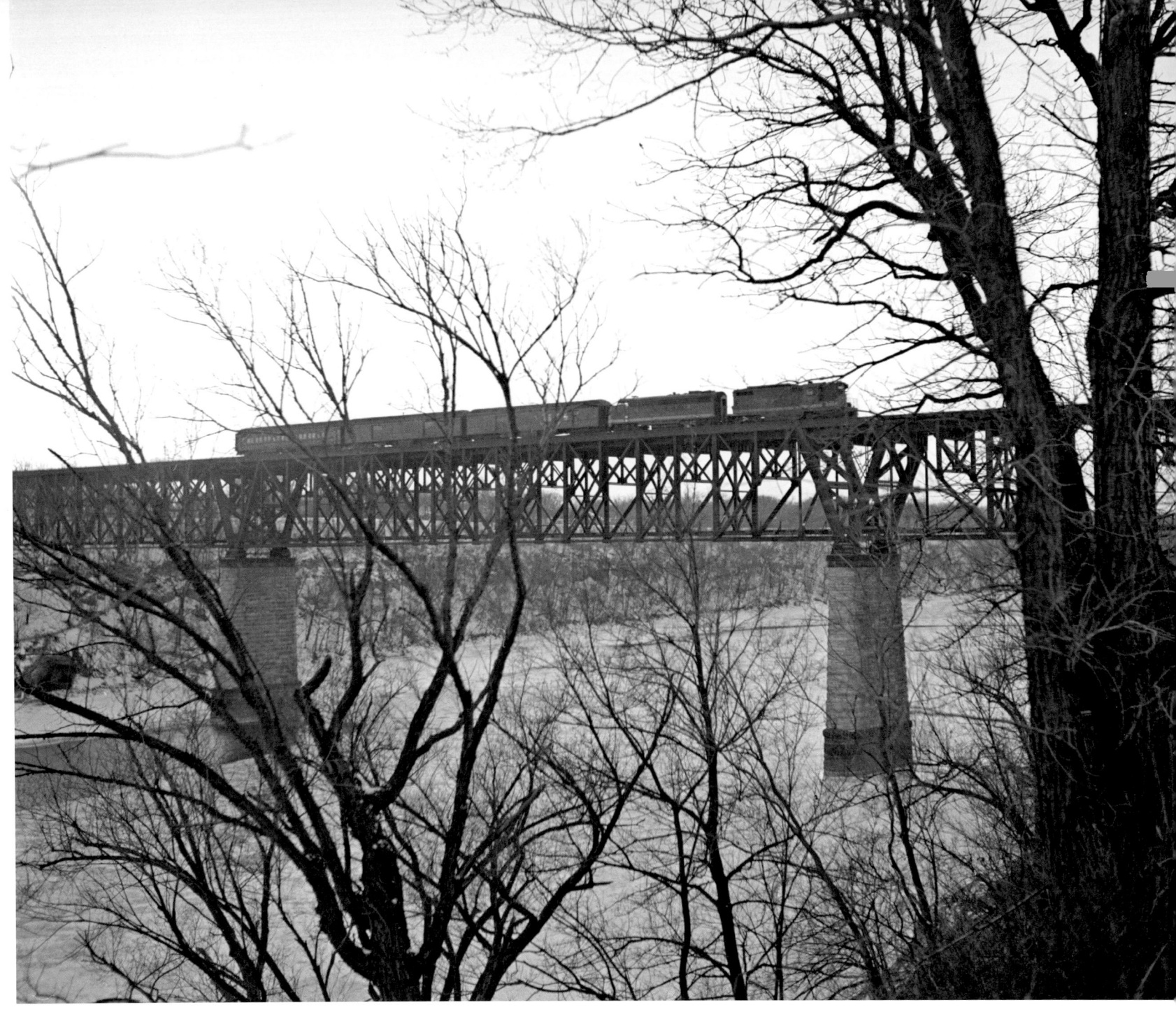

Last run of train no. 8, remnant of the *Atlantic Limited* that had become a nameless night train from Minneapolis to Sault Ste. Marie, Michigan, crossing the Milwaukee Road's Short Line Bridge over the Mississippi River in Minneapolis on March 4, 1960. Westbound counterpart no. 7 arrived two days later for the final time, closing the book on this service. Before the decade ended, no dedicated passenger trains would be left on the Soo Line.

under his own Pinon Productions imprint. The book is a useful, functional history of the Soo during Abbey's time there. More importantly, it's a showcase for Abbey's brand of photojournalism, proving that, as Abbey writes, "railroading can be enjoyable as well as useful."

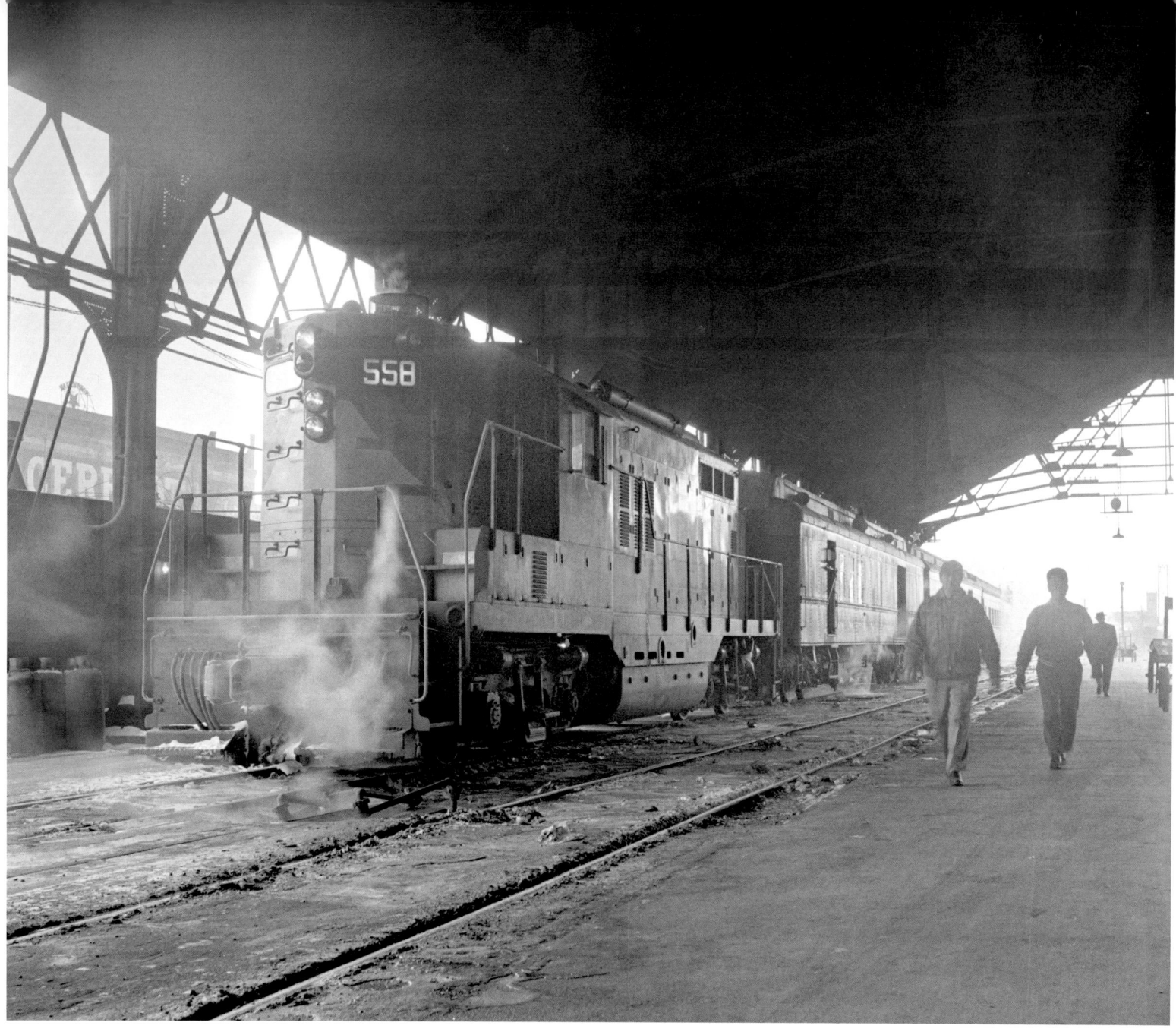

Above: Train no. 7 has just arrived for the last time at the Milwaukee Road depot in downtown Minneapolis, Minnesota, on March 6, 1960. The nameless night train from Sault Ste. Marie, Michigan, was a remnant of the *Atlantic Limited* that had once linked Minneapolis directly with Montreal and Saint John, New Brunswick. Eastbound counterpart no. 8 had departed two days earlier for the final time.

Facing: The Wisconsin Central Railroad's ore dock in Ashland, Wisconsin, with the lake boat *Denmark* in April of 1960. WC built the dock in 1916 to transload iron ore from rail-served mines in northern Wisconsin to lake boats for shipment to steel mills located farther down the lakes. The original dock was 900 feet long; WC lengthened it to 1,800 feet in 1925. The dock became part of the Soo Line in 1961 but operated for just four more years, handling its last ore in 1965. It would sit idle for nearly half a century before most of it was demolished in 2013, with only the concrete base left standing.

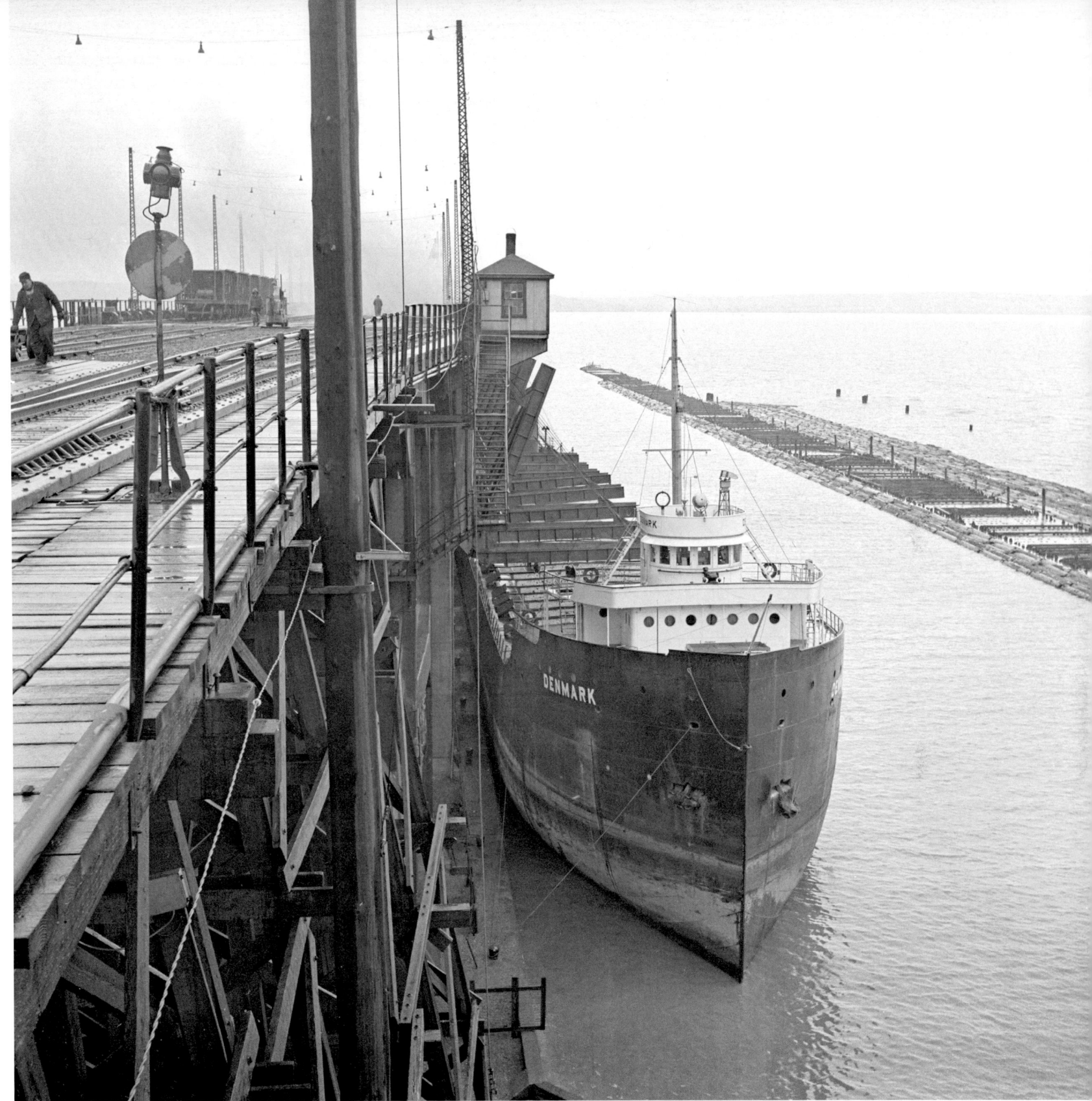

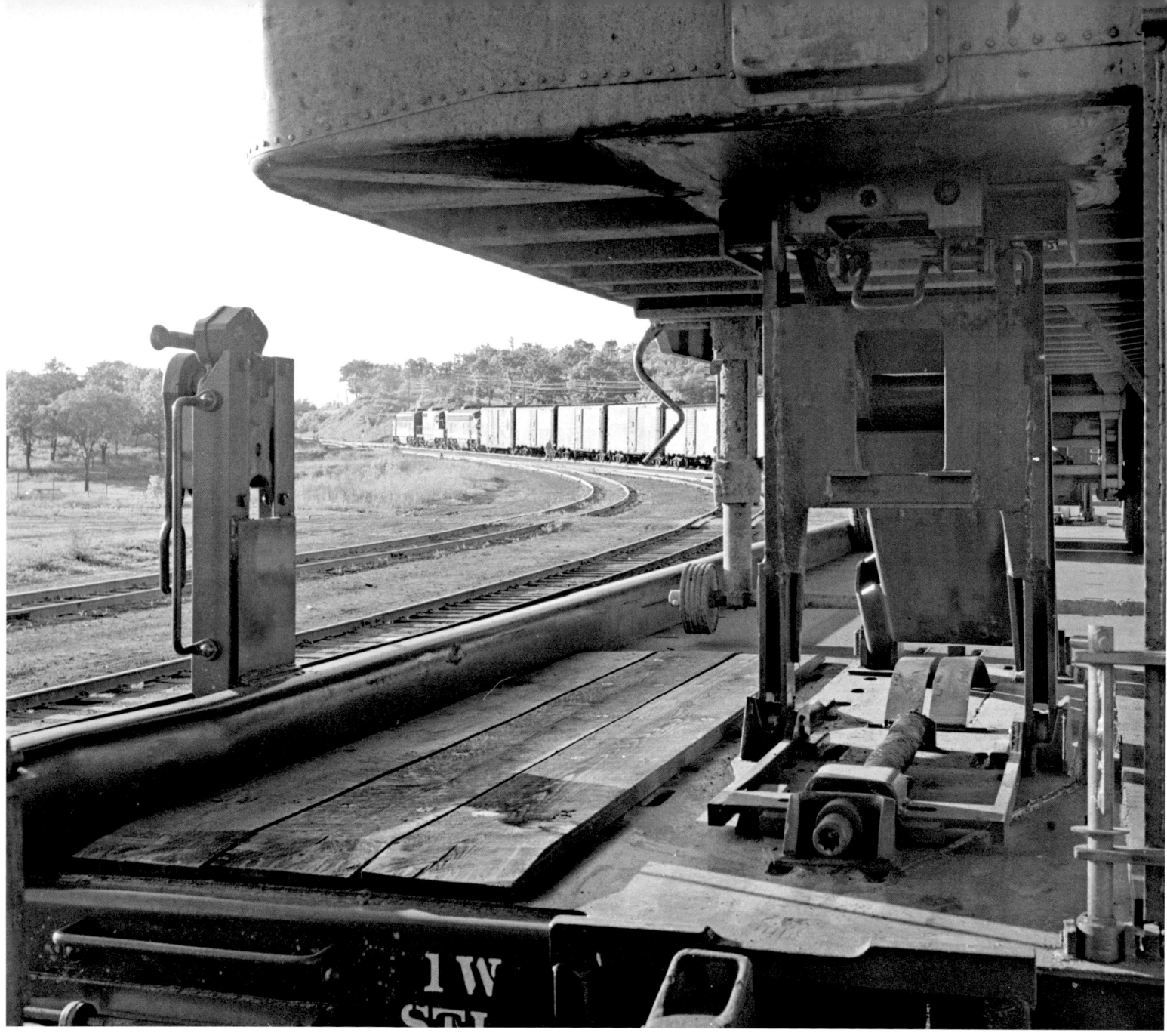

Above: Close-up view of a "piggyback" load—a truck trailer on a flatcar—on eastbound freight train no. 24 leaving Minneapolis's Shoreham Yard in 1960. Piggyback business comprised less than 1 percent of U.S. rail freight in the 1950s, but managers of the Soo and many other railroads saw an opportunity for growth. Today, intermodal traffic—both truck trailers and shipping containers—comprises nearly one-quarter of all revenues of North America's freight railroads.

Facing: Westbound freight train crossing the Camden Place Bridge over the Mississippi River on May 4, 1961. Located on the north side of Minneapolis, the 904-foot-long bridge opened in 1905 and carried the Soo's main line out of the Twin Cities to the Canadian border. It remains a vital link today on the Canadian Pacific Railway's route between Chicago and the West Coast.

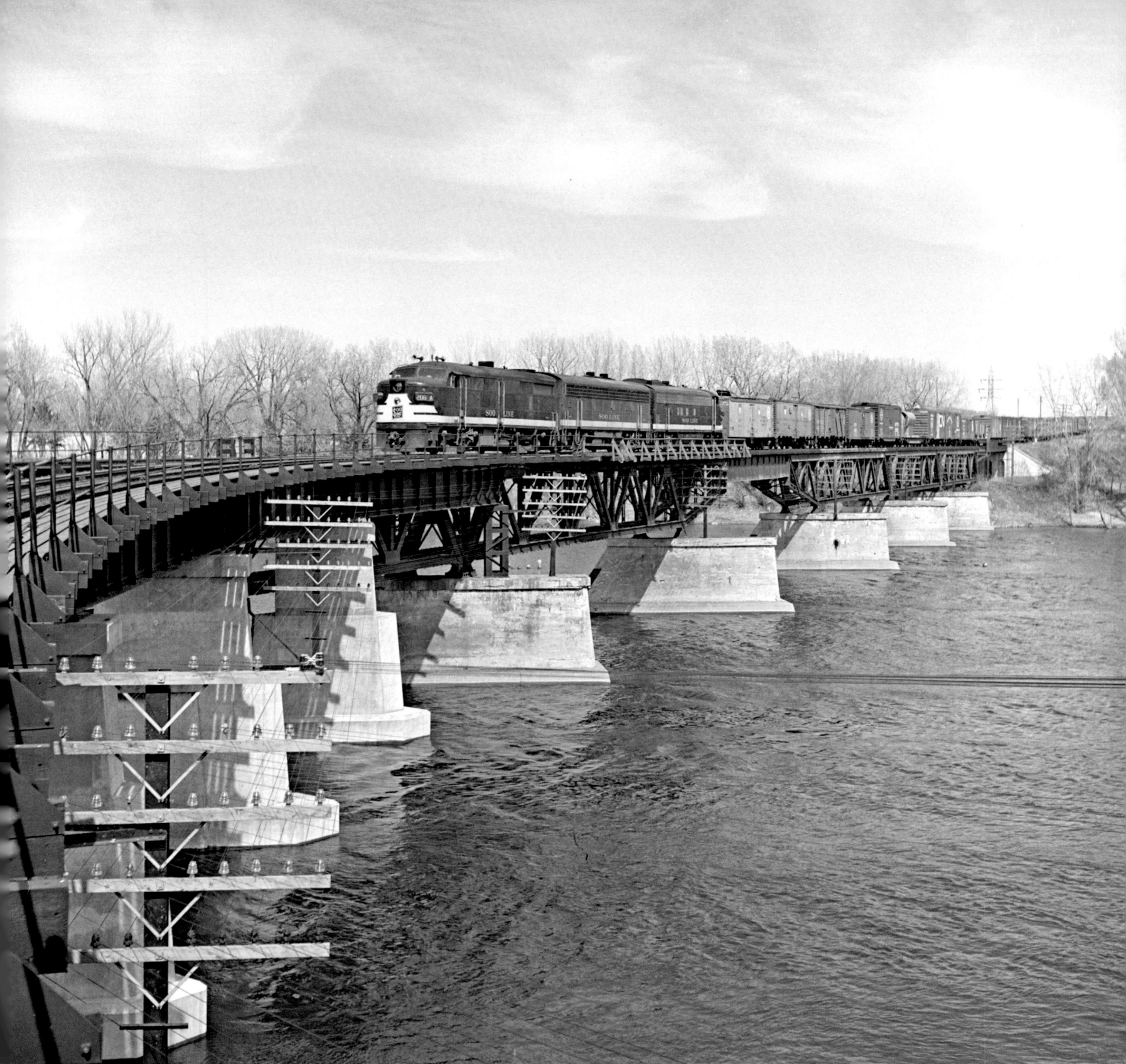

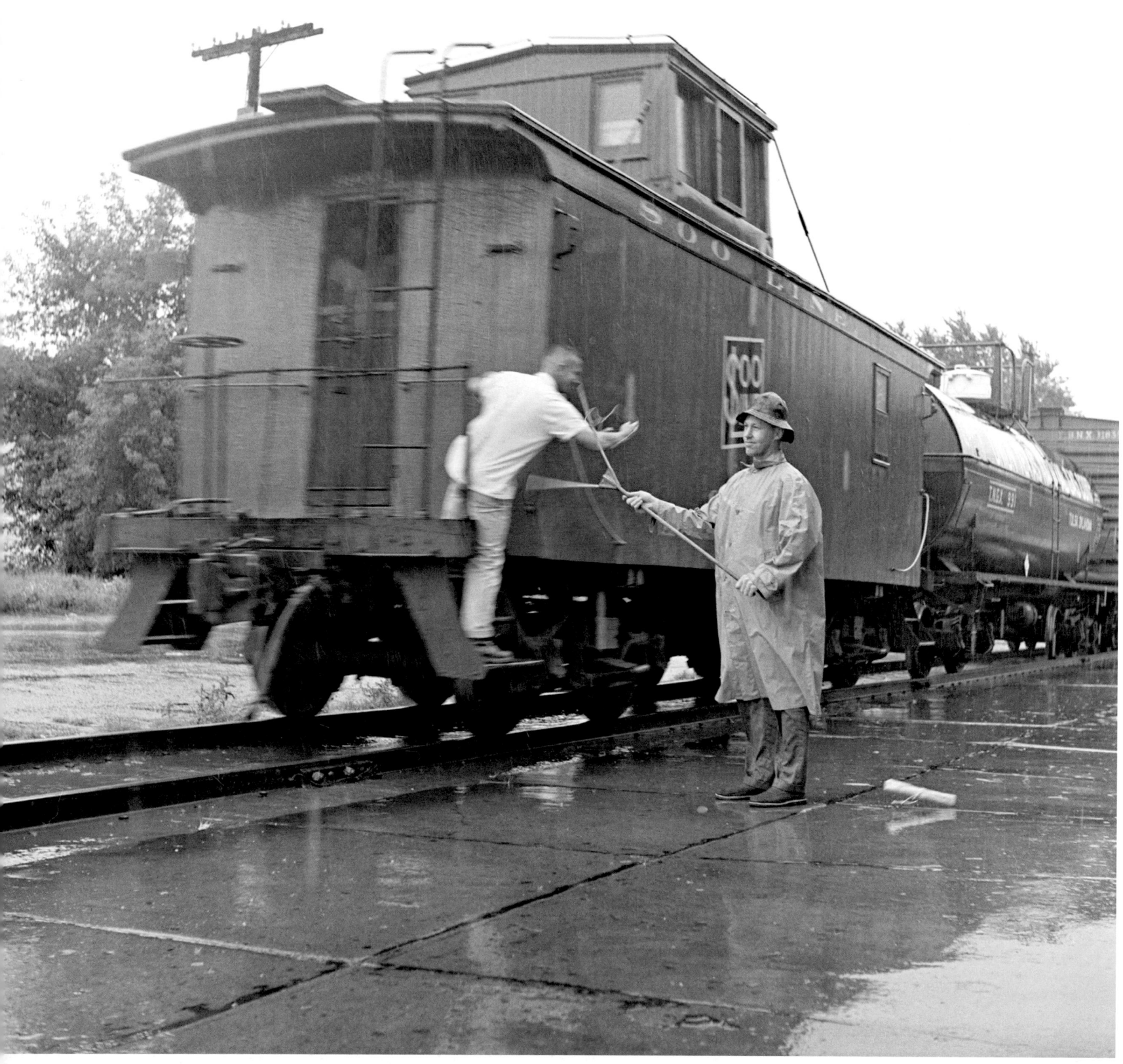

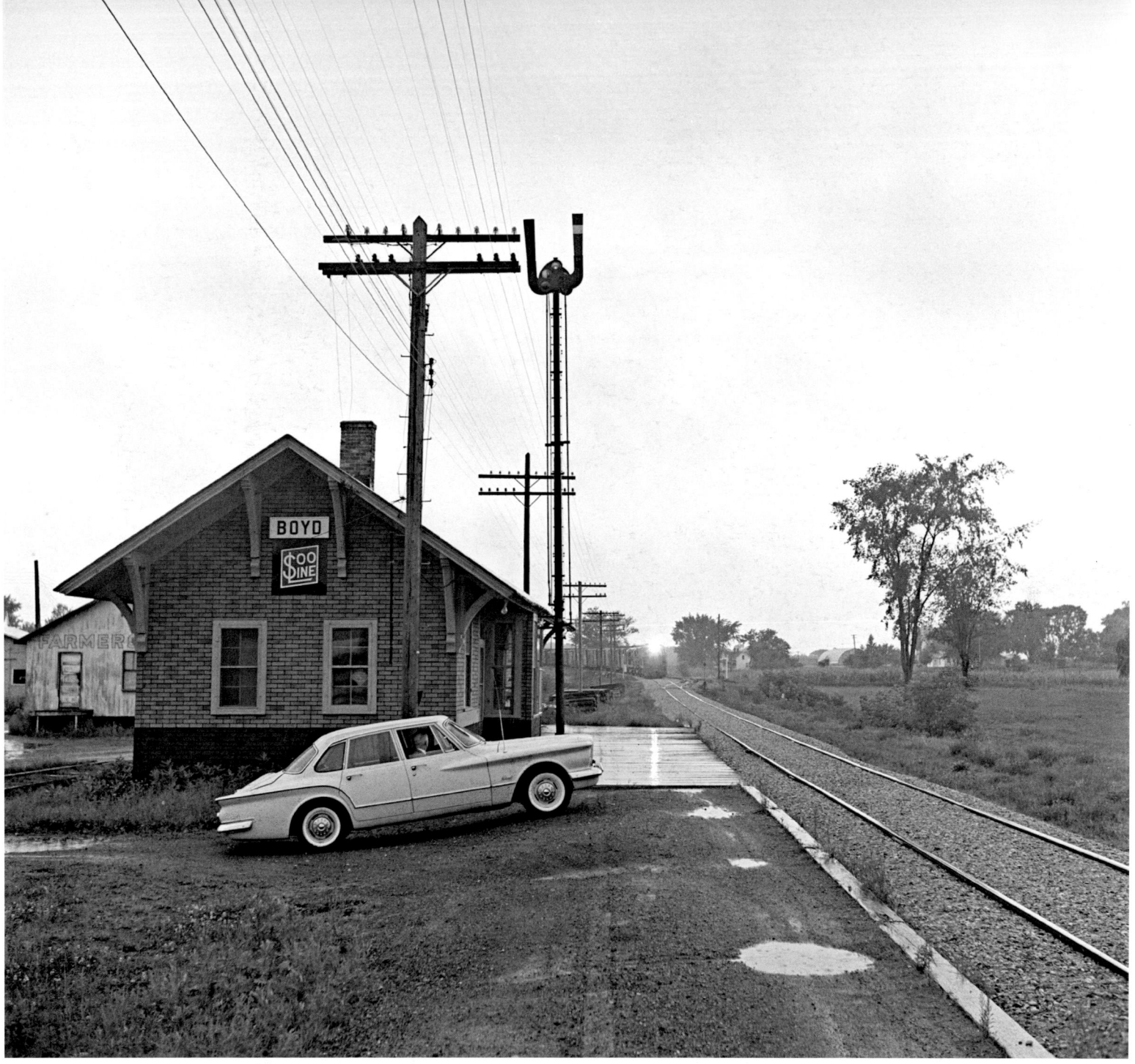

Facing: The conductor of a westbound freight train grabs orders "on the fly" from the operator at New Richmond, Wisconsin, during a summer downpour in 1961. From this end of the train, the scene nearly looks as if it could have taken place in the 1930s. Modernization was coming soon to the railroad, though, and Abbey would document much of it.

Above: *Trains* magazine editor David P. Morgan watches from inside Abbey's Studebaker as an eastbound Soo Line freight train bears down on the depot at Boyd, Wisconsin, on a gloomy summer day in 1961. Following his departure from *Trains* in 1954, Abbey maintained a friendship with Morgan that more than once led to the editor visiting Abbey on the Soo Line.

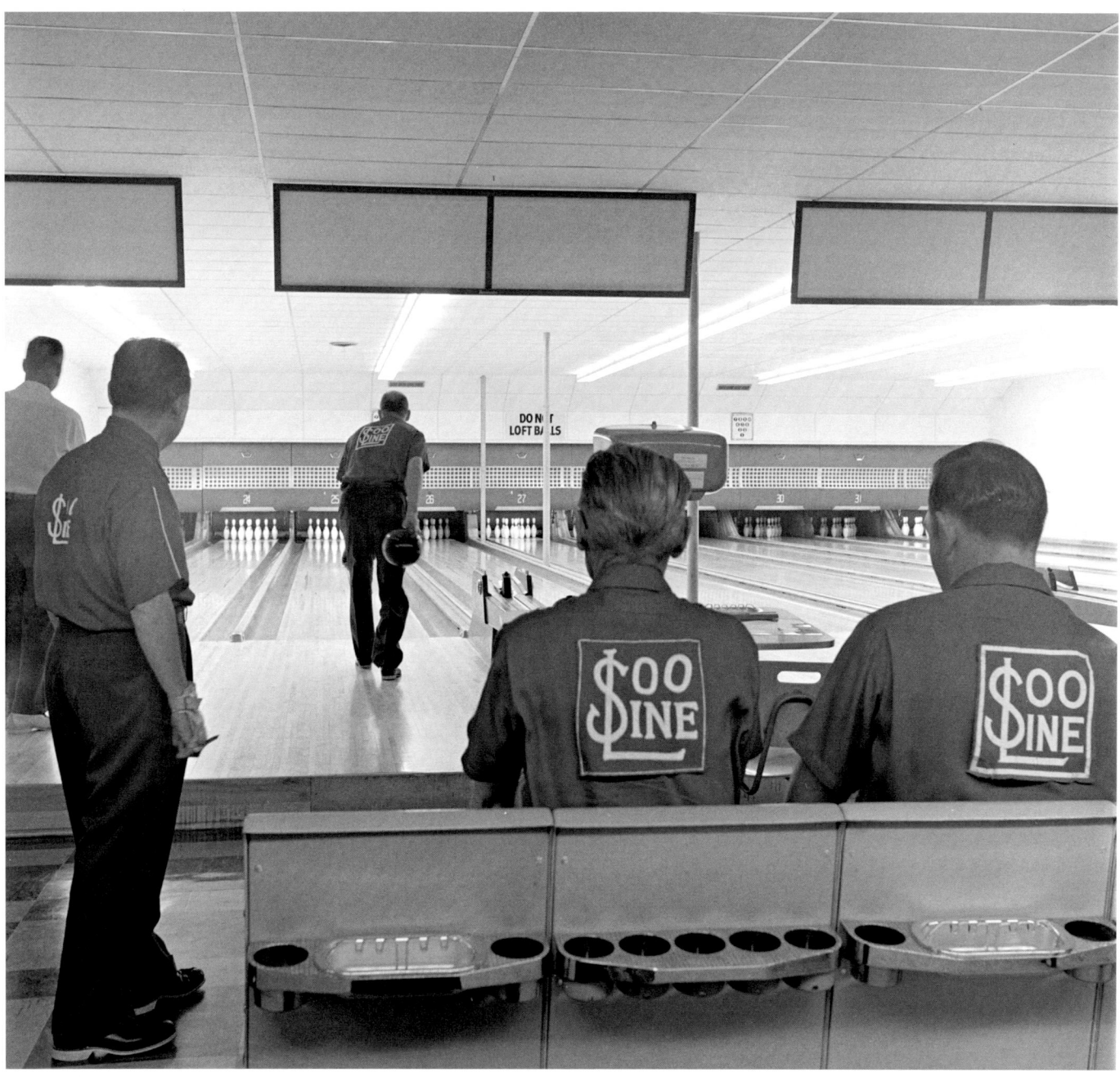

Above: Very few aspects of the Soo Line escaped Abbey's attention during his eleven-year stint with the railroad. It should come as no surprise, then, that he accompanied the Soo's bowling team to the lanes one October evening in 1961 for photographs.

Facing: The moon shines above the snowy tracks at Camden Place, on the north side of Minneapolis, on a winter night in 1962. The main line curves to the left to cross the Mississippi River and enter Shoreham Yard. This view looks south, toward Minneapolis, down a branch line that served industries clustered along the west bank of the river.

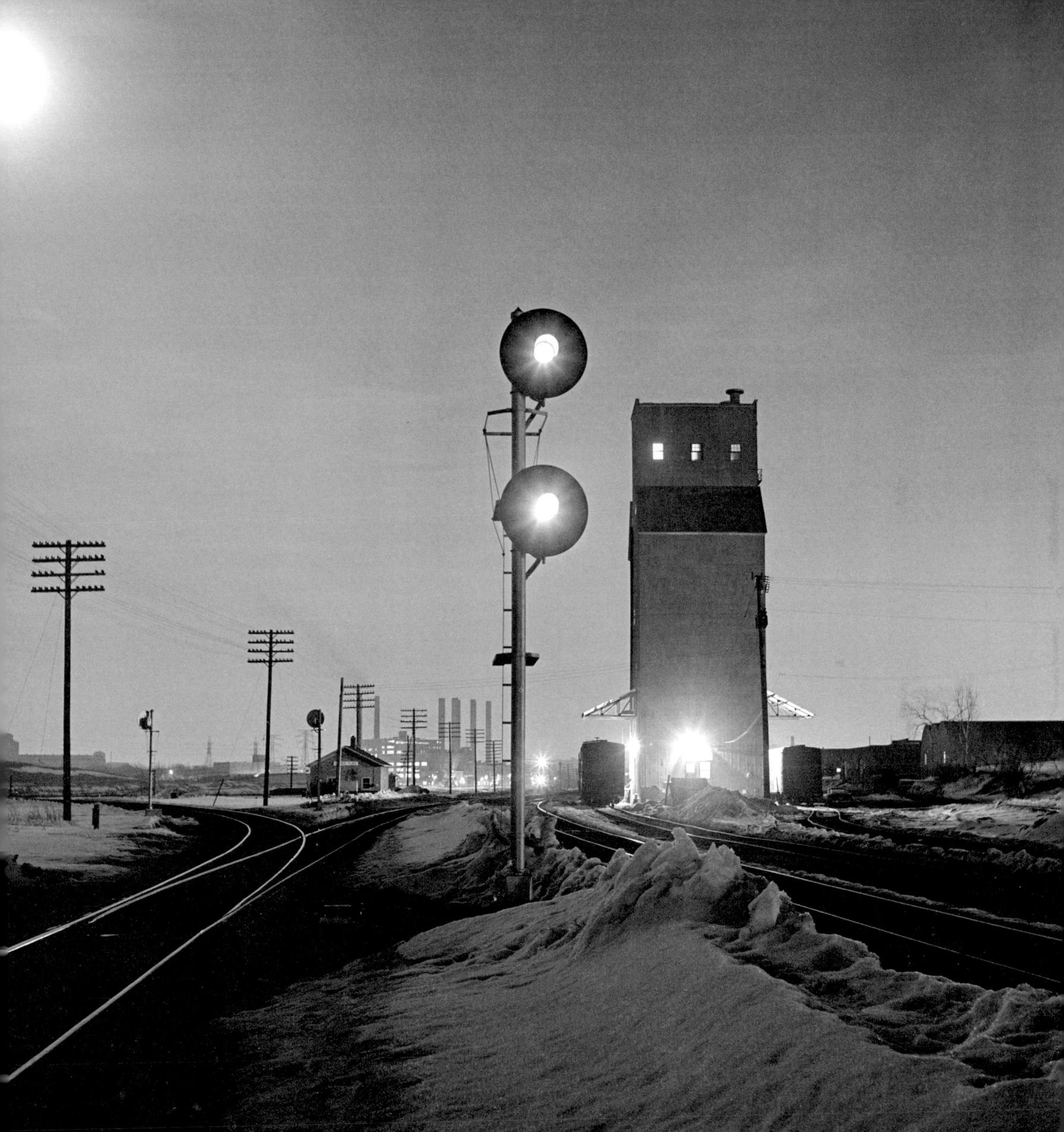

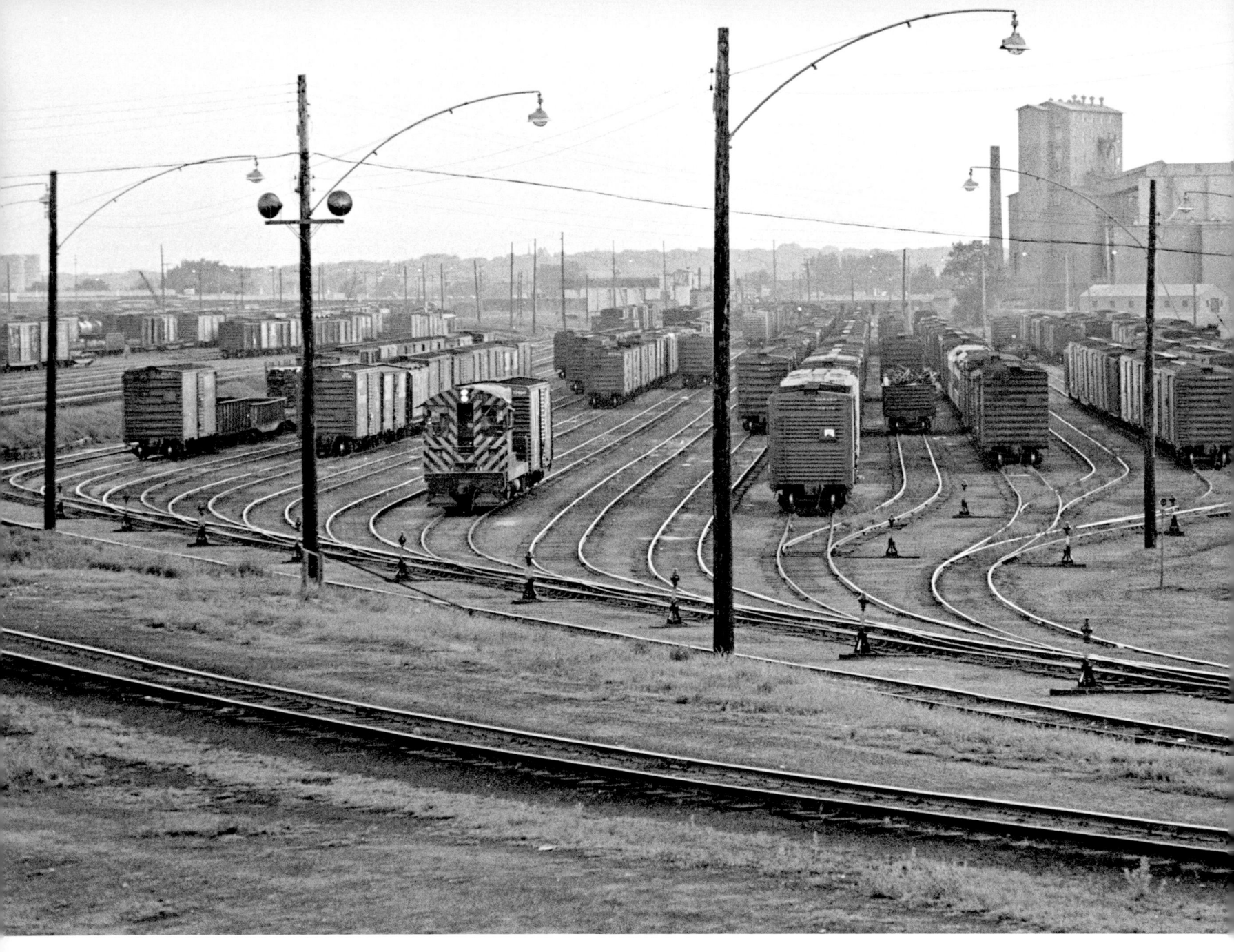

Above: A Fairbanks Morse switcher shuffles freight cars at Shoreham Yard in Minneapolis on a June day in 1962. Abbey made this view from the ice house platform, used to load fresh blocks of ice into refrigerator cars with rooftop hatches—several are visible on one of the tracks at far right. By the 1970s, mechanical "reefers" had replaced most icing operations.

Facing: On an August afternoon in 1962, westbound freight train no. 125 rumbles across the Camden Place Bridge over the Mississippi River on Minneapolis's north side, taking empty grain cars back to the prairies. Part of the Great Northern Railway's Northtown Yard is visible in the distance. The view is from the top of a concrete elevator along the Mississippi's western bank. The bridge remains a vital link on Canadian Pacific's main line from Chicago to the West Coast, although the leg branching off to the right is no longer in service.

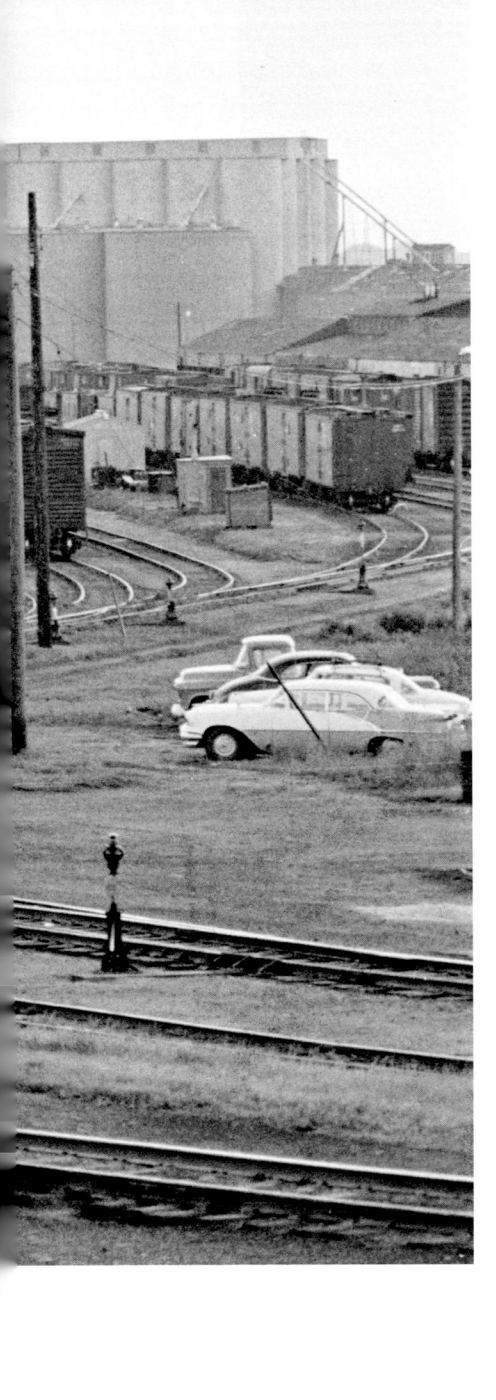

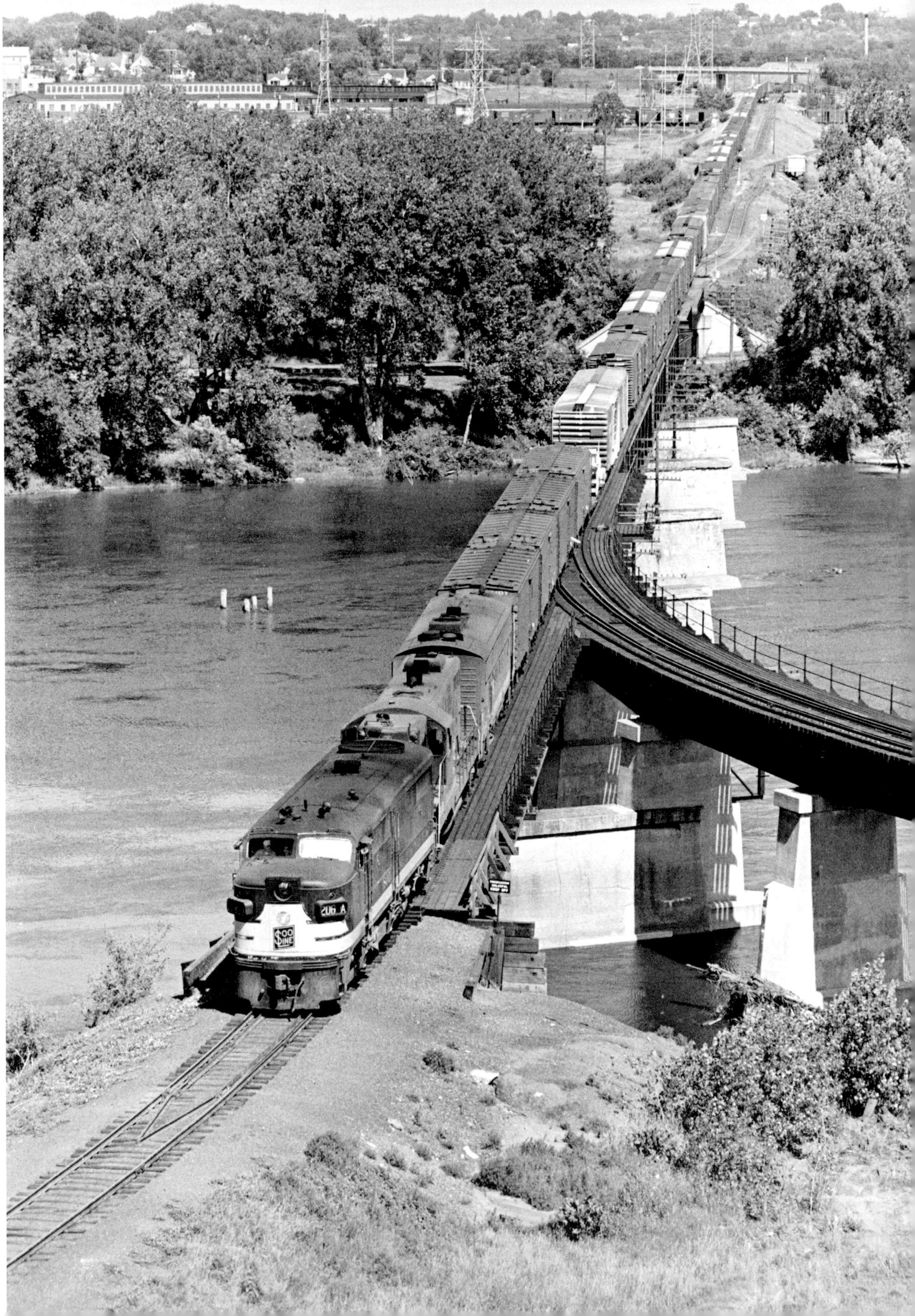

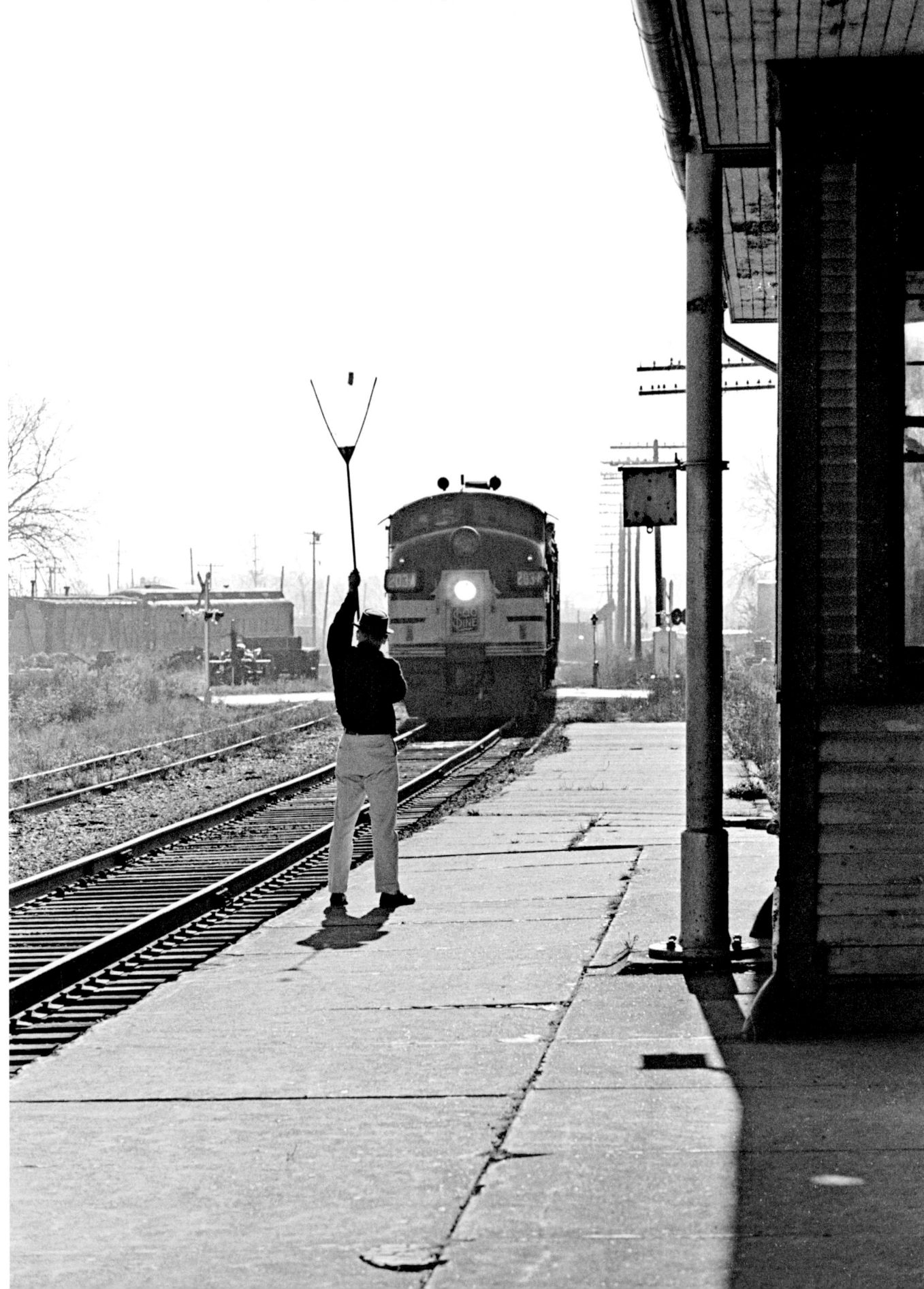

Facing: Tony Kunst, the relief operator at Mundelein, Illinois, holds up a hoop with a train order for a westbound freight, led by F3 no. 203A, on November 10, 1962. Kunst received the order over the phone from the railroad's dispatcher and then copied it onto the paper he is handing up to the train crew. Mundelein is 40 miles north of downtown Chicago and is today a passenger stop on Metra's North Central Service commuter operation.

Below: The "New Soo's" first new locomotives, Alco RS-27s nos. 415 and 416, blast through Wendell, Minnesota, with train no. 26 from the Canadian border town of Portal, North Dakota, on April 23, 1963. Abbey recorded that railroaders called these locomotives the "Dolly Sisters." The 2,400-horsepower units served the Soo for nineteen years, but ultimately the railroad would order most of its locomotives from the Electro-Motive Division of General Motors.

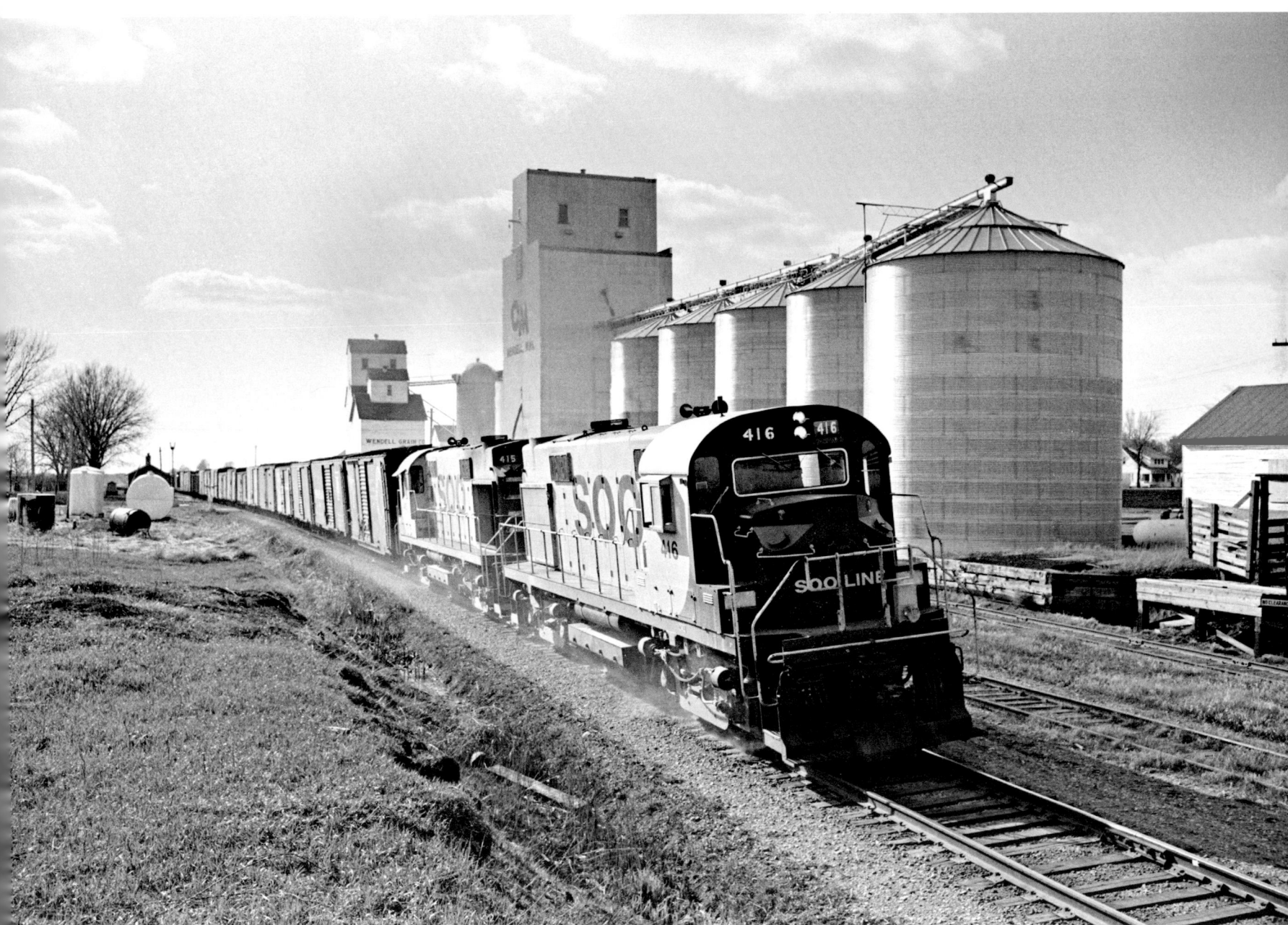

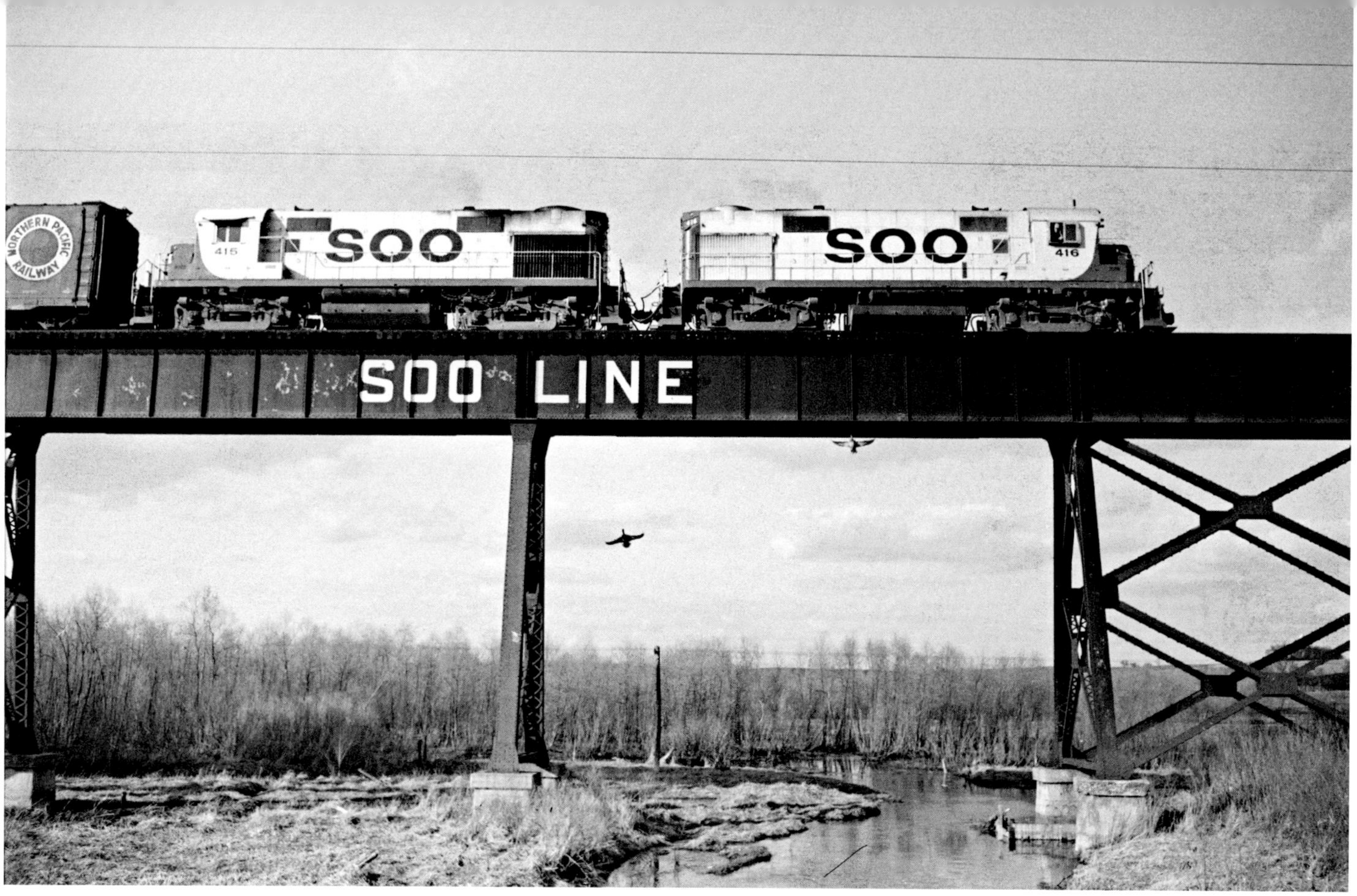

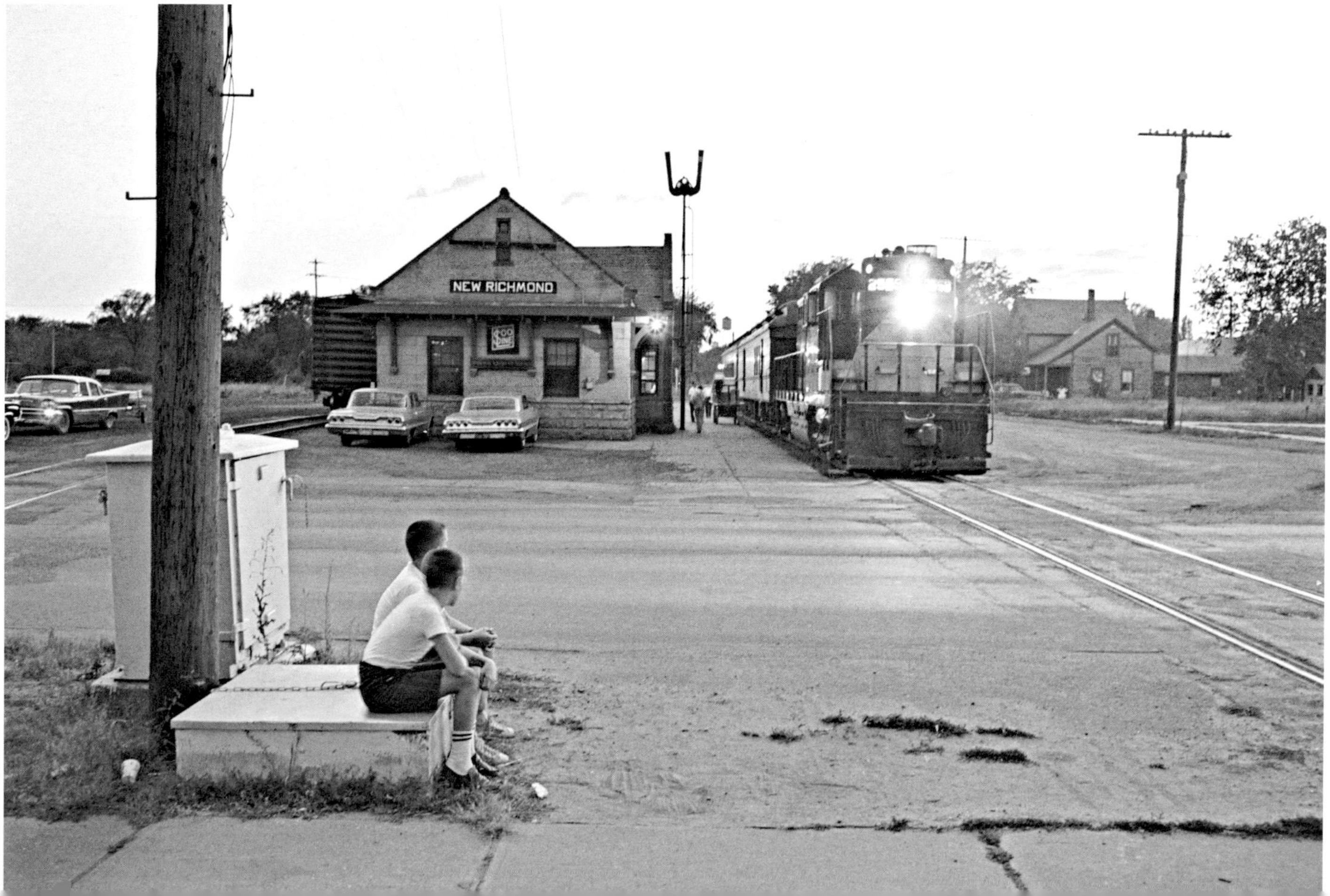

Facing top: Geese take flight as Soo Line RS-27s nos. 415 and 416 lead eastbound freight train no. 26 across the Crow River at Rockford, Minnesota, on April 23, 1963. Today this route is part of Canadian Pacific Railway's main line between Chicago and western Canada.

Facing bottom: Two boys in New Richmond, Wisconsin, watch as two-car train no. 6 pauses at the depot on the evening of August 5, 1964. No. 6 originated in St. Paul and connected in Owen, Wisconsin, with the *Laker*, which ran between Duluth and Chicago. Beset with a longer route between the Twin Cities and Chicago, the Soo never attempted to compete with the streamliners of the Burlington, Milwaukee, and North Western. After losing its mail contract, the *Laker* and its connections made their last runs in January of 1965.

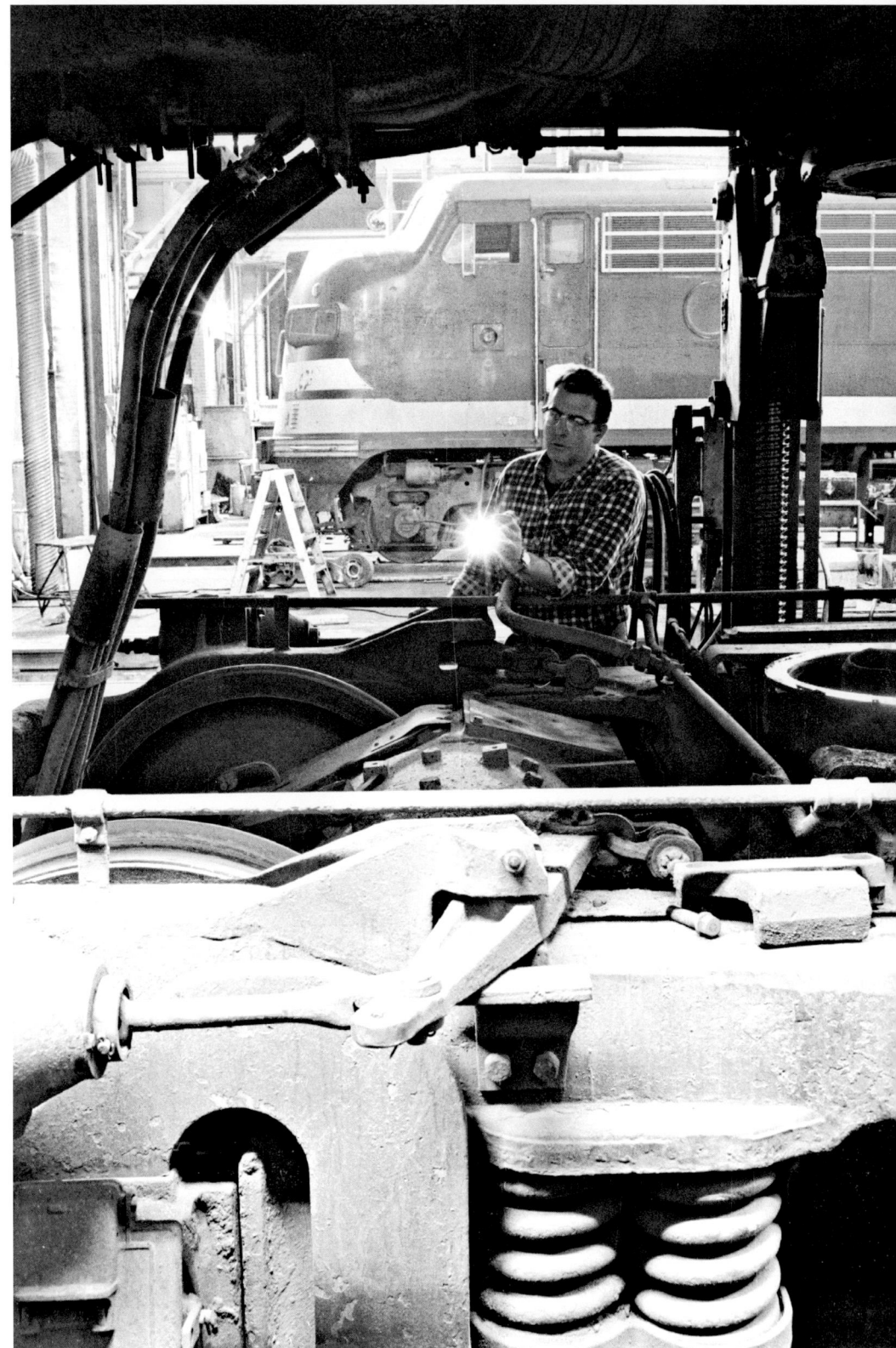

Right: Inside the diesel shop at Shoreham Yard in Minneapolis, a worker inspects the trucks from an Alco locomotive on a December evening in 1964. When the Soo ordered new GP30s and GP35s from EMD in the early 1960s, it opted to have EMD rebuild and reuse the trucks from older Alcos, a decision, Abbey wrote, "the Soo would soon regret." Eventually, second-generation EMD power allowed the retirement of venerable F-units like the one in the background.

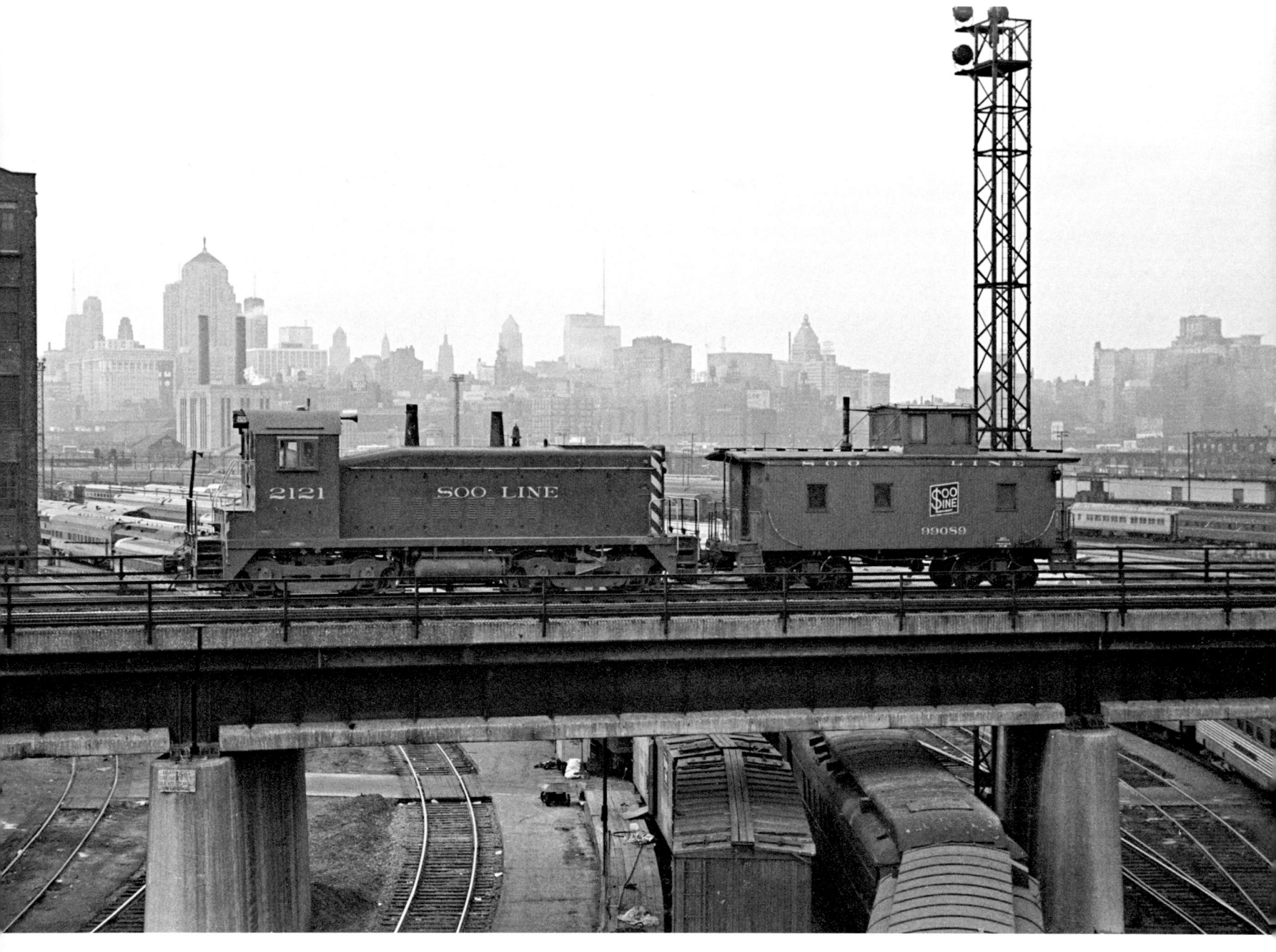

Above: After delivering cars to the Illinois Central, SW1200 no. 2121 and caboose head back to the Soo's yard at Schiller Park via the St. Charles Air Line in downtown Chicago on an April evening in 1962. The elevated tracks of the Air Line connect the IC tracks along Lake Michigan with the Chicago, Burlington & Quincy main line to the west, passing above congested streets, several busy railroads, and the Chicago River.

Facing: A dog watches from the banks of the St. Croix River as two brand-new GP30 locomotives and an F-unit lead westbound train no. 25 across the Arcola High Bridge at Somerset, Wisconsin, on April 26, 1963. No. 25 ran from Schiller Park in Chicago to Shoreham Yard in Minneapolis. The GP30s had just arrived on the property as part of the "New Soo's" first major order for new locomotives.

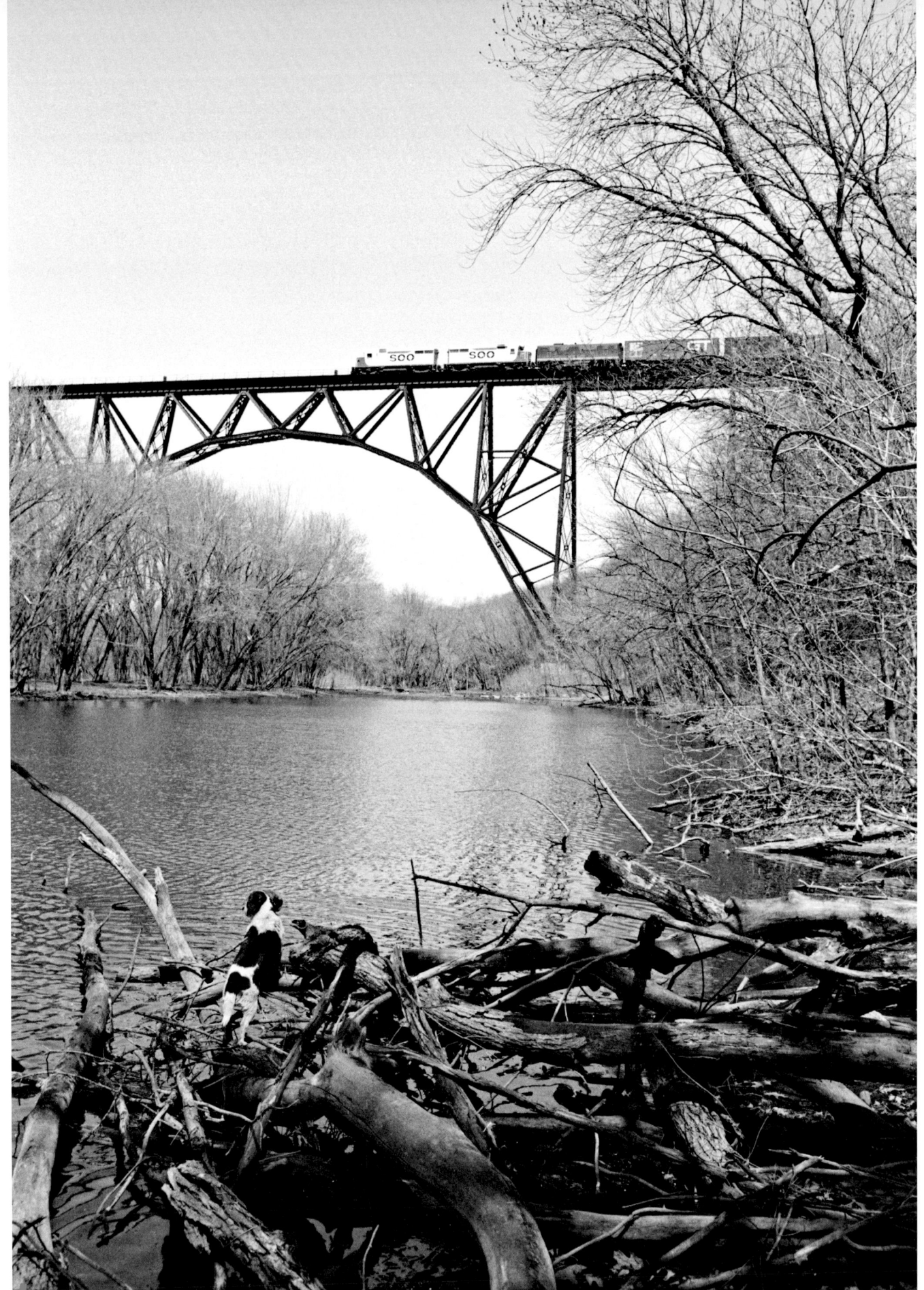

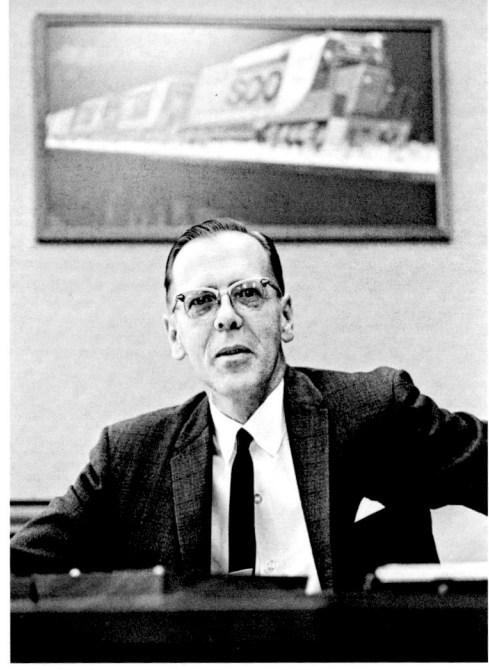

Left: Leonard H. Murray, president of the Soo Line, sits at his desk in Minneapolis in 1965, in a portrait Abbey made for an ad in *Railway Age* magazine. A painting of Soo GP30s by Tom Fawell hangs on the wall behind him; Fawell created advertising art for EMD for two decades. Murray was president of the Duluth, South Shore & Atlantic when it was merged into the "New Soo." Murray was selected to lead the new company, and did so capably for the next seventeen years, the longest tenure of any Soo president.

Below: SD45 no. 4353 departs Shoreham Yard on the night of April 3, 1967, with a transfer for St. Paul. In the early spring of 1967, three of EMD's "demonstrator" SD45s spent several days proving their capabilities to the Soo Line, which was in the market for new, six-axle locomotives. Ultimately, the Soo's first order went to General Electric, but the railroad came back to EMD in late 1968 with an order for ten SD40s—followed by several more orders for SD40s and SD40-2s.

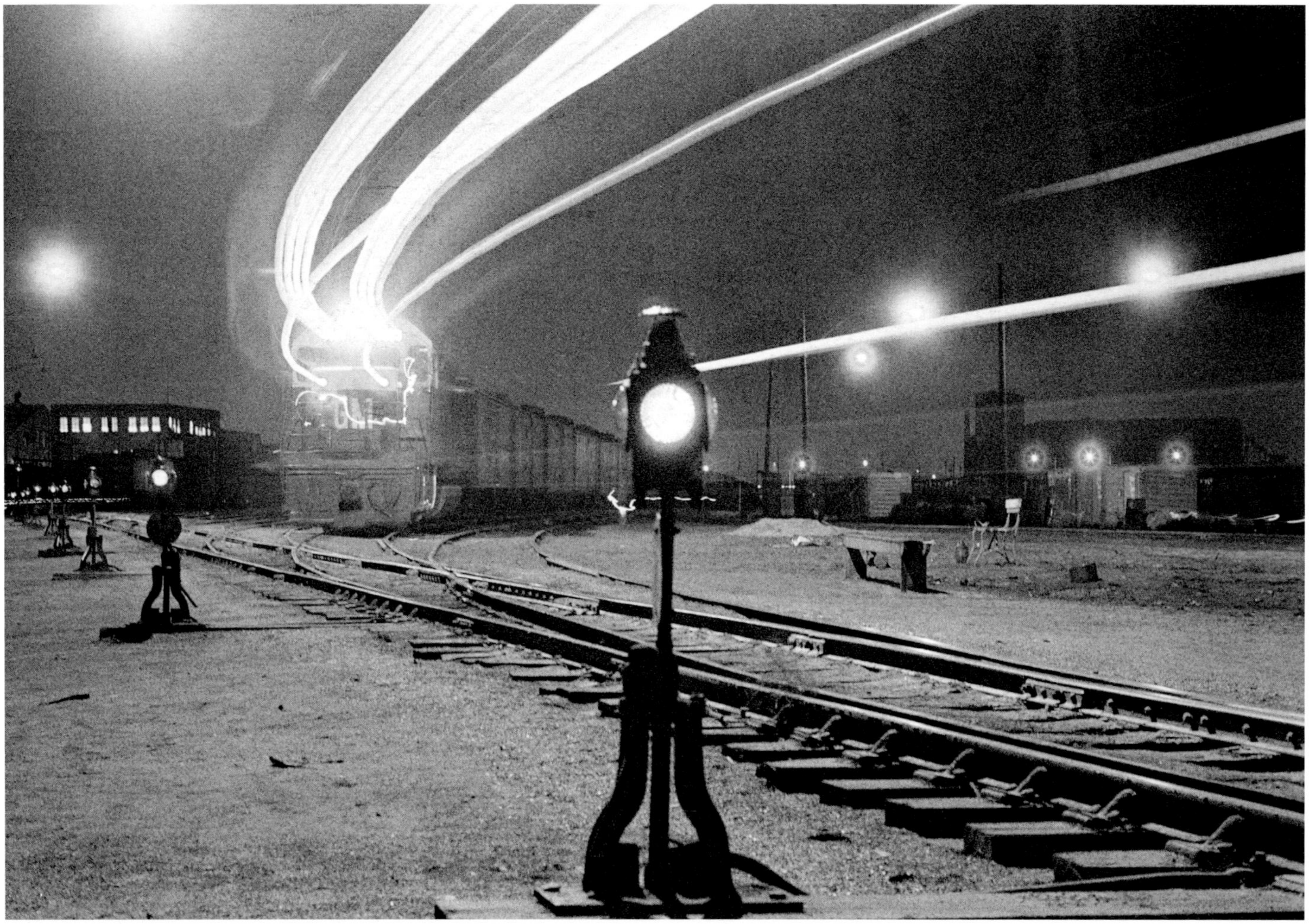

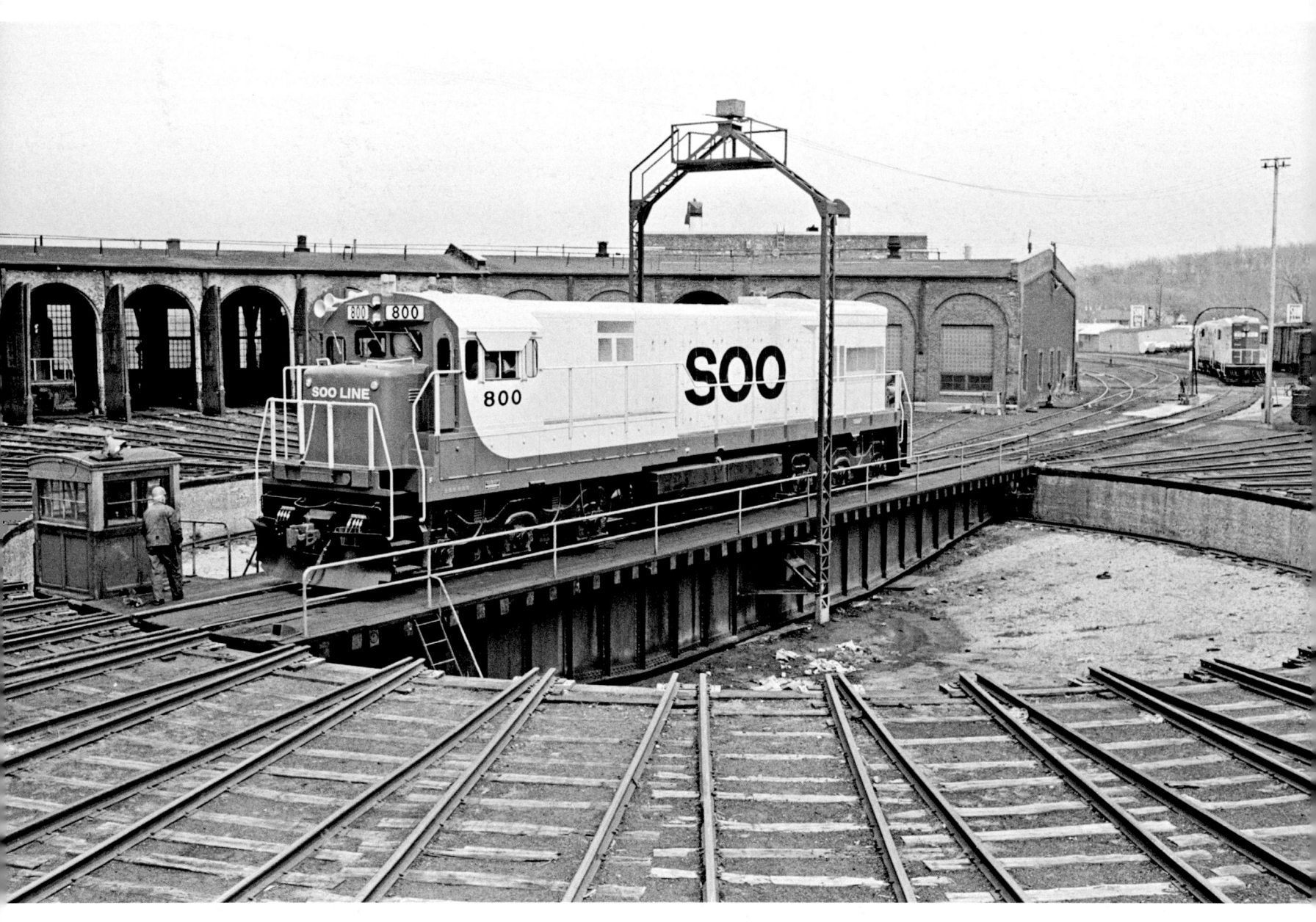

Fresh out of the General Electric erecting shop in Erie, Pennsylvania, U30C no. 800 poses in Minneapolis on Shoreham Yard's turntable on April 27, 1968. The railroad acquired ten of the big 3,000-horsepower locomotives that year, the first new, six-axle power for the "New Soo." The Soo leased these locomotives for fifteen years from the State Mutual Life Assurance Company of America, and would ultimately buy out the lease and trade them in to EMD in the early 1980s.

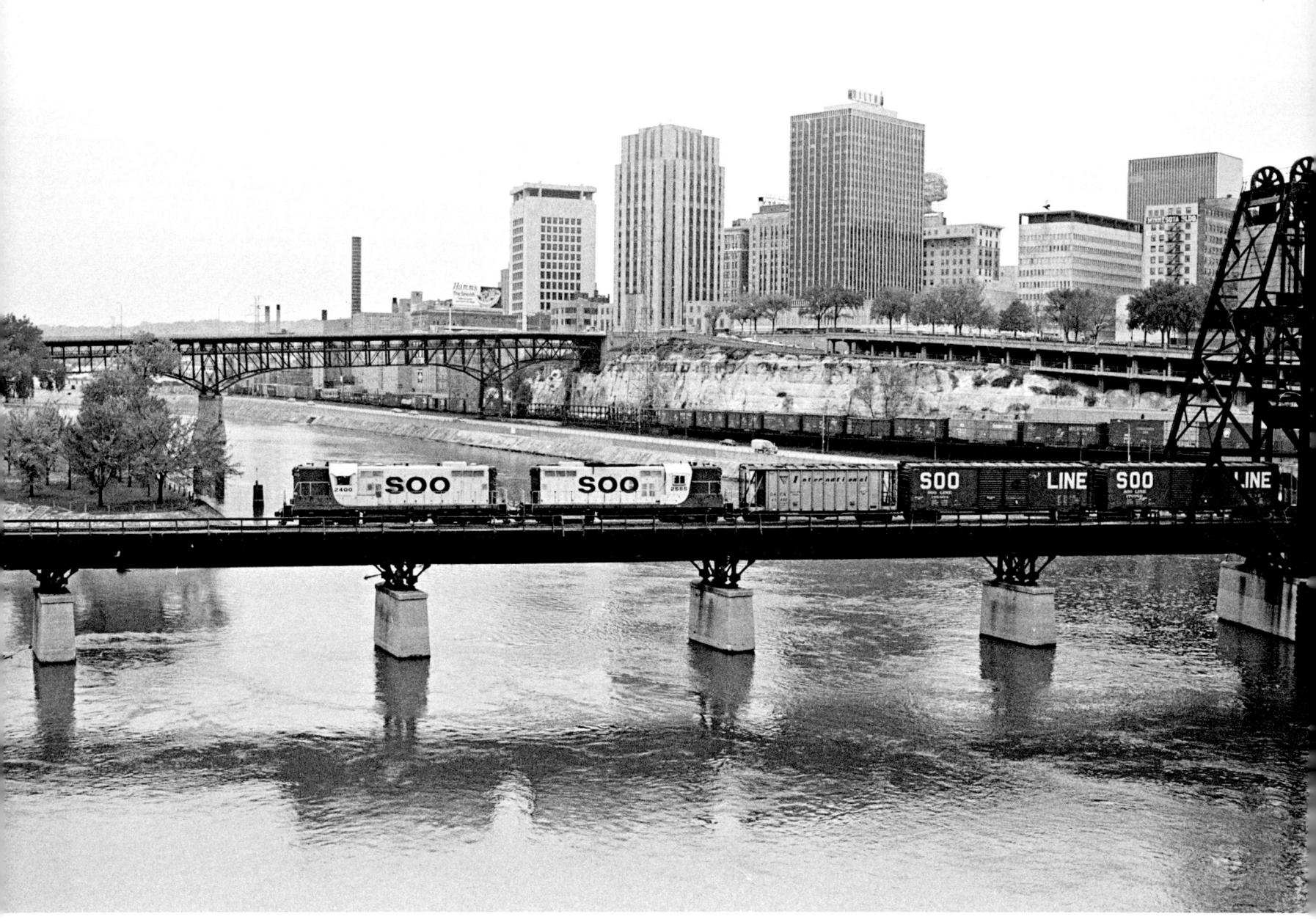

A pair of GP9s leads a local freight train across the Robert Street Bridge over the Mississippi River in downtown St. Paul, Minnesota, on October 14, 1968. Built in 1913 by the Chicago Great Western (CGW), the bridge became part of the Chicago & North Western when it acquired the CGW on July 1, 1968. As a condition of the merger, the Soo gained access to industries in Roseport, just south of St. Paul. This is the first day of that service, and the second Soo train making the run.

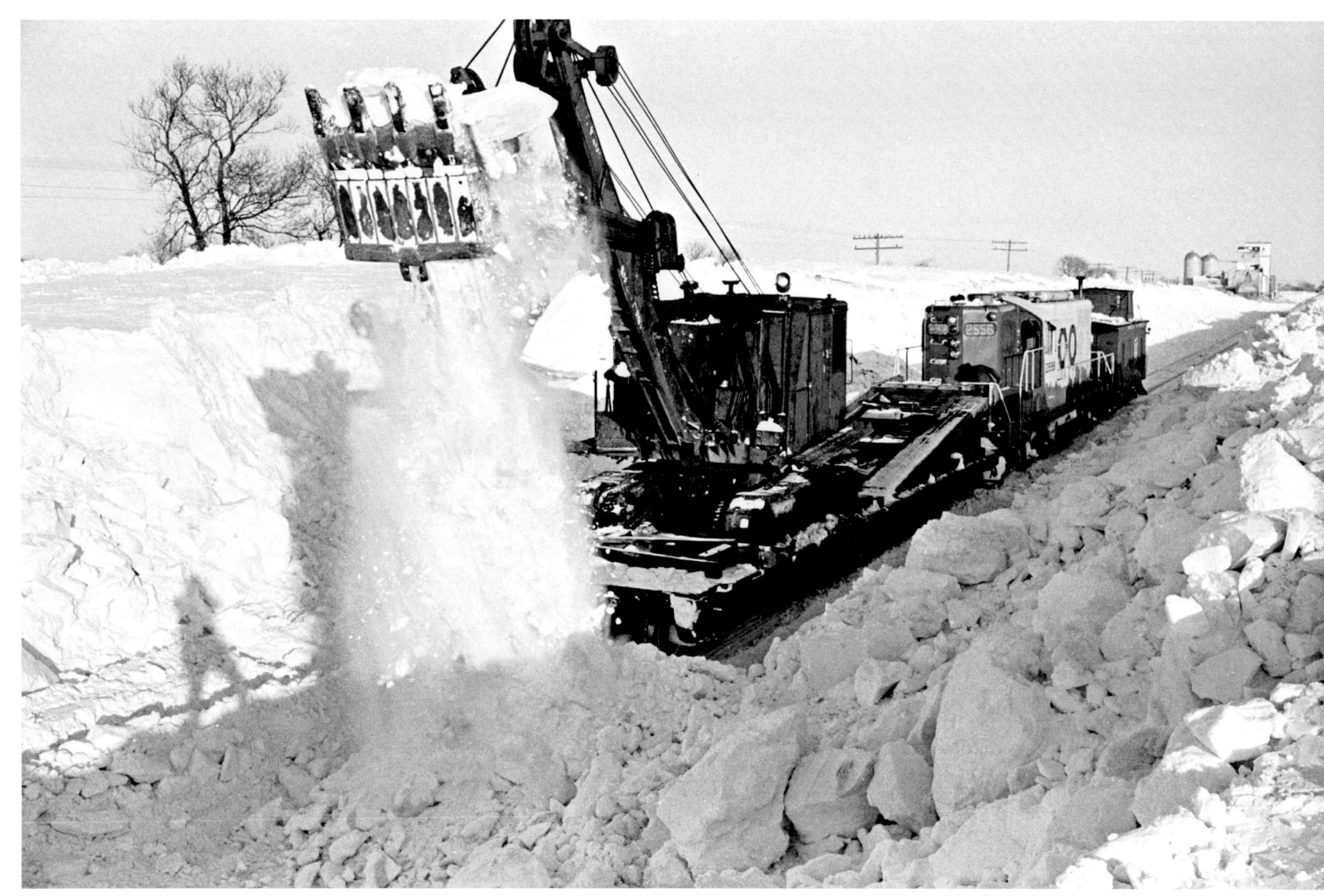

The winters of 1967–68 and 1968–69 were especially challenging for the Soo Line. Deep cuts, like this one at Wendell, Minnesota, were particularly prone to filling up with drifting snow. When locomotives and plows could not keep the line open, the Soo had to get creative to keep its trains running—like loading an excavator onto a flatcar and pushing it into position to clear the snow. The February sun on this clear day in 1969 casts a perfect shadow of the photographer at lower left.

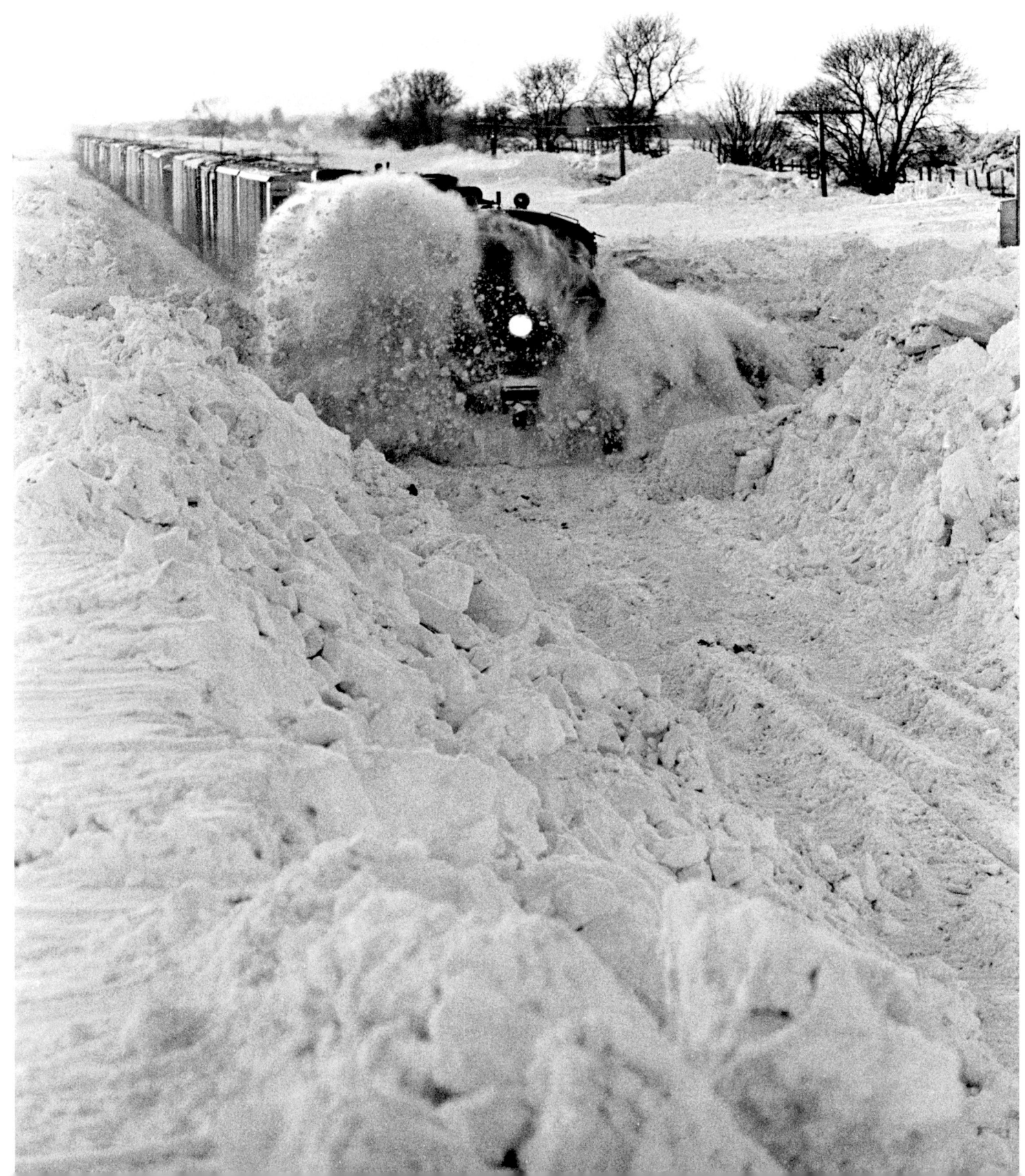

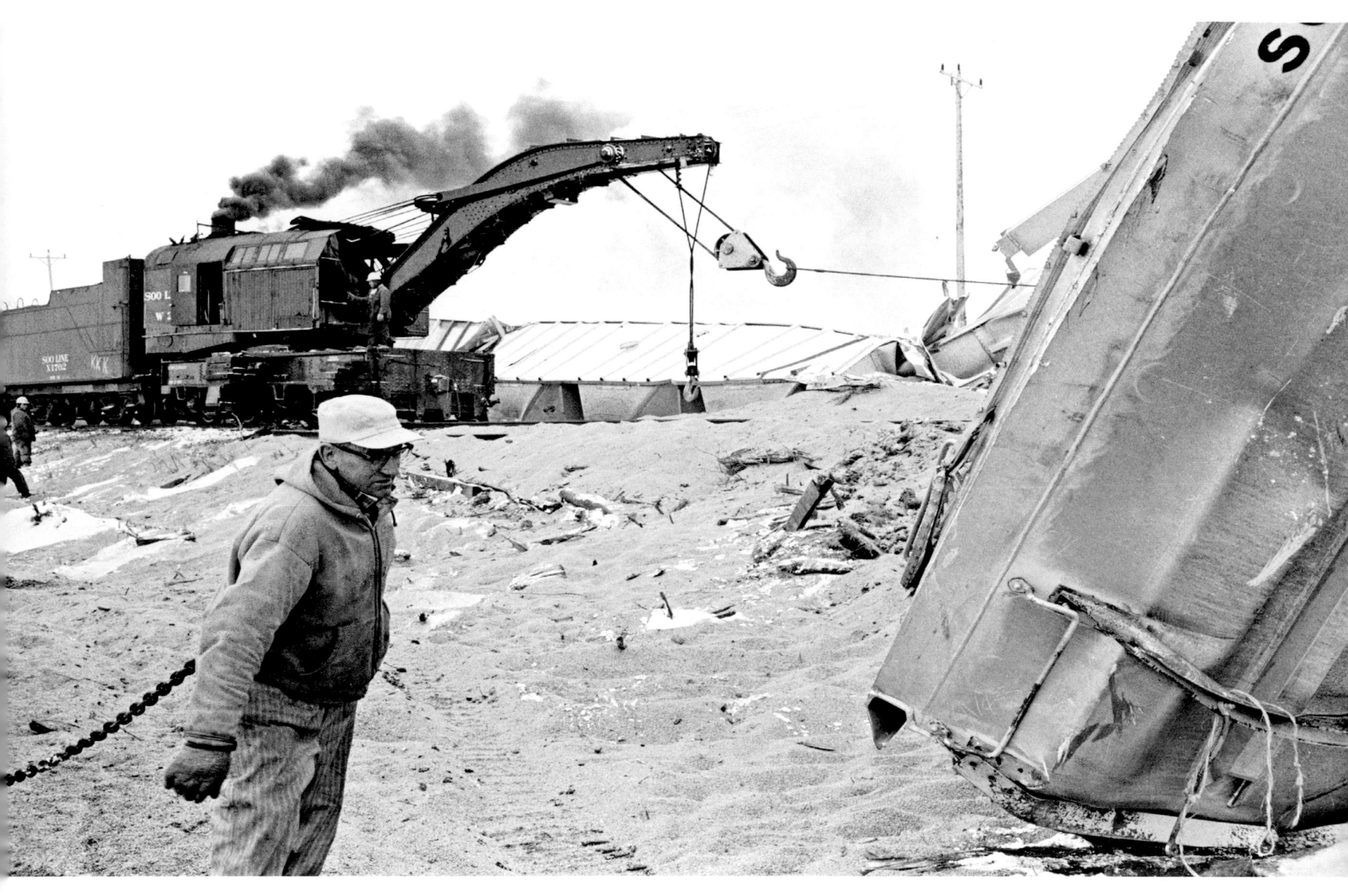

Facing: Toward sunset on a February day in 1969, the lead F-unit of this eastbound freight train plows drifted snow at Wendell, Minnesota. Snow posed challenges to Soo operations every winter, with this one being particularly difficult. Tread marks visible at lower right show that the railroad had to bring an excavator here to clear the worst of the snow before any trains could pass.

Above: Workers wade through spilled grain from a 1969 derailment at Duplainville, Wisconsin, while steam crane no. W2 tugs on the wrecked hulk of a covered hopper car. Abbey photographed several derailments during his time with the Soo Line. The railroad likely would have wanted photographs for insurance purposes, but Abbey's journalistic sensibilities led him to also portray the hard work that went into these clean-up operations.

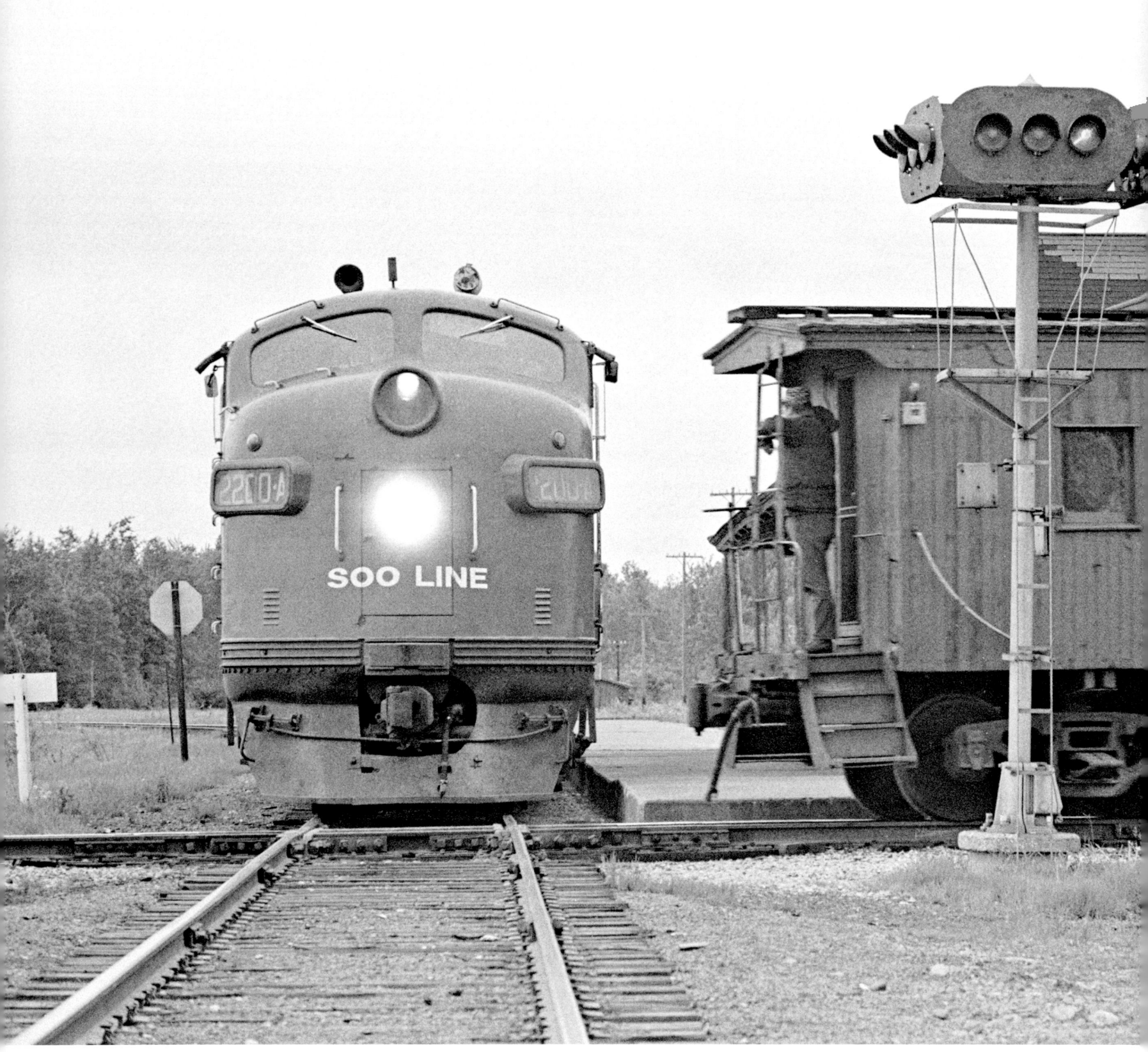

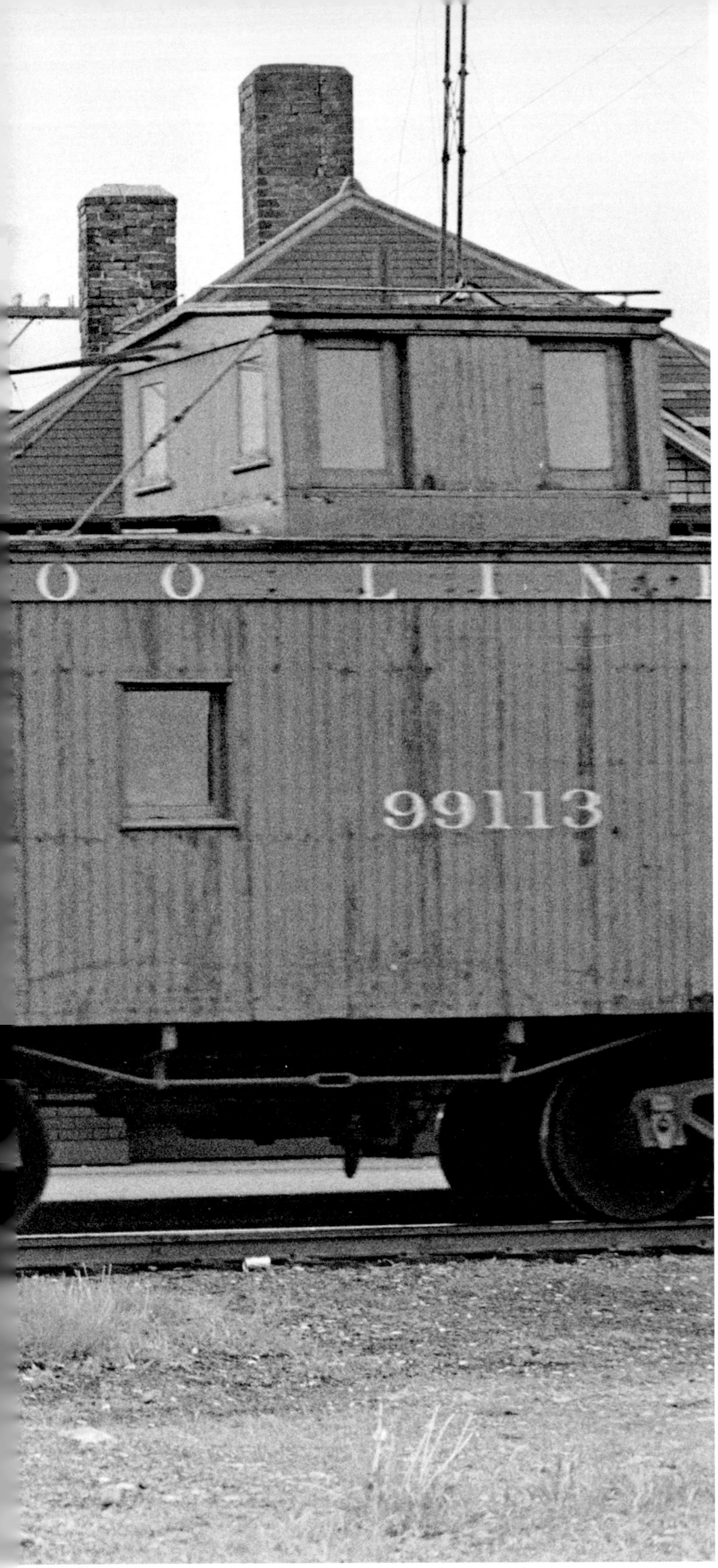

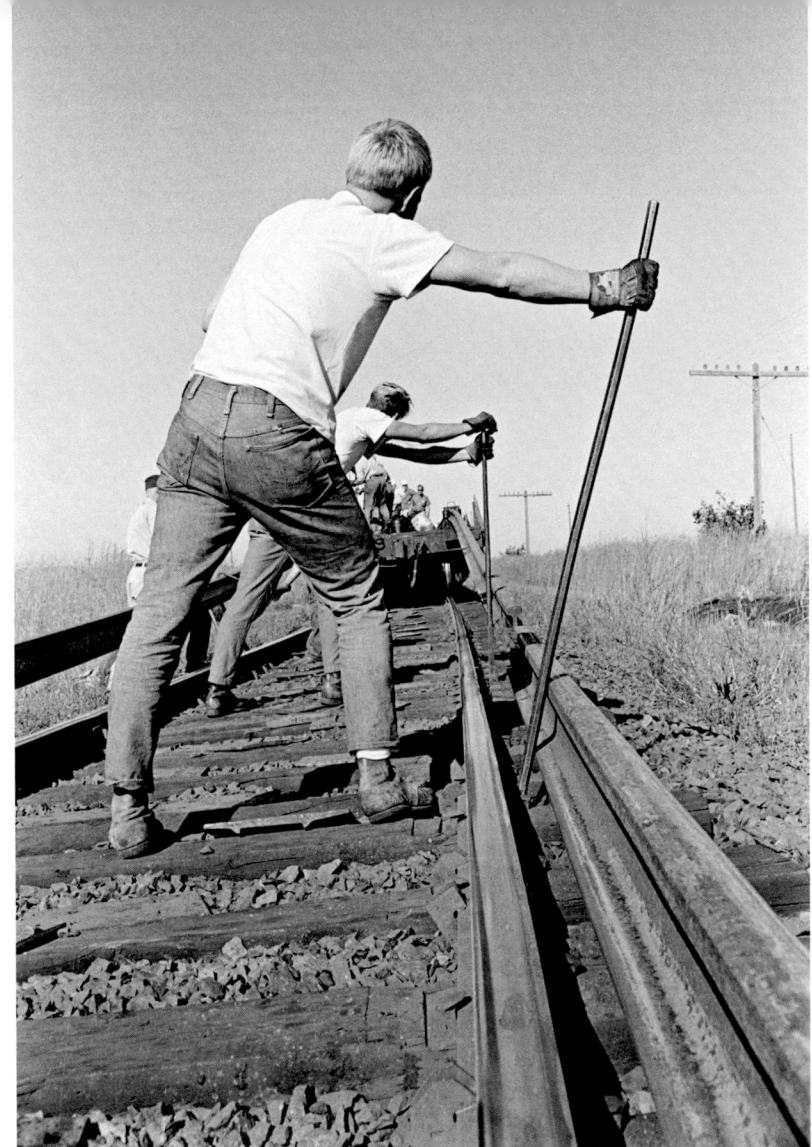

Facing: Soo Line trains pass at Prentice, Wisconsin, on a June day in 1969. The view looks east, where a westbound train led by F3 no. 2200A waits as the wooden caboose of a southbound clears the crossing. The caboose hides the depot, which still stands, built to serve both railroads. The north–south line, originally part of the Wisconsin Central, connects Ashland and Spencer, Wisconsin. The east–west line was the original Soo's main line to Sault Ste. Marie, Michigan.

Above: Track workers unload new continuous welded rail at Wheeler, Wisconsin, on September 2, 1969, as part of an upgrade to the main line east of the Twin Cities. Wisconsin and Minnesota residents often joke about having two seasons, winter and construction. The same is true for the region's railroads, which struggle to keep their lines clear of snow and ice, and then hustle to do as much maintenance and upkeep as possible during the warmer months.

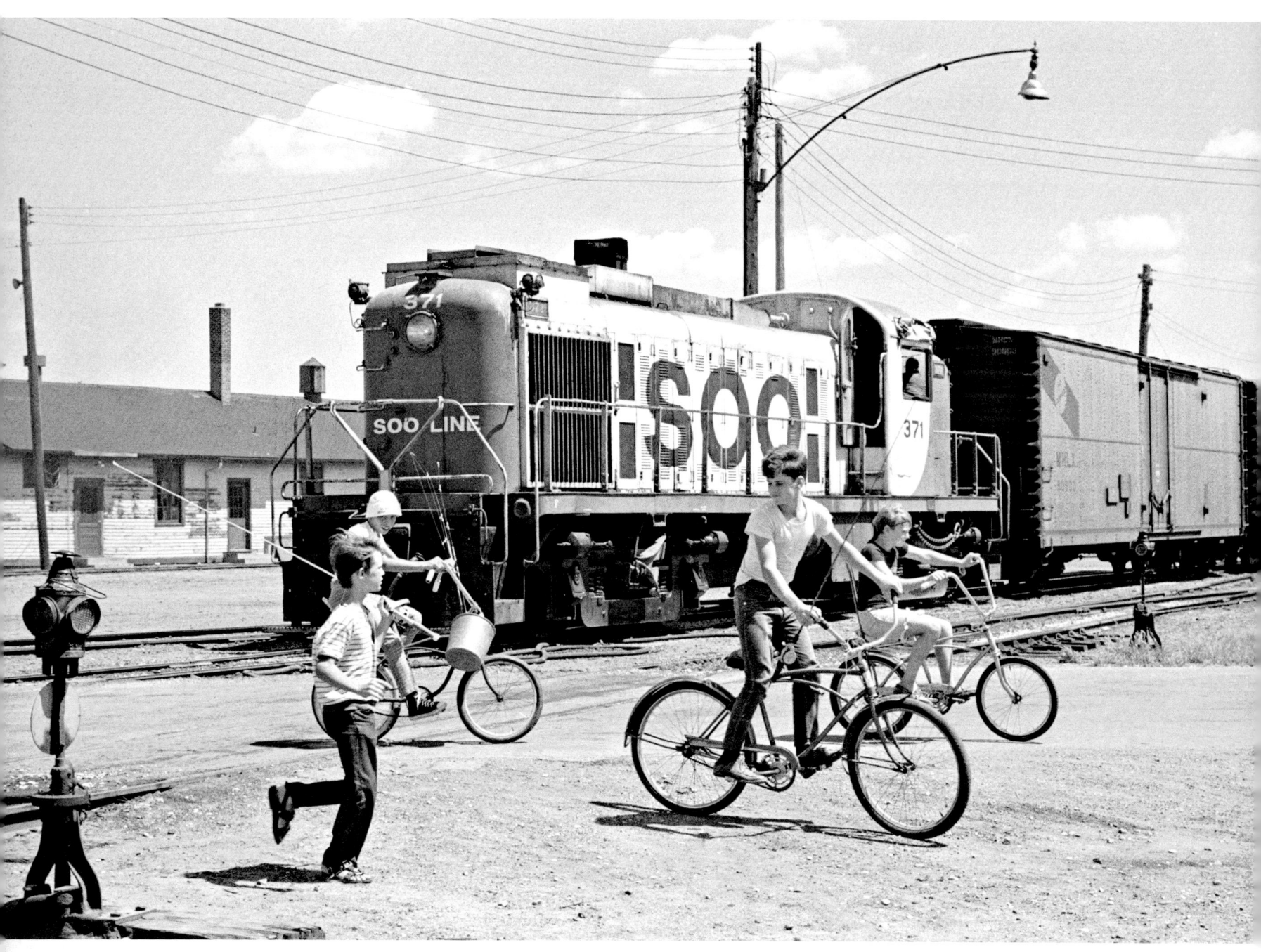

Shoving cars into Shops Yard in North Fond du Lac, Wisconsin, RS-2 no. 371 has just cleared the Lake Shore Drive crossing next to the yard office, allowing a group of kids to scurry across the tracks in the summer of 1971. The location and their equipment suggest they are returning from fishing in Lake Winnebago, the largest lake located entirely within the state.

Running south in the setting sun, train no. 418 led by GP38-2 no. 4421 rolls through Duplainville, Wisconsin, and across the Milwaukee Road main line on September 15, 1979. The Milwaukee had filed for bankruptcy two years earlier and faced an uncertain future. While much of its western lines would be abandoned, its core in the Midwest would ultimately become part of the Soo Line in 1985, giving the Soo a much shorter route between Chicago and the Twin Cities—and making Duplainville the spot where the "New Soo" crossed the Old Soo.

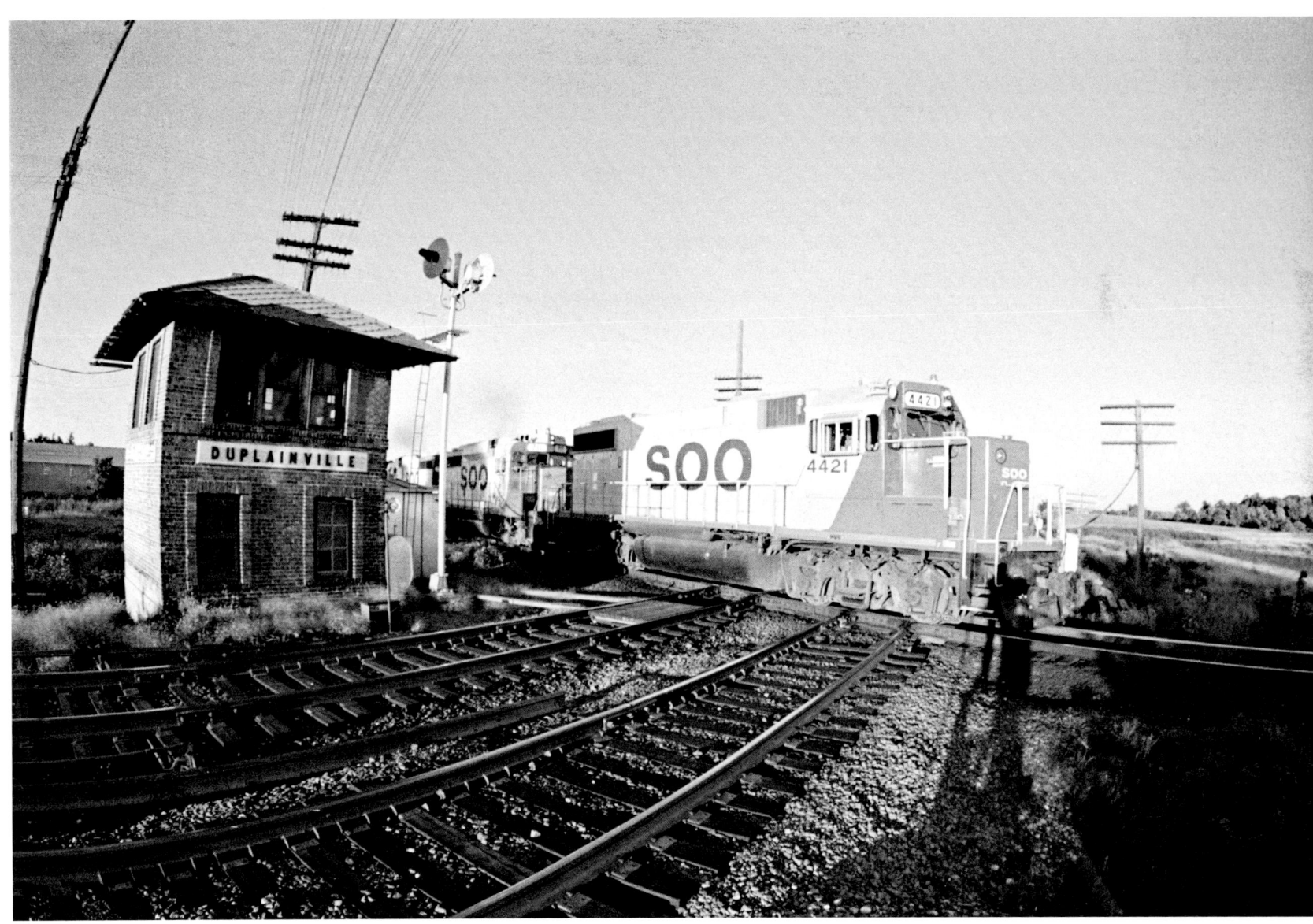

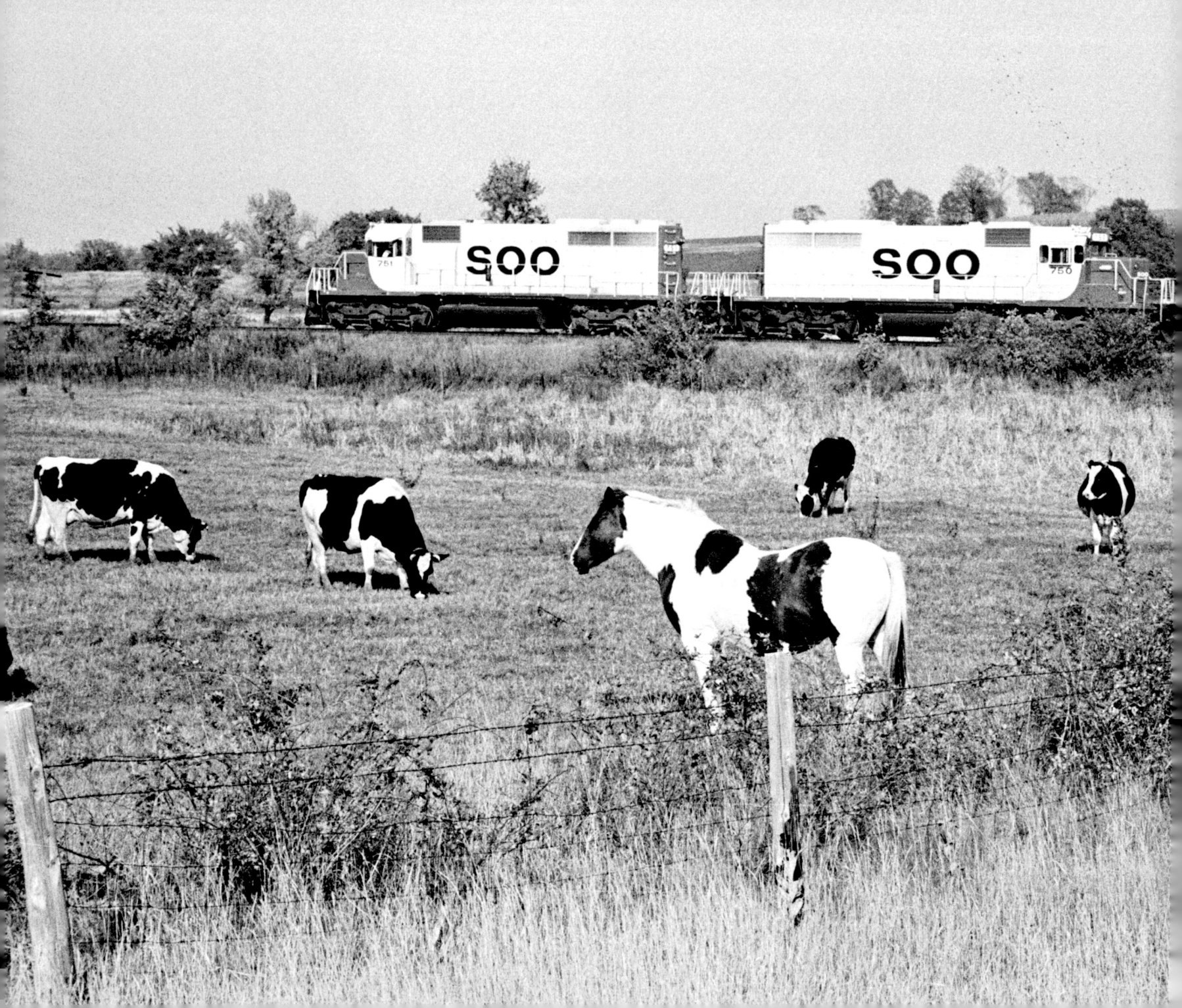

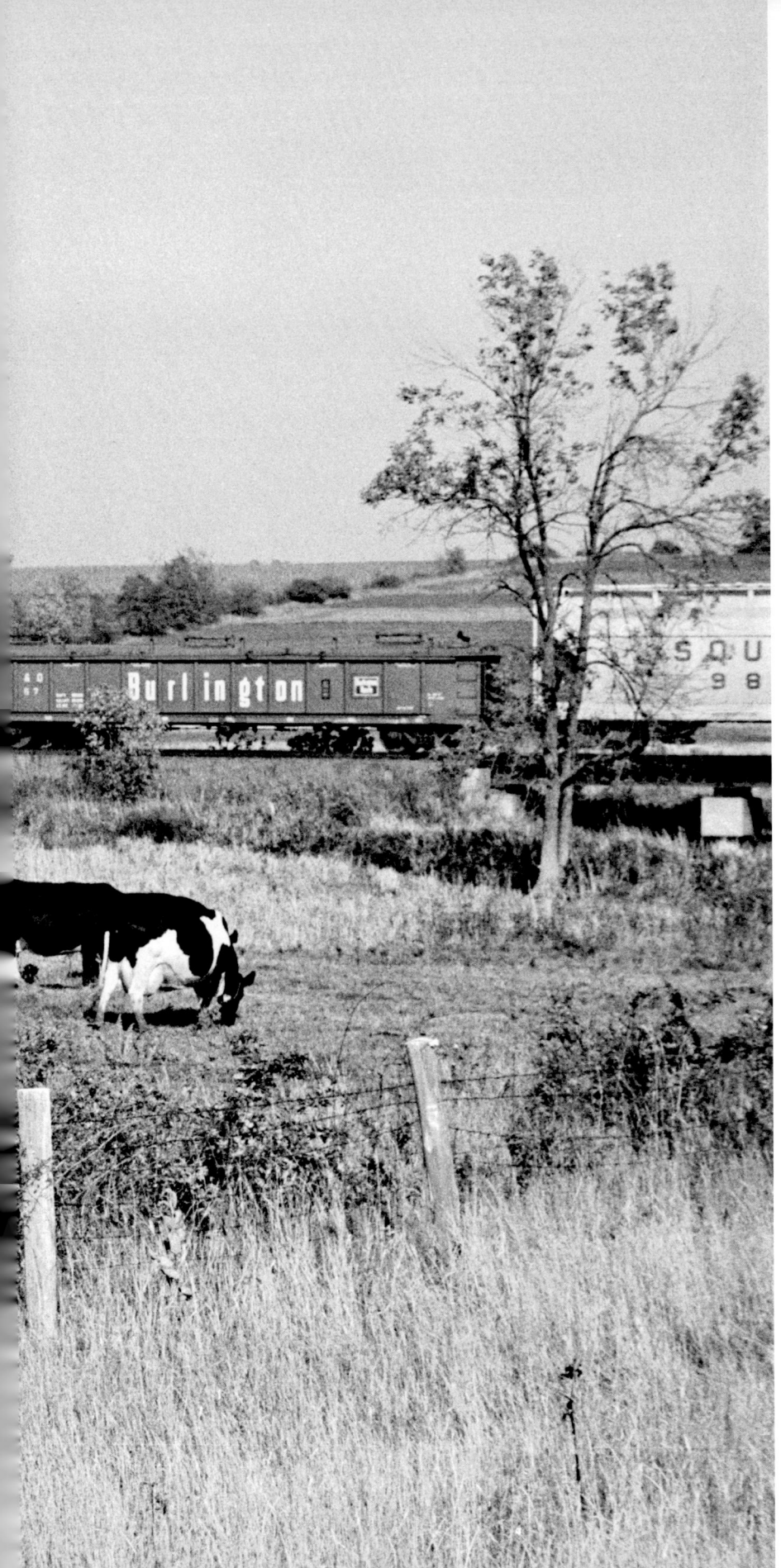

Brand-new SD40s nos. 750 and 751 lead a westbound train past cows and a horse at Turtle Lake, Wisconsin, in the summer of 1971. Electro-Motive's SD40/SD40-2 model series was among the most successful lines of North American diesel locomotives; more than 5,700 were built for some forty railroads between 1966 and 1988.

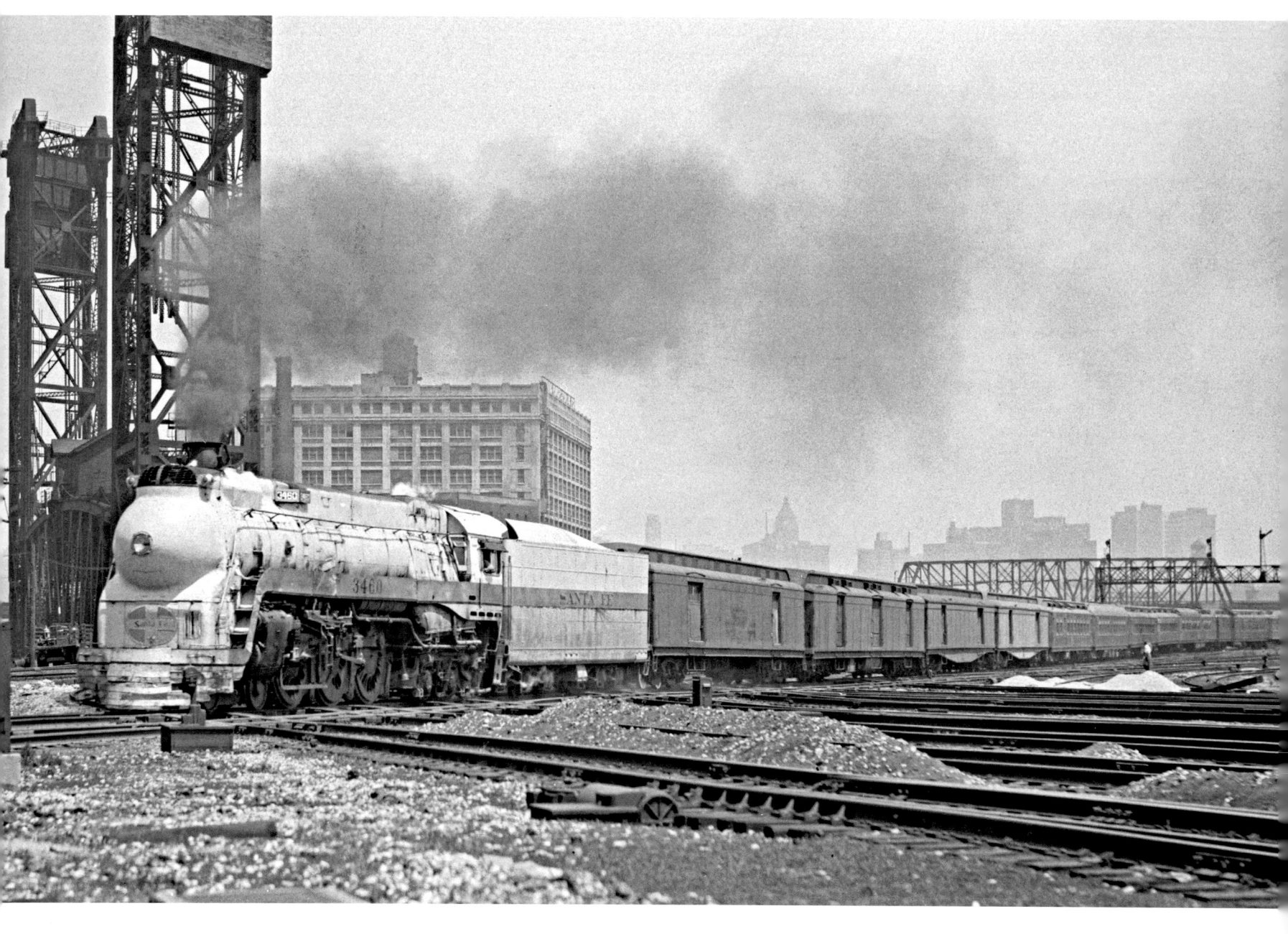

FOUR

CHICAGO AT ITS ZENITH

CHICAGO ALWAYS LOOMED LARGE IN WALLY ABBEY'S MIND. How could it not? Growing up in the north shore suburb of Evanston, Abbey spent a significant part of his childhood watching trains at the Chicago & North Western station over on Davis Street, just a few blocks from his house, or boarding Santa Fe trains downtown at Dearborn Station for family visits to Kansas. For a child growing up in Chicago in the 1930s, trains were a pervasive, inescapable, awesome presence.

The love affair intensified in high school as Abbey began to experiment with a 35mm Argus camera, a step up from the Kodak Brownie of his earlier years. High-school friends introduced Abbey to the wonders of Roosevelt Road, the wide, elevated east–west avenue that crossed the throat tracks leading to four of the city's great stations, Union, Grand Central, LaSalle Street, and Dearborn. There, Abbey could spend hours watching and photographing literally hundreds of passenger trains.

Abbey started making a paycheck off Chicago railroading in June 1944 with his summer job at Santa Fe's 21st Street enginehouse. He tried something completely different the following summer when he hired out with Chicago, Burlington & Quincy as a filing clerk in the freight claims department at the railroad's general offices on West Jackson Boulevard.

It was in the immediate postwar years that Abbey and Chicago made their mark together. This was the railroad capital at its zenith, with the postwar flood of GIs returning home and business booming in the Loop and along Michigan Avenue, the "magnificent mile." The city's train stations hummed with life

Santa Fe passenger train no. 23, the westbound *Grand Canyon* for Los Angeles, led by streamlined 4-6-4 steam locomotive no. 3460, crossing the Pennsylvania and the Chicago & Western Indiana railroads at Chicago's busy 21st Street Tower on June 22, 1946. Painted light blue and nicknamed the "Blue Goose," no. 3460 was the only streamlined steam locomotive on the Santa Fe roster. It was originally intended to pull matching streamlined passenger trains, but as diesels took more of those assignments, the "Goose" often powered trains with older, heavyweight equipment.

as many of the twenty-one passenger-carrying railroads serving Chicago enjoyed the last great surge of varnish before the interstate highway. A passenger train left the city every fifty-one seconds, a freight train every thirty-five seconds. The streets were crowded with Parmelee taxis ferrying travelers from station to station. It was the sprawling, brawling city writer Nelson Algren captured perfectly in the title of his epic prose poem of 1951, "Chicago: City on the Make."

For several years, from the late 1940s into the 1950s, Abbey himself was on the make in Chicago. It became his artistic stomping ground, just as he was coming into his own as a significant photographer, first as a college student coming home every summer, later as a professional journalist.

In June 1947, Abbey hired out with the Chicago & North Western for the first of two summers as a relief leverman, which means he managed train movements through junctions, called interlockings. The job required Abbey to learn the railroad's operating rules, master its various signal indications, and control traffic under extremely busy conditions. The places he worked were icons of the Chicago scene: Canal, at the junction of a branch line in Evanston; Clybourn, a tower near the city's Wicker Park neighborhood; Barrington, in the northwest suburbs where C&NW crossed the Elgin, Joliet & Eastern; and, perhaps most memorable of all, Mayfair, on the northwest side, the junction with the Milwaukee Road's main line, a racetrack for both the C&NW's *400* fleet and the Milwaukee's *Hiawatha*s.

Those leverman's jobs were like a graduate education in railroading. Later he looked back in amazement: "Comfortable though I was with my abilities and growing experience, sometimes, when a train full of people roared past the tower windows while another train waited impatiently on an intersecting track, I wondered, should a kid really be doing this?"

When he wasn't working, Abbey roamed the vast city. By this time he had an intimate knowledge of Chicago's dense railroad network, so he always knew the best places to go. Some of his favorites were the expected postcard panoramas: views of the city's iconic skyline from Roosevelt Road and the sweeping curve into North Western Terminal; dark, moody glimpses of life under the train sheds of the big stations, where passengers scurried past locomotives, observation cars, and bumping posts.

But Abbey loved the gritty, operational side of railroading and the workers who made it tick, so he also descended on engine terminals, freight yards, and interlocking towers. He was a habitué at 21st Street, the multitrack crossing of several railroads along the Chicago River south of Union Station. He made wonderful images at the North Western's Chicago Avenue roundhouse on the north side, and Santa Fe's engine terminal at 21st Street where he worked. He often headed for the edge of the city, shooting the Burlington on its racetrack through the western suburbs, or the Santa Fe and the Rock Island from the spacious platforms at Joliet Union Station, or the interior of the gigantic State Line tower in Hammond, Indiana, where crossed the Erie, Nickel Plate, Monon, Chesapeake & Ohio, and Indiana Harbor Belt.

Although Abbey apparently never wrote specifically about his love for Chicago, his affection for the city was often palpable in short, occasionally poetic phrases that appeared in his feature articles. In "The Last Outpost" from the December 1952 issue of *Trains & Travel*, he described a pressure-packed night at Mayfair, where snow and sleet had conspired to wreak havoc on train operations, especially for a callow, third-trick, fill-in operator forced to contend with late trains, urgent train orders, and fifty-five interlocking levers. Finally, when the storm subsided, he found a moment to reflect.

"The snow and sleet had stopped; it wasn't cold at all—just below freezing I estimated. The world was gray and quiet; down on Cicero Avenue there was next to no traffic and the street was rutted and snow covered. The reflection of countless neon signs tinged the sky a subtle red over downtown Chicago, and a searchlight was playing on the low clouds. I began to feel some of that relaxed, satisfied feeling I'd felt on less trying nights when the busiest part of the trick was past and the city was asleep."

Of course, Chicago was rarely asleep. The Windy City landscape was abuzz in those halcyon years with crowded station platforms, gleaming streamliners, bustling freight yards, simmering roundhouses. Abbey's visual document of that world is definitive.

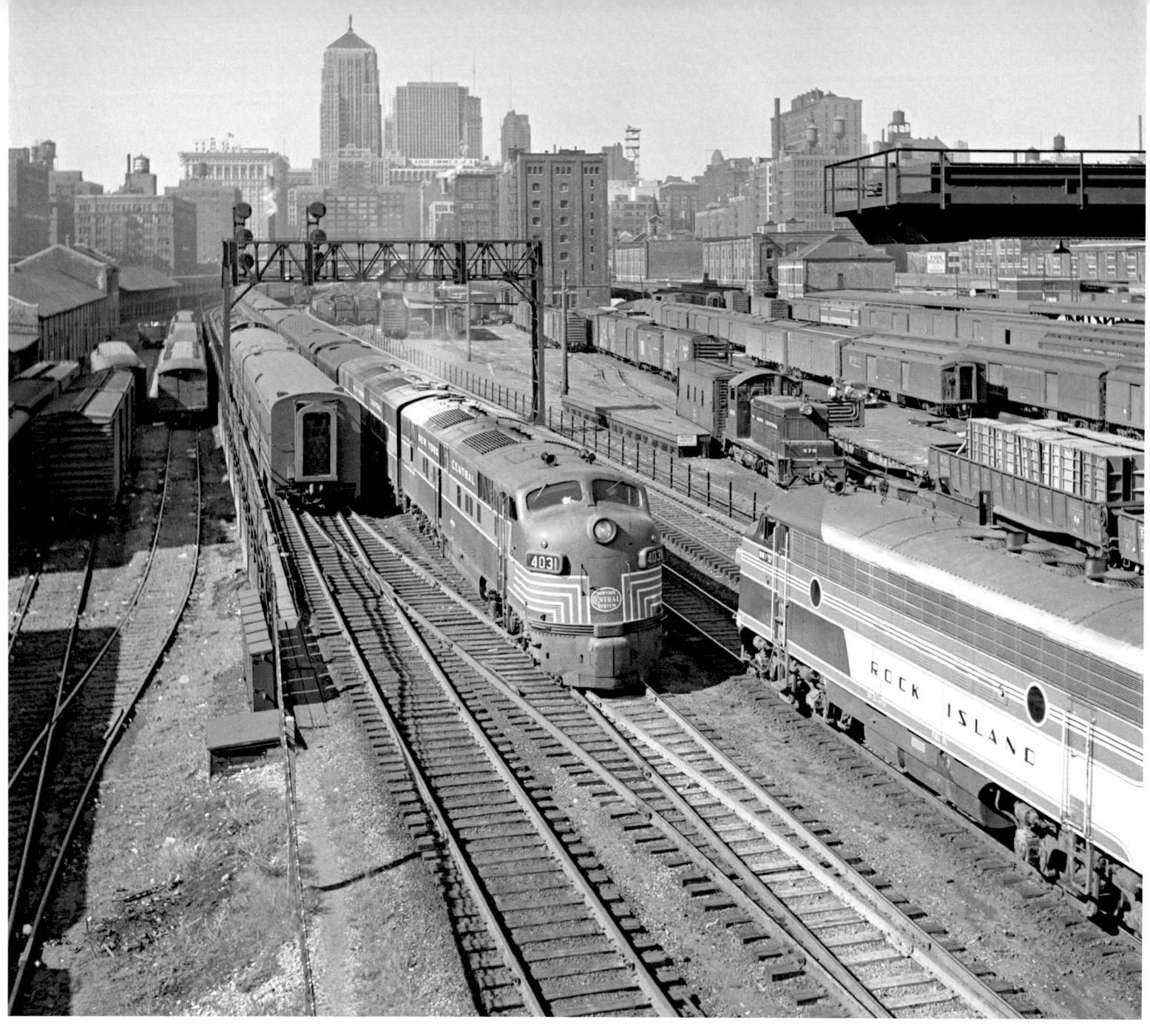

In a view befitting Chicago's title of the nation's railroad capital, one of its most famous trains—New York Central's *20th Century Limited*—leaves the Windy City amid a flurry of activity in August of 1950. At right, an inbound Rock Island train heads for LaSalle Street Station, while a switcher moves two passenger cars on the track at left and a second switcher works in the yard at far right. Another Chicago icon, the Board of Trade Building from 1930, dominates the skyline in the distance.

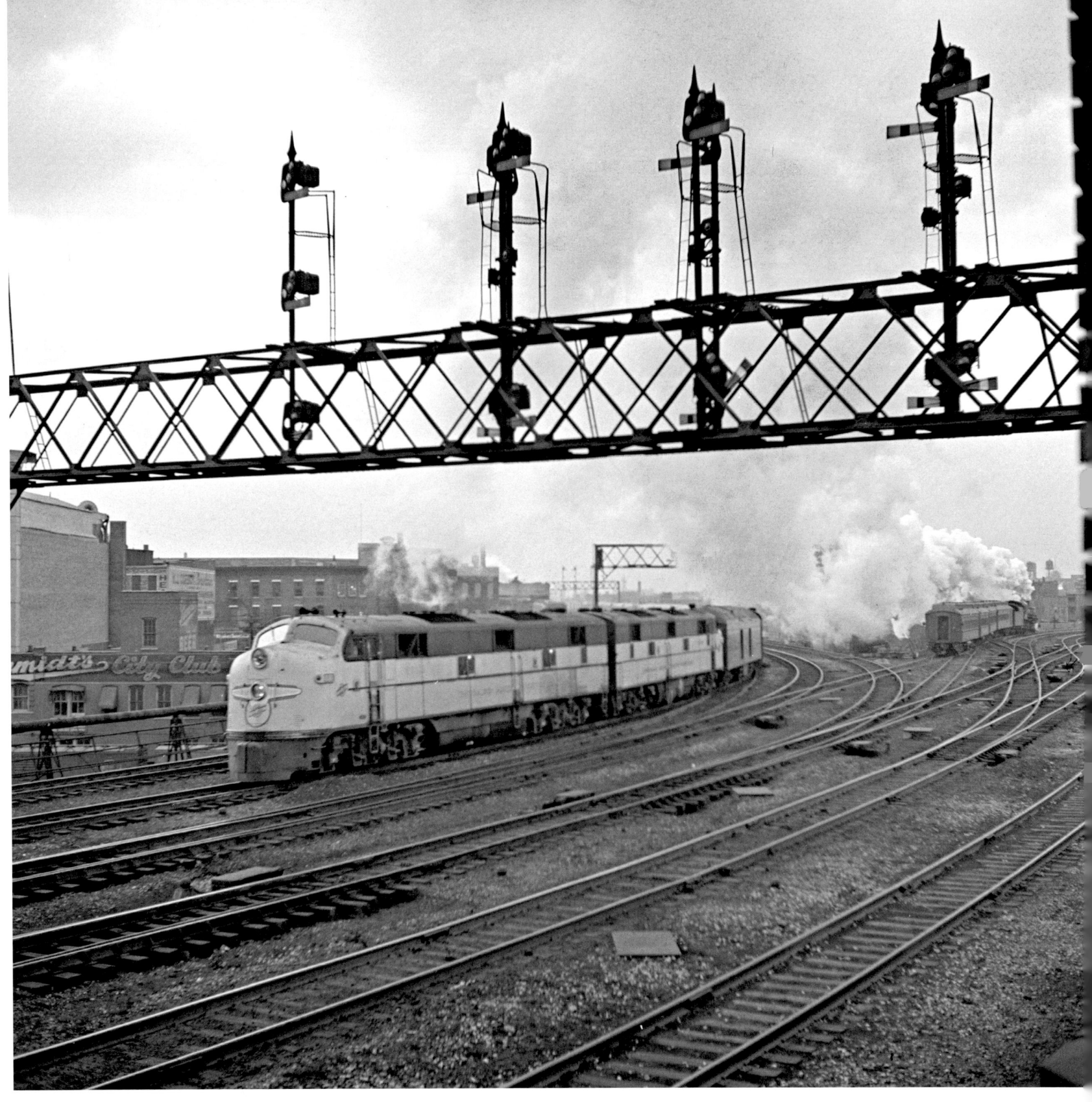

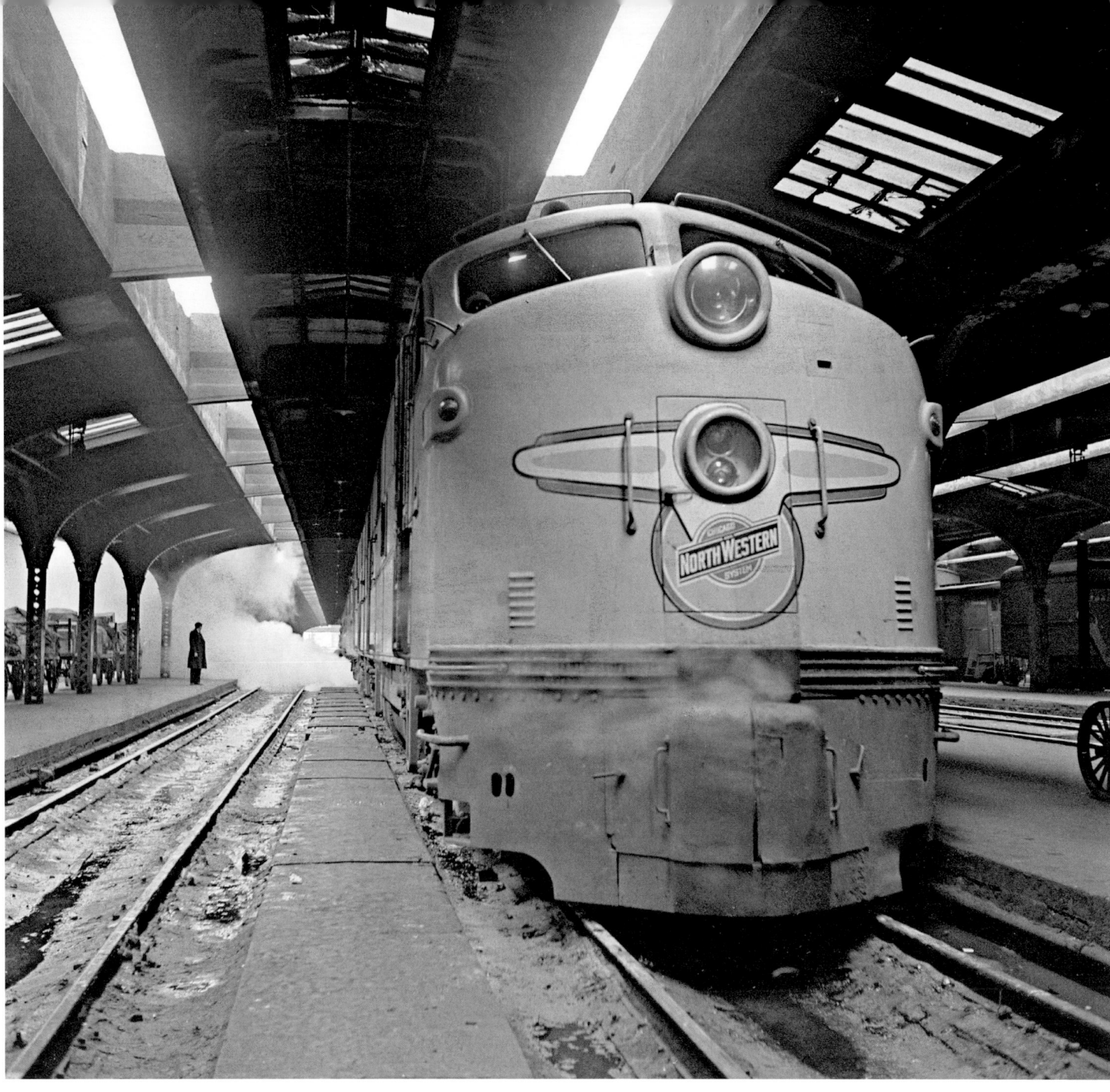

Facing: Steam and diesel passenger trains on the Chicago & North Western pass at Canal Street Tower, where Abbey had worked as a college student, in November of 1951. At left, an A-B pair of Electro-Motive E7s brings in train no. 28, the eastbound *San Francisco Overland* from the Union Pacific, while a 4-6-2 at far right steams away with an outbound commuter train heading for North Side suburbs.

Above: One of Chicago & North Western's E7A locomotives stands at the head of train no. 28, the eastbound *San Francisco Overland*, which has just arrived at the North Western Terminal in Chicago on November 2, 1951. Steam from the train's heating system silhouettes a lone passenger on the adjacent platform. Long-distance passenger trains no longer use these tracks, but they remain busy with Metra commuter trains in what is now the Ogilvie Transportation Center.

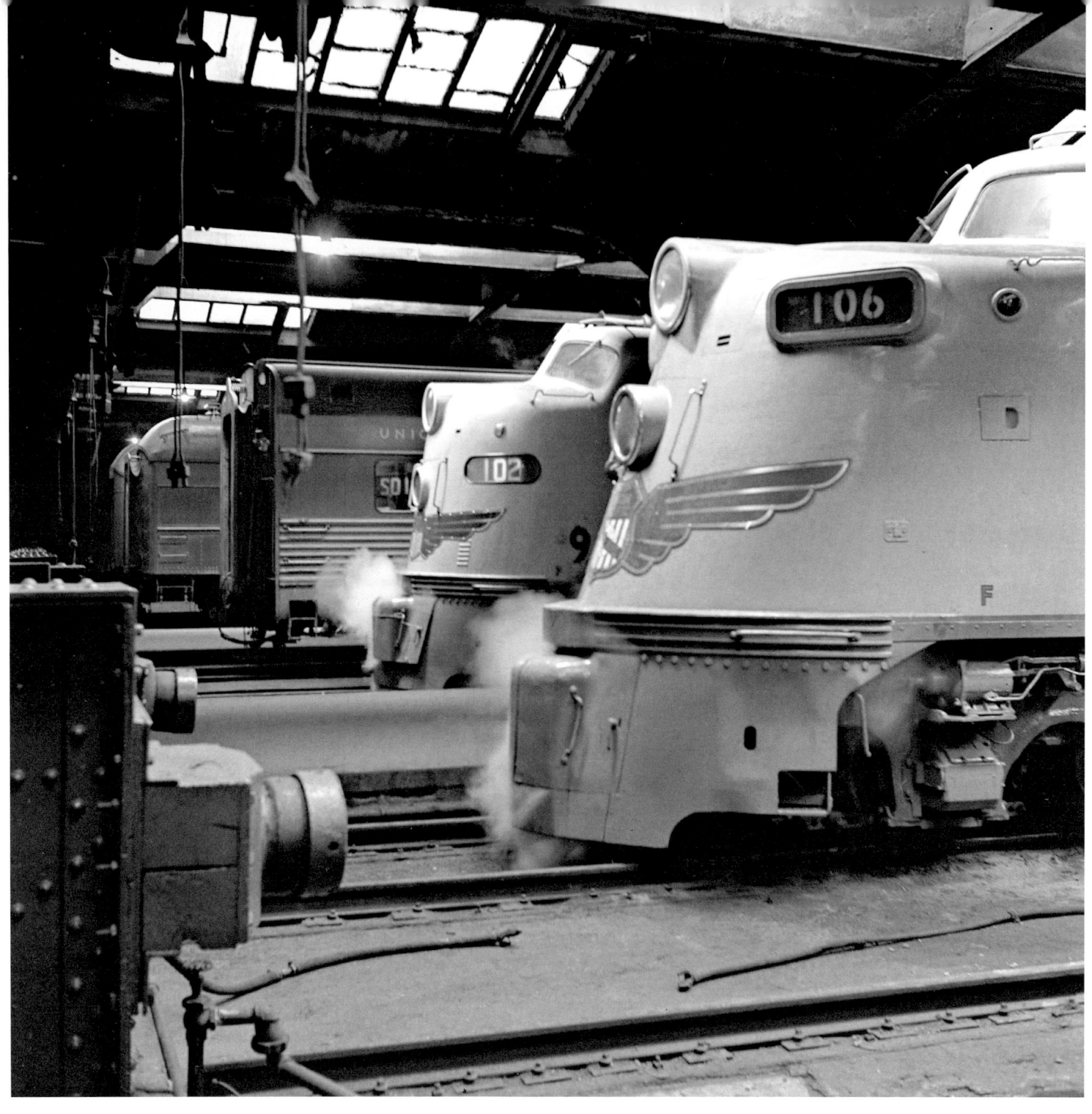

Two streamlined passenger trains from the West Coast rest at North Western Terminal on November 2, 1951. No. 106 is the *City of Portland* and no. 102 is the *City of San Francisco*. Both are Union Pacific trains, which at the time used the Chicago & North Western between Omaha and Chicago.

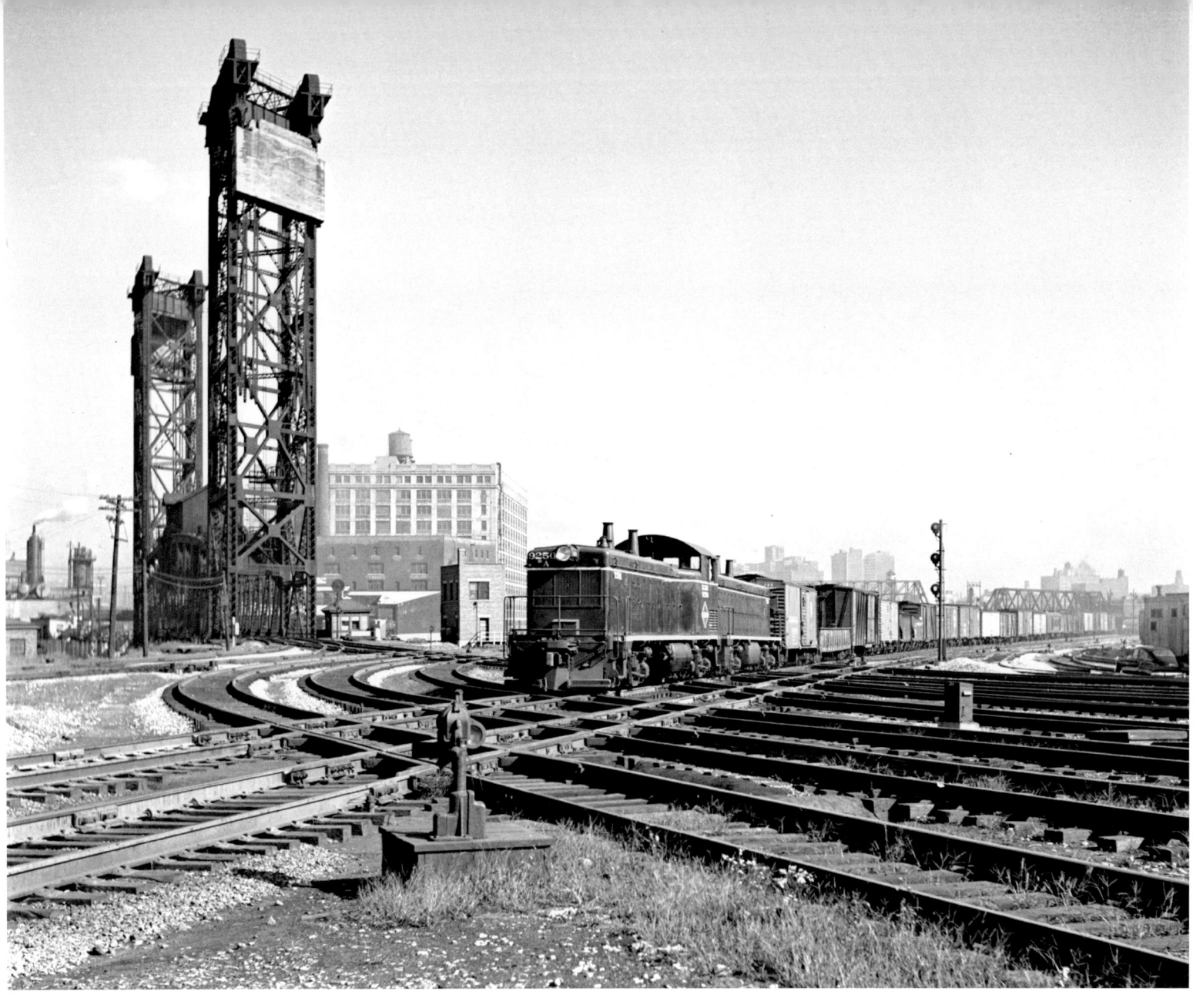

A pair of Illinois Central diesel switchers leads a transfer freight train through the spaghetti bowl of track that was Chicago's 21st Street Tower—one of the most complicated railroad junctions in the world. At its peak, the junction had twenty-six diamonds and hosted more than 150 trains per day. The two IC tracks cross five curving tracks of the Chicago & Western Indiana, and all of those are crossed by two tracks of the Pennsylvania Railroad, whose lift bridge over the Chicago River stands at left. Connecting tracks added to the total number of crossings and complexity. Abbey spent two days here in October of 1950, photographing the activity for his employer, *Trains* magazine.

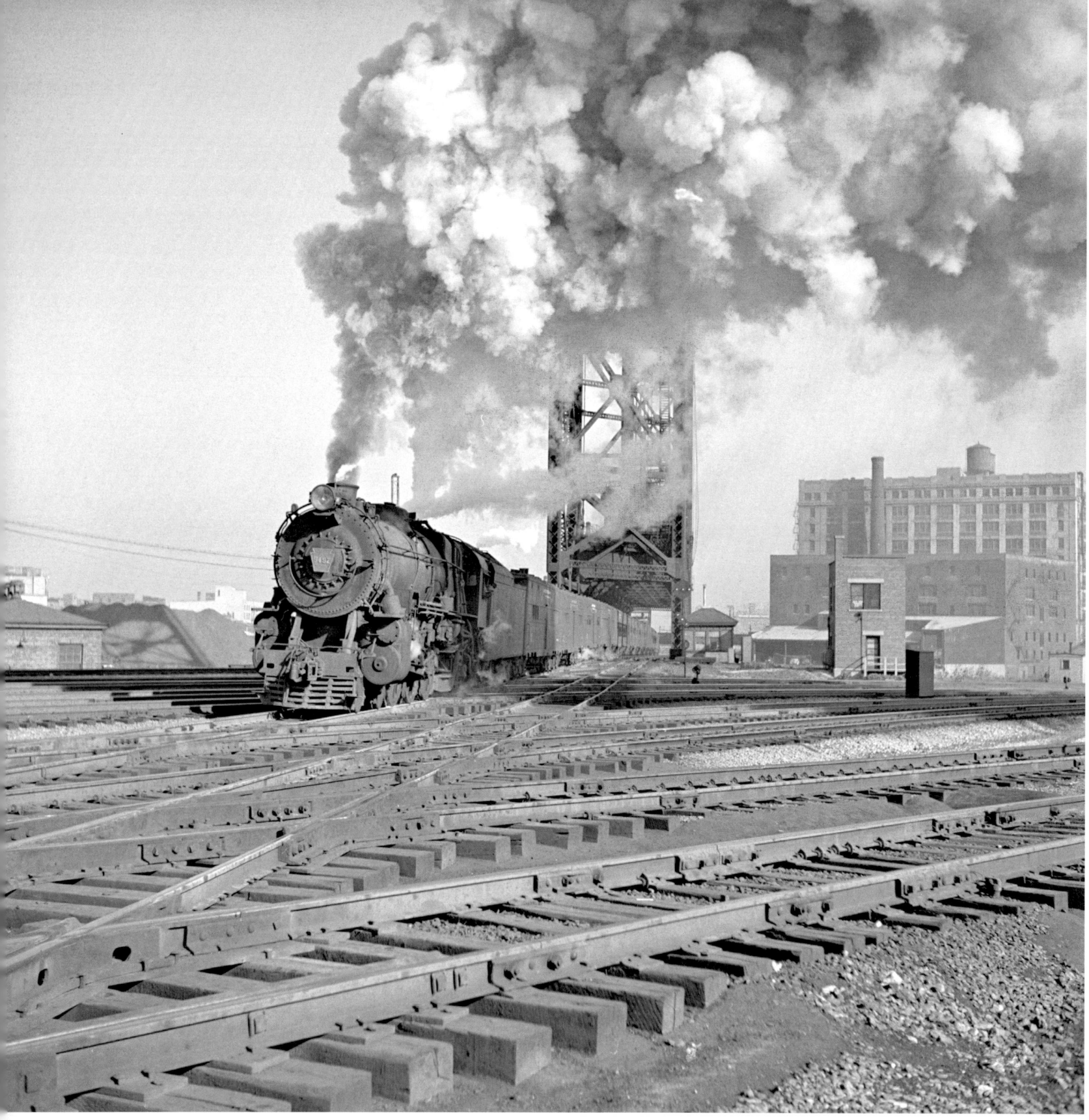

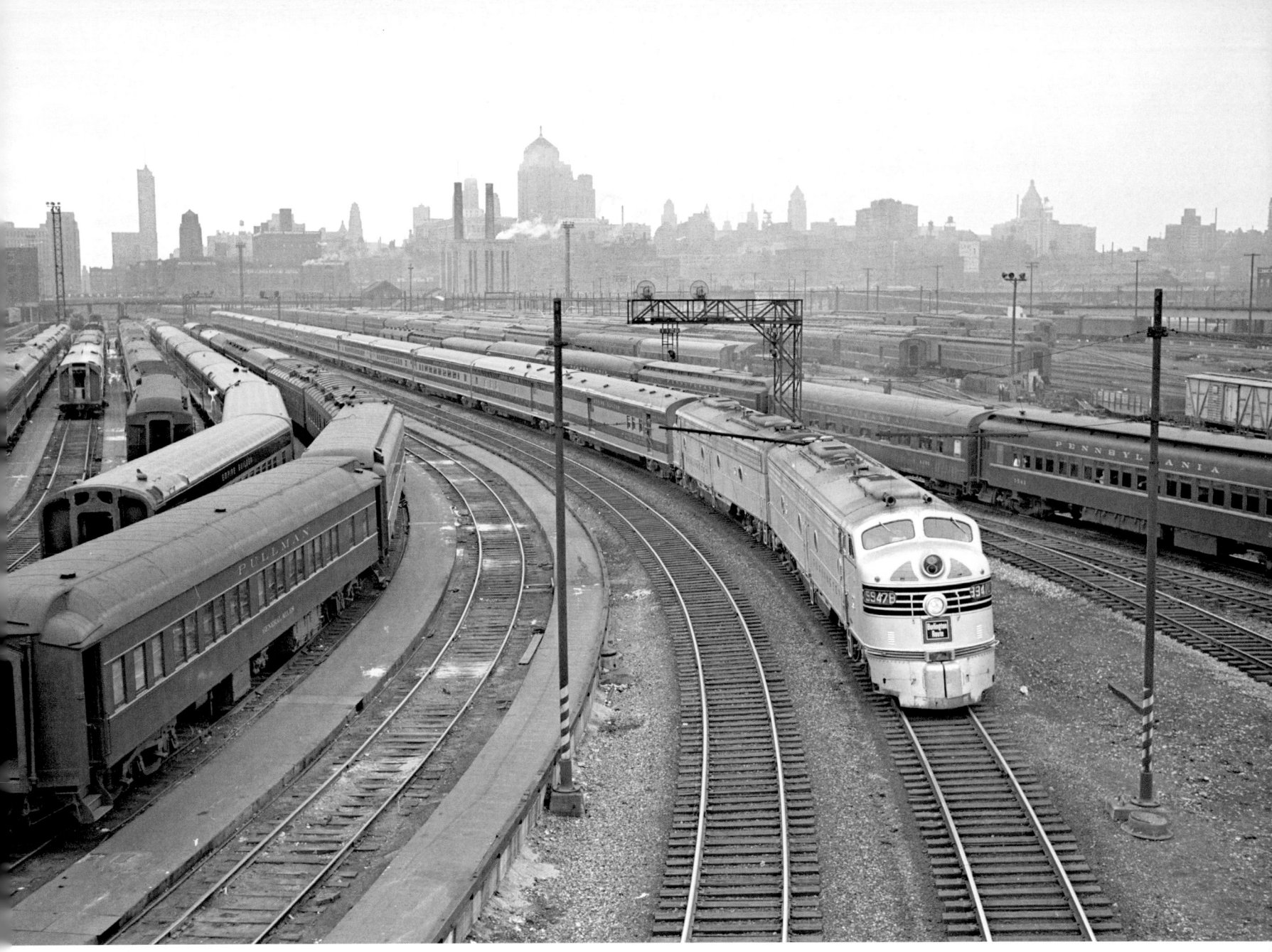

Facing: One of the Pennsylvania Railroad's legendary K4-class 4-6-2 steam locomotives leads an eastbound passenger train out of Union Station at 21st Street Tower on October 3, 1950. The cars are strung out across the lift bridge over the Chicago River, and the locomotive is crossing the tracks of the Illinois Central Railroad. The Pennsy was the major eastern railroad at Union Station, and its trains offered direct connections to much of the Midwest and the West via the Burlington; Gulf, Mobile & Ohio; and Milwaukee Road, which also used Union Station.

Above: With optimism for rail passenger traffic that would sadly prove unfounded, the Great Northern Railway ordered all-new cars for its premier train in 1951. Dubbed the "Mid-Century" *Empire Builder*, the fifteen-car train passes the 14th Street coach yards on its inaugural run to Seattle on June 3. Two Chicago, Burlington & Quincy E8A locomotives lead the train, which ran on the Burlington from Chicago to St. Paul, Minnesota.

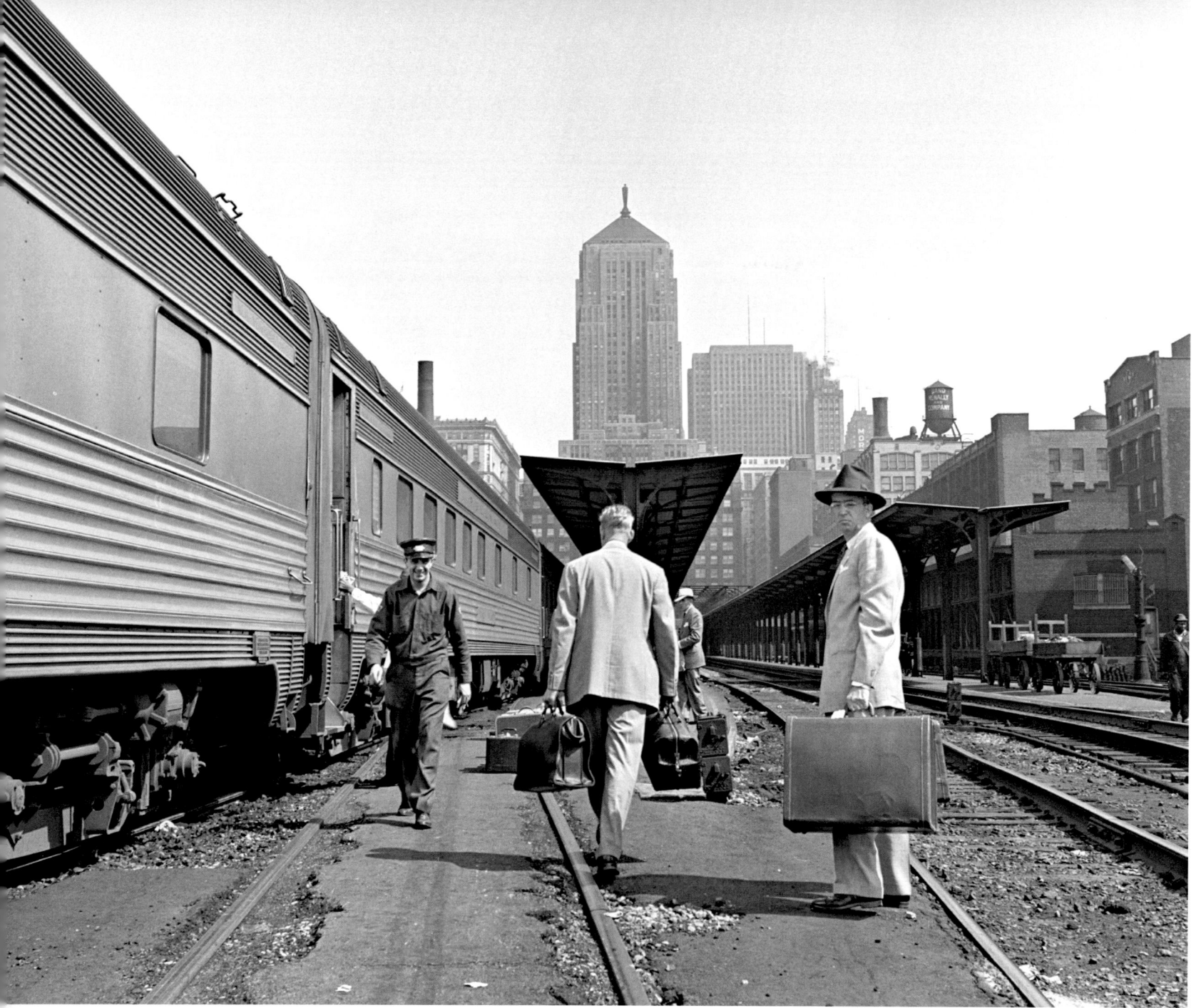

Above: Passengers alighting at LaSalle Station face a little longer walk than usual on this summer day in 1951. New York Central's *New England States* from Boston exceeds the platform by a few car lengths, but a "red cap" baggage handler at left is approaching to assist these heavily-laden travelers. The iconic Chicago Board of Trade Building rises directly behind the center platform.

Facing: Grand Trunk Western streamlined 4-8-4 no. 6409 storms out of Dearborn Station with a Michigan-bound train on a damp day of heavy skies in February of 1952. The Canadian National subsidiary's passenger service may not have been as well known as that of some other roads in Chicago, but engines like this one would make even the casual observer take notice. The 6409 was one of six in the U-4-b class delivered by Lima in 1938.

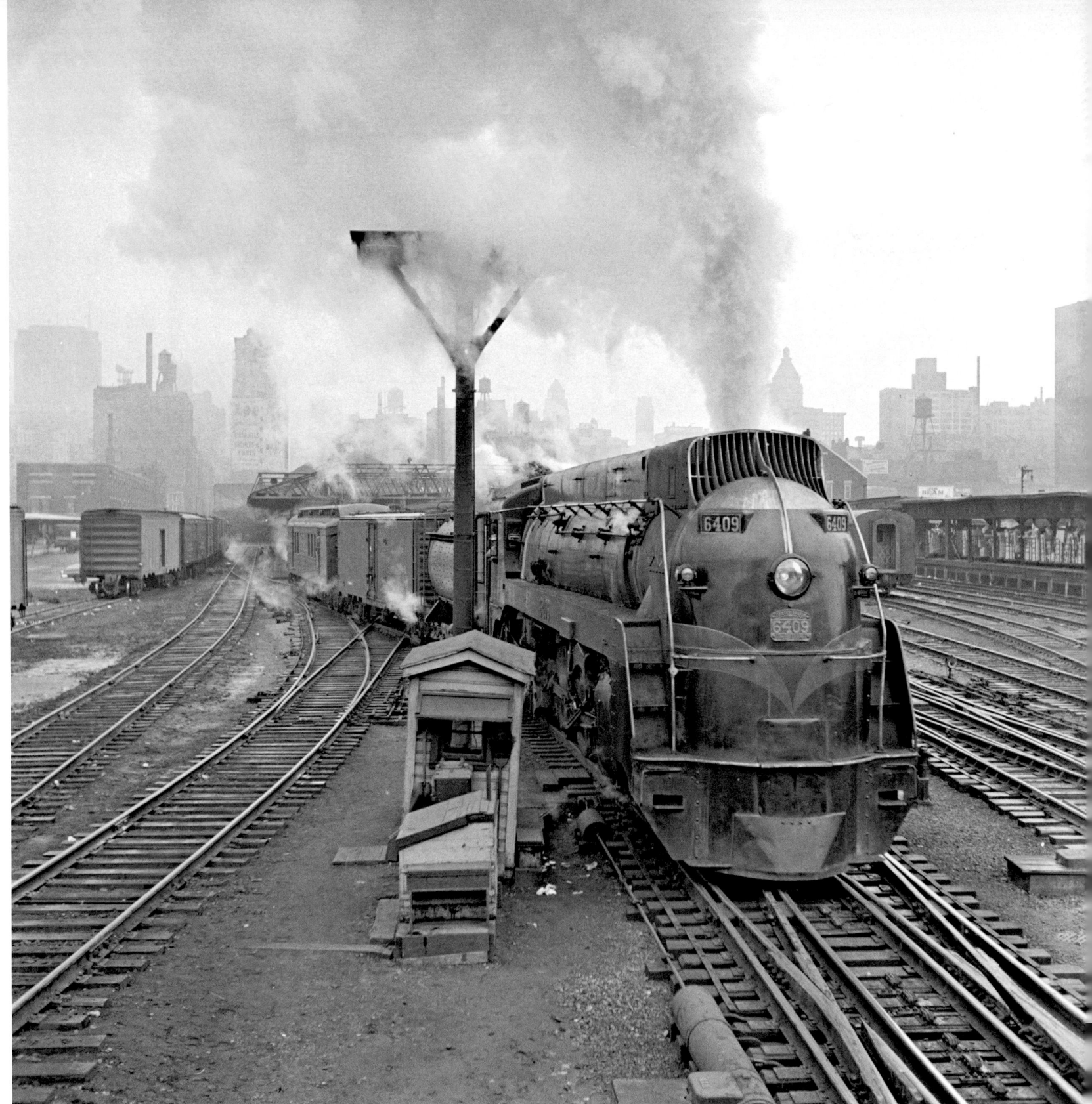

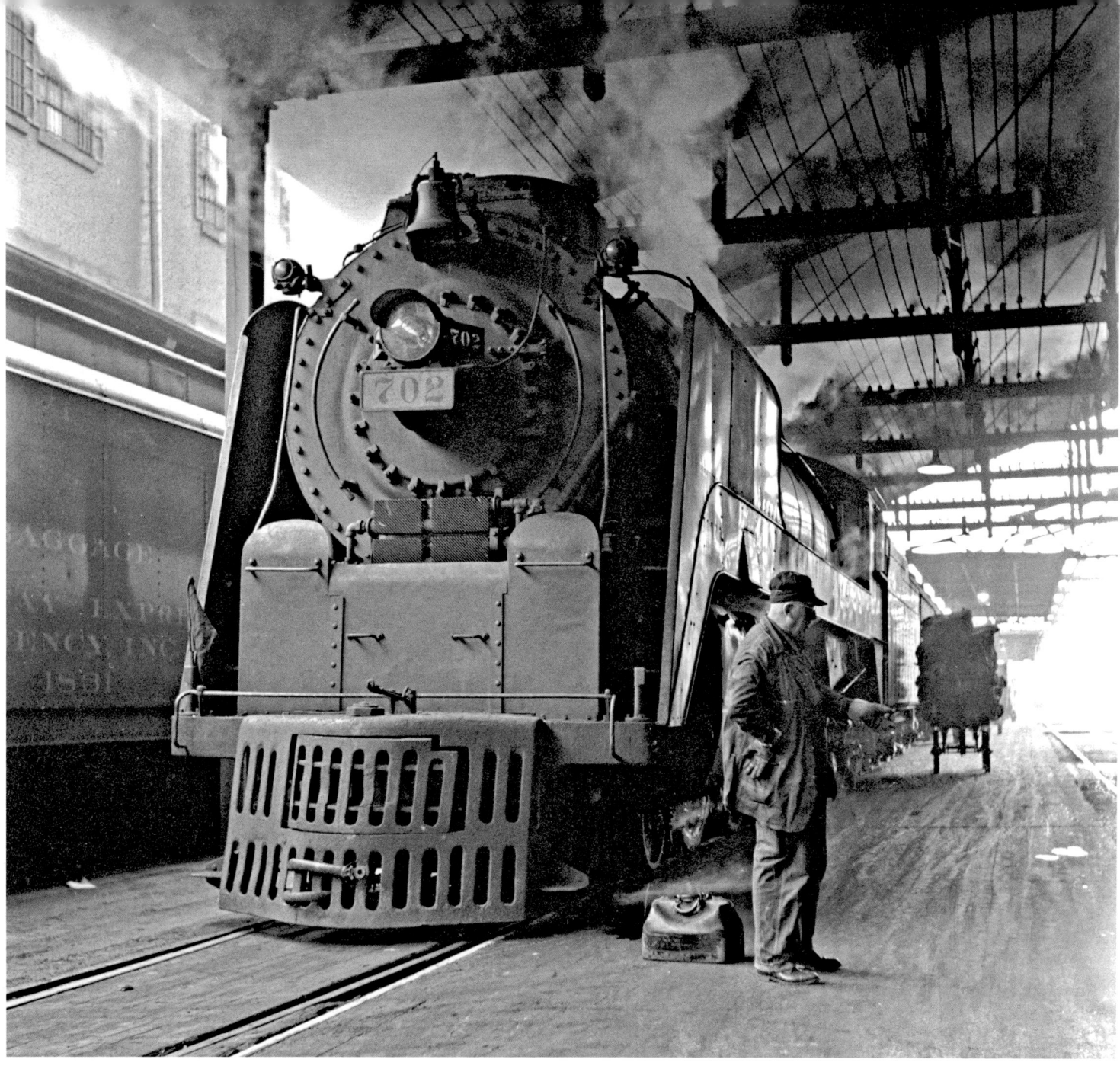

Above: A man and his machine: Wabash engineer and 4-6-4 no. 702 under the train shed at Dearborn Station on February 2, 1952. They have just brought eastbound train no. 10, the *Banner Blue*, in from St. Louis. The Wabash's five 4-6-4s were originally 2-8-2s built by Alco in 1925 and converted to passenger engines by the road's Decatur Shops in 1943. They were scheduled to make the 285.7-mile run from St. Louis in as little as five hours and twenty-five minutes.

Facing: One of steam's last great citadels in the Windy City was the North Western's Chicago Avenue roundhouse on the near north side. There the C&NW maintained a sizable fleet of 4-6-2s for suburban commuter service in a half-circle structure. Halstead Street passed almost directly above the turntable, providing easy access for spectacular views like this one of no. 514 in 1952.

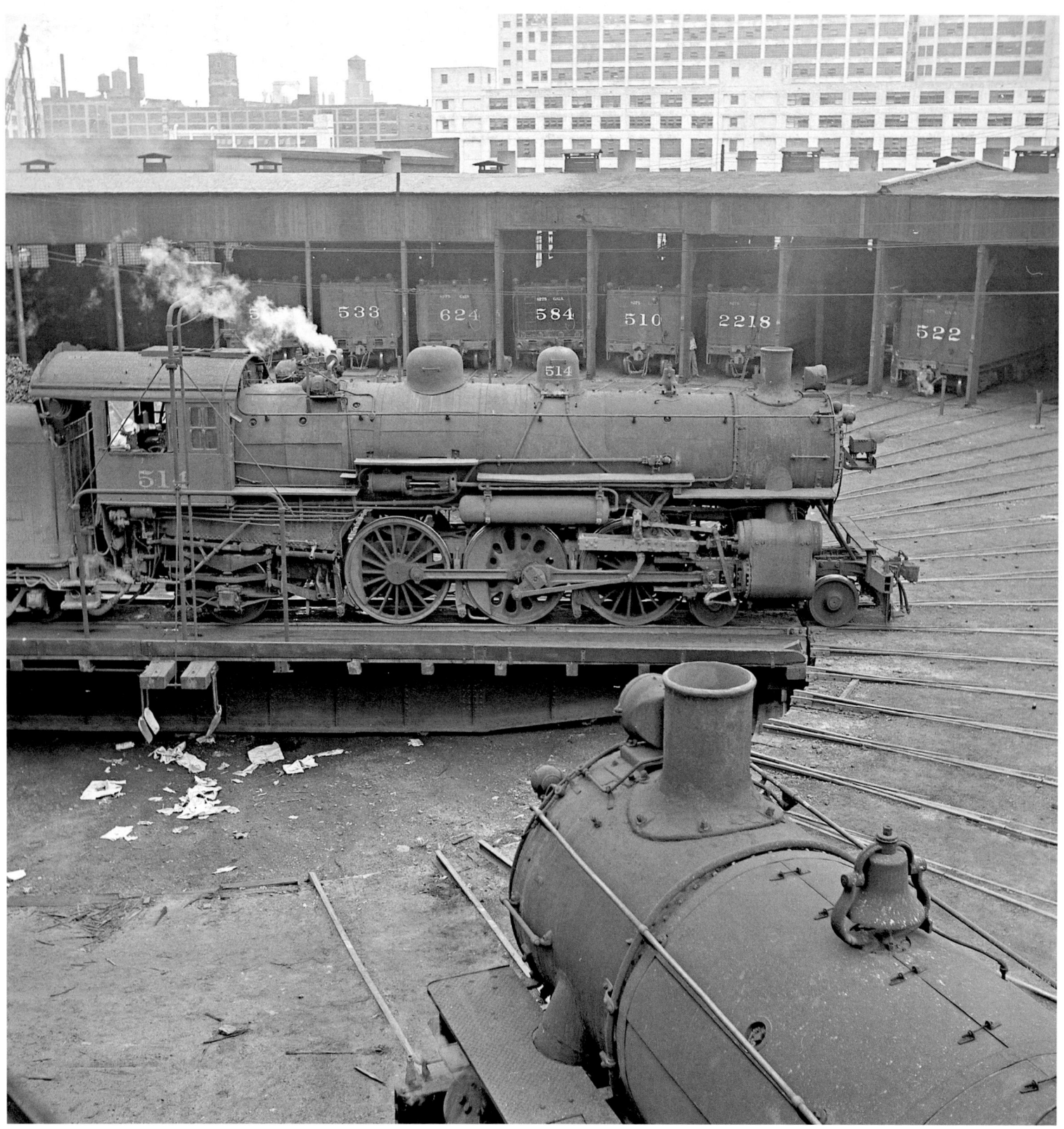

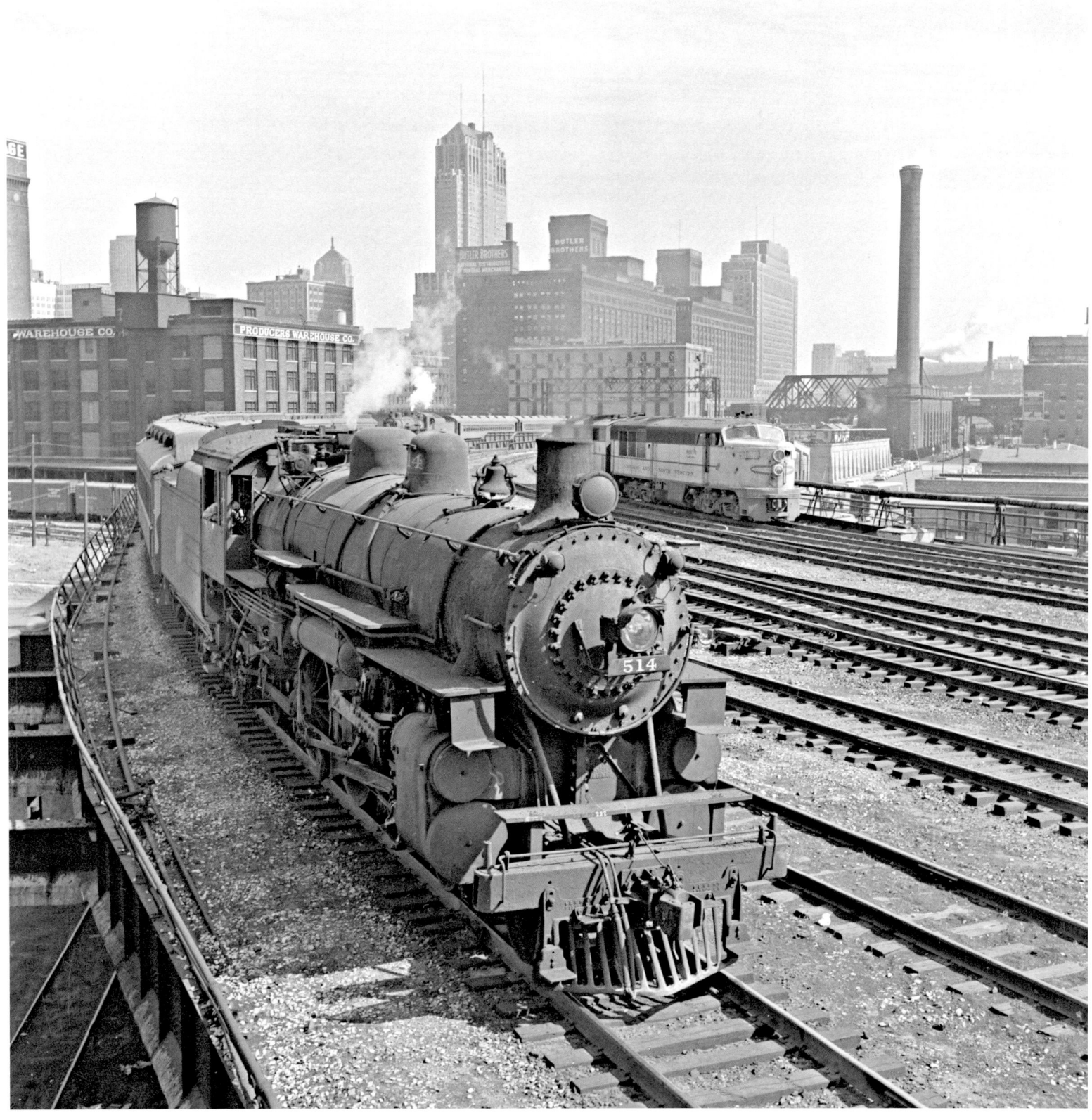

Facing: In this view of the famous curve just north of the North Western Terminal, frequently used for Chicago & North Western company photographs, the afternoon rush is underway as 4-6-2 no. 514 leads a westbound commuter train. Another steam-powered suburban train is visible in the distance, while Fairbanks Morse "Erie Built" diesel no. 6001B is on the far track. The truss bridge in the background carries one of Chicago's famous rapid-transit "L" lines over the North Western tracks.

Below: Santa Fe steam and diesel power congregates at the road's 18th Street engine facilities in Chicago in 1947. No. 90 leads a brand-new A-B-A set of Fairbanks Morse "Erie built" diesels, the only ones the Santa Fe would ever own due to their reliability issues. Abbey had spent a summer in high school working at the shops, which primarily serviced power for long-distance passenger trains.

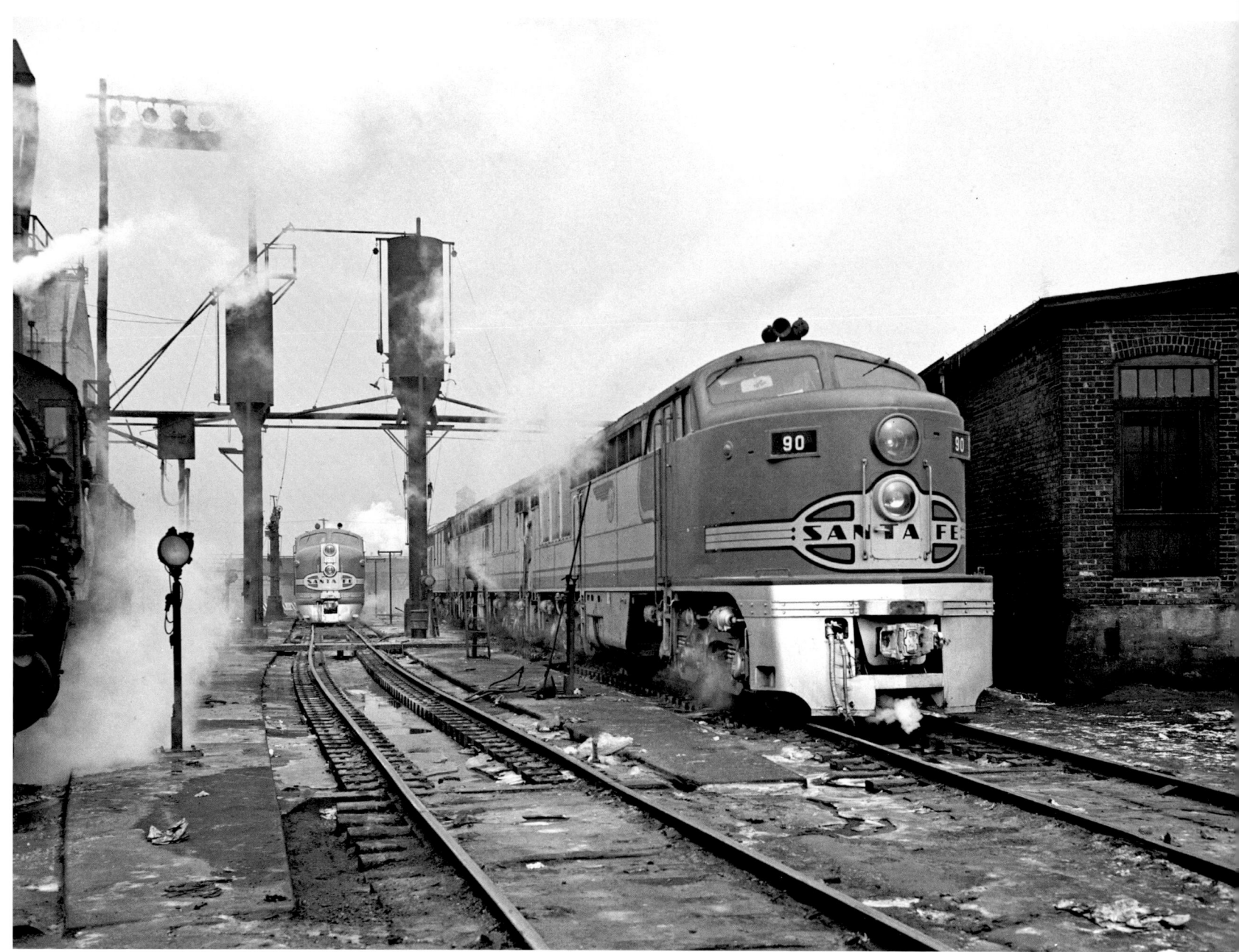

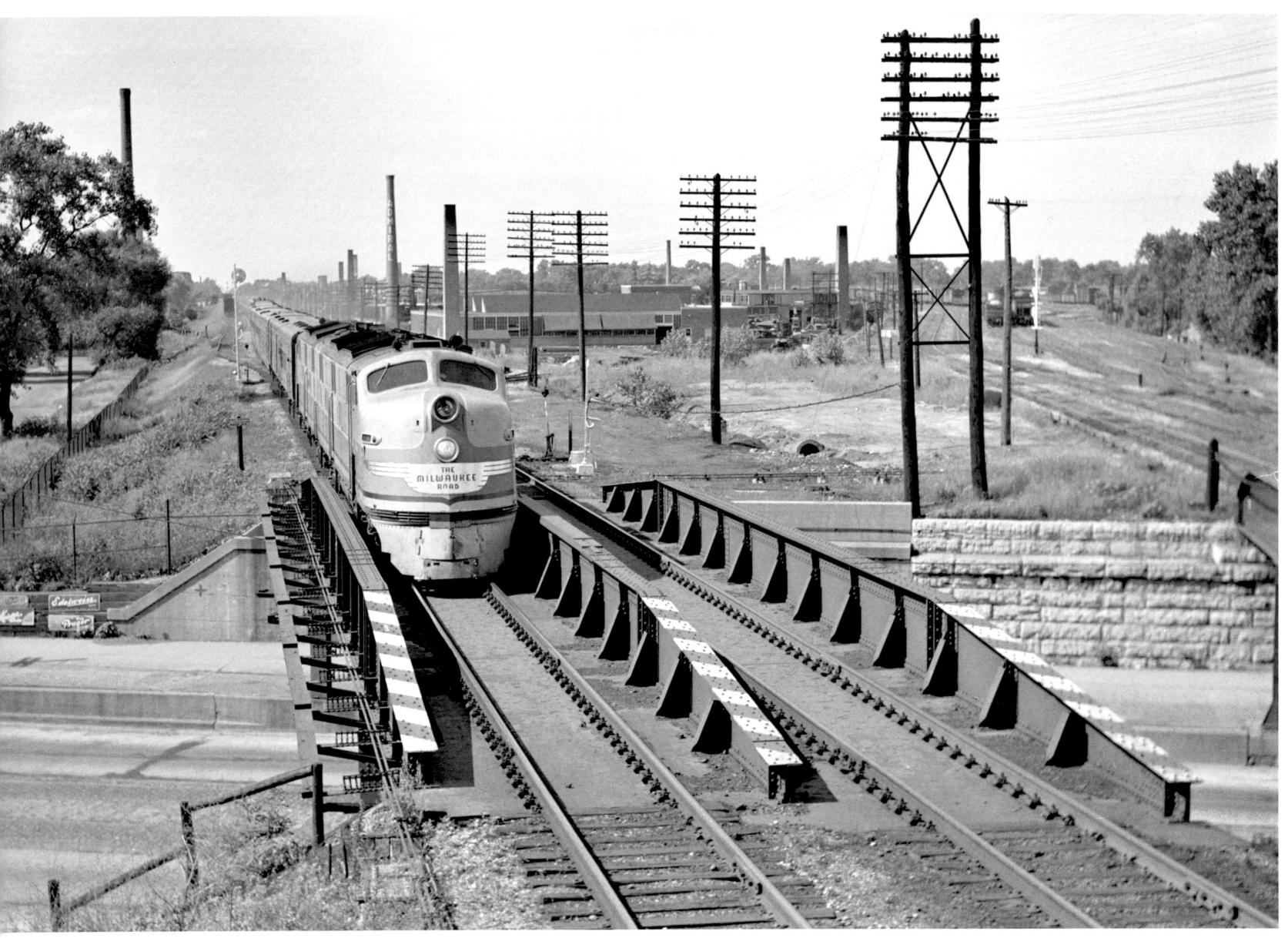

On a summer afternoon in 1947 on Chicago's North Side, Milwaukee Road passenger train no. 6, the *Morning Hiawatha* from Minneapolis, approaches Grayland Tower near the end of its 421-mile, six-hour and fifty-minute run to Union Station. The tower controlled an at-grade crossing with a Chicago & North Western line, visible at right; both lines cross West Irving Park Road on overpasses.

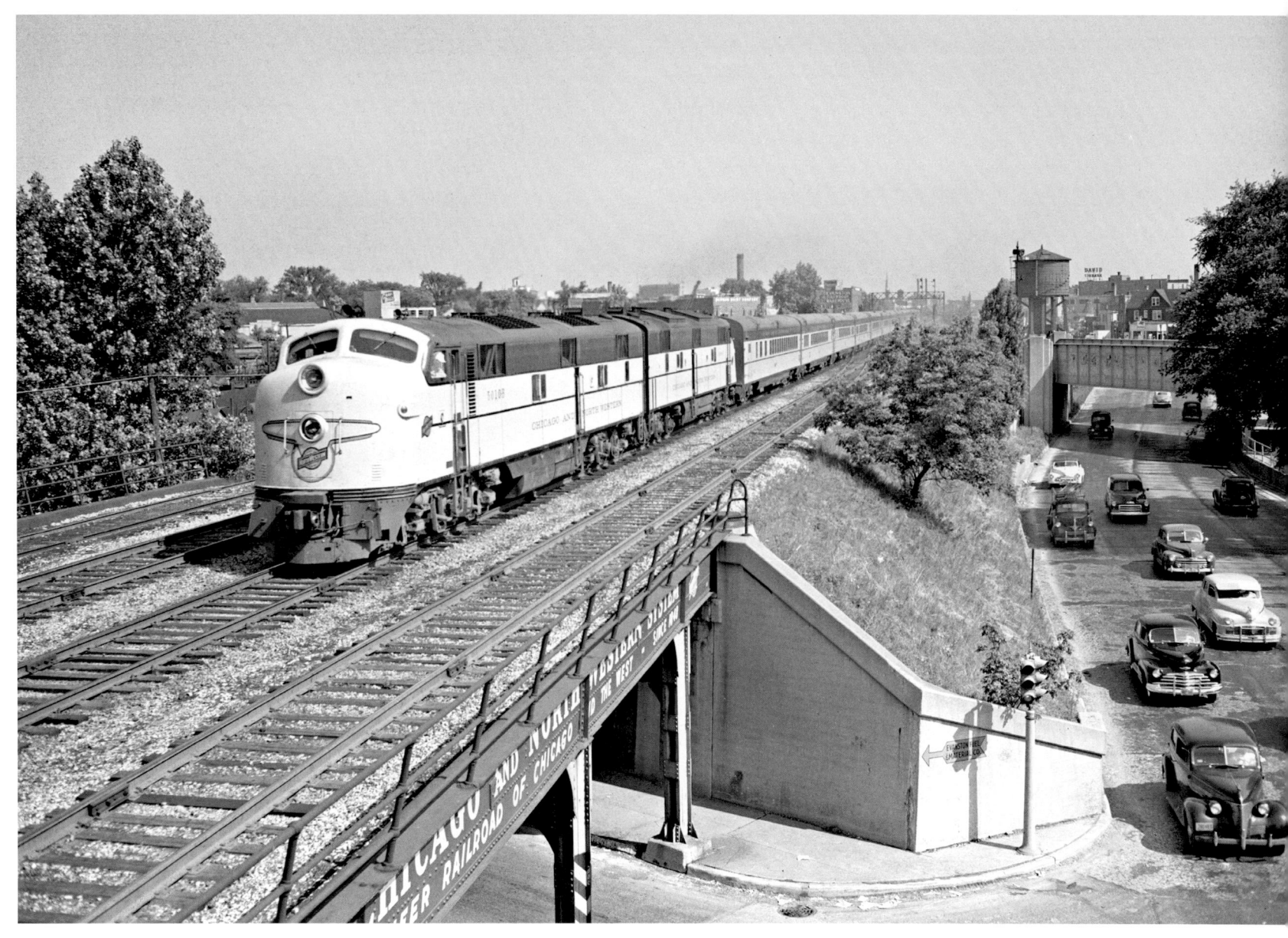

Chicago & North Western outbound train no. 401, the *Twin Cities 400*, hustles through the interlocking plant of Canal Tower in Evanston, Illinois, on a sunny July afternoon in 1948. E7A locomotives nos. 5010B and 5006B lead the train, which is undoubtedly outpacing the traffic below on Green Bay Road. Leaving Chicago at 2:45 p.m., the train was due into Minneapolis at 9:30—407 miles in 405 minutes and the reason behind the train's name.

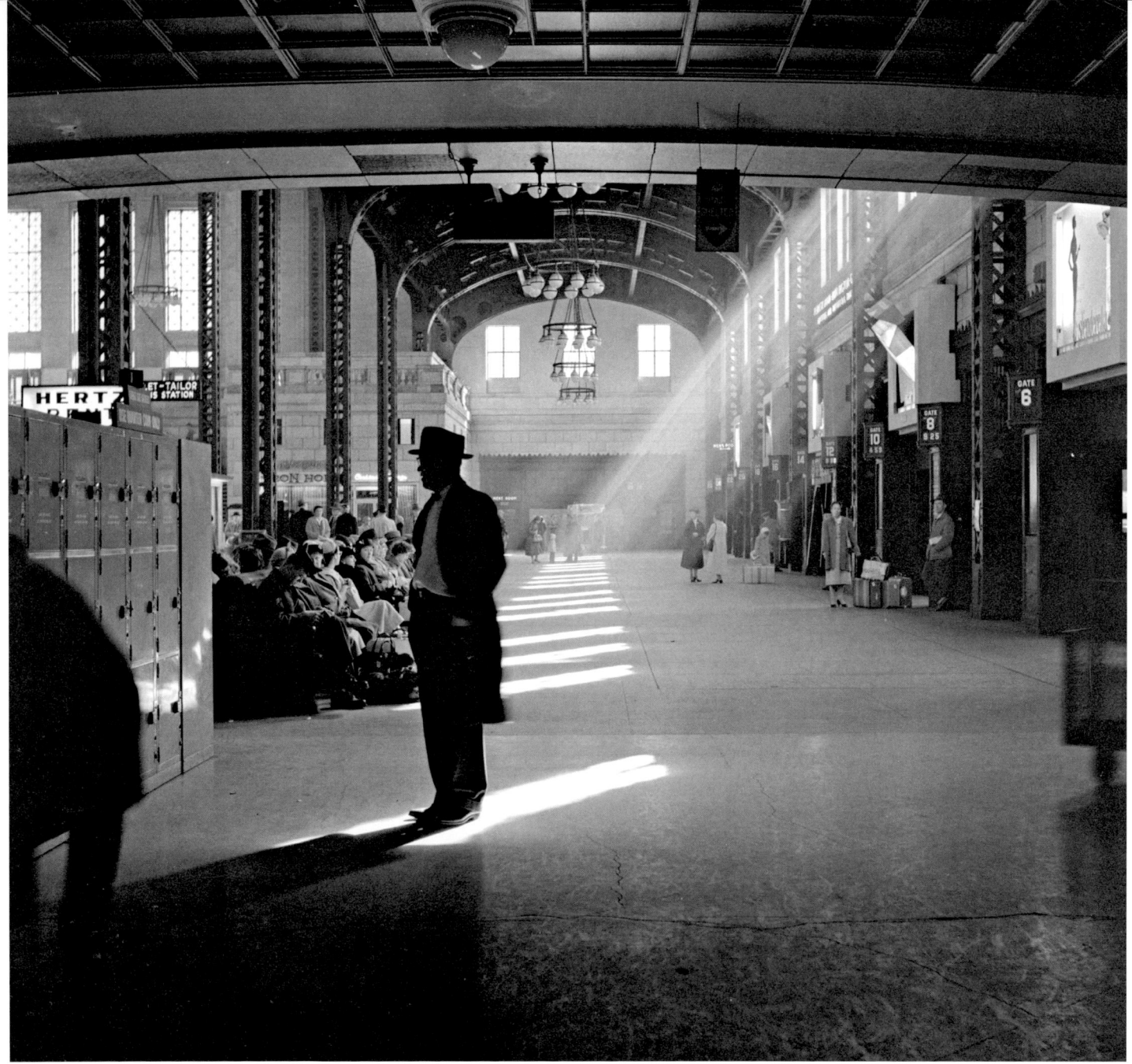

Morning sun streams into the concourse of Union Station, silhouetting a single traveler studying the lockers on March 29, 1957. A dozen years earlier, at the end of World War II, the station had handled as many as 300 trains and 100,000 passengers a day, but traffic had declined sharply by the time Abbey made this picture. A dozen years later, the concourse would be demolished and replaced by a much smaller structure to make way for a modern office tower. Business has partially rebounded, though, with more than 50,000 people using the station on an average day in the twenty-first century.

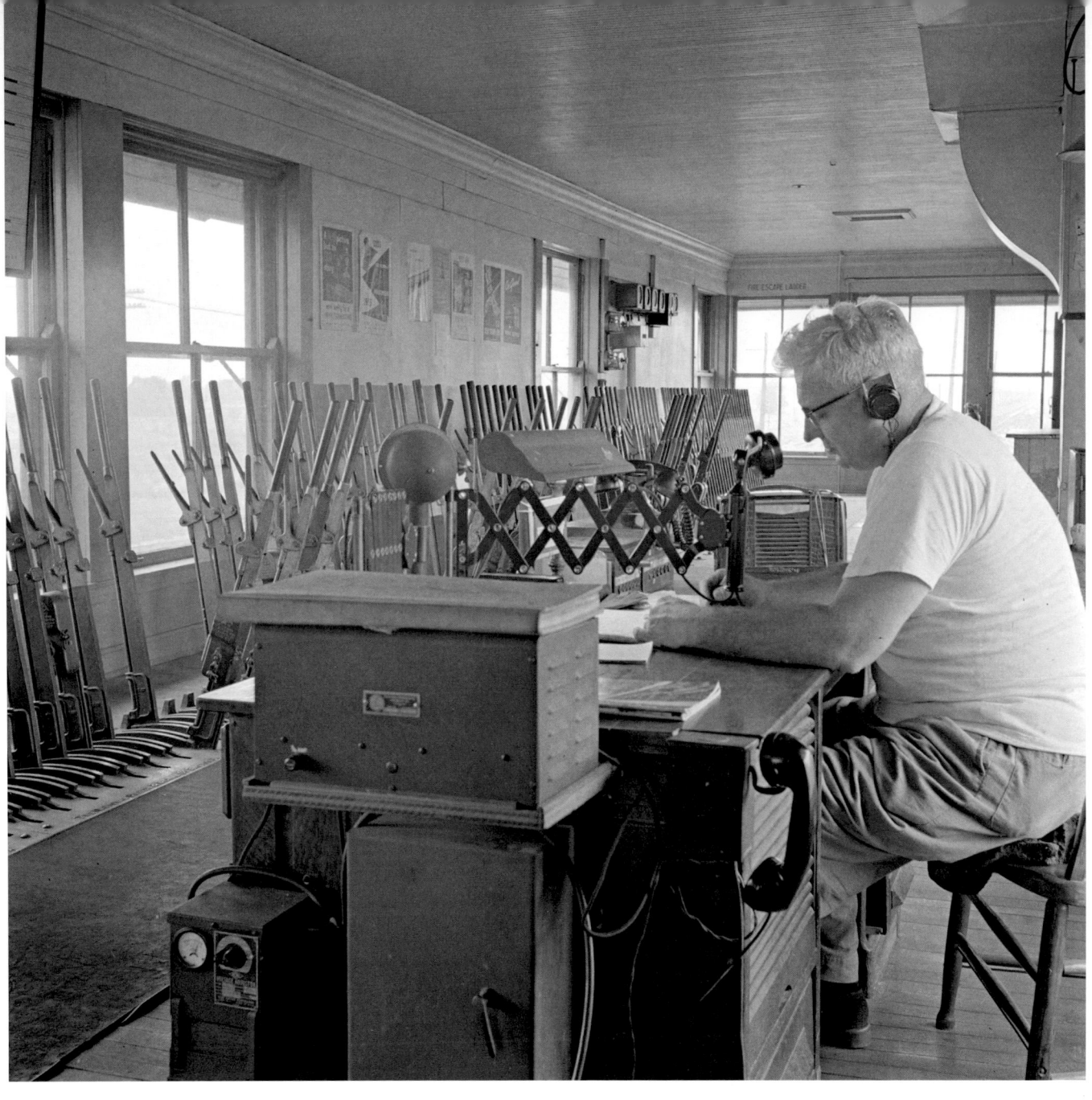

The operator inside the Chicago & Western Indiana's State Line Tower in Hammond, Indiana, on September 9, 1956. He controlled a maze of tracks at this southeastern entrance to Chicagoland on the Illinois-Indiana border. The Chesapeake & Ohio, Erie, and Monon all came in from the southeast and used the C&WI into the city. Running parallel was the Nickel Plate Road's main line, and everything crossed both the Baltimore & Ohio Chicago Terminal main line and a branch of the Indiana Harbor Belt.

Left: Travelers walk past Union Pacific's *City of Portland* passenger train, shrouded by steam from its heat line, while preparing to depart from Union Station in April 1957. In 1955, the Milwaukee Road took over operating Union Pacific's streamliners between Chicago and Omaha; previously the Chicago & North Western had handled this traffic, with the trains calling at North Western Terminal a few blocks north of Union Station.

Facing: Pedestrians walk briskly along the Loop in downtown Chicago, heedless of a North Shore Line train rumbling overhead on the "L" tracks above Wabash Avenue on a summer day in 1957. With more than 100 miles of routes, service dating back to 1892, and twenty-first-century ridership of three-quarters of a million per weekday, you could say the "L" is as Chicago as icy winter winds, hotdogs with relish, and ivy-covered outfield walls. Yet Abbey rarely photographed it—he made these views specifically for a story in *Railway Age*, where he worked for three years before beginning his tenure with the Soo Line.

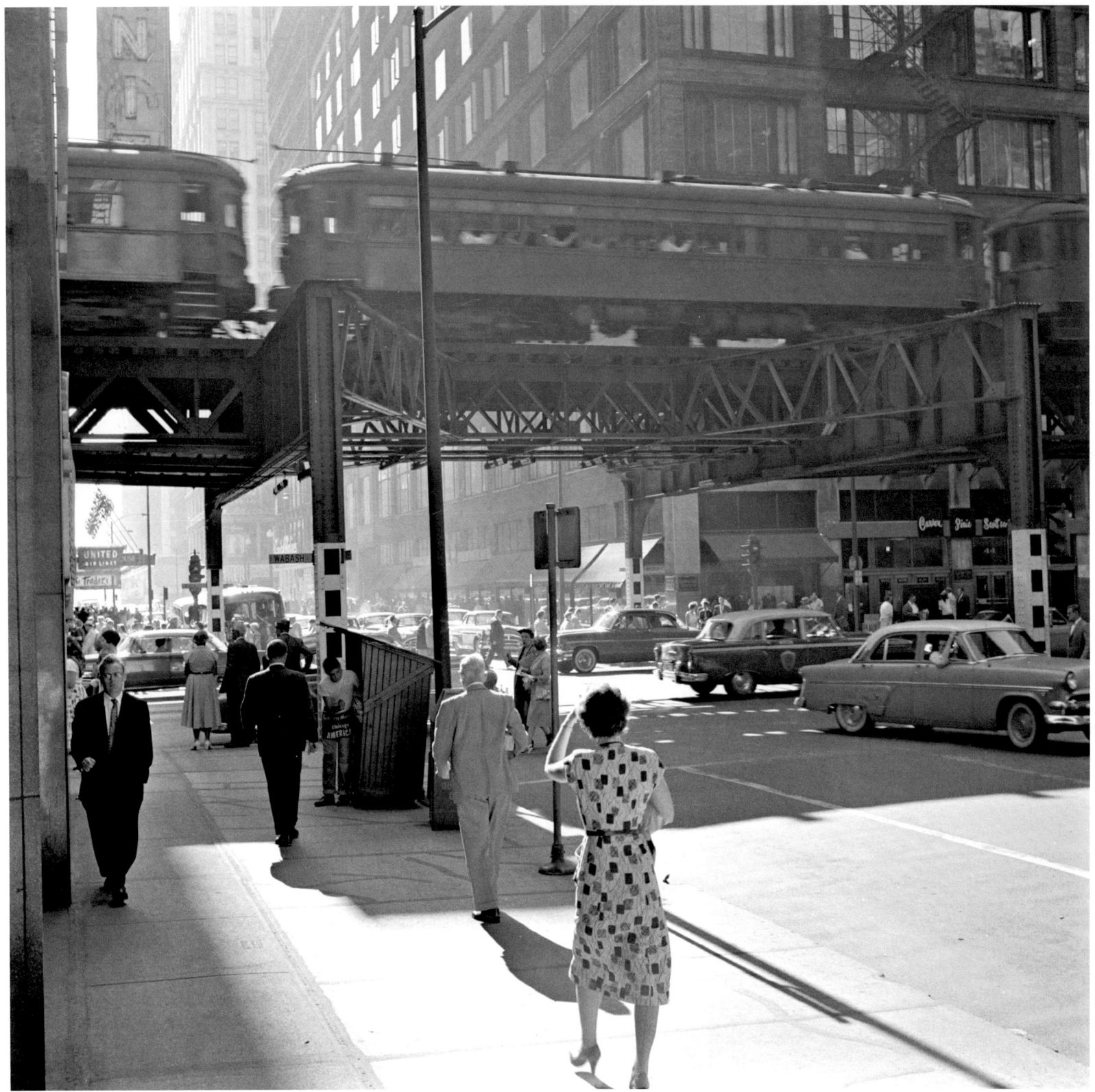

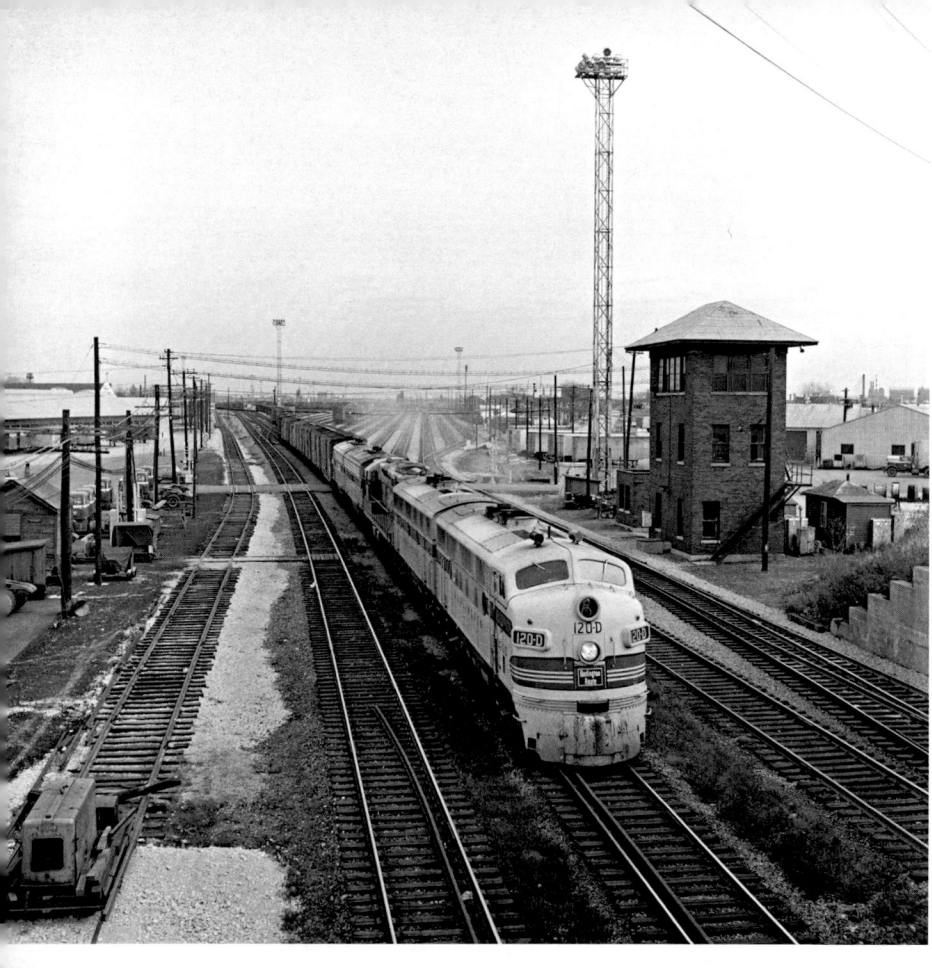

Chicago, Burlington & Quincy's westbound CD freight train to Denver departs Cicero Yard behind five locomotives on November 9, 1958. At the time Cicero was the Burlington's primary classification facility for its traffic coming into and out of Chicago. In the 1980s, successor Burlington Northern shifted nearly all its mixed freight classification 200 miles southwest to Galesburg, Illinois, and converted Cicero into a dedicated intermodal facility.

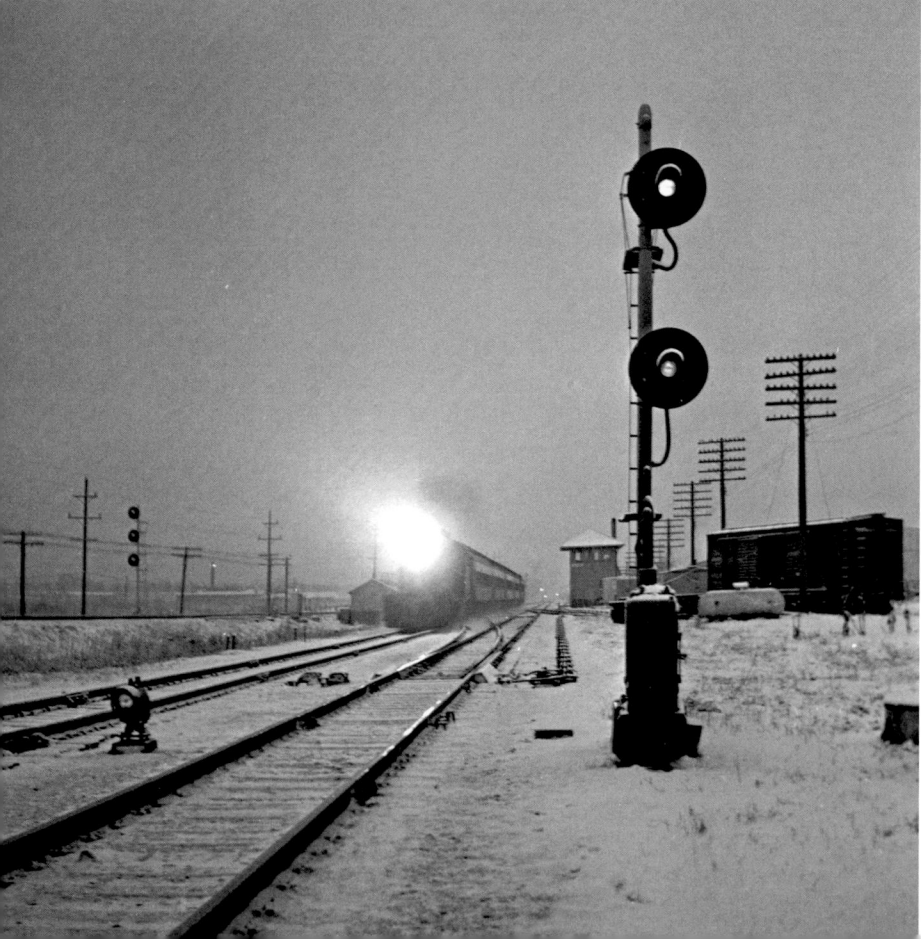

Left: Inbound Milwaukee Road commuter train passing Tower A-20 at dusk on March 24, 1959. The name comes from the railroad calling its route between Chicago and Milwaukee its "A" line, and this location being 20 miles from Chicago Union Station. Located at Techny Junction, the tower controlled a connection with a Chicago & North Western line that passed above the Milwaukee. The connecting track is visible at left.

Facing: Passengers from a Baltimore & Ohio train walk through Grand Central Station in April of 1959. Despite its name, Grand Central was the smallest of Chicago's six major passenger terminals. Besides the B&O, it also served trains of the Chesapeake & Ohio and the Soo Line, as well as the Chicago Great Western until 1956, when that road ended its Windy City passenger service. Facing declining patronage and political pressure, Grand Central's remaining trains were transferred to other facilities by 1969, and the station closed. It was demolished two years later.

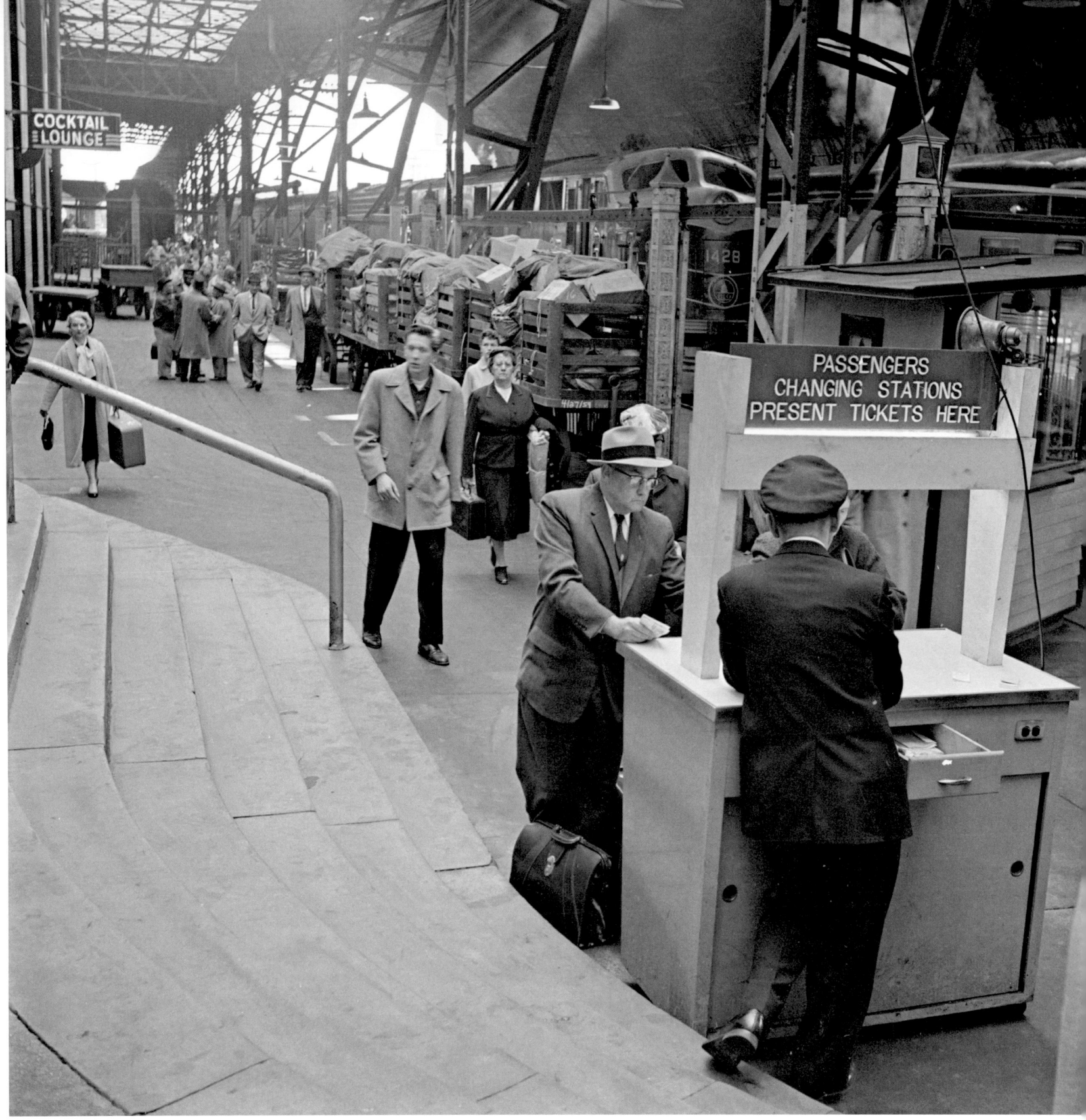

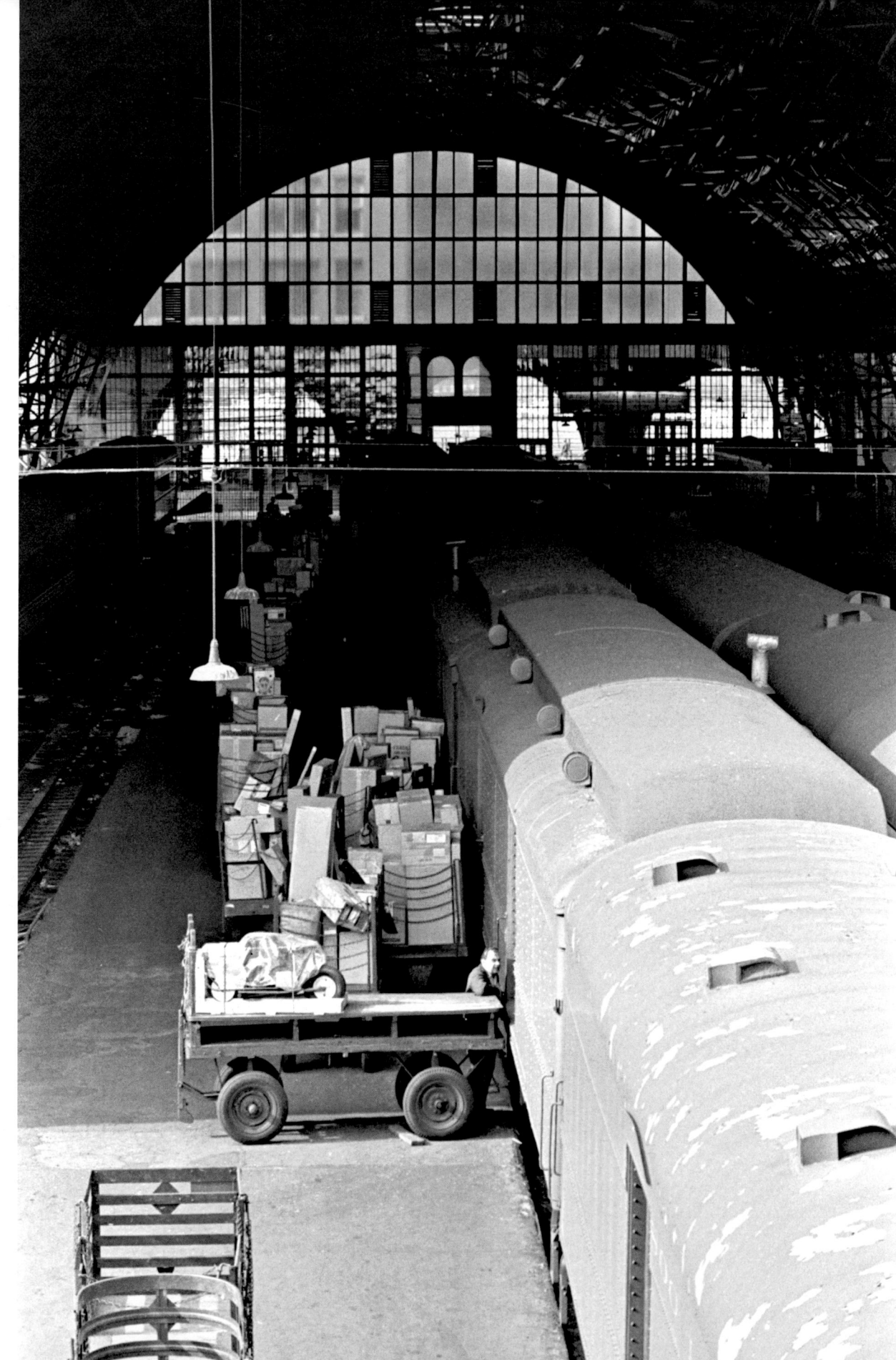

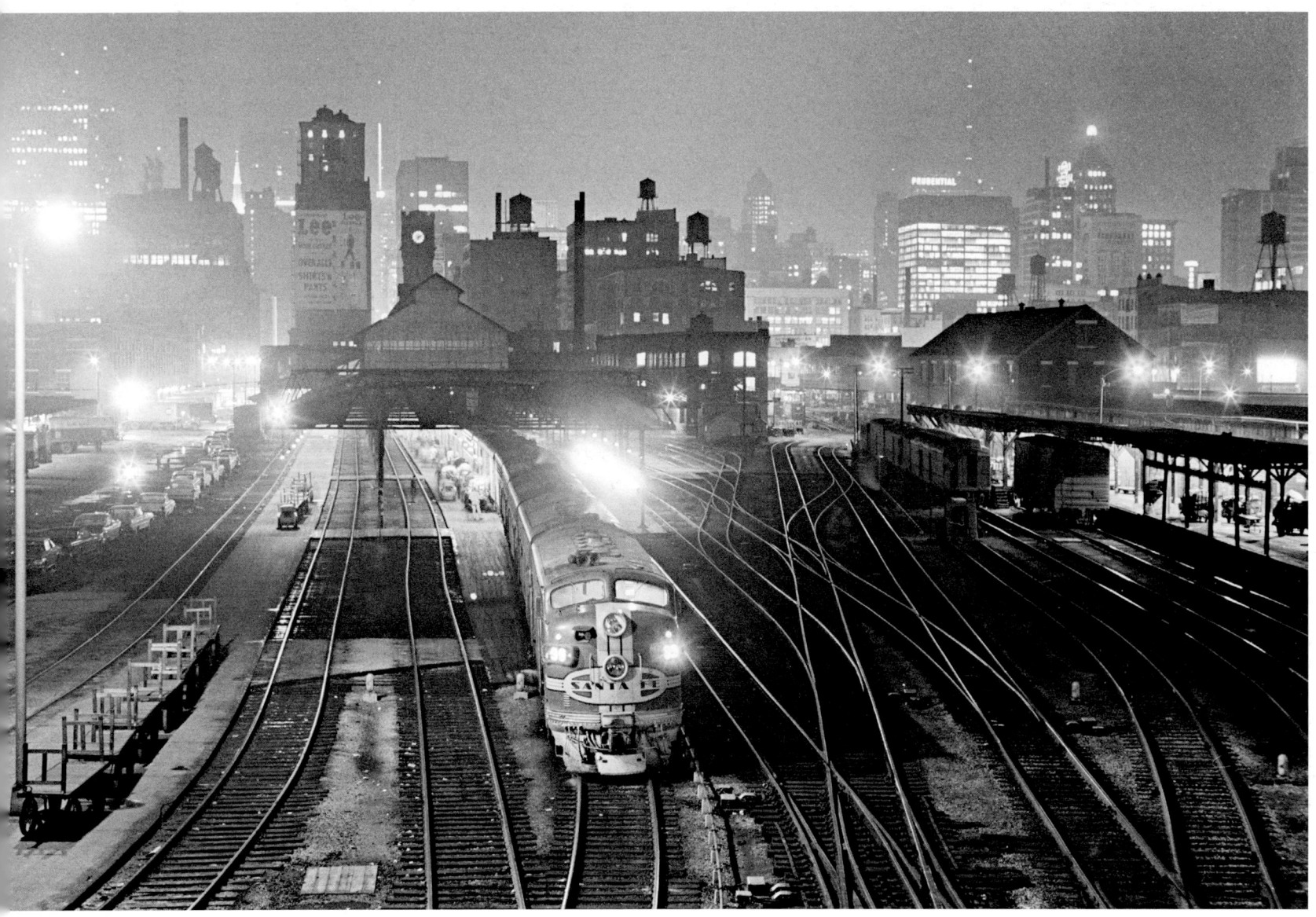

Facing: Workers at Grand Central Station load mail onto the Soo Line's *Laker* passenger train for Duluth on the evening of April 17, 1962. This was the last full year that the train would use Grand Central. In 1963, the Soo transferred its remaining passenger business to Central Station, a few blocks to the southeast. The move would be short-lived. Changes by the US Post Office Department in 1964 removed most of the mail from the *Laker*, and the train made its last run on January 15, 1965.

Above: With Chicago's skyscrapers glowing like palaces, Santa Fe's combined *Super Chief–El Capitan* prepares to depart Dearborn Station on the evening of October 22, 1965. Rail passenger patronage was in steep decline across the nation by the mid-1960s, but the Santa Fe still operated an impressive service. While it had combined these two trains in 1958, the railroad still offered four other departures from Chicago every day for the West Coast. That would last for two more years, until the Post Office Department canceled nearly all its mail contracts in October of 1967, leading to deep cuts in the railroad passenger business.

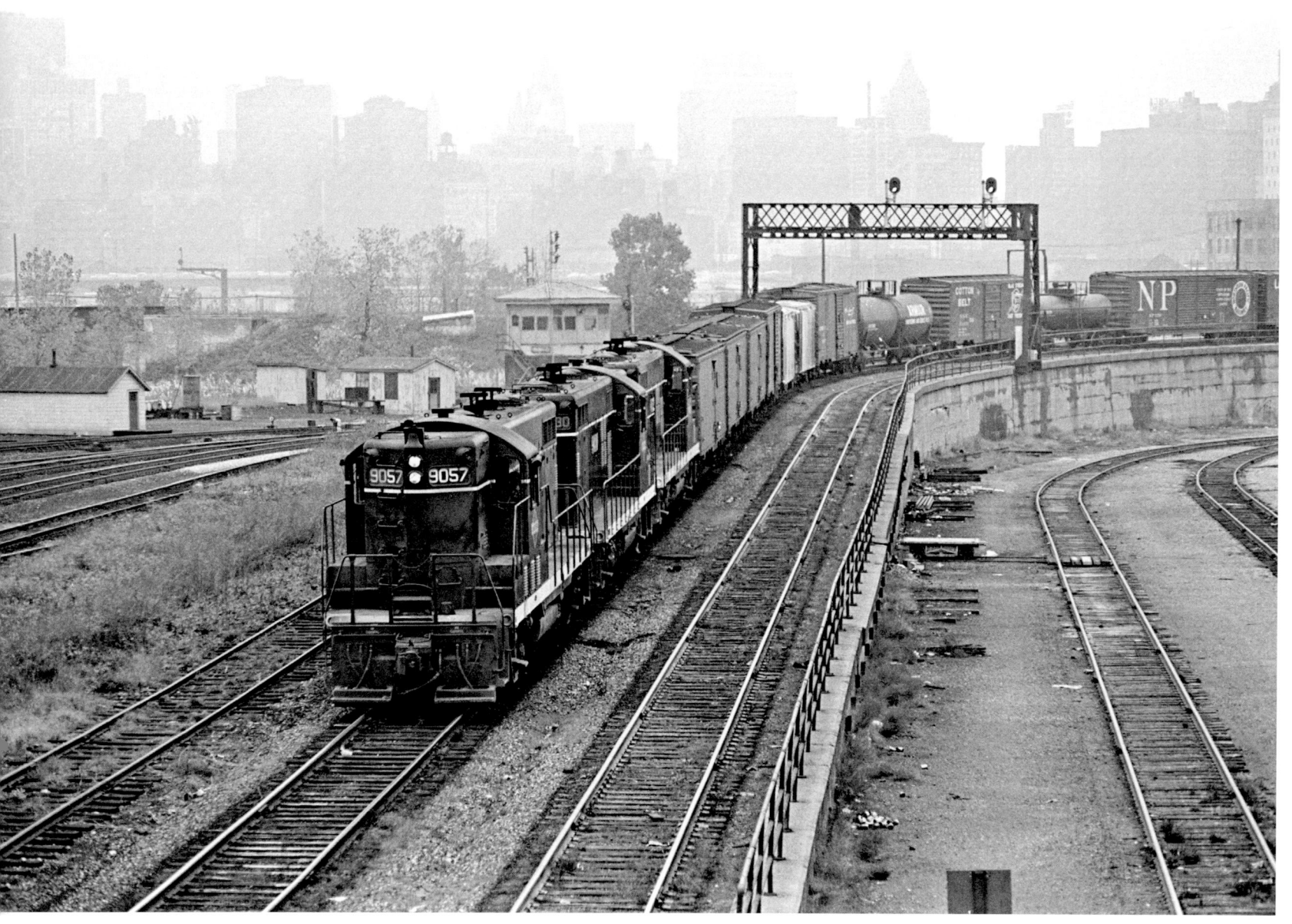

An Illinois Central freight train from Iowa comes down the ramp from the St. Charles Air Line, heading south for Markham Yard in south-suburban Homewood, Illinois, on October 22, 1965. Three GP9s lead the train, which includes three refrigerator cars, likely carrying Iowa beef, directly behind the locomotives. The Air Line passes above the congested streets and railroads immediately south of downtown. The IC owned one-quarter of the route (along with the Michigan Central, Burlington, and North Western) and used it to get trains between its line to Iowa from the west and its line running south along Lake Michigan.

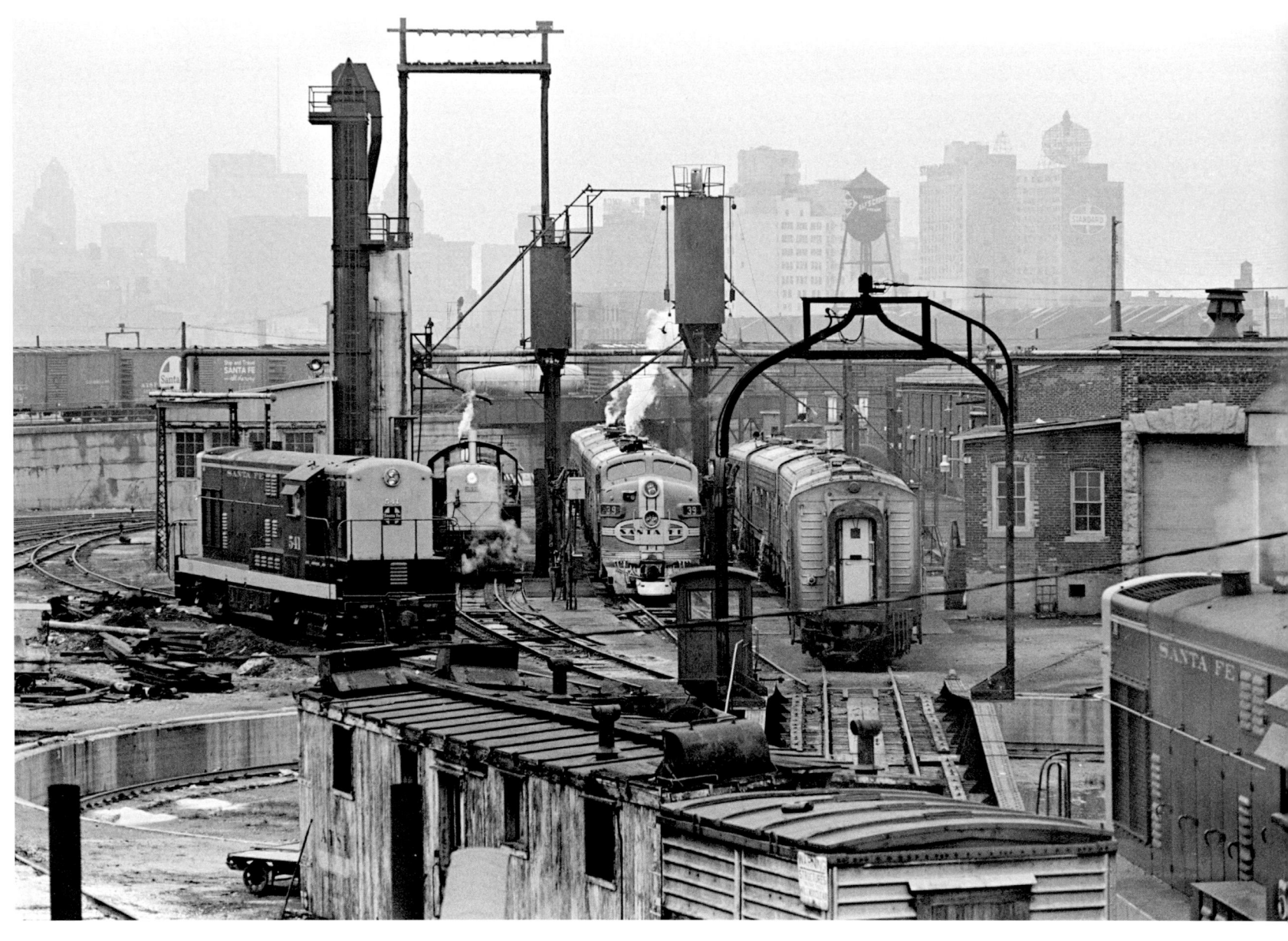

Santa Fe diesels from three builders rest between assignments at the railroad's 18th Street roundhouse. Fairbanks Morse switchers at far left and right bracket an Alco switcher and two sets of F-units. 18th Street primarily serviced power for the Santa Fe's passenger trains, and in 1965, the year of this photograph, that still included four streamliners and the *Fast Mail* every day between Chicago and the West Coast. As a high-school student, Abbey spent the summer of 1944 working here.

Passengers watch from Englewood Union Station as an eastbound Pennsylvania Railroad passenger train arrives on October 22, 1965. The tower at left controlled the crossing of four Pennsylvania tracks and three of the Rock Island. Out of view to the right, New York Central's main line curved from paralleling the Rock to the Pennsy. The station served all three railroads, as well as the Nickel Plate Road, which used NYC's tracks.

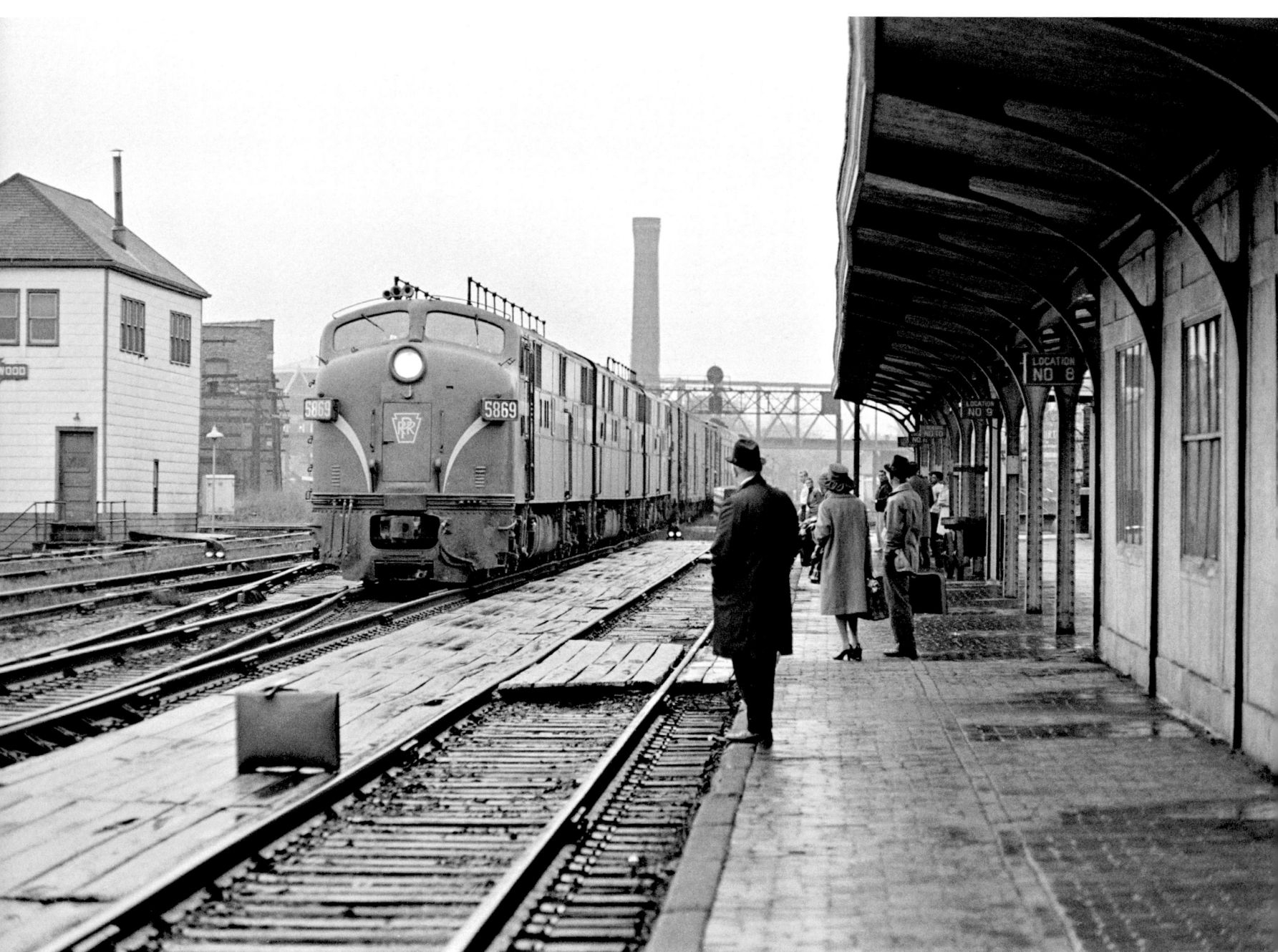

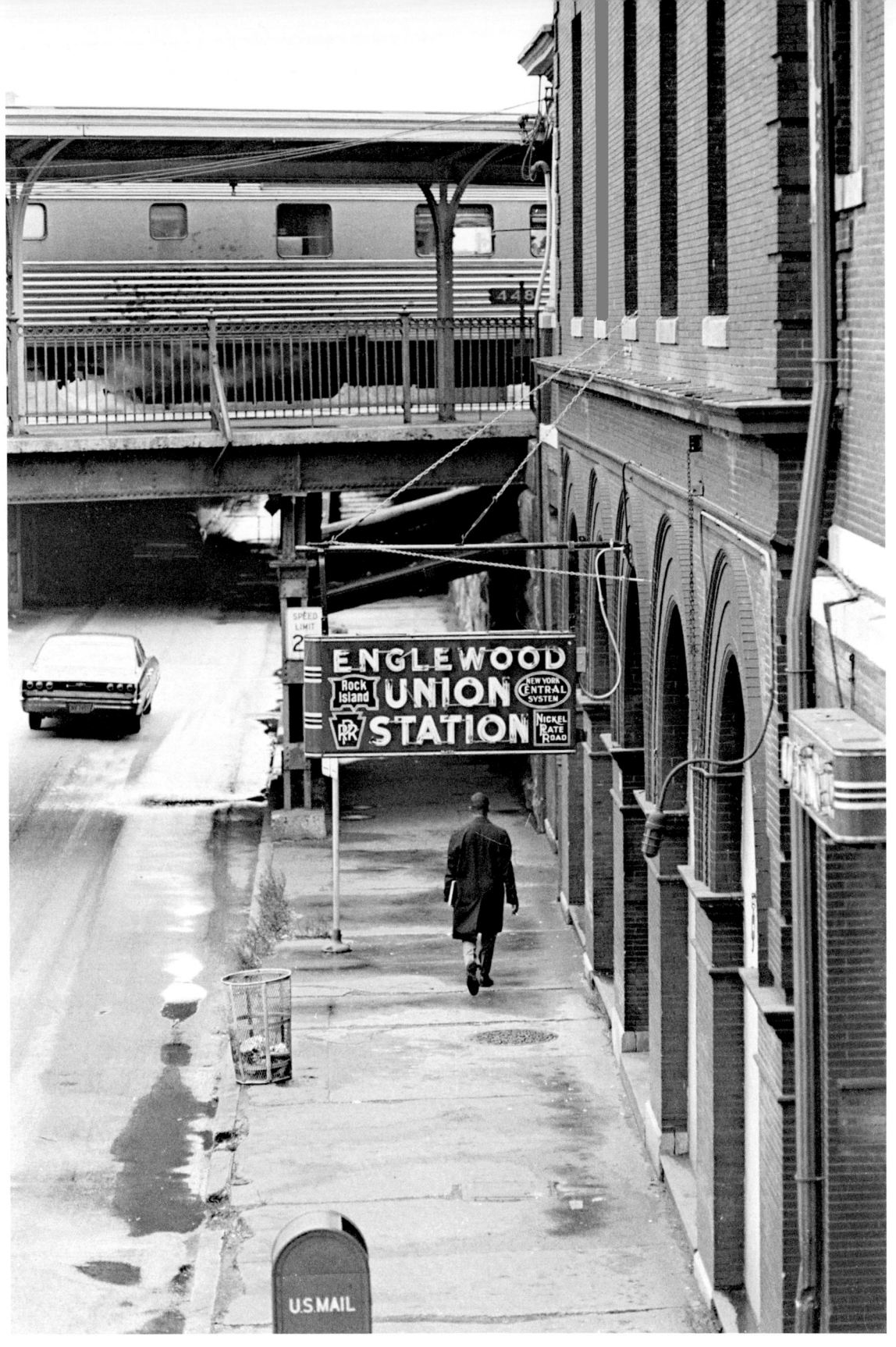

A lone pedestrian walks east along 63rd Street, passing Englewood Union Station and about to go under a New York Central passenger train. The view looks east from the platform serving the Rock Island; the Pennsylvania tracks were on the other side of the station to the right. Trains of the fourth railroad, the Nickel Plate, used the NYC tracks. The station was a convenient place for making connections just outside of downtown, but it was closed and demolished in the 1970s. Metra commuter and Amtrak intercity passenger trains still pass through Englewood, but they no longer stop here.

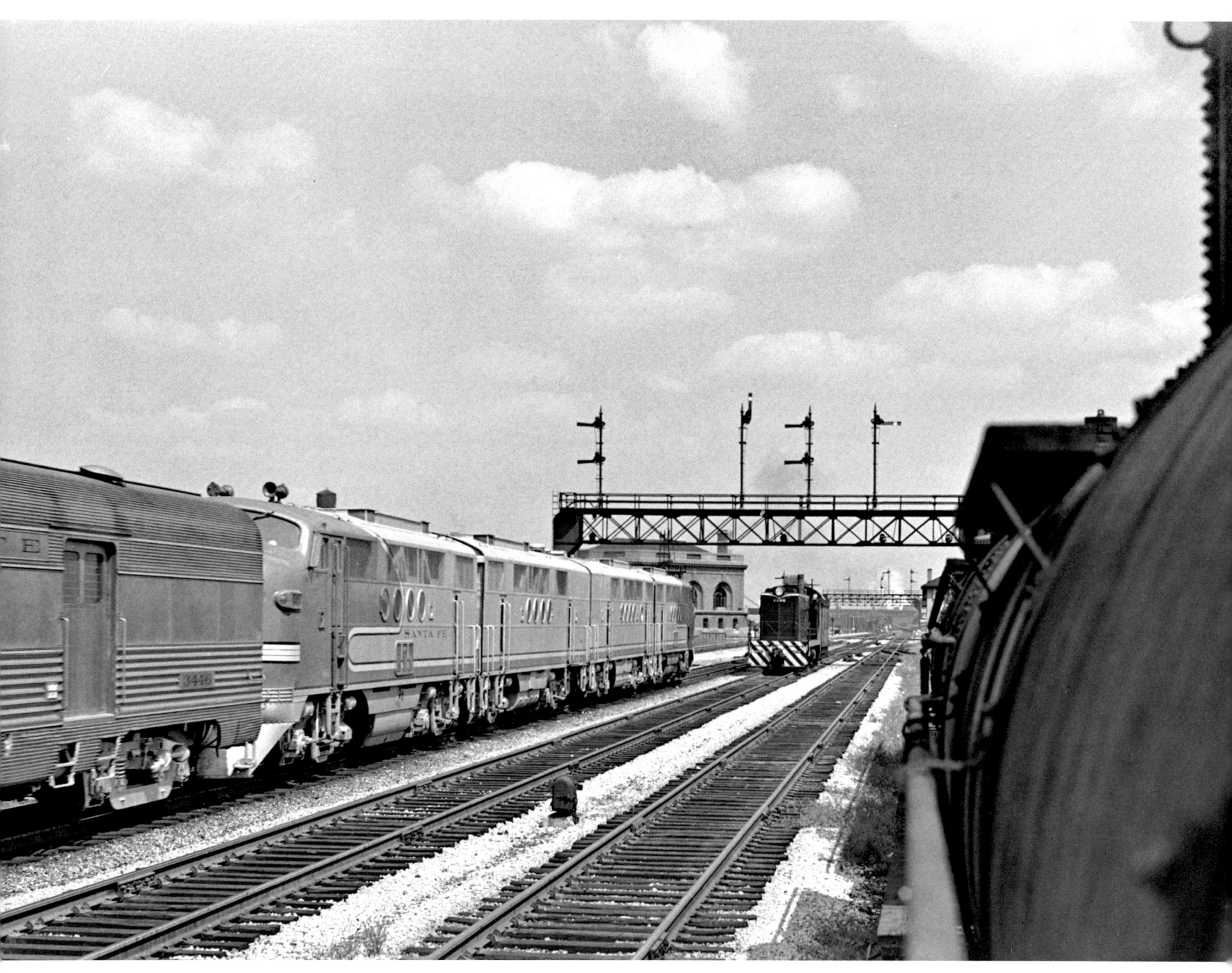

FIVE

CLASS BY ITSELF

Located forty miles southwest of Chicago, the busy junction of Joliet, Illinois, was one of Abbey's favorite places for photography in the late 1940s and early 1950s. The Santa Fe's main line to California crossed the Rock Island at grade in front of Joliet Union Station, and the mix of infrastructure, people, and heavy train traffic offered myriad photographic opportunities. In this view from a tank car in a freight train, Santa Fe's eastbound passenger train no. 20, the FT-powered *Chief* from Los Angeles, accepts a clear, "high-arm" semaphore signal at the Rock Island crossing and moves toward the station while a switcher waits on an adjacent track.

WALLY ABBEY KNEW HIS WAY AROUND THE STEAM LOCOMOTIVE, and his photography proved it. Whether it was a 4-8-4 roaring across the prairie or an 0-8-0 shuffling cars in a freight yard, he depicted the iron horse with perception and insight. He reveled in the sensations of being around steam—the hiss of air compressors, the smell of rod grease, the heat from a boiler—and he loved to portray the men who made it all happen.

But Abbey was never an antiquarian, not as a professional railroader, and certainly not as a photographer. In that influential salon of trailblazing photographers in the November 1955 issue of *Trains* magazine, Abbey even made a point of it in a statement attributed to him: "The dieselization of the railroads is merely a means and not an end—a means of keeping the railroads abreast ... of continuing change in the world of trade and transportation. Having dieselized, if a railroad then ceases to modernize and to change, it might as well pull up its rails."

That was Abbey: rational, clear-eyed, optimistic. It informed his photography, and it informed his career. Unlike many of his camera-carrying contemporaries in the late 1940s and early '50s, he embraced the diesel.

That's also why his favorite locomotive undoubtedly was the Electro-Motive FT, the pioneering diesel-electric that in a few short years changed the course of railroading. Introduced in 1939 as the 5,400-horsepower, four-unit demonstrator No. 103, the FT successfully made the case for standardized, mass-produced motive power on its historic barnstorming tour of several railroads. But for World War II putting locomotive development largely on hold, the FT might have led to steam's extinction even sooner than the mid-1950s. Abbey's friend David P. Morgan, editor of *Trains*, put the first FT in perspective in the November 1965 issue of his magazine: "No. 103 was the biggest change in railroading since the air brake."

Abbey came by his own appreciation of the FT honestly, with oil under his fingernails to prove it. There was his summer job in 1944, at age sixteen, working as a diesel repairman's helper for the Santa Fe at 21st Street. The young high school kid earned a princely eighty-two cents an hour, eighty-four cents if he did the job of oiler. He usually worked the second trick, 3 to 11 p.m., officially on a schedule of seven days per week, but usually only five or six.

The shop was there to perform running repairs on Santa Fe's passenger locomotives, mostly Electro-Motive E1 and E3 models in the railroad's new "Warbonnet" paint scheme. The gleaming red-and-silver racehorses ran out of Dearborn Station, only a couple of miles or so north of the shop. For a budding diesel fan, it was the perfect apprenticeship.

The work could be difficult, as Abbey recalled. "Mostly, I carried the diesel repairman's toolbox, or turned over the big diesel engines for piston-ring tests by standing on a long steel bar inserted in the flywheel, my back against the locomotive's ceiling, or applied various kinds of lubricants where they were needed. It was hard, hot, dirty work. But I enjoyed it."

He also wasn't satisfied to learn only what his narrow job required. He submersed himself in textbooks by John Draney, published by the American Technical Society, a Chicago-based organization that at the time was devoted to helping industrial workers in the war effort. Draney's two volumes from 1943, *Diesel Locomotives: Electrical Equipment* and *Diesel Locomotives: Mechanical Equipment*, became bedtime reading for the young railroader and fed his relentless curiosity. "I'm sure I annoyed others in the shop with my questions."

Then came a formative experience. One day in 1945, he got word that the 167, one of Santa Fe's first FTs, had made a rare visit to Chicago. And he'd missed it! In their early years, the FTs stayed way west, mostly working the desert territory between Winslow, Arizona, and Barstow, California, where they could make the best case for supplanting steam. But that September some of them began showing up around Chicago.

Abbey recalled his first sighting on the southwest side. "The diesel, we'd been given to understand, was out in Arizona, winning the war against Japan, that we'd actually seen only in the literature of the time—unexpectedly, that magic, mystical machine had materialized out of the mists of McCook!"

Over the next few years, Abbey would photograph the FTs as often as he could. But the diesels were an elusive quarry, and Abbey's nascent journalism career would begin taking him in different directions. By the early 1950s, the FTs were giving way to newer locomotives such as the F3 and the GP7 hood unit, and the last FT was retired by Santa Fe in 1966. In his early 1950s travels for *Trains*, though, he did get a chance to shoot FTs on the North Western, Burlington, and Erie.

Decades after he photographed the FTs, Abbey turned to them once again, this time to write what he likely considered his most important book, *Class By Itself*, an exhaustive history of the first FTs on the Santa Fe. Alas, the book never saw publication; the huge manuscript awaits the ministrations of a capable editor willing to finish what Wally Abbey started. But even in its unpublished form, Abbey got down on paper what he thought was one of railroading's essential stories.

"If it weren't for progress in dieseldom," he wrote, "there would be no railroads to enjoy at all. But here and now, and sounding quite like a railfan, I want to declare that if there is an all-time classic diesel-electric locomotive—classic much more for how it played its designated role than for how interesting it might have been to the locomotive-watcher—it is the Santa Fe's 100-class FT."

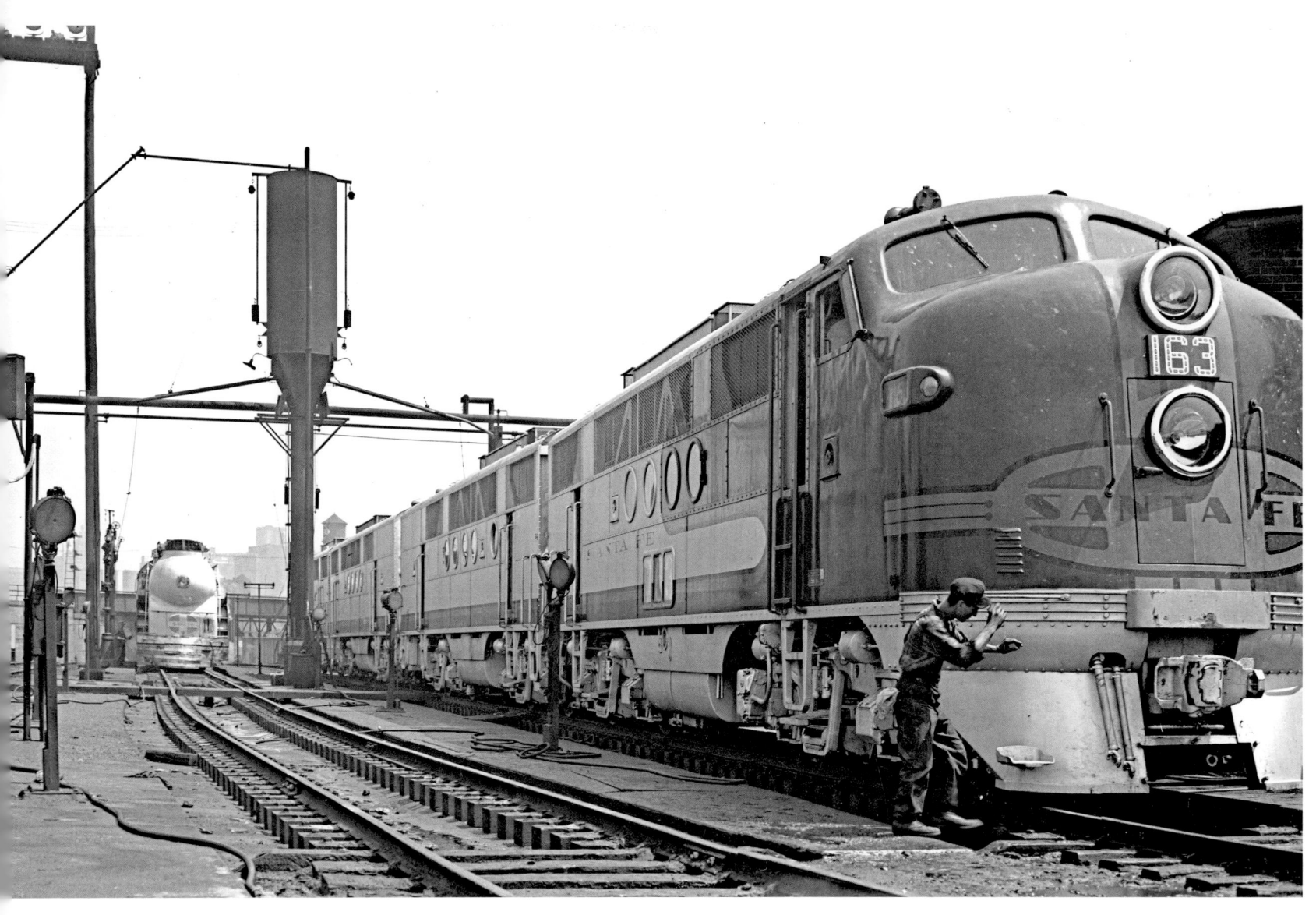

A worker at Santa Fe's 18th Street Roundhouse in Chicago inspects FTA no. 163 in the summer of 1946. No. 3460, the railroad's only streamlined steam locomotive, stands in the distance beyond the sanding towers. The early success of Electro-Motive's diesels on the railroad's premier passenger trains contributed to the lack of streamlined Santa Fe steam power. As a high school student, Abbey had spent the summer working at 18th Street two years earlier.

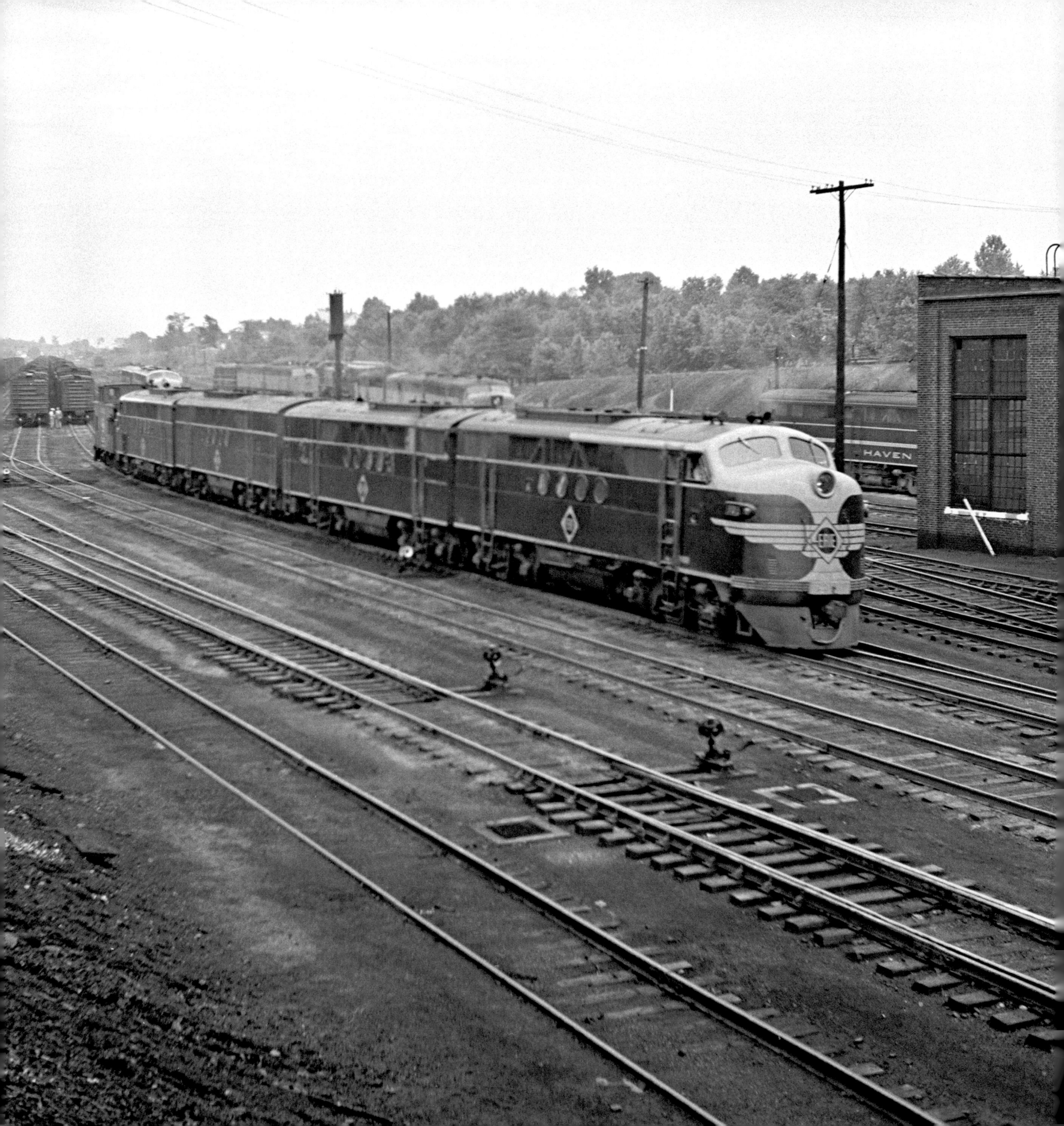

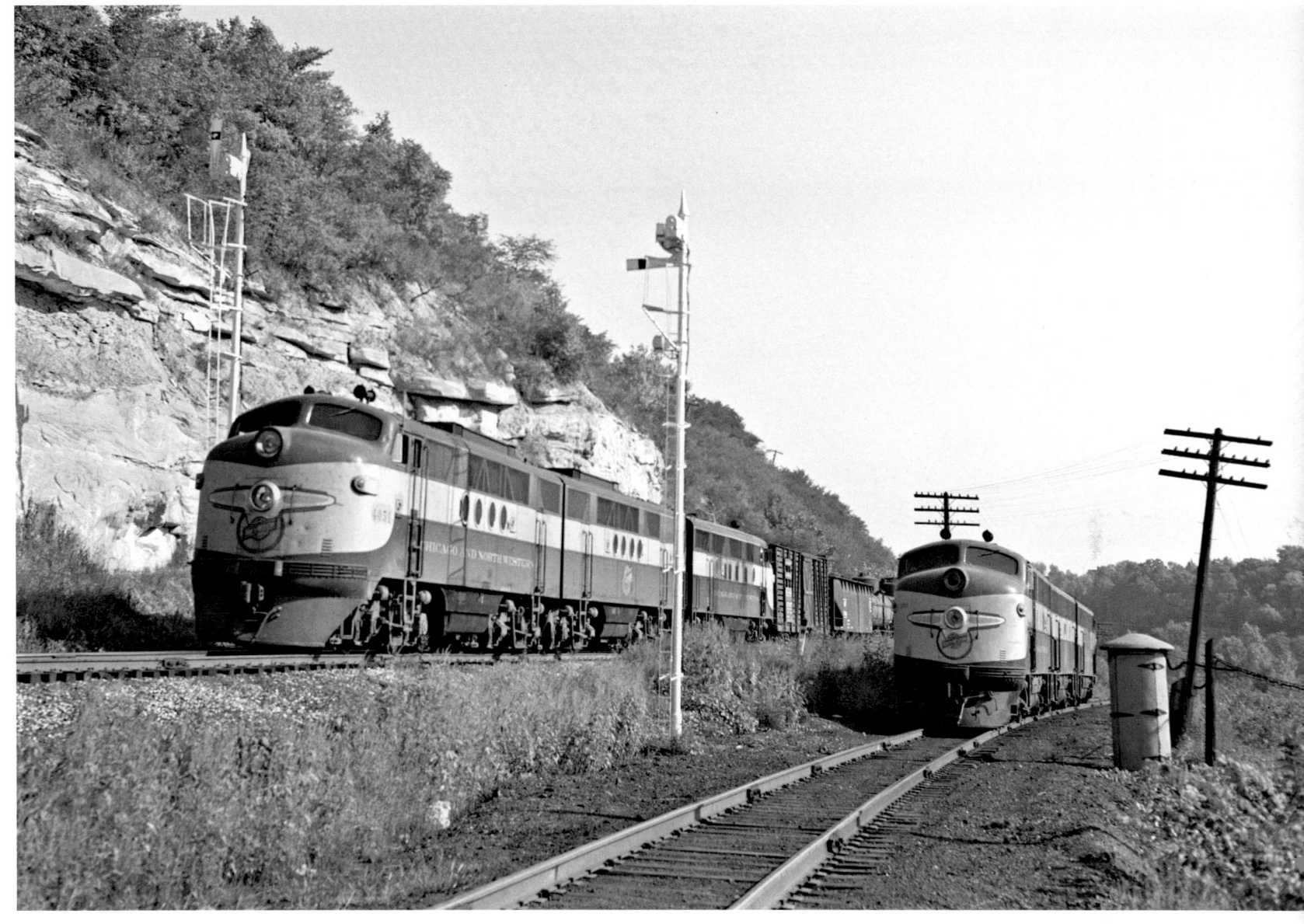

Facing: An A-B-B-A set of Erie Railroad FTs roll past the engine servicing facility at Maybrook, New York, in June of 1951. Maybrook was a major gateway for freight traffic moving between New England and the Mid-Atlantic. The New Haven came in from the east via the Poughkeepsie Bridge over the Hudson River and connected with the Erie; Lehigh & Hudson River; Lehigh & New England; New York, Ontario & Western; and New York Central. A fire closed the Poughkeepsie Bridge in 1974, and two years later all of the railroads were merged into Conrail. Today the only trace of the once-massive Maybrook Yard is a single running track at the edge of the property.

Above: To climb out of the Illinois River valley going north from Peoria, the Chicago & North Western used helper locomotives throughout the steam era and into the early diesel era. Abbey's photograph of this operation at Kickapoo Junction, Illinois, in 1949, allows a comparison of F-units. On the left, an A-B pair of FTs and an F3A arrive with a northbound freight; on the right, an A-B-A set of F3s waits to assist the train up the grade to Radnor.

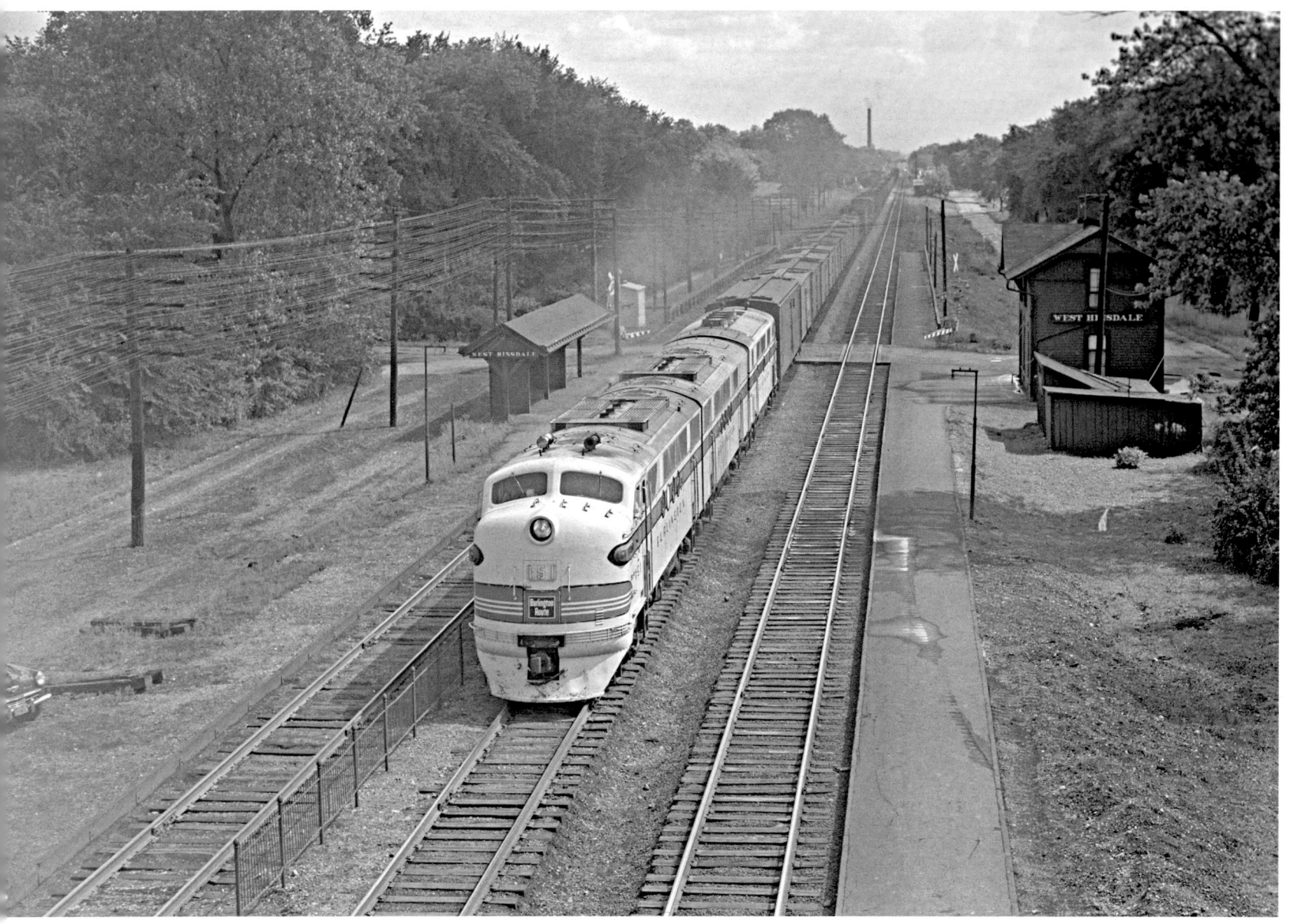

Above: An A-B pair of Chicago, Burlington & Quincy FTs leads an F3A on a freight charging down the middle of the Burlington's "Racetrack" through West Hinsdale, Illinois, in 1949. The three-track main line was—and is—a place for fast and frequent freight and passenger trains coming in and out of Chicago. This westbound has a large block of ice-cooled reefers behind the power—quite possibly filled with meat from the Windy City's sprawling Union Stock Yards.

Facing: Veteran Santa Fe engineer in the cab of FTA diesel locomotive no. 176 on a freight train in Arizona in 1953. While his name is lost, he surely spent most of his career running steam locomotives and, like many railroaders, took great pride in his appearance. While many "old heads" mourned the loss of steam engines and the craftsmanship of operating them, the cleaner diesels made spotless overalls and jackets much easier. Abbey was riding in the cab while on assignment for his "Super Railroad" story about the Santa Fe in *Trains* magazine.

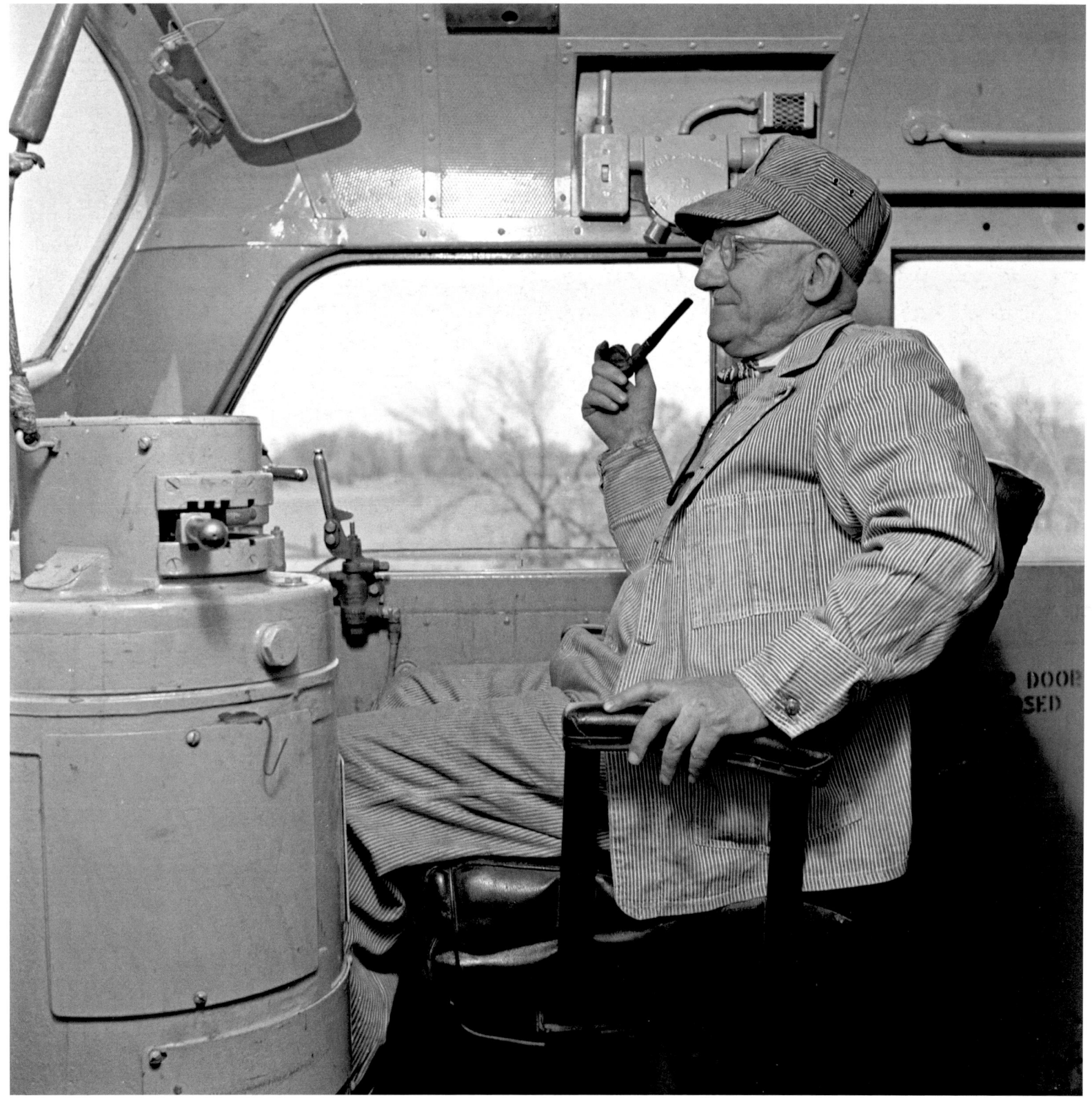

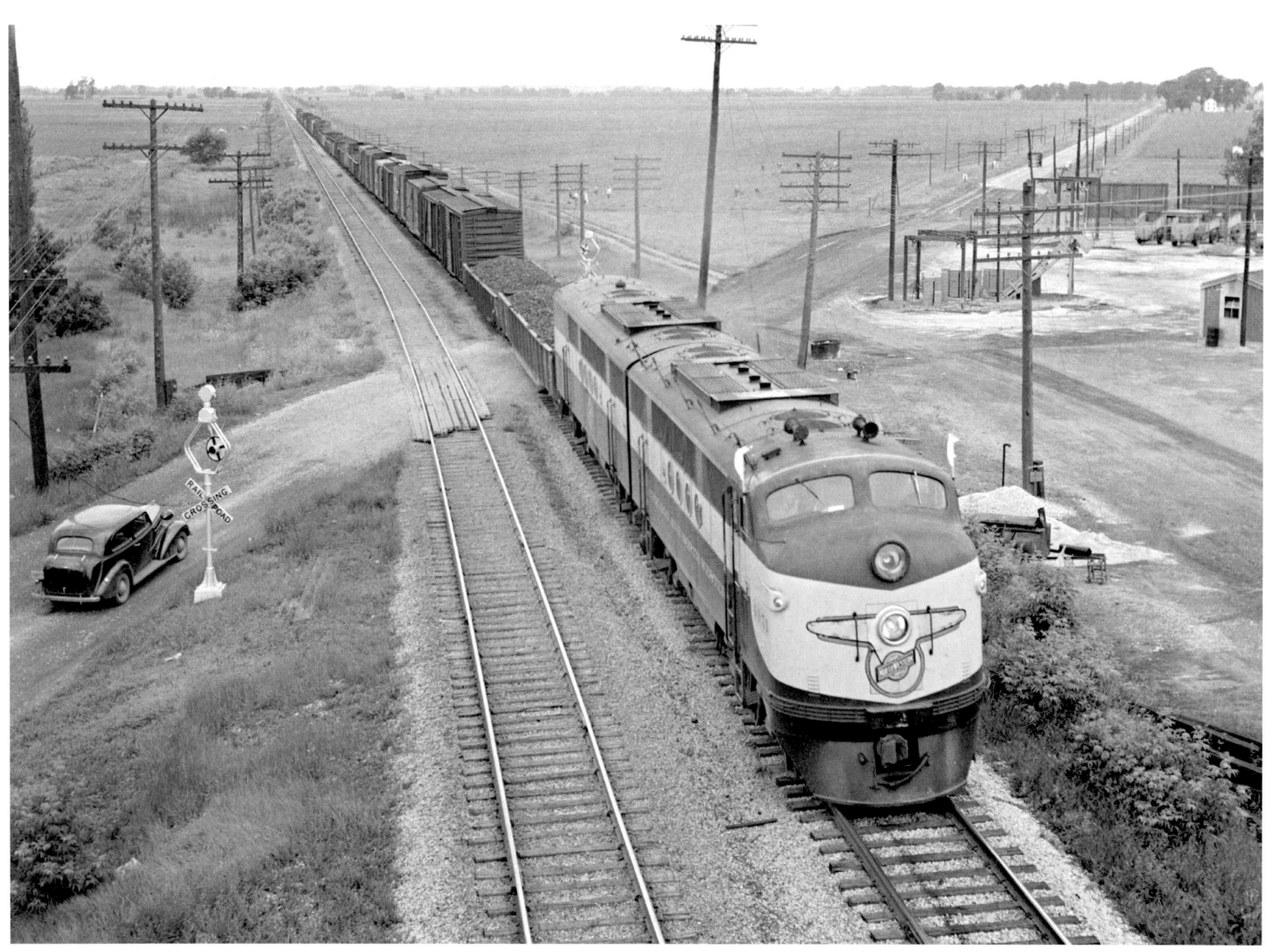

Above: Chicago & North Western FTA-B nos. 4051 and 4051B approach Rochelle, Illinois, with an eastbound freight train on June 20, 1948. The C&NW crossed the Burlington at Rochelle, which is even busier today as a crossing of the Union Pacific and BNSF Railway, respectively. This train is passing through what is today Union Pacific's Global 3 intermodal facility. Note the wig-wag crossing signal protecting the two-lane road.

Facing: The first section of Santa Fe train no. 7, the westbound *Fast Mail Express*, passes Turner, Kansas, on its way out of the Kansas City area on June 4, 1948. FTA no. 168 leads an A-B-B-A consist of locomotives. Train no. 7 and its eastbound counterpart, no. 8, handled express freight and mail between Chicago and Los Angeles. When business was heavy, they operated in multiple sections, as was the case on this day.

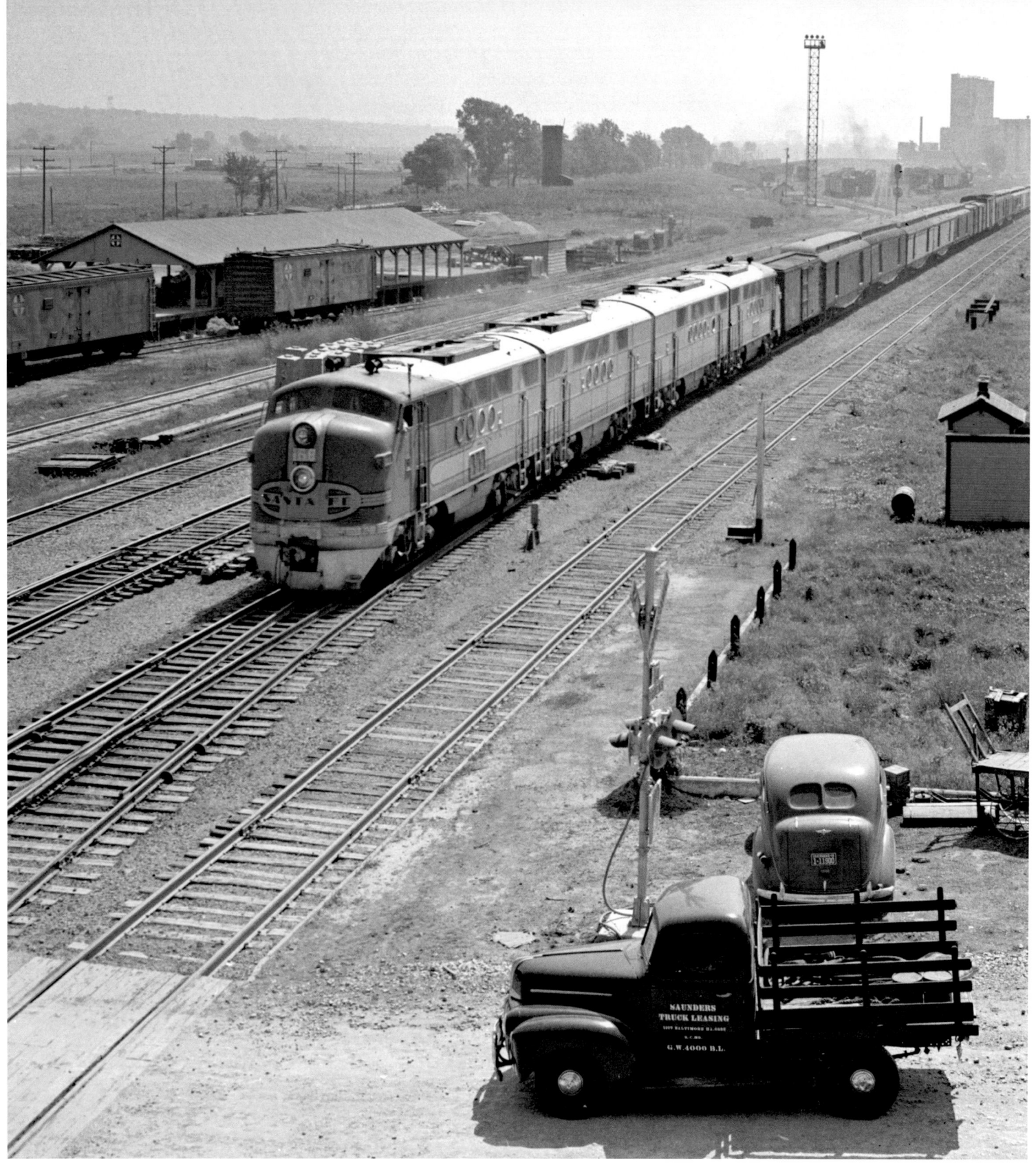

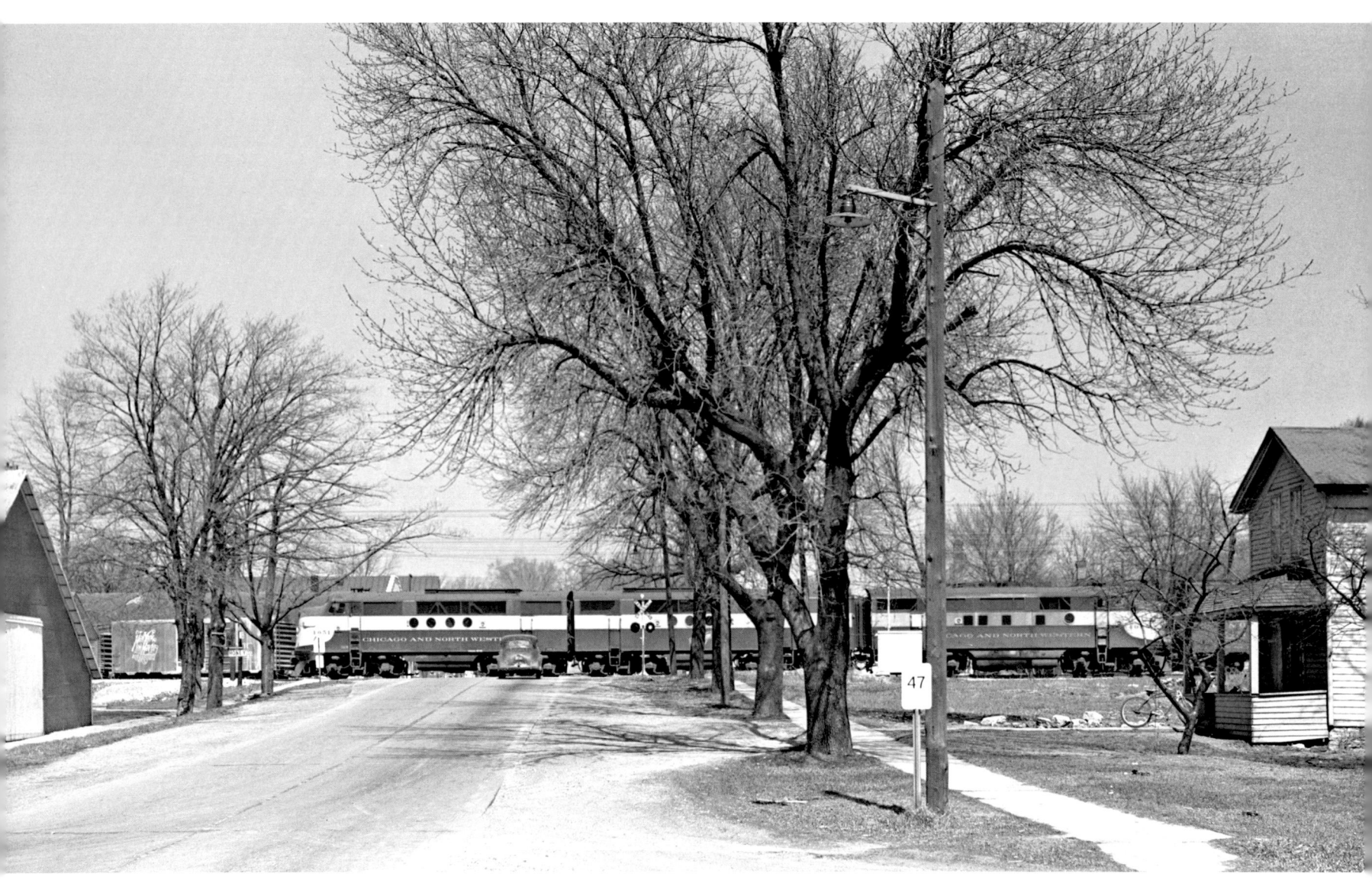

Chicago & North Western westbound freight train no. 381 for St. Louis crossing Main Street in Elburn, Illinois, on April 12, 1949. FT locomotives nos. 4051 and 4051B lead F3A no. 4055 with a train Abbey recorded as having 39 loaded cars and 48 empties, weighing 3,000 tons.

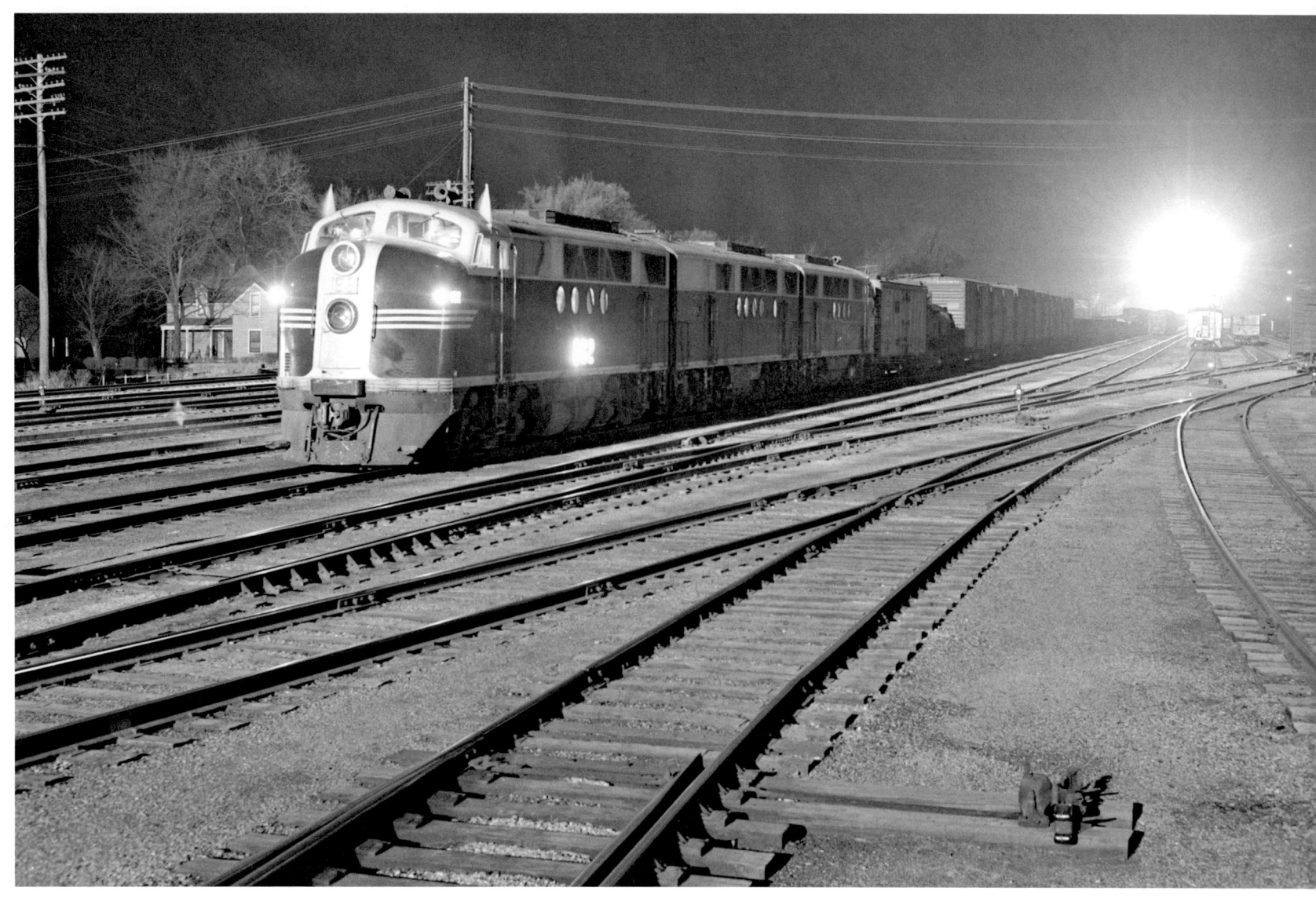

Santa Fe "time freight" no. 86, an eastbound train led by an A-B-A set of FTs, prepares to depart Chanute, Kansas, for Argentine Yard in Kansas City on a calm night in 1950. The first two units are among the relatively few FTs that were modified for passenger service. Note the second headlight, additional hoses flanking the coupler, the removable plate on the pilot covering the steam line, and the steam generator stack on the B unit. Located just north of Cherryvale, home of Abbey's maternal grandparents, Chanute was not on the Santa Fe's main line to California, but could still see heavy freight traffic at times.

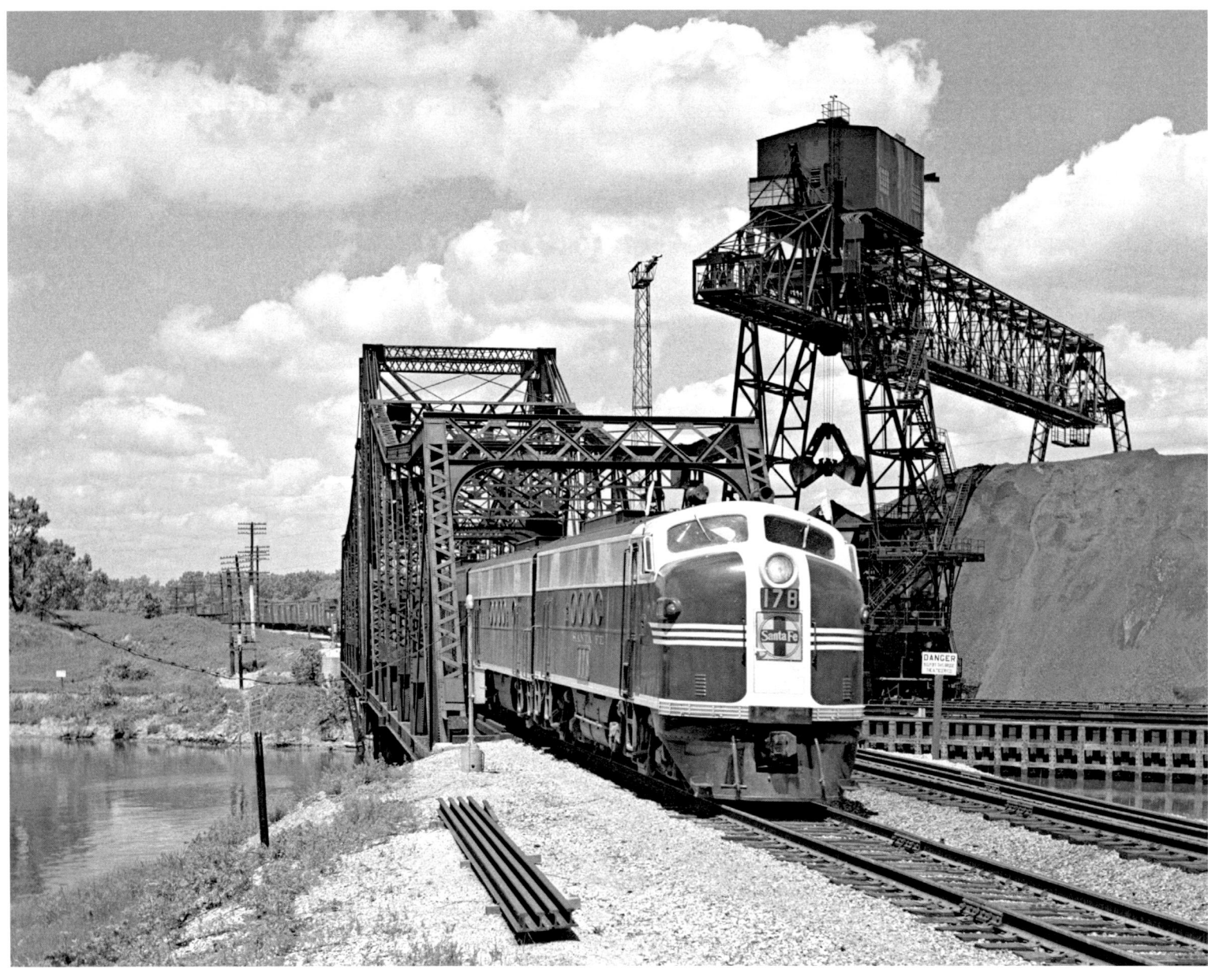

Above: Eastbound Santa Fe freight train crossing the Chicago Sanitary & Ship Canal at Berwyn, Illinois, on June 1, 1952. The 28-mile canal system opened in 1900, reversing the flow of the main stem of the Chicago River and sending it down the Des Plaines and Illinois rivers to the Mississippi. The main reason for the canal was to divert sewage out of Lake Michigan, source of Chicago's drinking water. The canal also replaced the earlier Illinois & Michigan Canal for navigation—the reason that Santa Fe's bridge is a swing design, pivoting on its center pier to allow vessels to pass.

Facing: Santa Fe no. 175 joins several other FTs and a set of F7s—the latter in the railroad's "Warbonnet" color scheme for passenger trains—by the coaling and sanding towers at Argentine Yard in Kansas City in the spring of 1953. A single steam locomotive, 4-6-2 no. 3427, is in the distance at far left. Santa Fe received its first FTs in the winter of 1940–41; a dozen years later, they had helped to almost completely replace steam on the railroad. The last steam operations for regular service on the Santa Fe occurred just four years later.

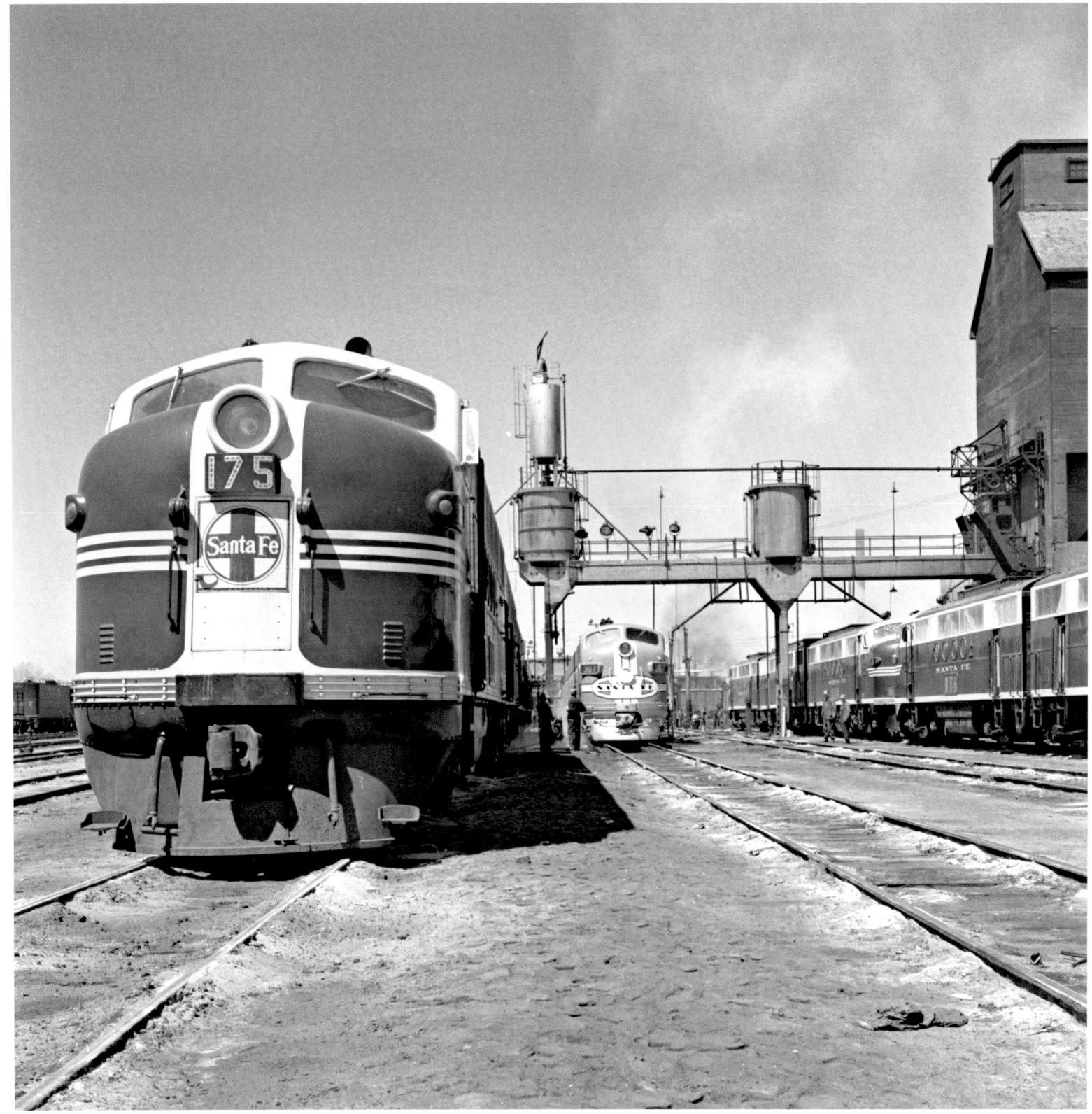

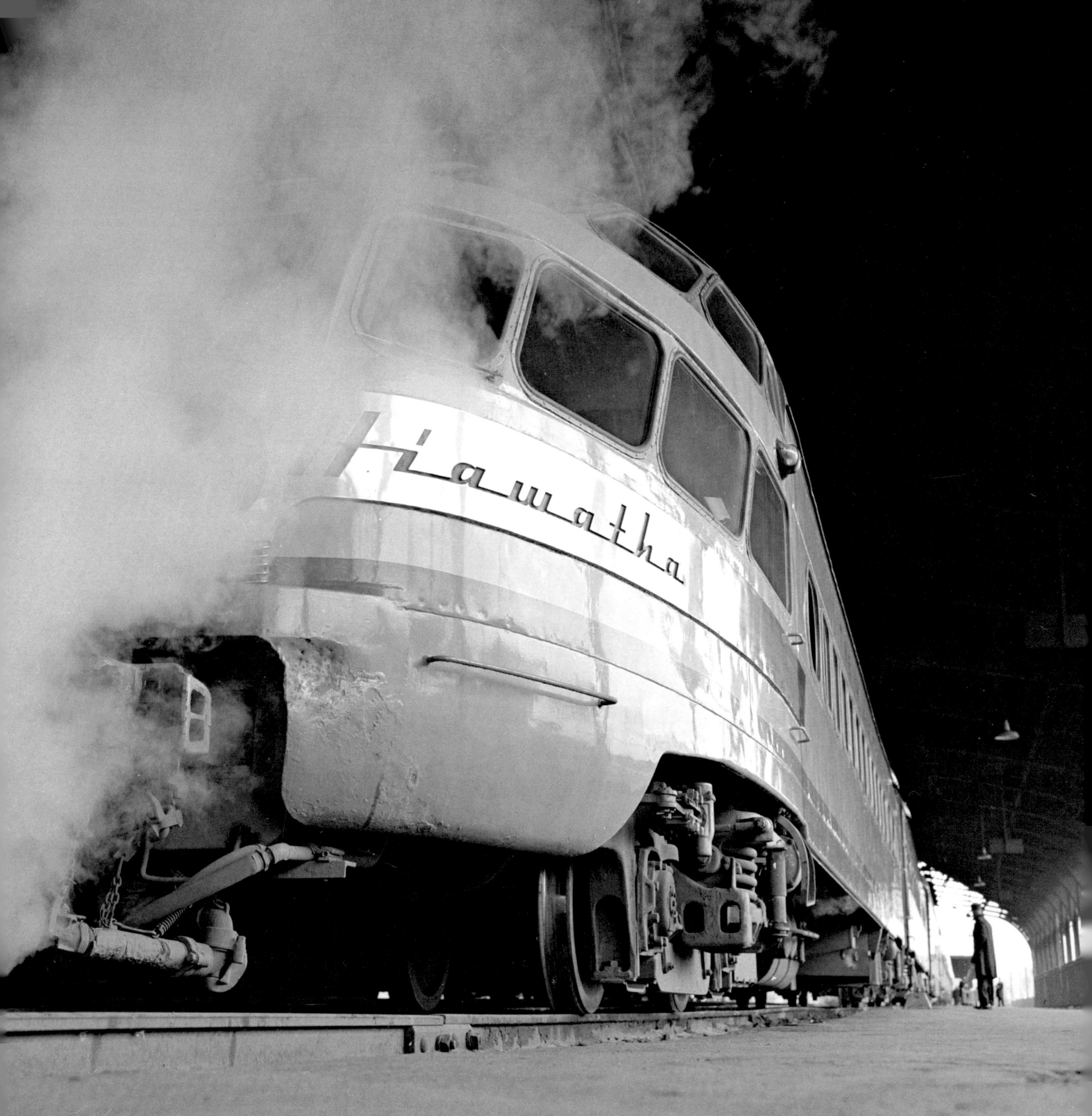

SIX

FIGHTING FOR THE MILWAUKEE ROAD

Facing: Steam from the train's heating line envelopes the Skytop parlor-observation car of the *Afternoon Hiawatha*, standing beneath the Minneapolis train shed ready to depart for Chicago on October 24, 1969. The train would make its final run just three months later. The depot closed in 1971 after Amtrak took over the Milwaukee Road's remaining passenger operations. While many of the nation's great train stations were demolished, this one is now a hotel. Even the train shed still stands to provide covered parking and, in the winter, shelter for a skating rink.

EVEN IF THE MILWAUKEE ROAD WASN'T WALLY ABBEY'S favorite railroad, you might have thought otherwise based on the body of work he created once he arrived at *Trains* magazine in 1950. From the magazine's office on the north edge of downtown Milwaukee, Abbey ranged across a railroad empire that often dominated the city's landscape.

Abbey's timing was perfect. The Milwaukee Road was flying high. It was the era of the *Hiawatha*s, the railroad's celebrated orange-and-maroon streamliners, new versions of which debuted in 1948. The Milwaukee was locked in a fierce battle with its key rivals for the Chicago–Twin Cities passenger trade, the North Western's *400*s and the Burlington's *Zephyr*s, and Abbey's newly adopted city was in the middle of the action.

A favorite vantage point was the Everett Street passenger station, a brooding, gothic rock pile a few blocks south of the *Trains* office. Behind the building, a lofty train shed was accessible at each end by sweeping curves of track, hemmed in by surface streets on all sides. For the photographer, it was a vantage point loaded with potential, and Abbey made the most of it, contrasting the sleek, modern *Hiawatha*s with a vintage cityscape looming beyond the platforms.

There was plenty more for Abbey to shoot. Just a mile or so west of the depot, the railroad's West Milwaukee shops sprawled across the bottom of the Menomonee River Valley, a vast panorama of freight yards, locomotive and car repair shops, office buildings, and two roundhouses, all easily visible from the 35th Street viaduct. Over the years Abbey also ranged far from the railroad's operating headquarters, photographing Milwaukee Road passenger and freight trains in the Chicago region and, later during his Soo Line years, in and around the Twin Cities.

Then there was the Beer Line, an Abbey favorite. This industrial branch reached down into Milwaukee from the north, hugging the west side of the Milwaukee River until it fanned out across a narrow corridor near downtown to serve the team tracks of the Schlitz, Pabst, and Blatz breweries, as well as several tanneries. The Beer Line was a singular stretch of railroad, emblematic of the city. An idiosyncratic fleet of exotic Alco and Fairbanks Morse diesel switchers tended its tangle of sidings, and the air smelled of malt and rendering. Abbey returned to photograph this quirky stretch of railroad again and again.

Abbey left Milwaukee in 1954 and moved back to Chicago for a job with the Association of Western Railways, but he sustained his ties to the Milwaukee Road, which was an association member. He got to know various company executives at countless meetings and conferences. Those contacts continued in his next job as a Midwest editor at *Railway Age*, and later in his public relations post at Soo Line, which shared much of the Milwaukee Road's territory.

Those contacts paid off in 1975. Abbey was a bit adrift, having difficulty drumming up new business for his Abbey Enterprises PR firm and, it seems, losing his passion for working for himself. He had closed an office he was renting and moved his work onto a desk in the basement at home. Then, he heard that the man handling Milwaukee Road's advertising and public relations was leaving. He knew Worthington Smith, then president of the railroad, and inquired about the position.

"Worth's reply to me was neither yes or no," recalled Abbey, who welcomed a move to 516 West Jackson in Chicago. "It was more like, 'When can you be here?' And so I assumed the new position of director of corporate communications for the Milwaukee Road. It wasn't evident, to me at least, but strenuous times were about to begin."

The strain was already showing on the company. By the mid-1970s the Milwaukee was locked in an existential financial struggle as traffic declined and a host of historical bad decisions began catching up on management, notably the railroad's money-losing Pacific Extension across Montana, Idaho, Washington, and into Seattle, opened in 1909. Deferred maintenance for track and locomotives had become obvious. The railroad's huge shop complex in Milwaukee was beginning to look rundown.

Abbey stepped into a public-relations situation that was equally problematic. "I had the responsibility for what had once been a sizable advertising campaign. But I had no advertising budget. I had a staff that on paper contained thirteen job positions, three of which were unoccupied. The Milwaukee was something of a laughing-stock in the railroad public relations trade." Still, he threw himself into the work, reporting directly to Smith and Chairman William J. Quinn.

Then came what Abbey called "the fateful, but not fatal, weekend," December 19, 1977, when the Milwaukee Road filed for bankruptcy. Suddenly Abbey was not only dealing with the usual challenges of running a railroad's corporate communications, but also explaining the railroad's troubles to key constituencies, not least of which was the bankruptcy court. He became a constant companion of the trustee, first Stanley E. G. Hillman and later Richard B. Ogilvie, both of whom believed the railroad's only salvation lay in abandoning the Pacific Extension and retrenching to a core Midwest system.

Abbey's responsibilities were weighty, but he embraced them. "The bankruptcy of the Milwaukee Road prompted continuous and nearly always erroneous assumptions, rumor, and misconstructions of fact," he later recalled. "To control the quality of the information output from his office, the Trustee appointed two official spokesmen: the president and me. The president was too busy at the time to be available very often. I thus became, in effect, the 'voice' of the reorganization process outside the courtroom."

It was a tough position to be in, but Abbey got high marks for performance under fire. Joseph A. Swanson, a professor at Northwestern University's Kellogg School of Management and a close observer of the Milwaukee debacle, admired his efforts. "Abbey was a guy who could put the best foot forward. The story was difficult to tell in a positive way, but that's exactly what he did."

Frustrating as the job likely became, Abbey still thought like a journalist. He knew he was uniquely qualified to document what

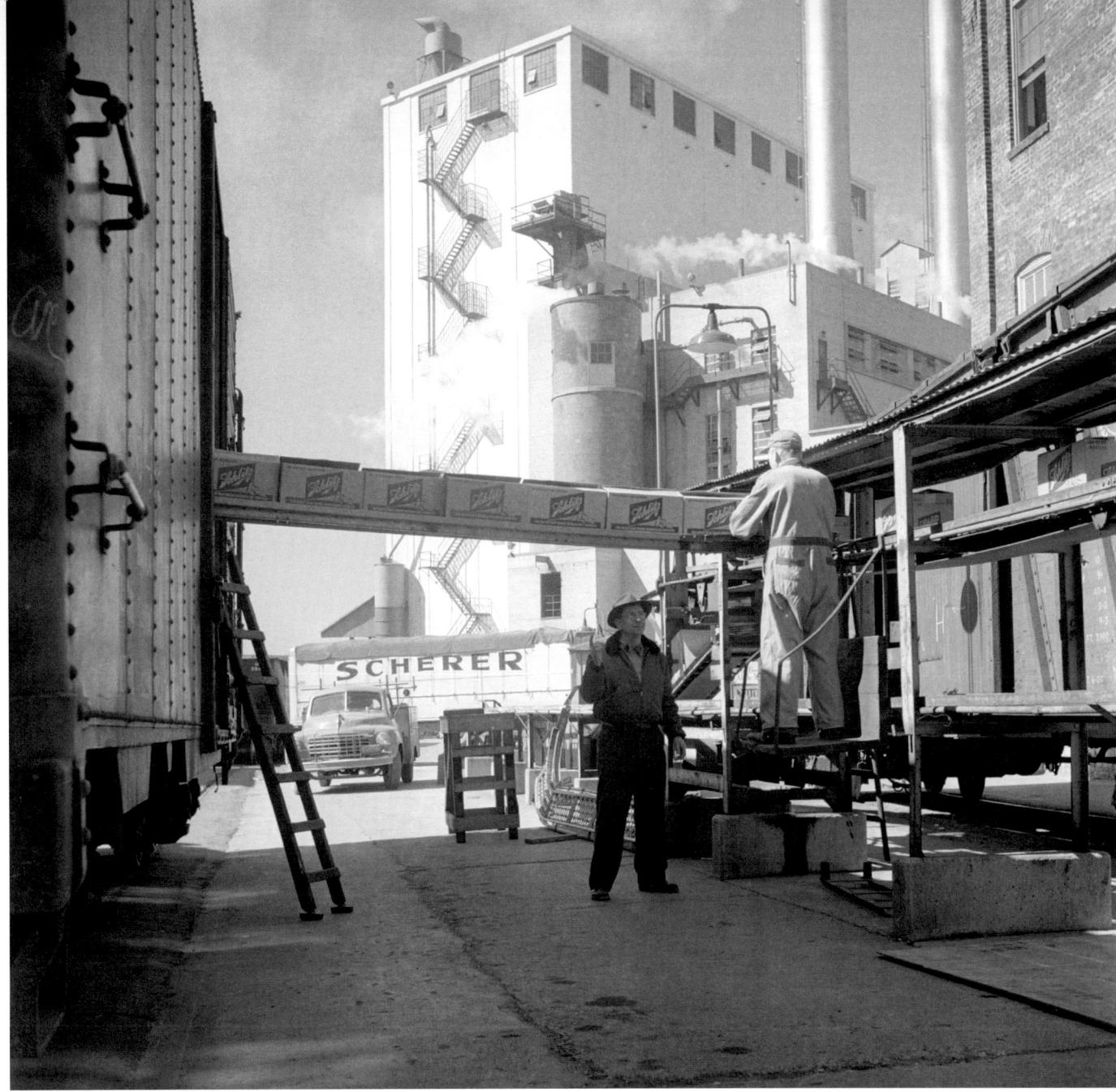

was happening, especially with his camera. Thus did he make a number of heartbreaking photographs of the railroad during a multiday inspection trip with the trustee, creating a sad record of worn-out diesels, deteriorating track, and the always-lovely scenery along the doomed Pacific Extension.

Years later, Abbey planned but never finished a book about the Milwaukee Road. Rarely the sentimentalist, he gave it the working title *Leaky Boat*.

Brewery workers load cases of beer into boxcars using roller conveyors at the Schlitz brewery in Milwaukee on April 7, 1952. When loaded, the cars will go out on the Milwaukee Road's "Beer Line," which also handled shipments to and from Pabst and Blatz. During the 1950s, the three breweries combined to ship out 50 cars of beer each day. Other industries on the line contributed another 50 daily cars, making this one of the railroad's most profitable branch lines.

Fighting for the Milwaukee Road

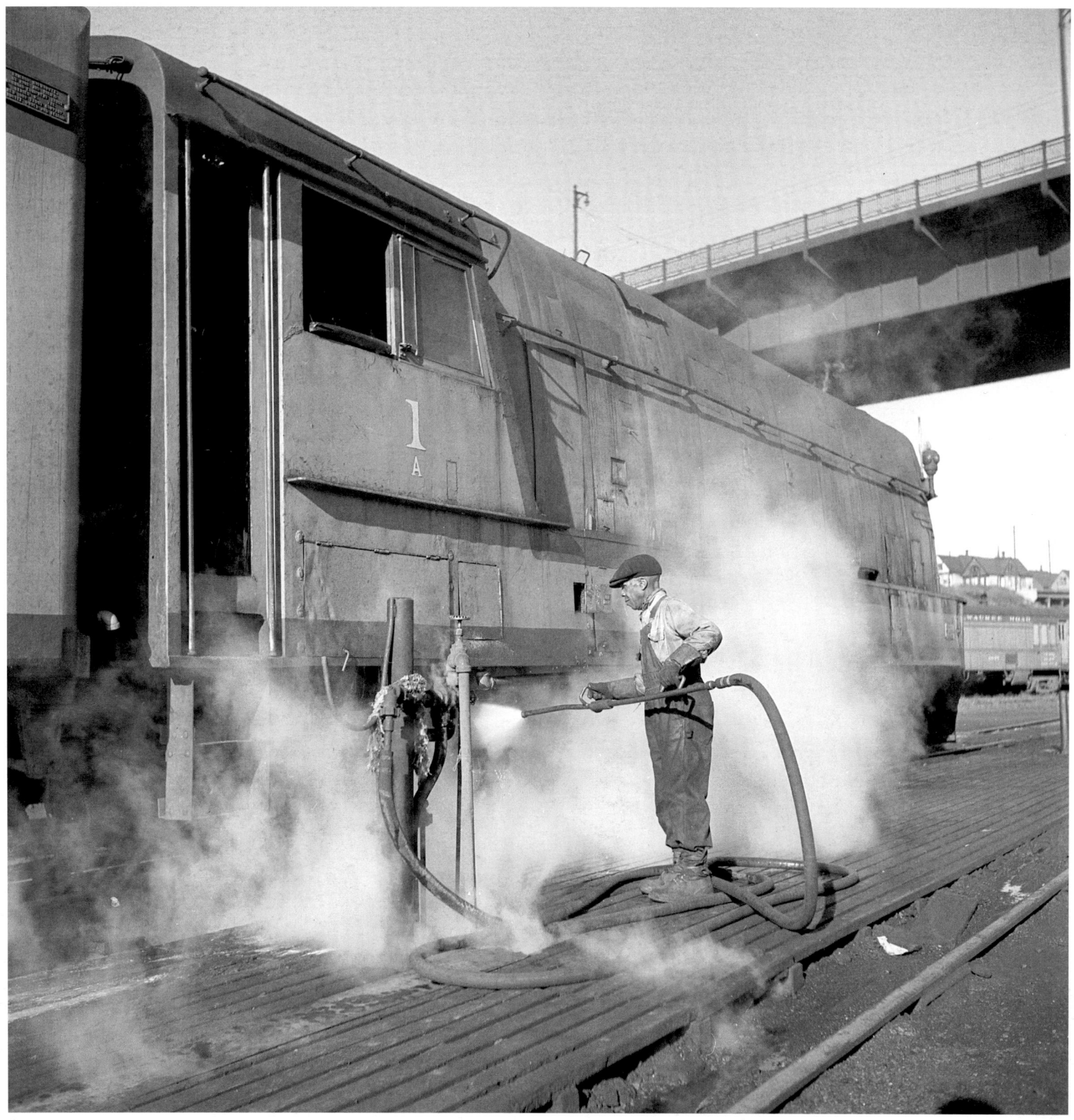

Facing: A Milwaukee Road worker steam cleans locomotive no. 1, a streamlined 4-4-2 from the railroad's inaugural *Hiawatha* passenger train of 1935, at the Milwaukee (Wisconsin) shops on October 9, 1951. As the *Hiawatha* trains became longer and heavier, the 4-4-2 locomotives were assigned to shorter (and still fast) local trains on such routes as Milwaukee to Madison, Wisconsin. No. 1 had little more than a year to go before it was retired from service, but the railroad still took pride in its appearance.

Below: The station clock shows 1:32 p.m. as a set of new Milwaukee Road diesel locomotives is about to pull out of Milwaukee, Wisconsin, with the *Morning Hiawatha* from Minneapolis. The train was scheduled to leave at 1:25 p.m. for the 85-mile, 75-minute nonstop trip to Chicago Union Station. In this era, the train would "make up time" and arrive in Chicago on time. The steam era is not yet over; a water column, to provide water for locomotive tenders, stands at the left.

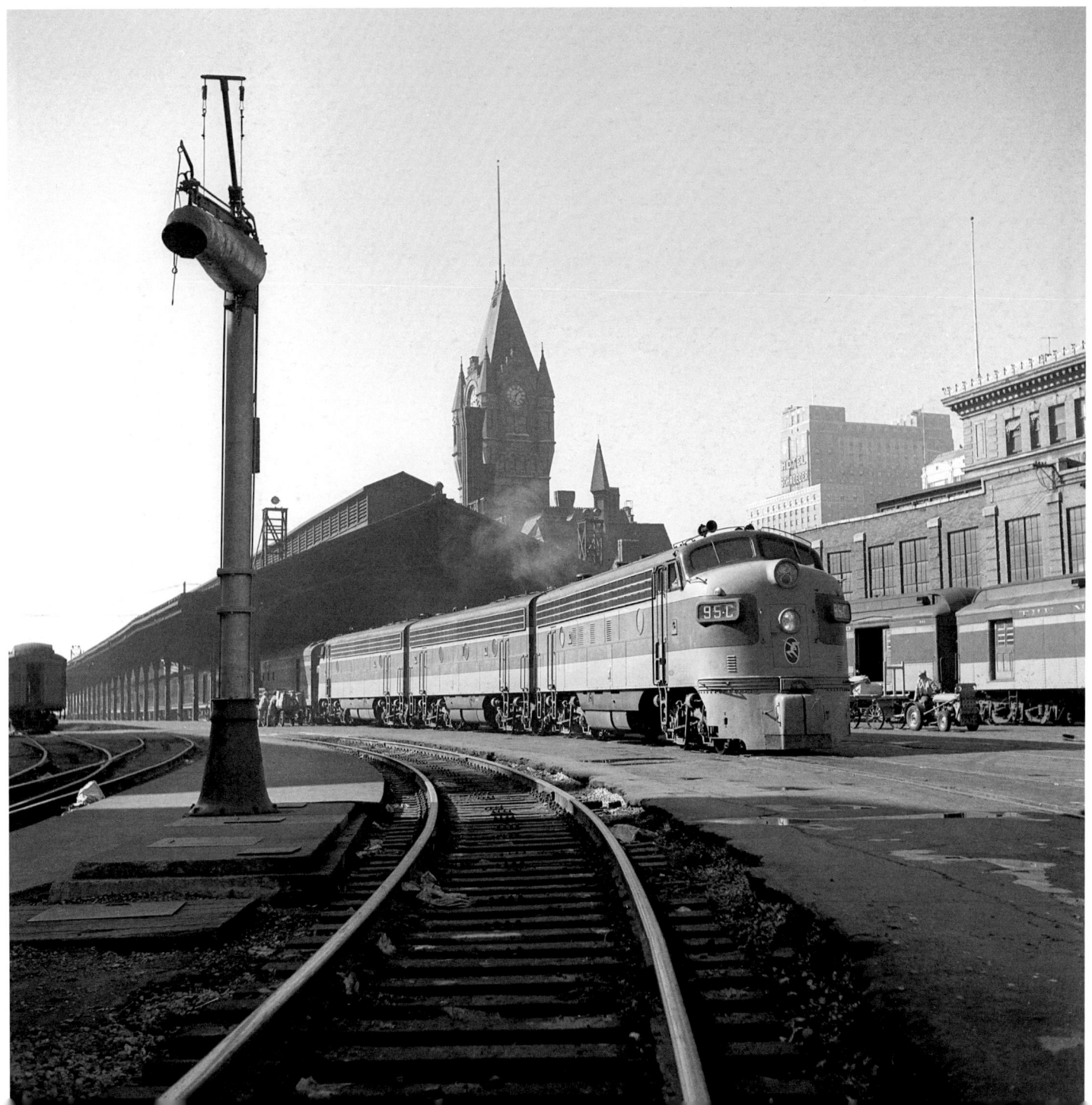

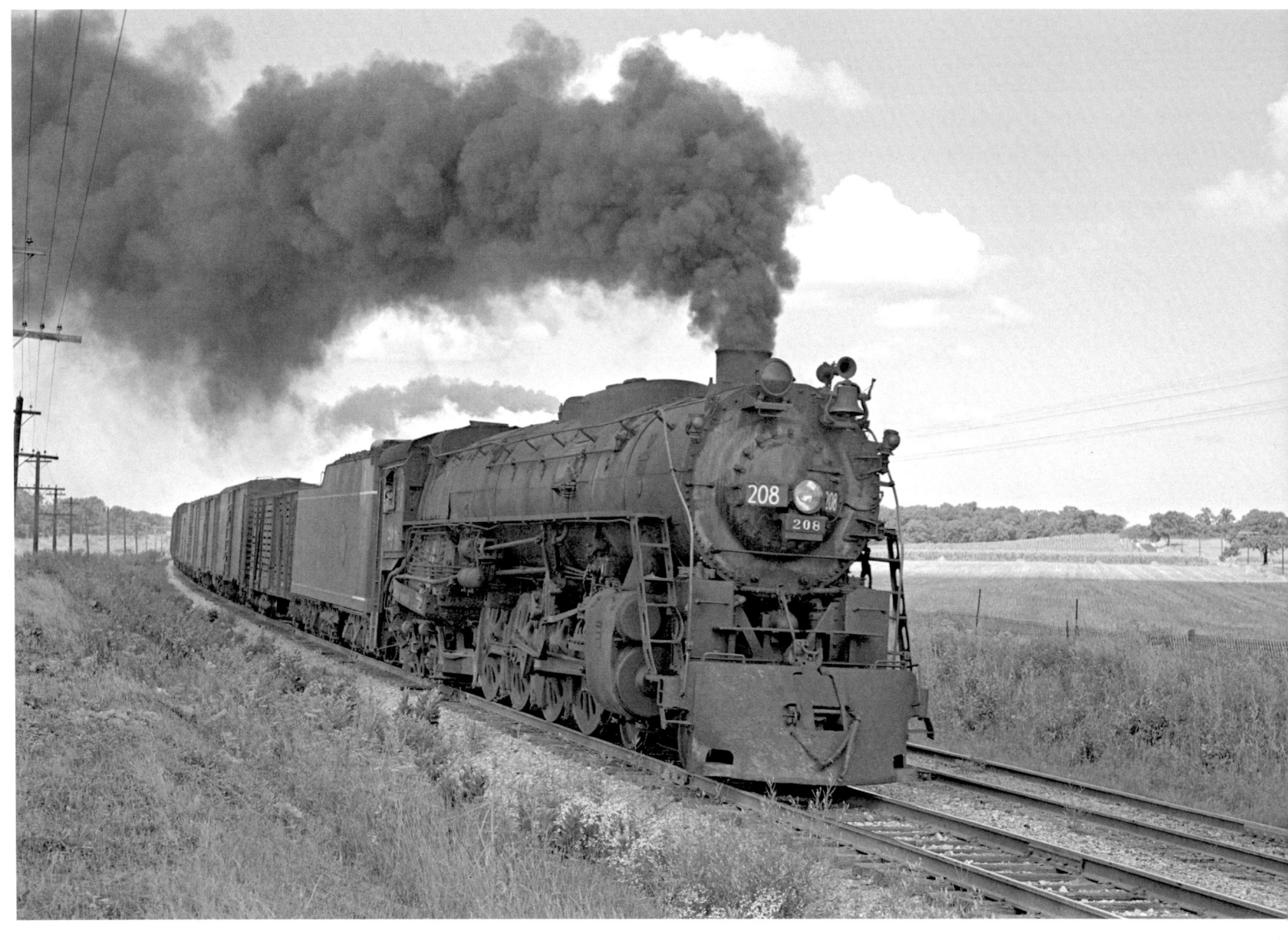

Above: Milwaukee Road S2-class 4-8-4 steam locomotive no. 208 leads an eastbound freight train through rolling farmland just outside of Elgin, Illinois, on August 5, 1948. The eleven-year-old locomotive was one of forty of the S2 class, designed in-house and built by the Baldwin Locomotive Works. The S2s typically handled freight trains between Bensenville Yard in Chicago and either Council Bluffs, Iowa, or St. Paul, Minnesota. They were actually slightly larger and more powerful than the later S3 class, to which well-traveled survivor no. 261 belongs.

Facing: Crossing the Elgin, Joliet & Eastern at Rondout, Illinois, Milwaukee Road 4-8-4 no. 221 leads a westbound extra freight train on October 14, 1955. Order boards for the EJ&E stand just beyond the locomotive, while the grade of the electric interurban Chicago North Shore & Milwaukee is visible in the background at far left.

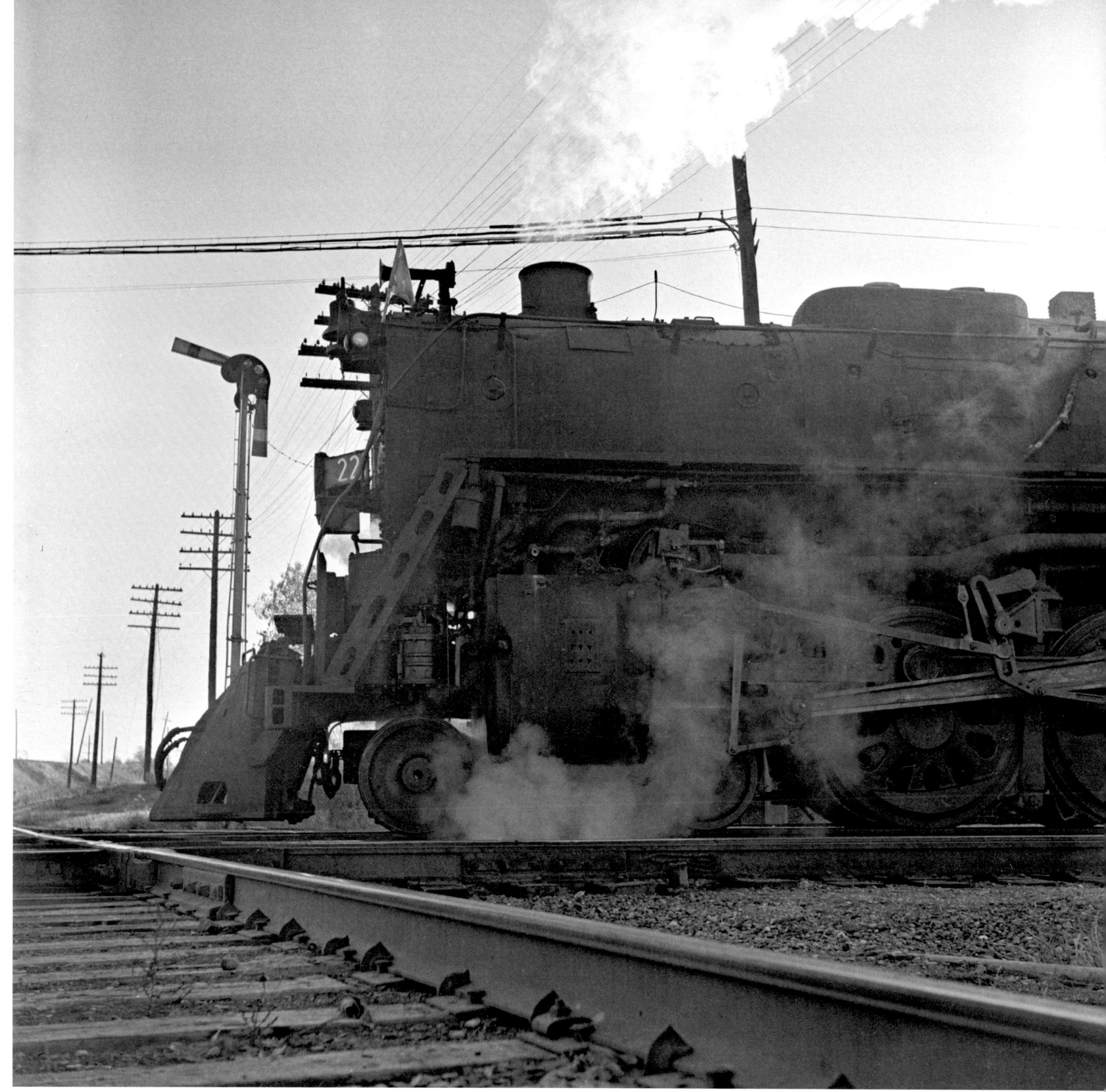

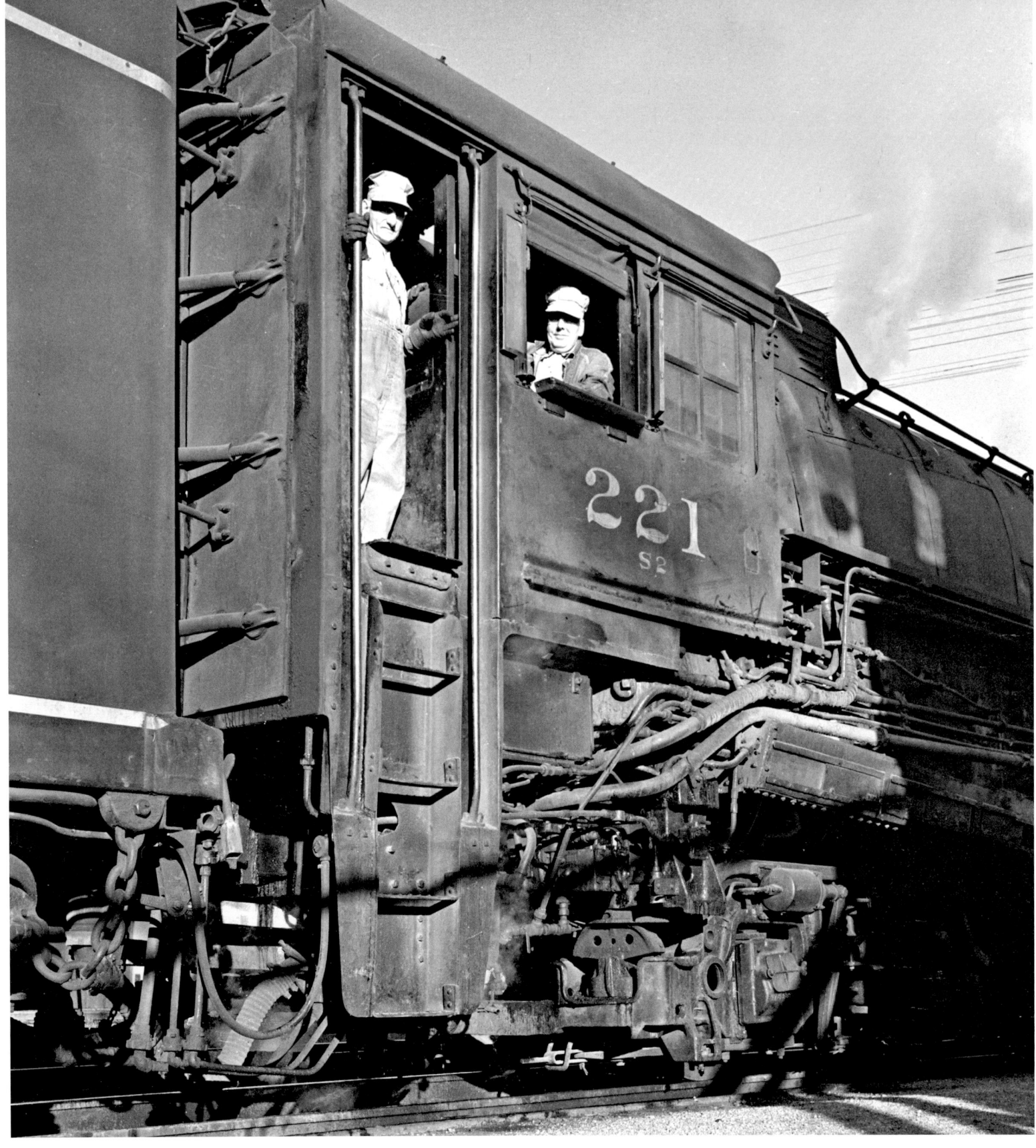

Facing: During a stop at Rondout, Illinois, in 1955, the engineer and fireman of a westbound freight train look down from the cab of S2-class 4-8-4 no. 221. The shadow of Rondout Tower is visible on the boiler, just in front of the cab. The railroad's main line from Chicago to Milwaukee crossed a branch of the Elgin, Joliet & Eastern at Rondout, and this train may have been stopped for an EJ&E train.

Below: Two streamlined *Hiawatha* passenger trains at Chicago Union Station, circa 1950, offer striking commentary on industrial design of railroading's streamlined era. Leading the train in the background is F7-class 4-6-4 steam locomotive no. 102, styled by Otto Kuhler. One of the famed Skytop observation cars, designed by Brooks Stevens, dominates the foreground.

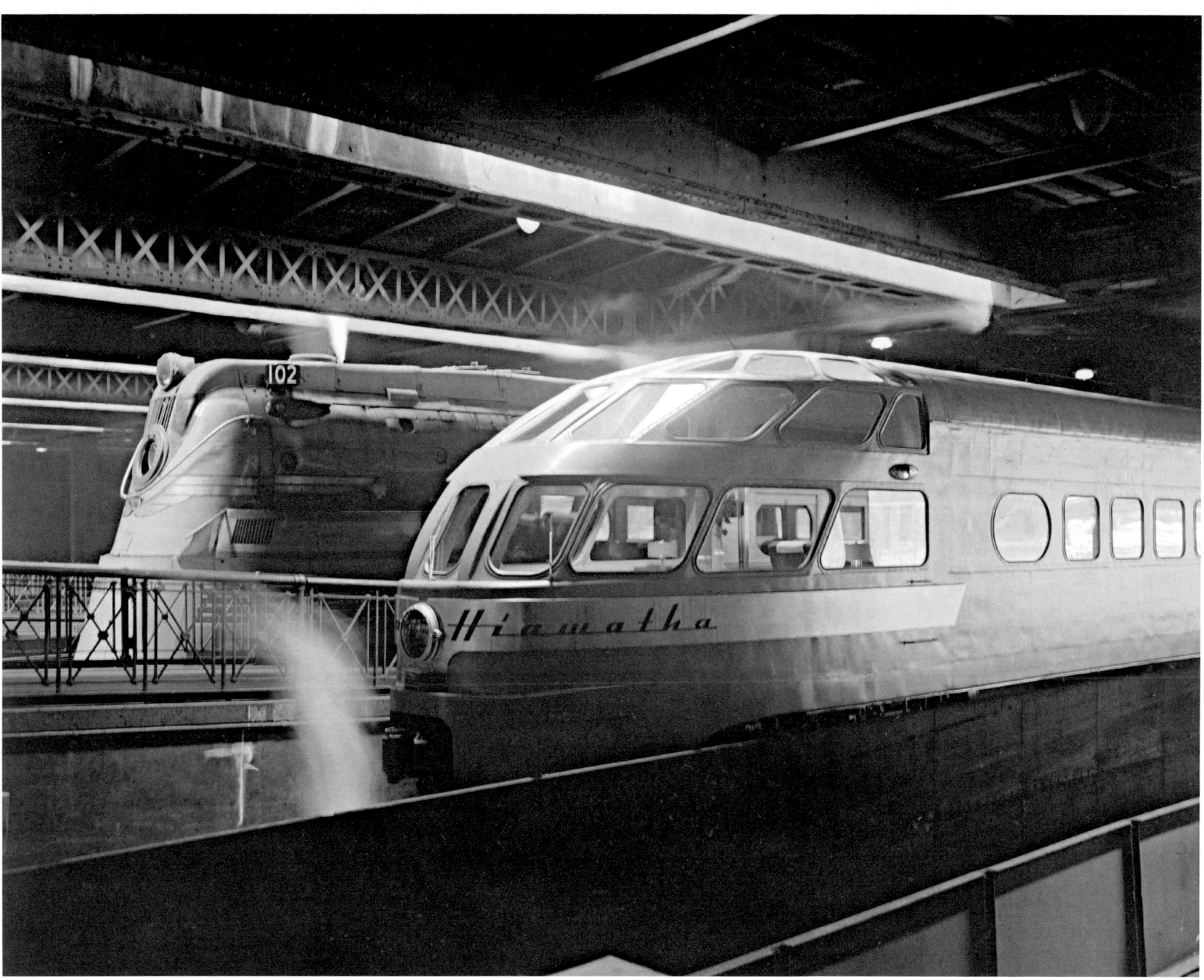

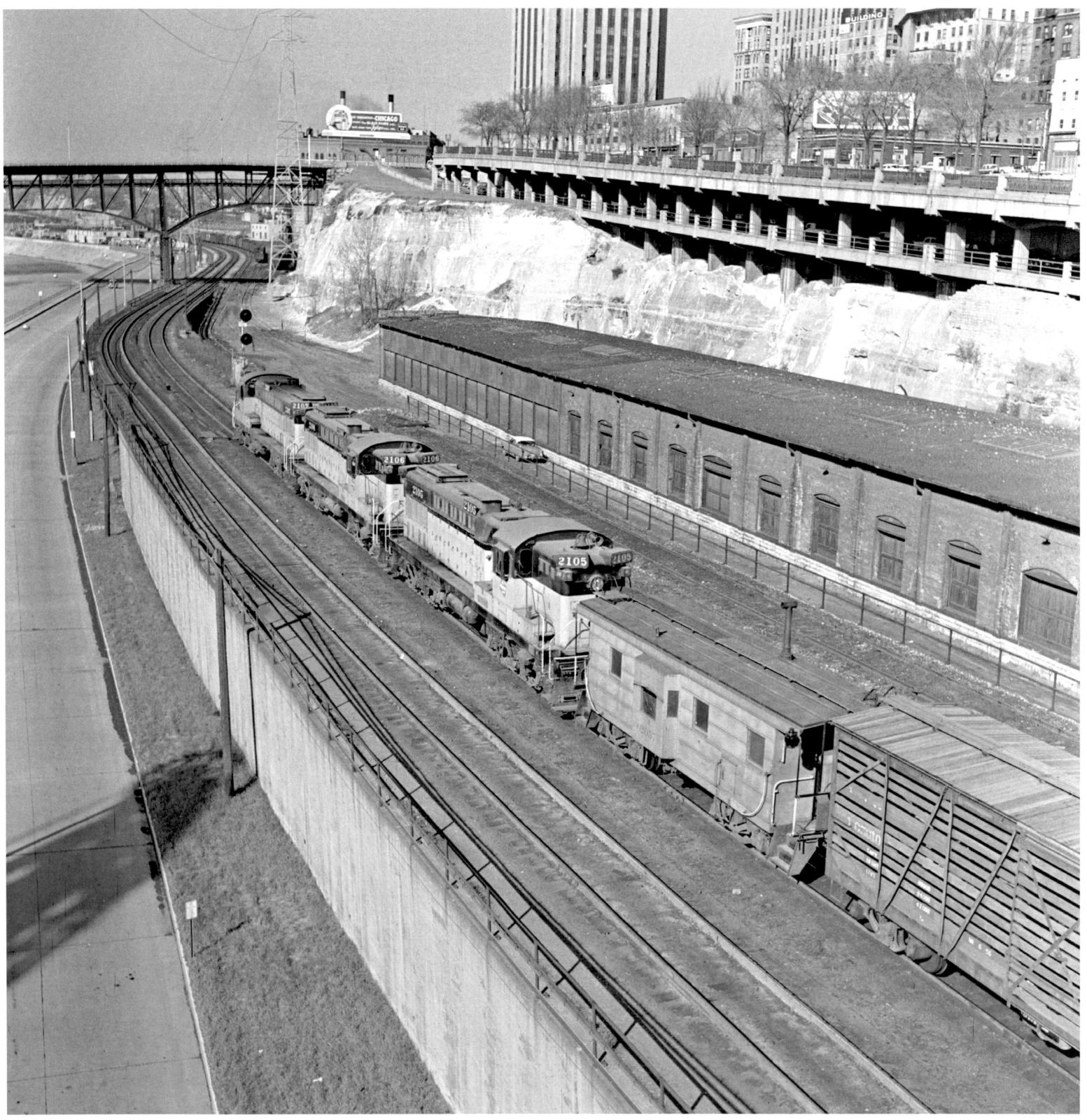

Facing: A trio of Baldwin AS-616 diesels digs into the grade up Short Line Hill along the Mississippi River in St. Paul, Minnesota, with a transfer freight for Minneapolis on March 24, 1959. Short Line Hill allowed the railroad to bypass a long bend in the river between the Twin Cities. The 1889 High Bridge, which carries Smith Avenue and state highway 149, stands in the background. It was closed in 1984 over structural concerns and replaced in 1987 with a steel arch bridge.

Below: The Milwaukee Road's main Twin Cities facility was this sprawling yard in the Mississippi bottomlands below Dayton's Bluff along the eastern edge of St. Paul. It was locally known as Pig's Eye Yard, a name going back to Pierre "Pig's Eye" Parrant, the first European to live in what would become St. Paul. Blind in one eye, he distilled liquor inside a cave and opened the city's first business—a tavern, naturally. Abbey's view from 1965 looks southeast.

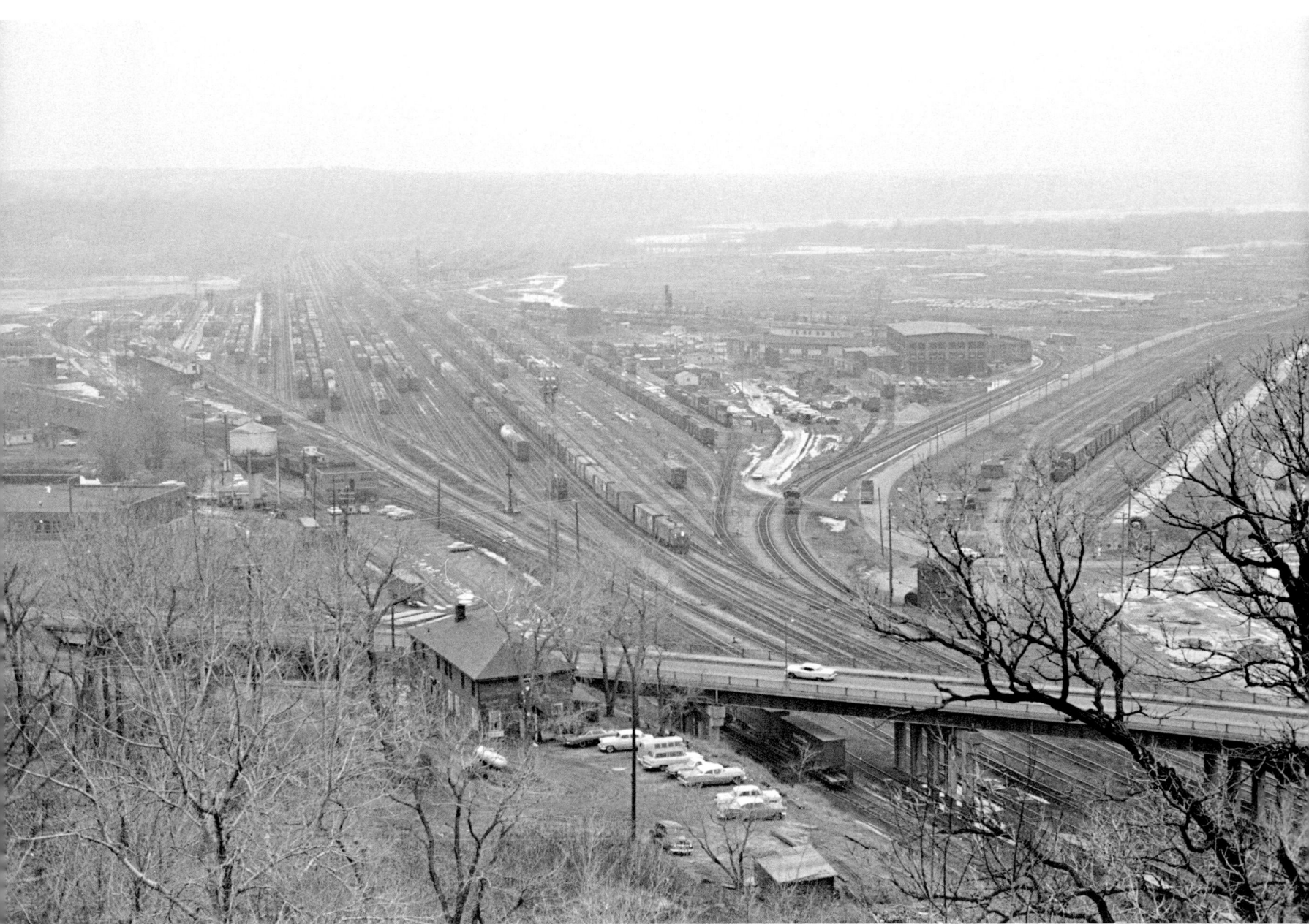

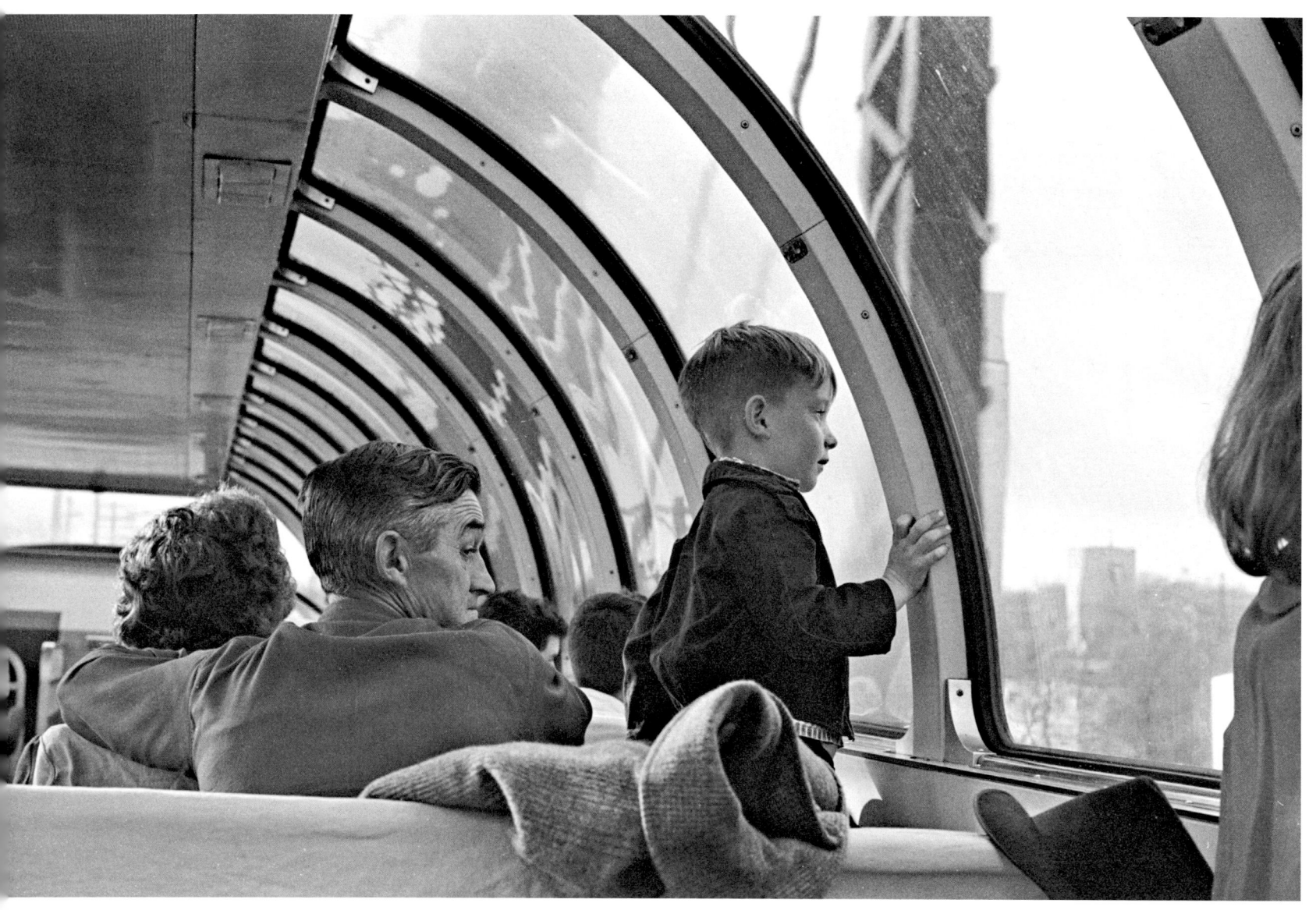

A young passenger looks out the window of the full-length dome car on the *Morning Hiawatha*, en route from Minneapolis to Chicago on October 20, 1965. The railroad still ran five daily trains each way between the two cities, but that frequency would last for less than four more years. Amtrak took over what was left of the Milwaukee Road's passenger service in 1971, and today runs just one train between Chicago and the Twin Cities.

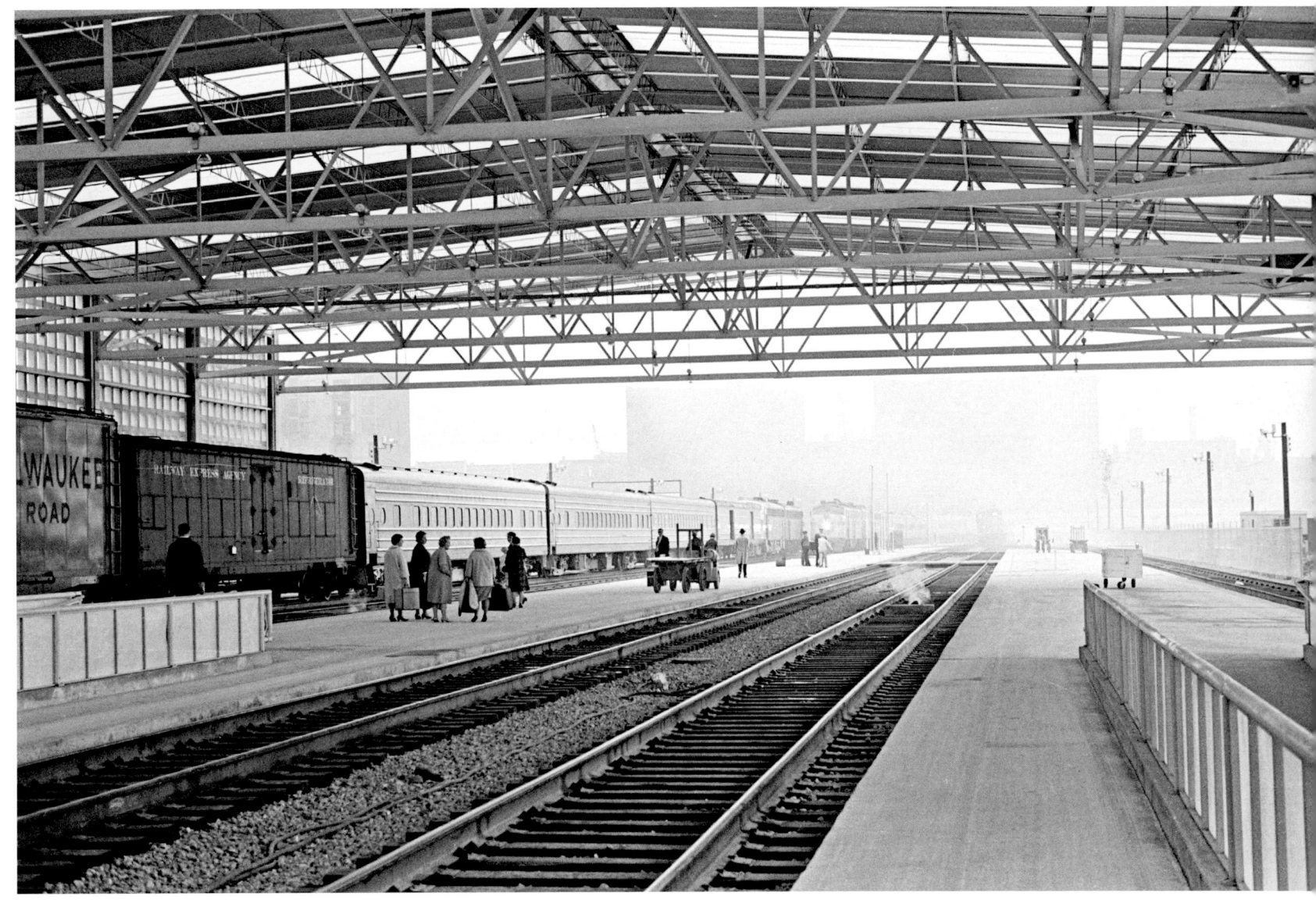

The eastbound *Morning Hiawatha* meets westbound local train no. 55 at the brand-new Milwaukee Road station in Milwaukee, Wisconsin, on October 20, 1965. The facility had opened less than three months earlier, replacing the city's Everett Street Depot, a grand structure in the Gothic Revival style built in 1886 and featuring a 140-foot clock tower. Extensively renovated and renamed Milwaukee Intermodal Station in 2007, the 1965 structure continues to serve Amtrak and bus patrons today.

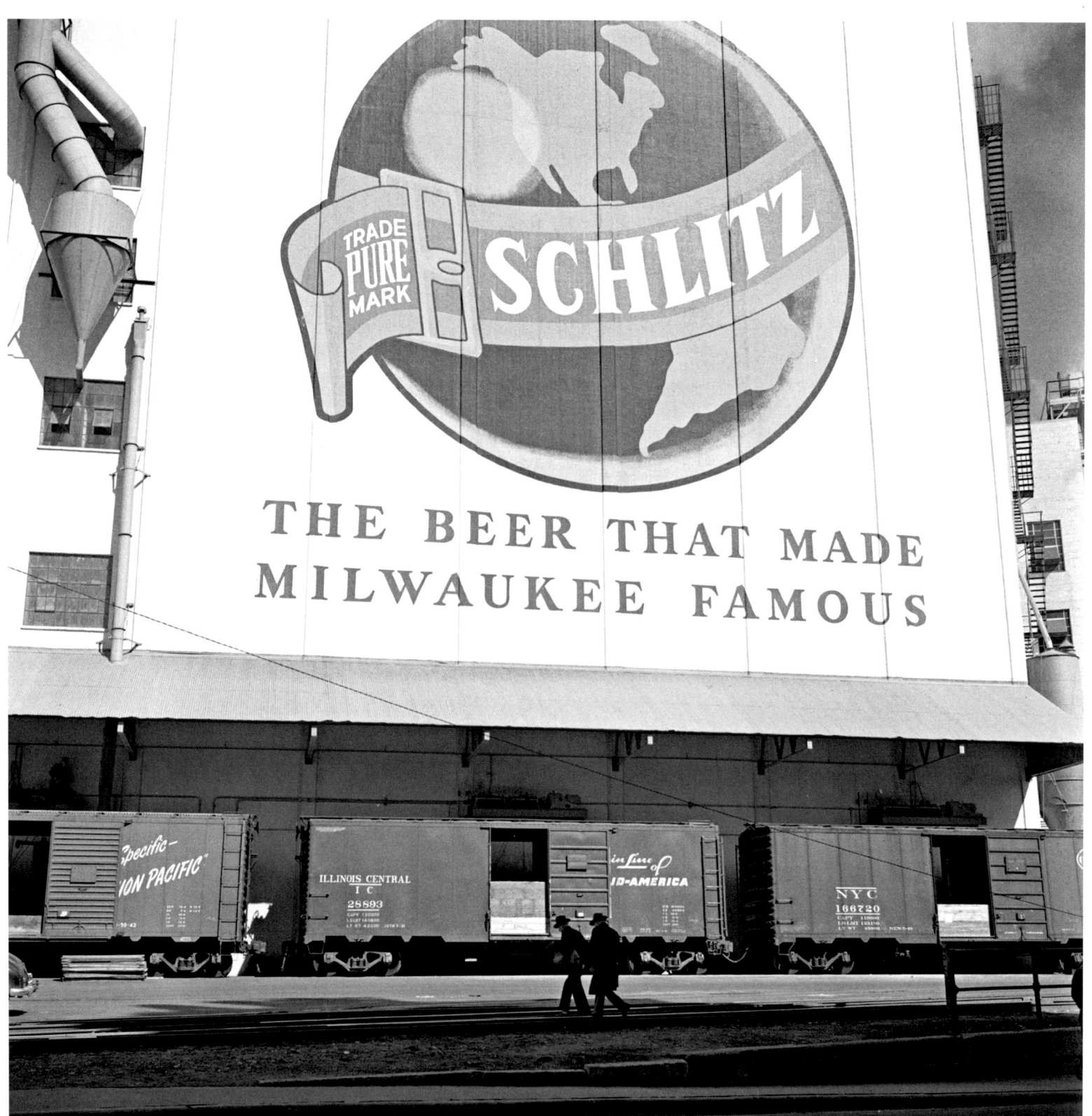

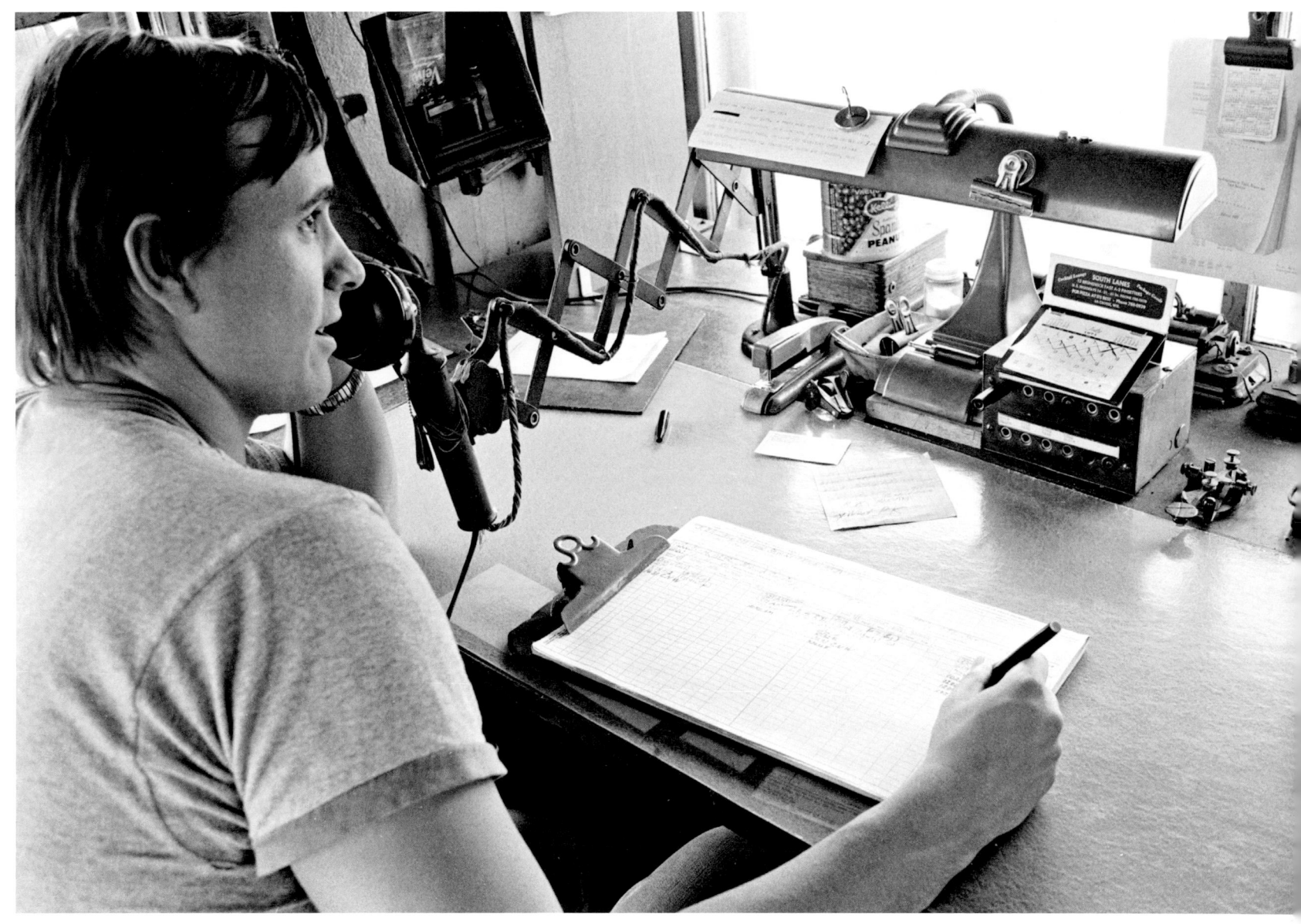

Union Pacific, Illinois Central, and New York Central boxcars spotted for unloading at the Schlitz brewery in Milwaukee, Wisconsin, on April 7, 1952. A Milwaukee Road line—originally the main line of the Milwaukee & La Crosse Railroad—that wound through the north side of the city reached the Schlitz brewery. It also served the Pabst and Blatz breweries via team tracks, leading to its nickname, "The Beer Line." Both grain and hops arrived by rail.

Above: The young operator at Grand Crossing Tower in La Crosse, Wisconsin, talks on the company phone line while updating his train sheet on July 9, 1971. Phones were still the primary means of communication, but railroads were beginning to use radios more widely. Radios allow dispatchers to communicate directly with train crews and, along with centralized traffic control, led to the demise of operators at most towers and stations along the line by the 1980s.

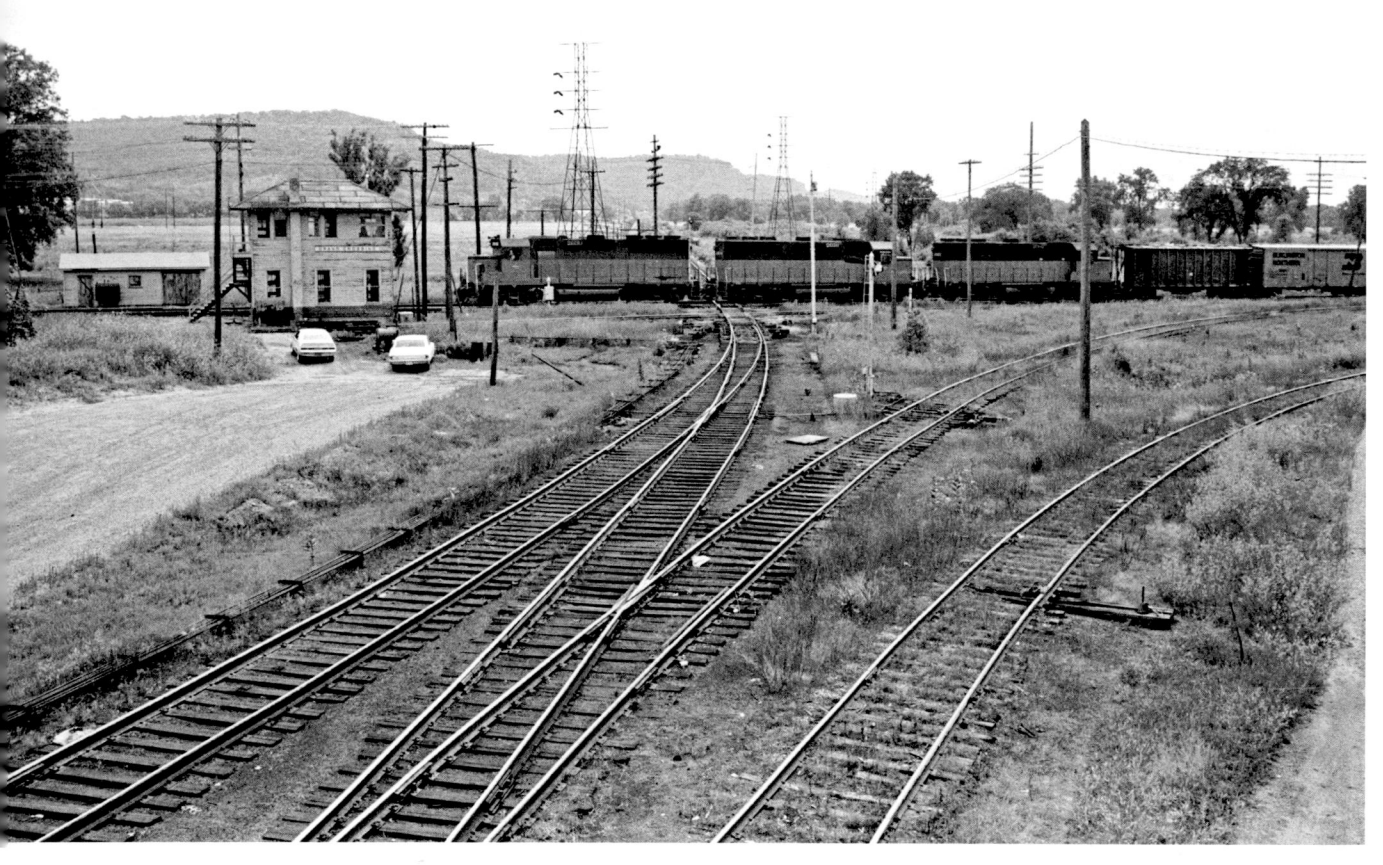

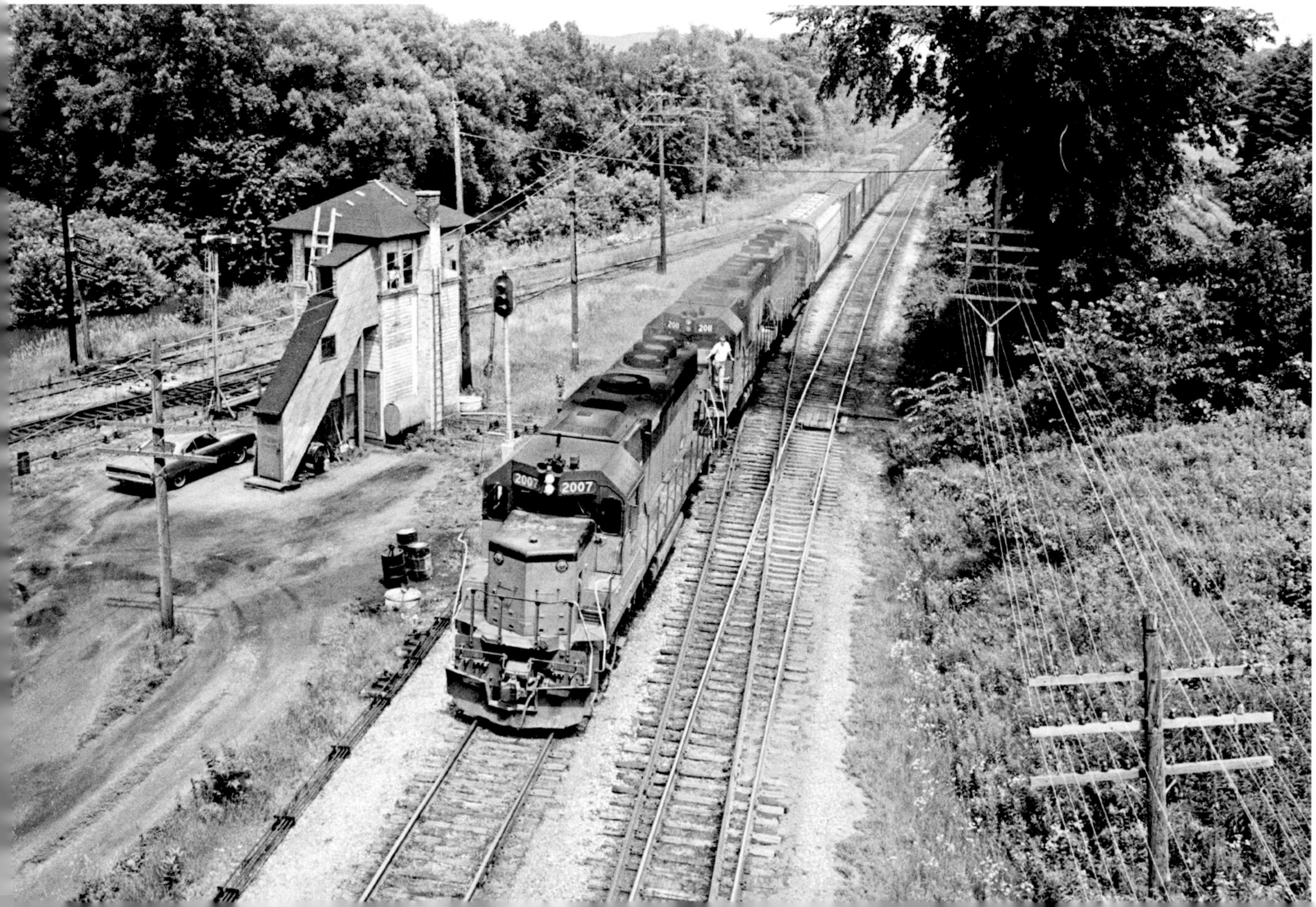

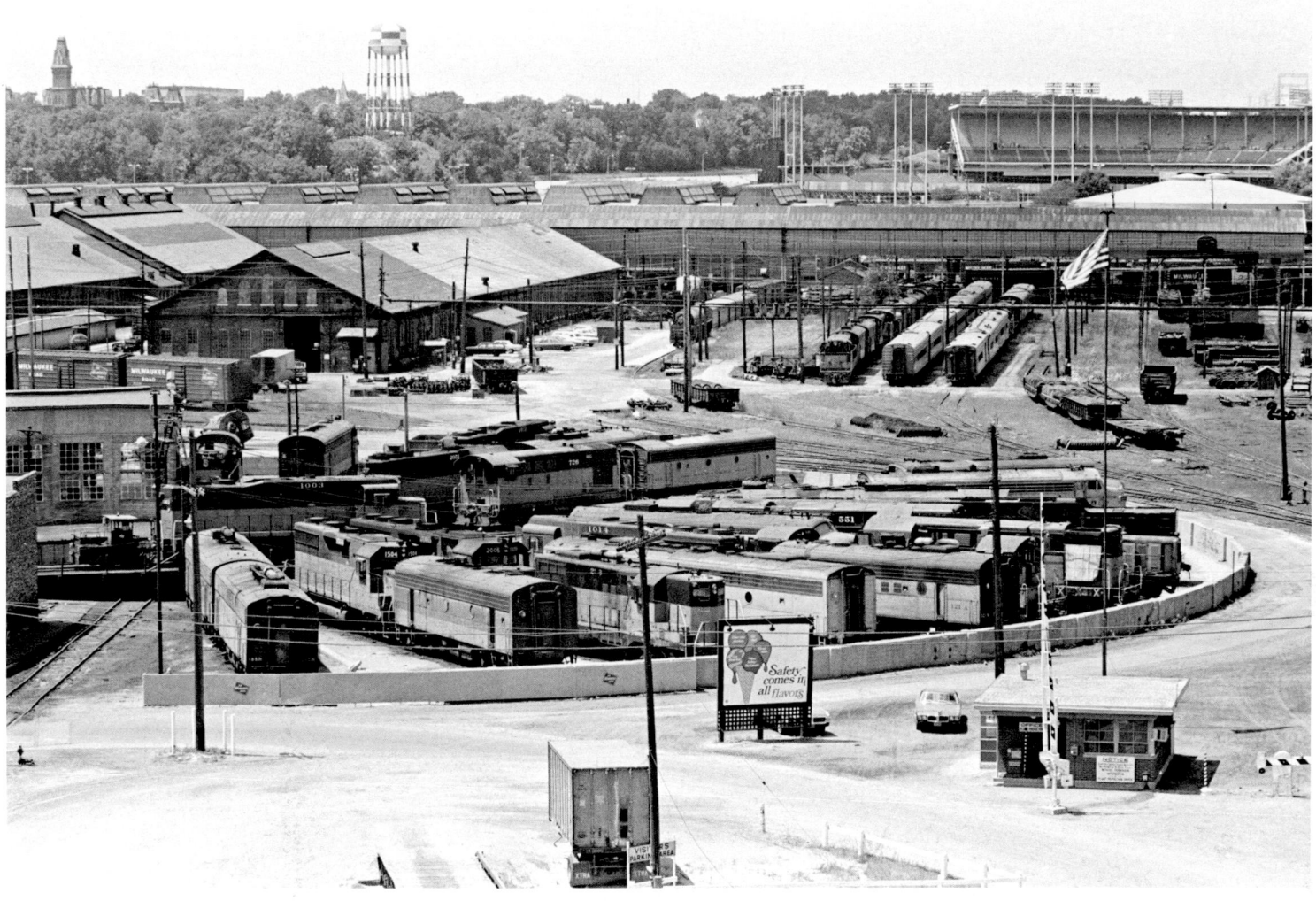

Facing top: An eastbound freight led by three GP40s rumbles across the Burlington Northern and passes Grand Crossing Tower in La Crosse, Wisconsin, in July of 1971. The high bluffs of the Upper Mississippi Valley stand to the south in the hazy distance. A Chicago & North Western branch line also crossed these two busy main lines here. Those tracks have since been removed, the tower demolished, and a new highway overpass built almost directly above the crossing. The Milwaukee and BN tracks remain, now part of Canadian Pacific and BNSF Railway, respectively, and they are both busy links on main lines to the west coast.

Facing bottom: Three GP40s lead a westbound freight across the Chicago & North Western and past Medary Tower on the outskirts of La Crosse, Wisconsin, on a July afternoon in 1971. Today, Canadian Pacific freights and Amtrak's *Empire Builder* still ply the former Milwaukee Road route, but the tower is long gone and the North Western tracks have been removed, the right-of-way turned into the Great River State Park Trail. Abbey was looking east off the state route 16 overpass.

Above: At its peak, the Milwaukee Road's network covered more than 11,000 miles, stretching from the Ohio River to Pacific Tidewater, but its largest shops were always in its namesake Wisconsin city. Sprawling out across the Menomonee River bottomlands west of downtown, the shops handled everything from light maintenance to building new cars and even locomotives. In this view from the early 1970s, first- and second-generation diesels from Electro-Motive and Fairbanks Morse line the "garden" tracks surrounding the turntable. Milwaukee County Stadium, home of the Brewers baseball team, stands at right in the distance to the west.

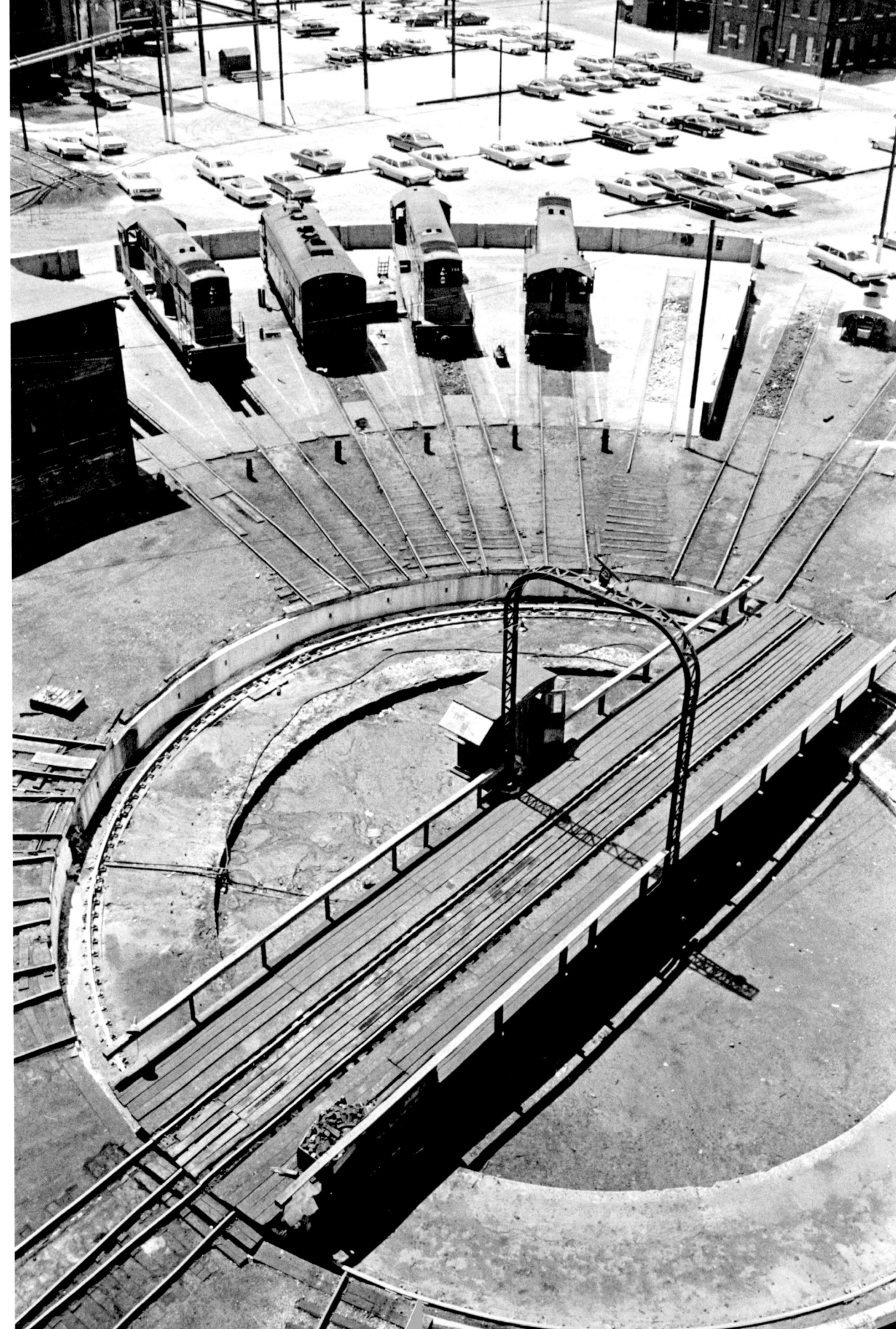

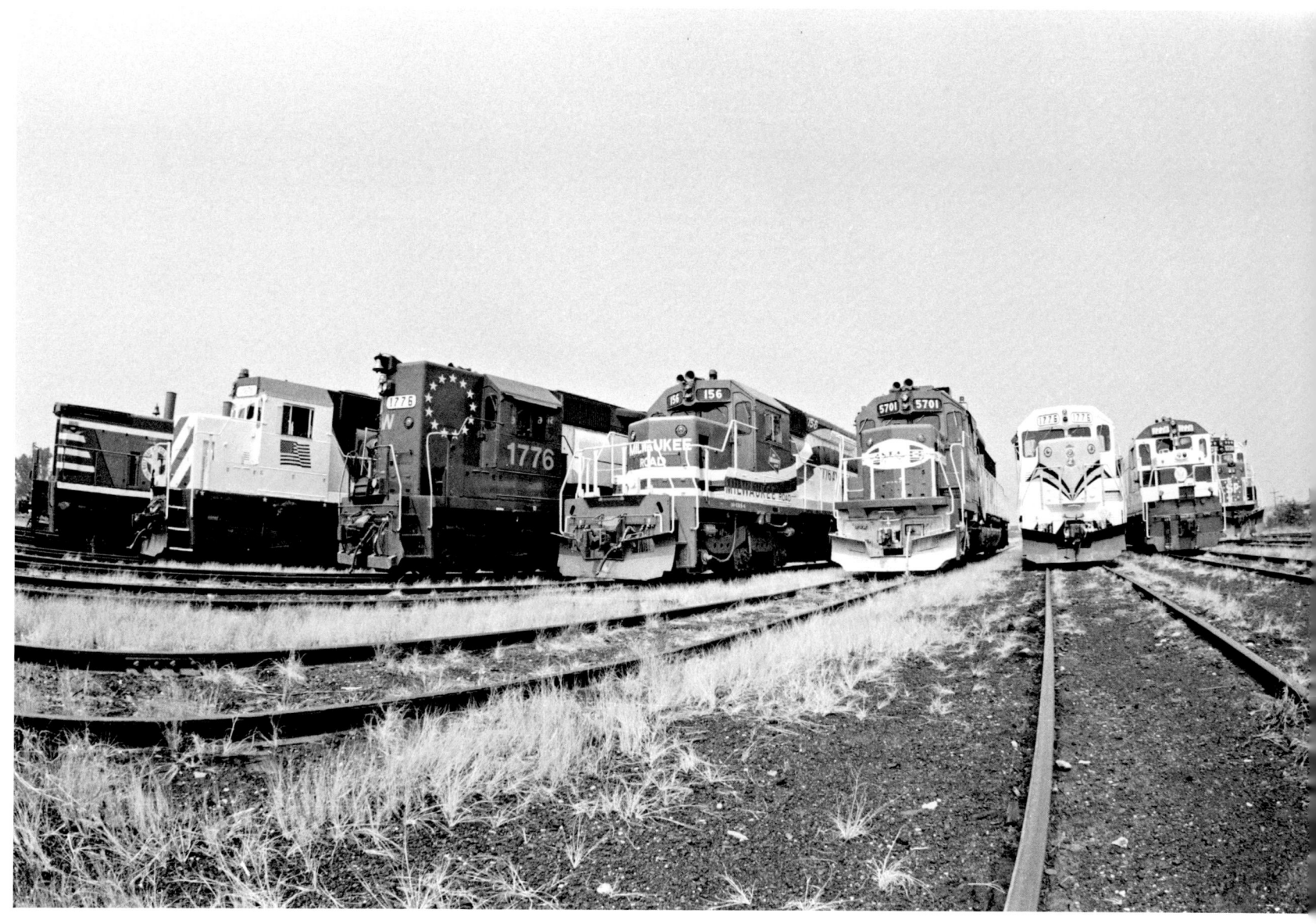

Facing: Milwaukee Road Fairbanks Morse switchers bracket a single Electro-Motive F-unit on the garden tracks at the railroad's shops in its namesake Wisconsin city. The Milwaukee Road was still a busy and successful railroad when Abbey recorded this view in the early 1970s. The railroad's fortunes declined swiftly in the latter half of the decade. After the Soo Line purchased what was left of the Milwaukee in 1985, these once-bustling shops became redundant. Scarcely a trace of them remains today.

Above: To celebrate the nation's bicentennial in 1976, many railroads painted locomotives in special color schemes. Eight railroads assembled their bicentennial locomotives for a special event organized by *Trains* magazine at the Belt Railway of Chicago's 87th Street Yard on July 31, 1975. Milwaukee Road SD40-2 no. 156 is in the middle, flanked by Norfolk & Western and Santa Fe units.

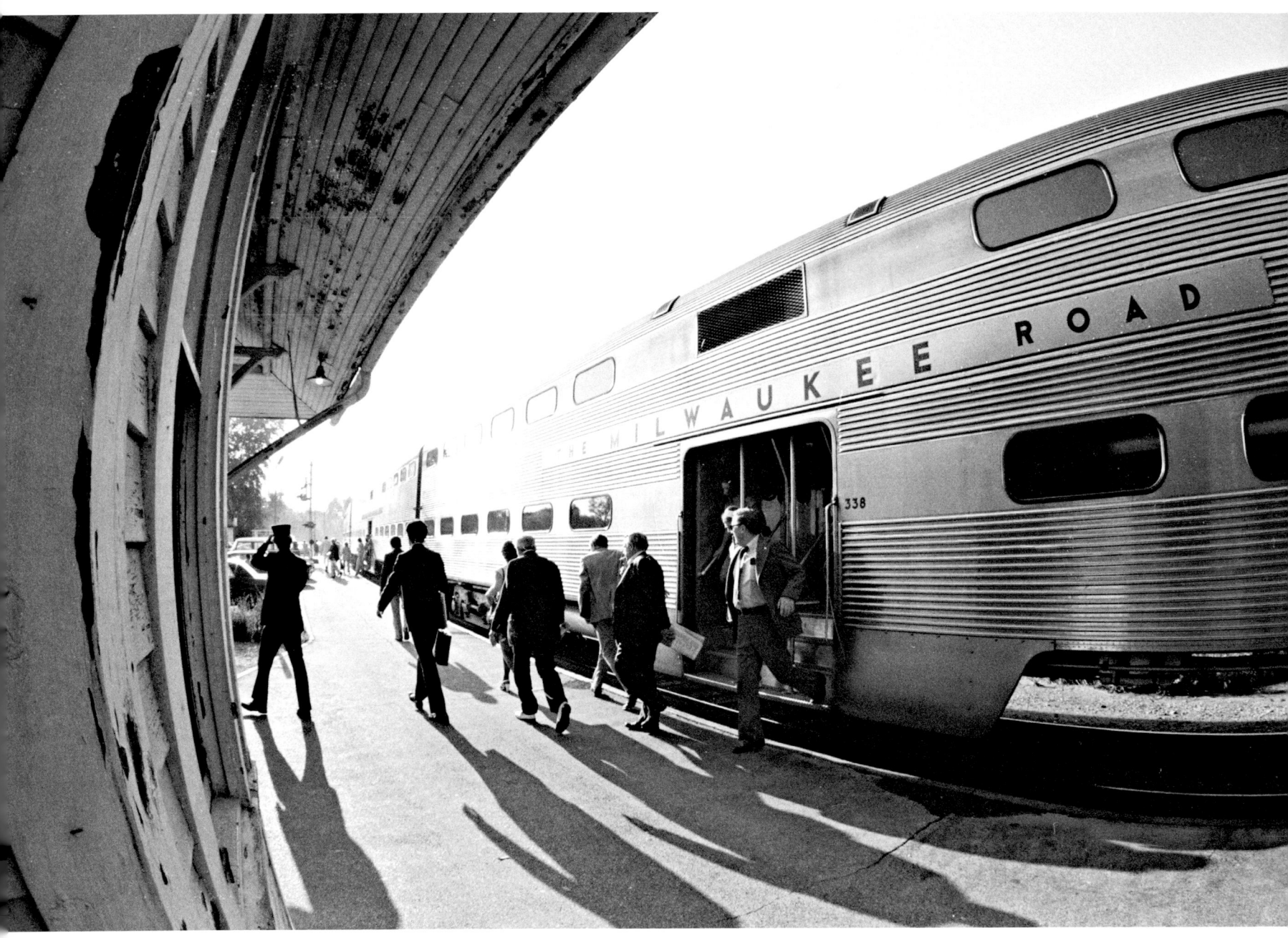

Above: Passengers disembark from an outbound commuter train at Libertyville, Illinois, on the afternoon of August 4, 1975. The Milwaukee Road operated commuter trains in and out of Chicago Union Station on two lines, west as far as Elgin and north to Fox Lake, Illinois, and Walworth, Wisconsin. Libertyville is on the latter route; it is the first stop north of Rondout, where this line splits off from the main line to Milwaukee. Metra commuter trains still run to Elgin and Fox Lake—and stop in Libertyville.

Facing: Operator Scott Porinsky hangs orders for a westbound Milwaukee Road train at Duplainville, Wisconsin, as the sun sets on September 15, 1979. Abbey was documenting the end of an era. Within six years, what was left of the Milwaukee Road would become part of the Soo Line. The Soo would soon build a new connection at Duplainville and wire up the interlocking for remote control from an office in Milwaukee. The tower was razed in 1987.

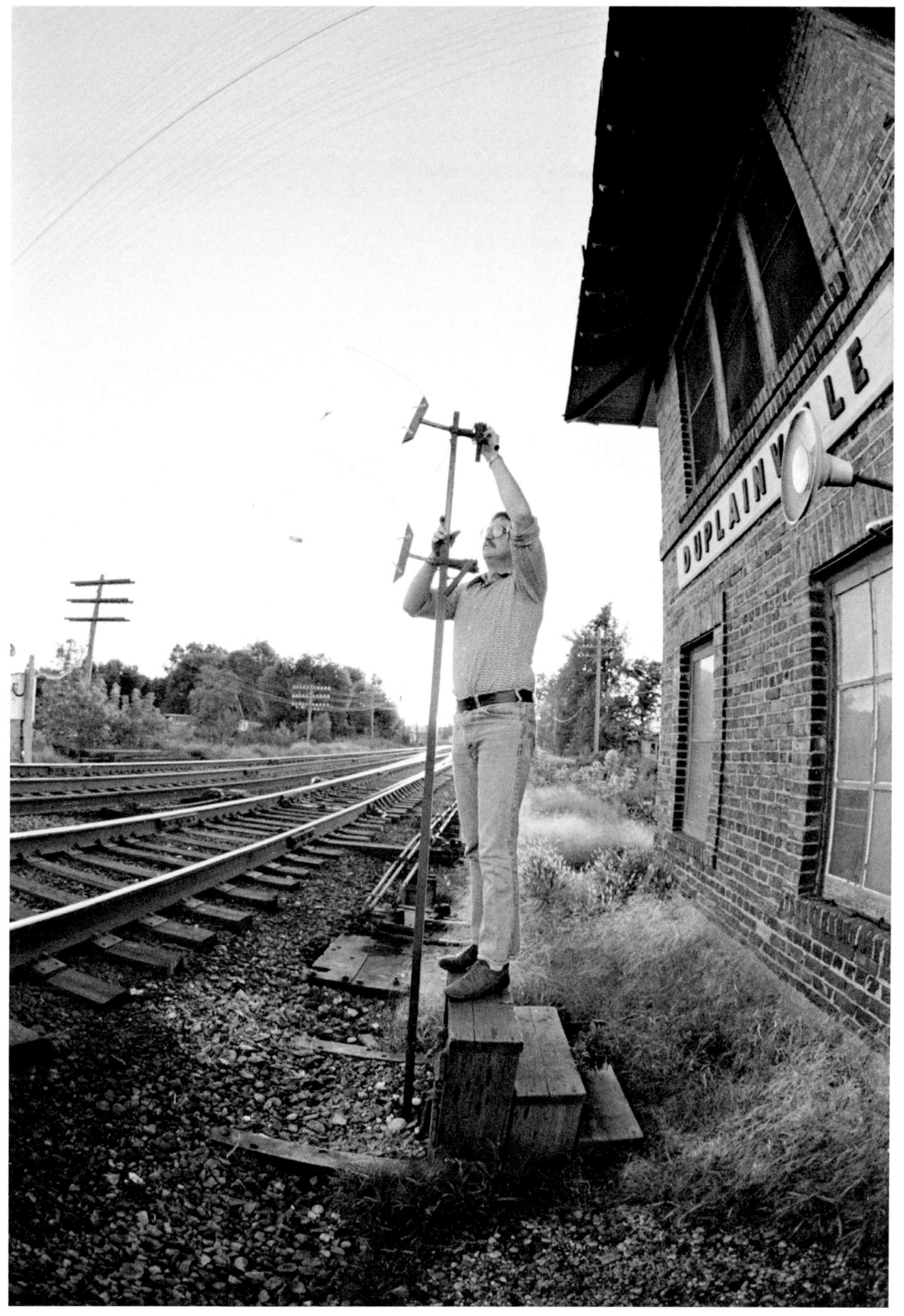

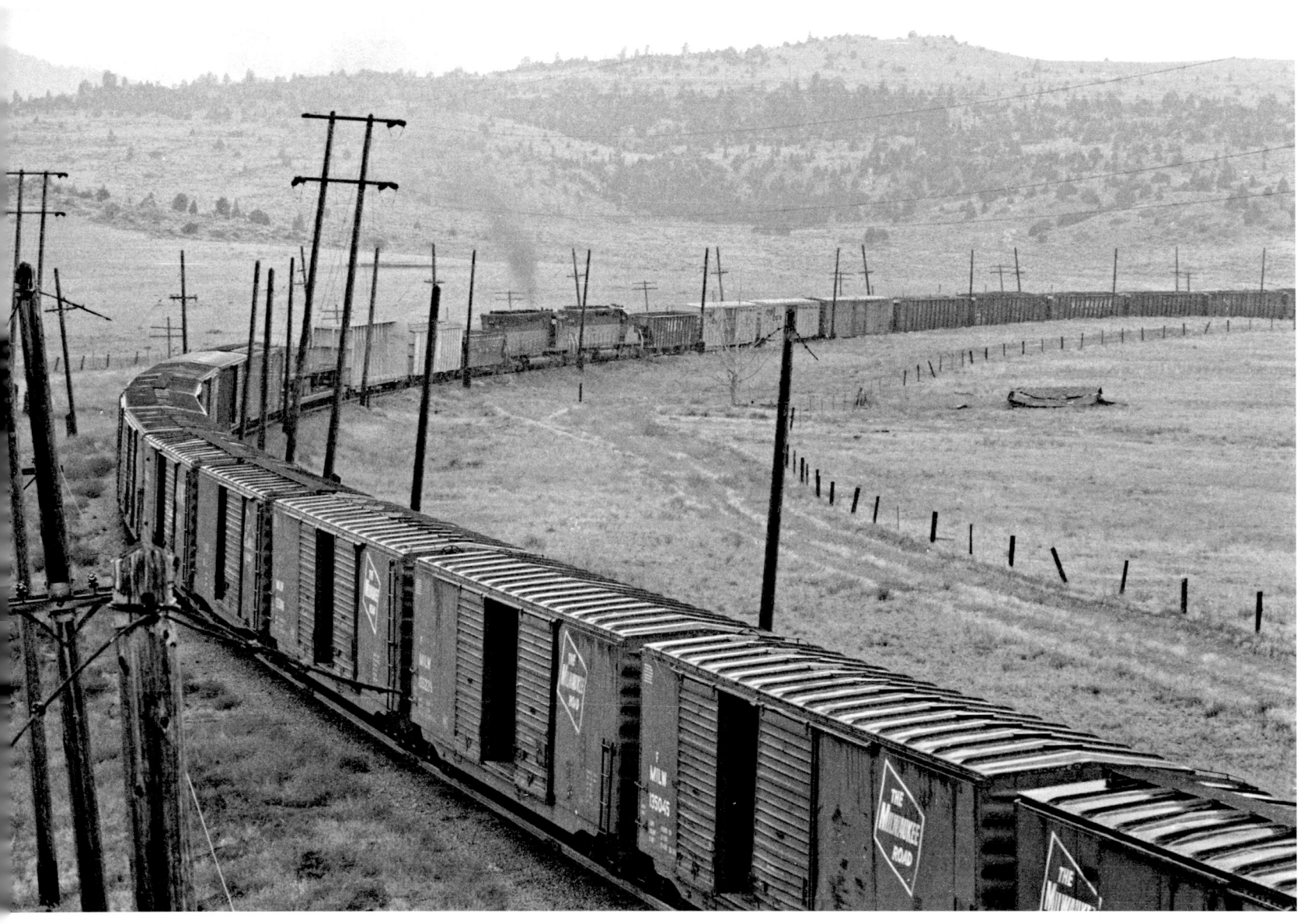

A westbound freight train rounds the horseshoe curve known as Vendome Loop in southwestern Montana during the summer of 1977. Mid-train helpers—an SD40-2 and SD45—are assisting the locomotives on the head end on the climb to the continental divide. The Milwaukee Road crossed the divide at Pipestone Pass with a 2,290-foot-long tunnel at an elevation of 6,347 feet. The line opened in 1908 with a temporary route over the tunnel, which was completed in 1909. Electrification followed in 1915 and lasted until 1974.

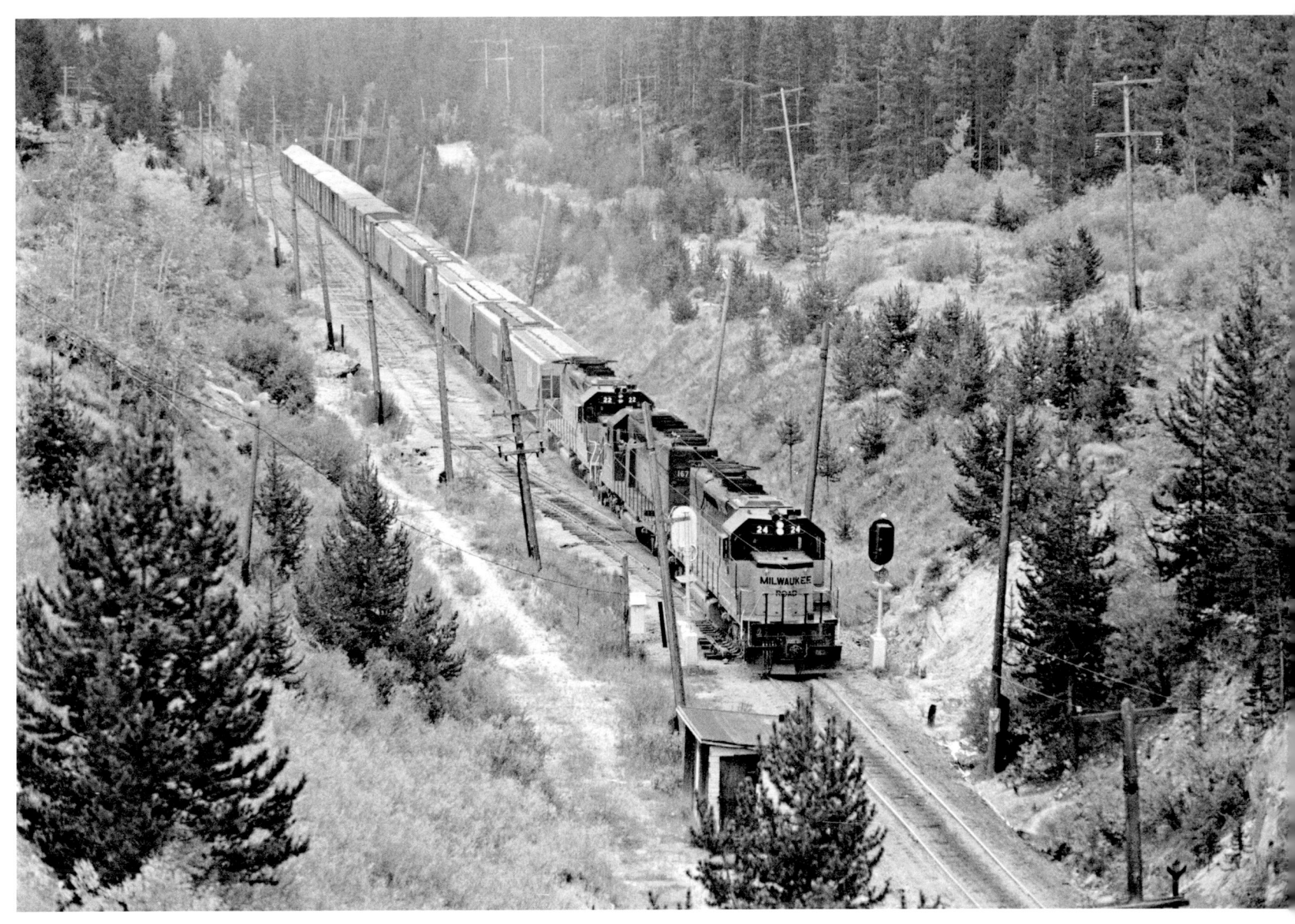

A westbound freight train passes the siding at Donald, Montana, nearing Pipestone Pass and the continental divide in the summer of 1977. The poles of electrification still stand along the tracks, but the wires are gone, the railroad having de-energized its entire Rocky Mountain Division on June 16, 1974, after nearly six decades of electric operations.

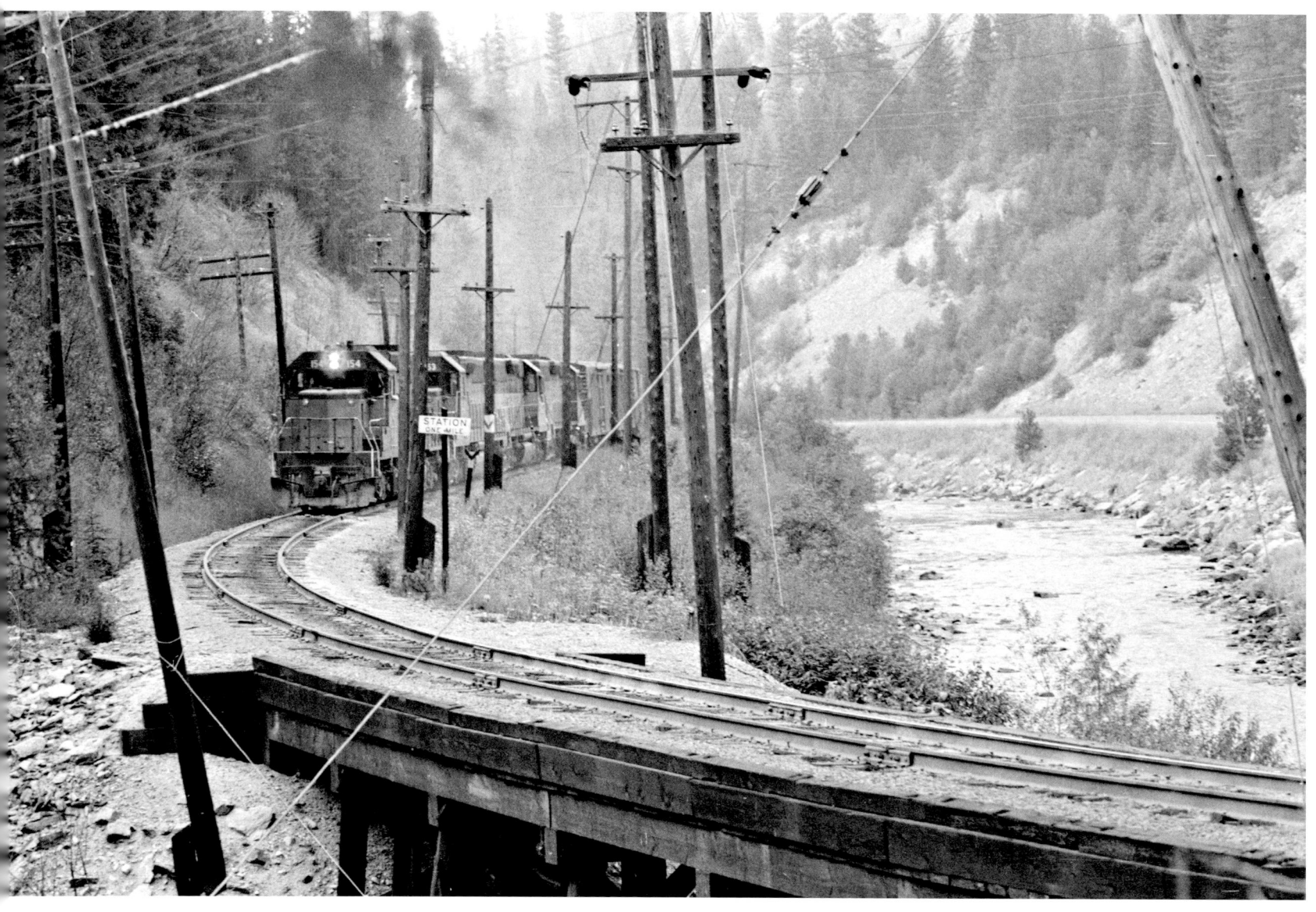

Above: An eastbound freight train negotiates the narrow canyon of the St. Regis River near the Montana town of the same name in September of 1977. Interstate 90 is visible across the river. The poles that carried electric catenary still stand, but the wires are gone.

Facing: Two SD40-2 diesels lead westbound freight train no. 211 across the snow-covered fields near Lanark, Illinois, on February 8, 1980. This is the Milwaukee Road's main line west from Chicago, crossing the Mississippi River at Savanna, Illinois, and ending at Council Bluffs, Iowa, where it connected with the Union Pacific. From 1955 until the creation of Amtrak in 1971, the Milwaukee handled UP's cross-country passenger trains on this route.

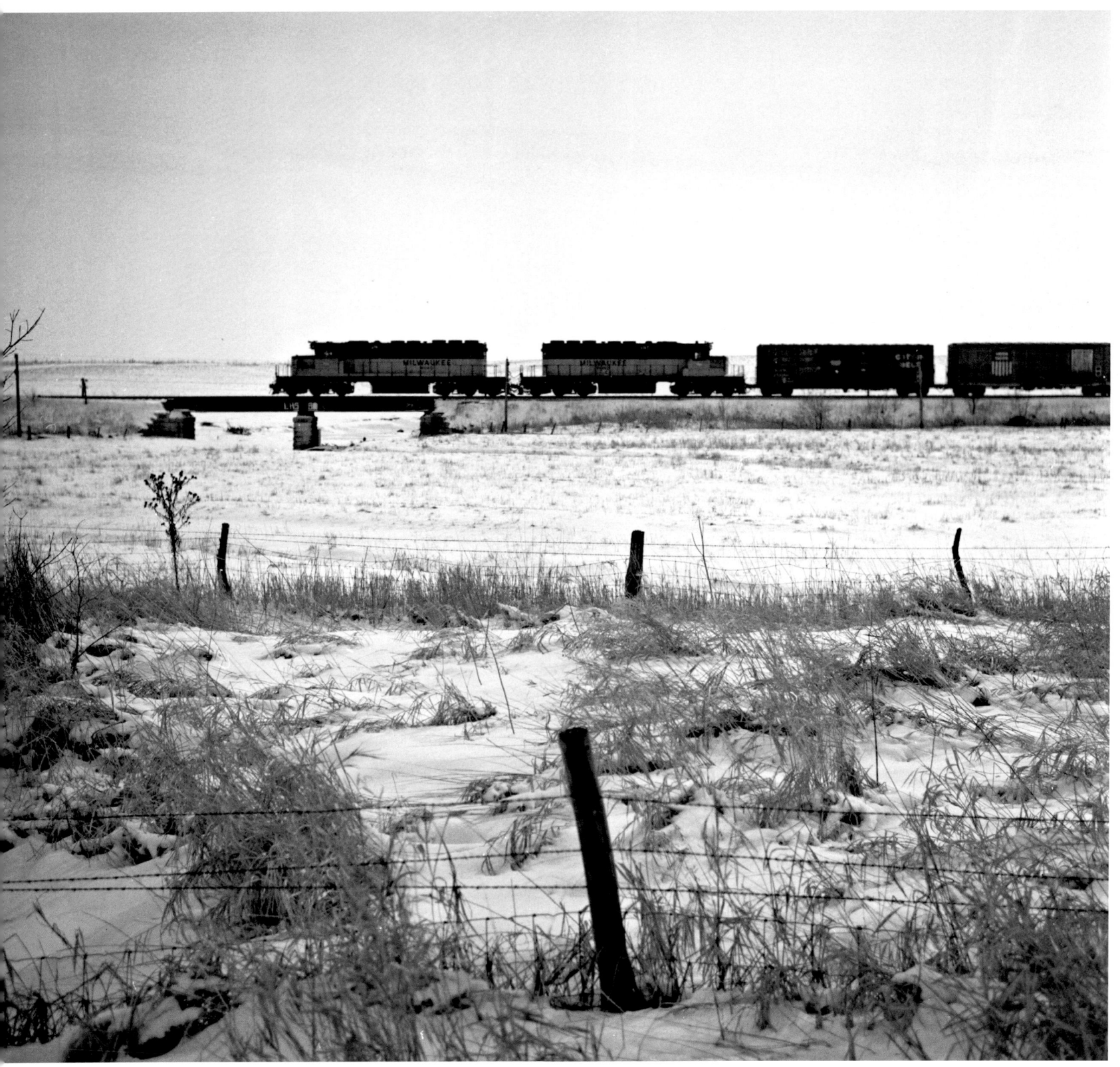

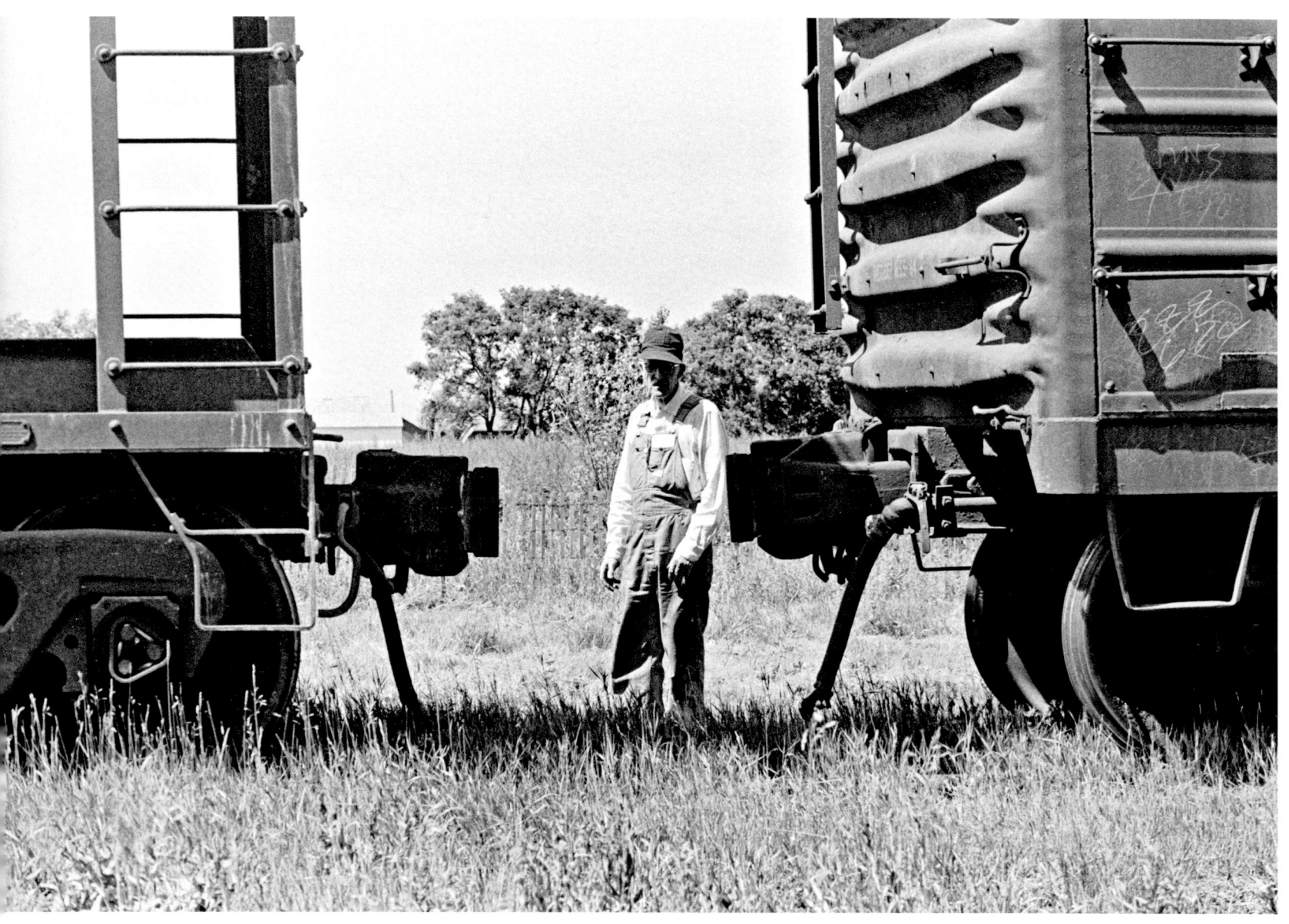

A trainman watches the coupling of two freight cars at Wheaton, Minnesota, on a summer day in the mid-1970s. The weed-grown track speaks volumes for the state of the soon-to-be bankrupt Milwaukee Road, despite the best efforts by its proud workforce to keep the trains running. Wheaton was a branch that ran north from the main line to Fargo, North Dakota. Train service ended in 1976, and the railroad pulled up the tracks four years later. Wheaton's depot became a museum in 1977 and gained recognition on the National Register of Historic Places in 1985 as a strong example of standard design and the railroad's impact on rural communities.

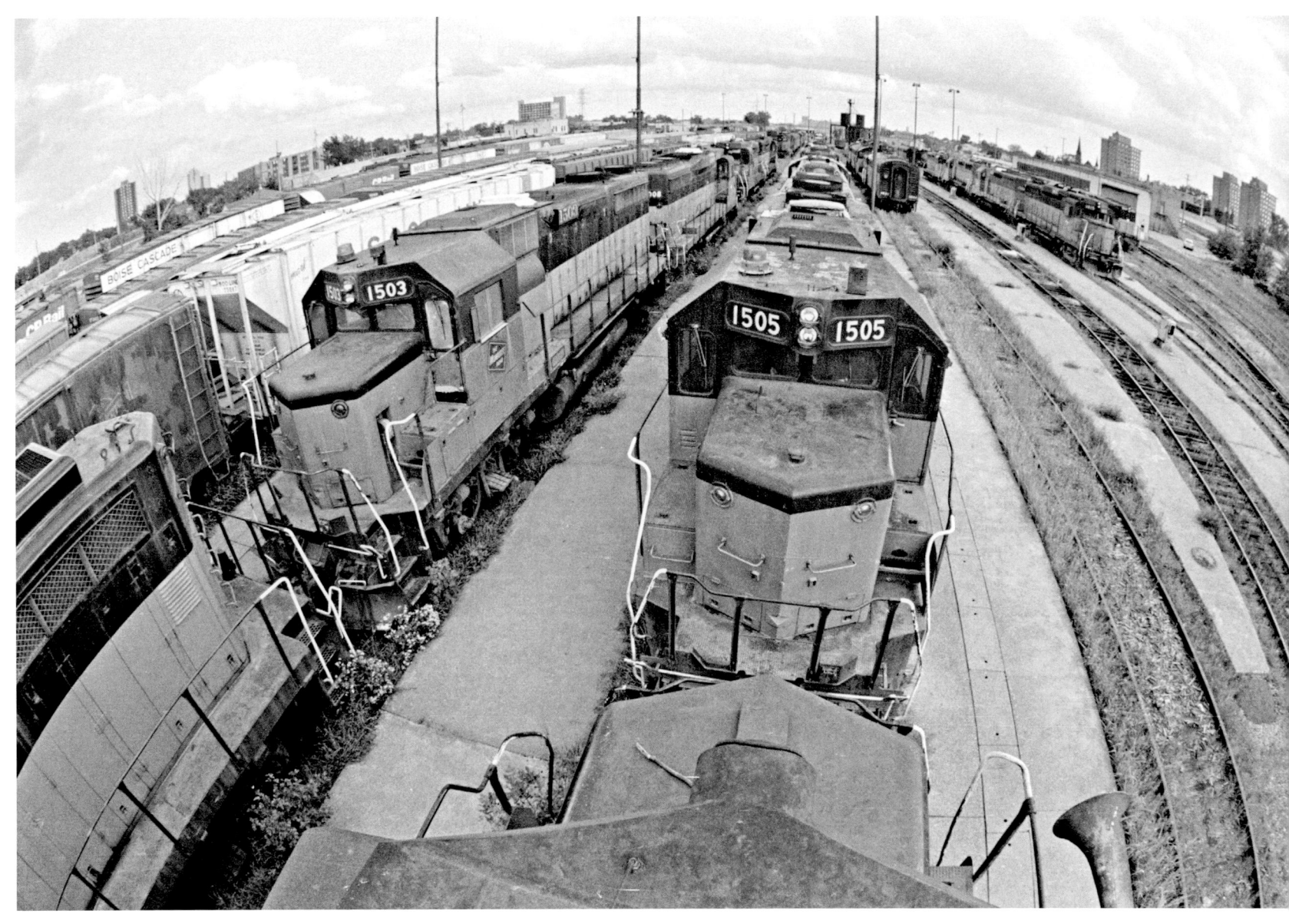

As business declined in the 1970s, Milwaukee Road's managers put locomotives into storage at yards all over the system. The extreme perspective of a fisheye lens takes in more than twenty stored diesels in St. Paul, Minnesota, in 1980 at another railroad's facility. This yard belonged to the Chicago, Rock Island and Pacific Railroad. That same year, these two railroads made the two largest trackage abandonments in U.S. history.

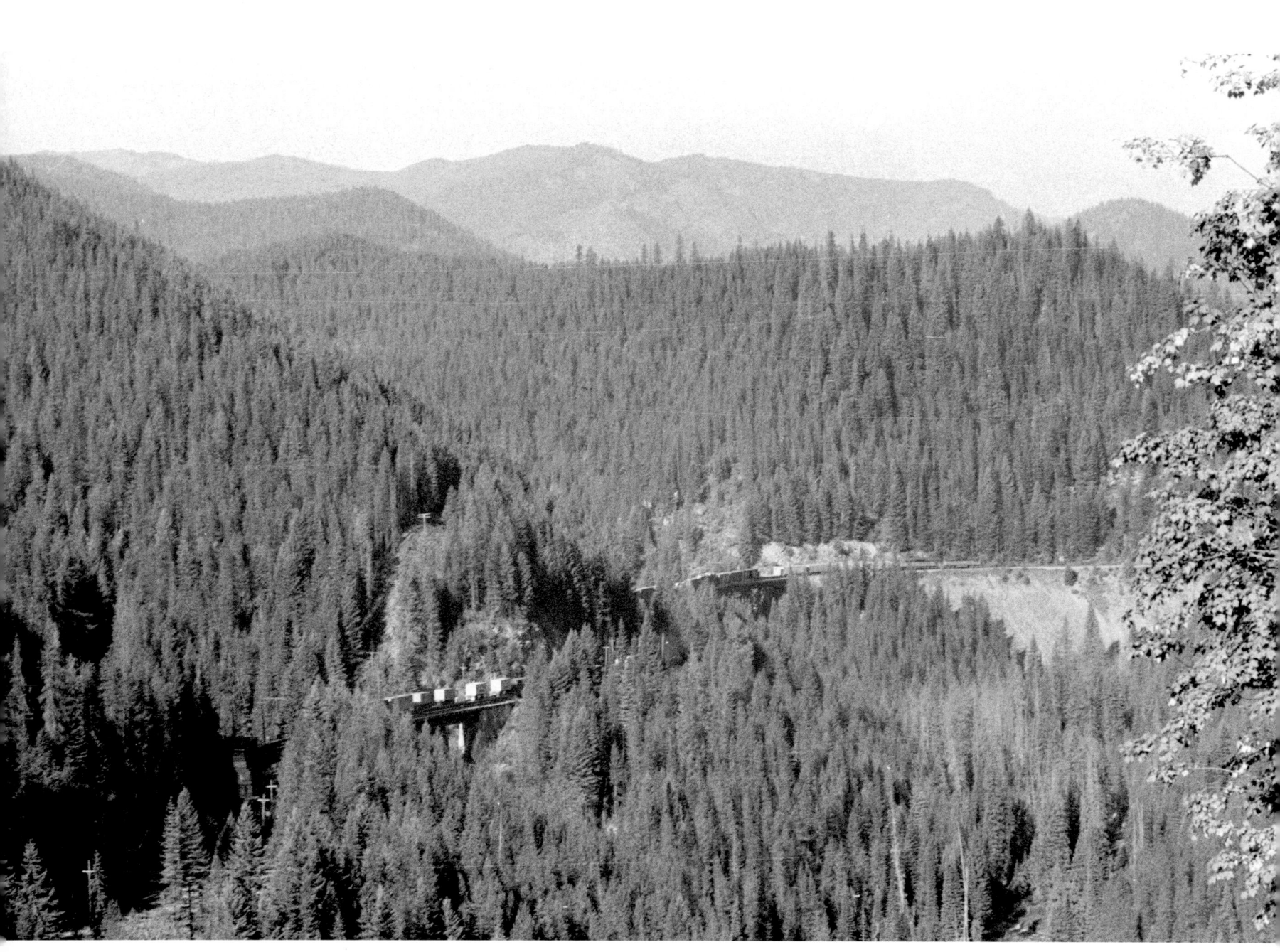

Facing: A westbound freight train descends the 1.7-percent grade through Idaho's Bitterroot Mountains in September of 1979. Opened in December of 1908 with the completion of the 1.66-mile tunnel beneath St. Paul Pass, this part of the railroad was electrified from 1915 to 1974. The last train would run less than six months after Abbey made this photograph, during the inspection trip with bankruptcy trustee Richard B. Ogilvie. In 2001, the "Route of the Hiawathas" biking and hiking trail officially opened on the railroad grade, including the summit tunnel.

Below: Westbound freight train at Haugan, Montana, viewed from over the shoulder of Abbey's pipe-smoking driver in September of 1979. They were both on an inspection tour with federal bankruptcy Trustee Richard B. Ogilvie, a former Illinois governor, who wanted to make personally sure of his abandonment recommendation for the Pacific Extension, and an embargo effective March 1, 1980. The inspection party traveled east from Seattle and Tacoma, Washington, to Roundup, Montana, mostly on the railroad in a Chevrolet Suburban outfitted as a hi-rail vehicle.

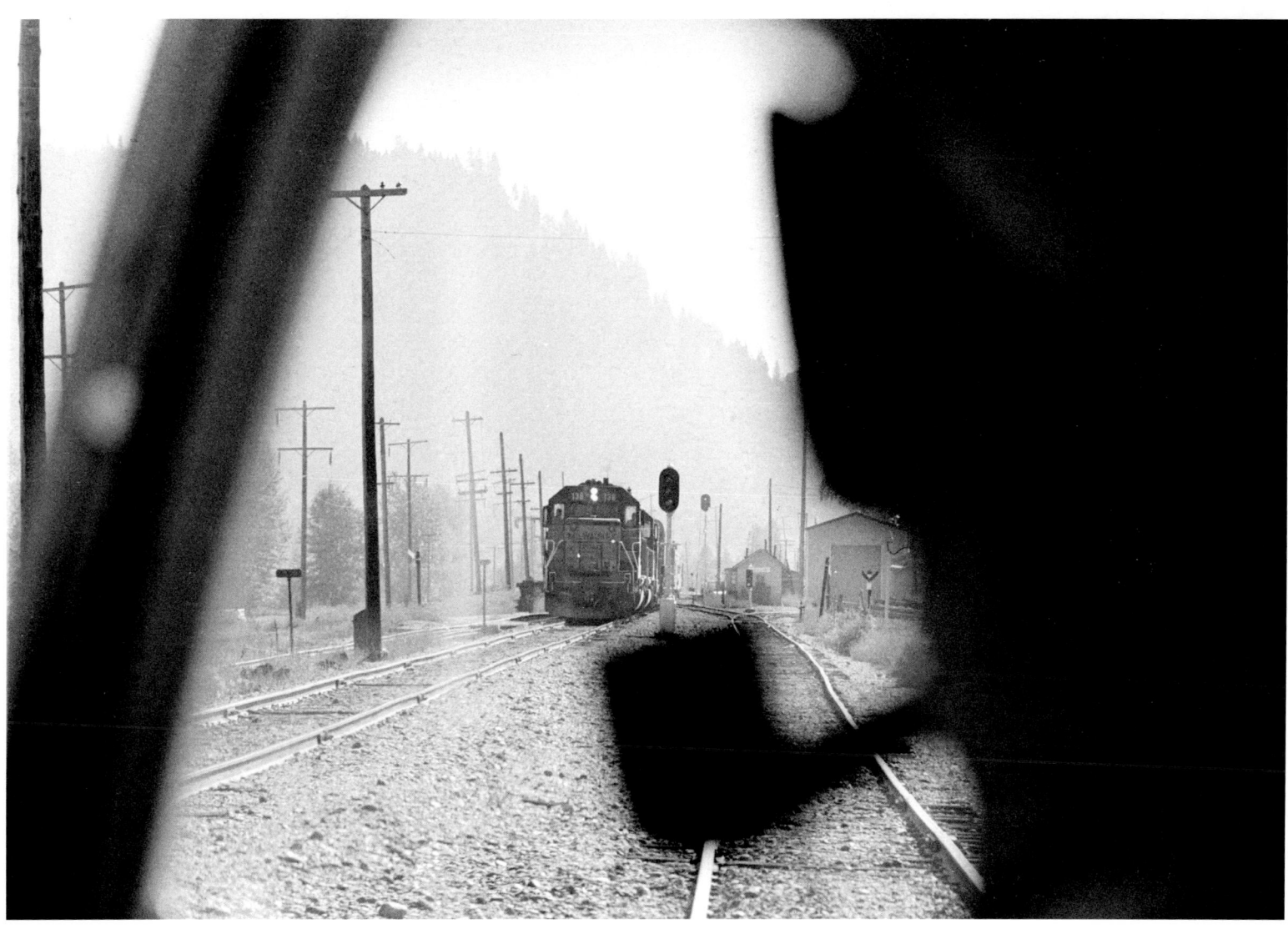

EPILOGUE

WALLACE W. ABBEY'S PHOTOGRAPHY RECEIVED A FRESH appraisal as the entire genre of railroad photography became the subject of deeper study. In 2003, the Railway & Locomotive Historical Society honored Abbey with its prestigious Fred A. and Jane R. Stindt Photography Award. In 2008, his haunting photograph of the redcap was included in a *Trains* magazine special publication, *100 Greatest Railroad Photos*. That Cincinnati photo was emblematic of Abbey's greatness, said Robert S. McGonigal, editor of *Classic Trains* magazine, in a 2017 interview. "Those CUT photos, made during the golden age of photojournalism, rank among the best of the genre. They make us weep, for the world they depict would soon vanish."

One person who recognized Abbey's importance was John Gruber, who in 1997 founded the Center for Railroad Photography & Art, based in Madison, Wisconsin. Gruber is himself an influential railroad photographer, with an extensive oeuvre showcased in dozens of railroad publications. His interest in finding a home for Abbey's archive coincided with a story he wrote about the photographer for *Classic Trains*.

Travelers in Cincinnati Union Terminal appear as silhouettes behind the east-facing windows of the rotunda. The Art Deco icon opened in 1933 and at its peak in the mid-1940s hosted 108 arriving and departing trains on seven different railroads. Business was still strong when Abbey visited in September of 1952, on assignment for what might be his best-illustrated article for *Trains*, "Temple of Transportation" in the May 1953 issue.

"My first impressions of the importance of his photography came from seeing his pictures taken while he was employed by mainline railroads and during the years he operated his own public relations business," said Gruber. "Since I had visited Wally at his office at the Milwaukee Road in Chicago and at his home in Pueblo, I knew him personally. I had written about his lifetime achievement award for photography given by the R&LHS. So it seemed only natural to approach Wally and his family about preserving his collection at the Center. Gratefully, after discussions, they said yes." Thus, in 2010, Abbey's entire collection of 25,000 black-and-white negatives and 10,000 color slides found a permanent home, to be preserved and curated for generations to come.

Scott Lothes, the Center's executive director since 2011, reviewed every one of Abbey's 25,000 negatives while selecting the photographs for this book. Laborious as the process was, it was another, perhaps deeper, way to appreciate Abbey's work.

"A true journalist, Abbey was at his best when people were in front of his lens," Lothes says. "From operators at out-of-the-way signal towers to passengers in big-city terminals, Abbey had a true gift for evoking the human drama of railroading. At this, in the history of railroad photography, he has had few peers—and, I would argue, no superiors. It is a privilege for the Center to be the custodians of his remarkable collection."

ACKNOWLEDGMENTS

RAILROADING IS AMONG THE MODERN WORLD'S MOST transformative technologies, but much of its work happens behind the scenes and out of the public eye. We might wave at the engineers and conductors in the locomotives, yet we rarely—if ever—see the dispatchers, track workers, mechanics, and the host of others who keep the trains running. One of the strengths of Wallace W. Abbey's photography is how he illuminated so many of these rarely seen aspects. Like railroading, archiving photographs and publishing books about them require the work of many people, most of whose efforts go unseen. Here we will illuminate as many as we can.

First and foremost is Abbey himself. Beyond creating a body of photography so richly deserving of a monograph, Abbey also left behind the documentation necessary for a book about his life's work. He recorded meticulous notes about many of his photographs, especially his earlier images. Almost as importantly, he kept detailed records and journals about his career—without which, constructing the narrative for this volume would not have been possible. Photographers, take heed!

Speaking of the possible, so much of what's in this book is the result of the enthusiastic participation of Abbey's daughters, Mary (Maggie) Abbey and Martha Abbey Miller. Over the years, Abbey created an unusually rich and detailed archive of personal papers—letters, memoirs, speeches, "to-do" lists—all of which were made available to us by Maggie and Martha. We couldn't have done this book without their help, but more than that, our correspondence with them turned the book into a warmly shared experience.

They also delighted us in bringing out aspects of their father's life beyond railroading. One thing we learned is that Wally's interest in railroads wasn't an overriding presence in family life. Instead, more often the topic was music, and specifically their dad's love of traditional country & western and Western swing. "It was really Dad's other enthusiasm," says Maggie. "We grew up surrounded by records, and he had quite a collection of CDs and old 78s in Pueblo." She recalled this telling moment: "A year or so before he passed away, the music therapist at his assisted living facility asked me if he had perfect pitch. I had no idea, but she said she had been tuning her guitar near where he was sitting and he kept shaking his head and grimacing... until she apparently got it right, and then he gave her a thumbs-up and a smile."

Finding a long-term home for Abbey's photography was also a family matter. John Gruber founded the Center for Railroad Photography & Art in 1997, with preserving significant images of railroading a core initiative. Recognizing the importance of Abbey's work, Gruber drew on the strength of his relationship with the photographer and the strength of the Center's work to arrange for the family to donate the collection to the Center.

From its early days, the Center has partnered with Lake Forest College, 30 miles north of Chicago, on archival work. While the Center performs much of its archival work in-house, the Archives and Special Collections of the Lake Forest College

Library did the heavy lifting for the 25,000 black-and-white negatives in the Abbey Collection. That included rehousing the negatives into archival-safe pages and binders, scanning them, and digitizing all of the caption information and other metadata. The project spanned the tenures of two archivists, Arthur Miller and Anne Thomason, both of whom deserve a great deal of gratitude. Several interns put hundreds of hours into processing the Abbey Collection, including Harris Miller, and, more recently, Jim Cascino and Colleen O'Keefe. The latter two are graduates of archiving master's degree programs, and their expertise and professionalism were invaluable in the latter stages of the processing work.

In the middle of processing the Abbey Collection, the Center had the great fortune of hiring its second full-time employee, Jordan Radke, who served as archives manager through 2017. Radke solved a lingering issue of the Abbey Collection by reorganizing the entire collection—an exceptional measure in the archives world, but one necessitated by Abbey's use of three different organizational schemes for his photography that were not fully compatible with one another.

Trains magazine, Abbey's one-time employer, selected the Center for their 2010 Preservation Award, a $10,000 grant that provided the initial resources to begin such high-caliber archiving of such a large collection. The editorial staff members at *Trains* and sister publication *Classic Trains* were great resources throughout the project, and Diane Laska-Swanke, Rob McGonigal, Brian Schmidt, and Jim Wrinn deserve special thanks for their great help in supplying missing caption information and answering other questions.

Indiana University Press deserves the gratitude of anyone interested in trains or railroading for becoming a guiding light of railroad publishing. This book would not have been possible without their interest and dedication. Thanks go to everyone on their staff, and especially to Sarah Jacobi and Ashley Runyon for their roles in this project.

We called on several of the Center's members and friends to help pinpoint unidentified photographs and check facts. Time and again they impressed us with their knowledge and generous lending of it. Those include Nick Benson, Marc Entze, Fred Frailey, John Kelly, Blair Kooistra, Rob Leachman, John Lucas, John Luecke, Joe McMillan, and Joe Swanson. Each of the Center's members contributed to the success of this project by supporting the Center. We thank each of them, and especially our board of directors for their guidance. Al Louer, in particular, encouraged our efforts. The Center is fortunate to garner the support of several foundations, and two of them, the Candelaria Fund and the Tom E. Dailey Foundation, support our archiving work directly.

Special thanks—of the kind that words cannot sufficiently convey—go to Bon French, who chairs the Center's board of directors. Bon's extraordinary generosity has enabled the institutionalization of the Center, including an endowment to ensure the long-term care and availability of such one-of-a-kind resources as the Abbey Collection. Bon's deep knowledge of the railroad industry, particularly in his native Illinois, also helped resolve questions about the locations and subjects of many of the photographs that appear in these pages.

The Wallace W. Abbey Collection is one of many in the Center's Railroad Heritage Visual Archive, which numbers more than 200,000 photographs. The Center is a not-for-profit arts and education organization whose mission is to preserve and present significant images of railroading. In addition to collecting and publishing, other activities include producing traveling exhibitions, hosting conferences and other events, and sponsoring an annual awards program. Learn more at www.railphoto-art.org.

As representatives of the Center, the authors are deeply grateful for the assistance of all the aforementioned people. We also acknowledge that any errors of fact or interpretation are ours alone.

—*Kevin P. Keefe and Scott Lothes,*
Madison, Wisconsin,
January 2018

Note: Photographs, unless otherwise noted, by Wallace W. Abbey, Collection of the Center for Railroad Photography & Art, www.railphoto-art.org

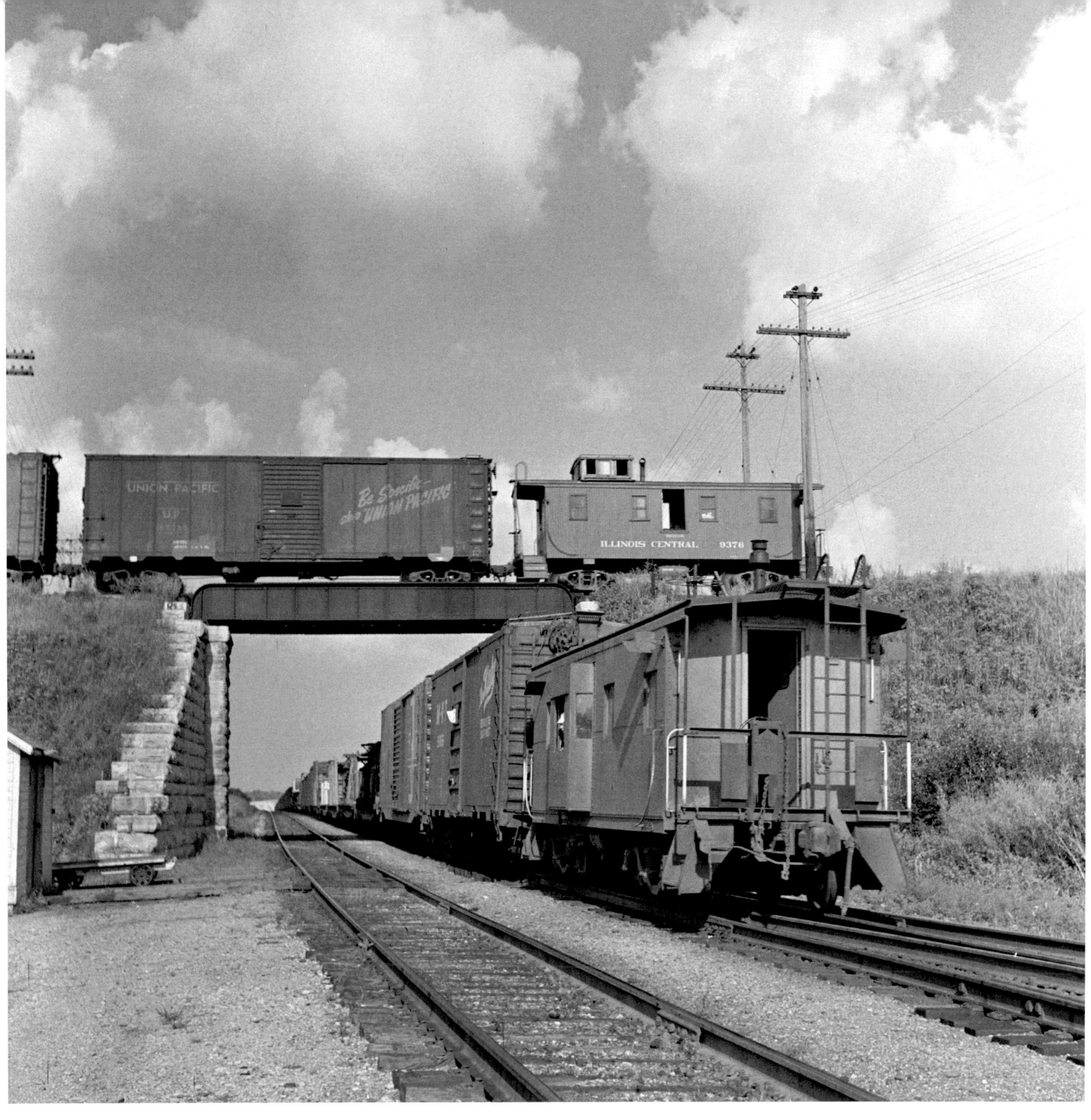

Cabooses bring up the rear of Milwaukee Road and Illinois Central freight trains at Forreston, Illinois, in the summer of 1957.

INDEX

Locators in italics indicate photographs.

Abbey, Margaret Squier, 4
Abbey, Martha Jewett, 5, 64; death, 10
Abbey, Wallace W., II, 4, 5
Abbey, Wallace W., III (biographical and personal material): Abbey Enterprises, 172; at Association of American Railroads, 10; at Association of Western Railways, 9, 64; at C&NW, 9, 25, 128; at CB&Q, 9, 127; childhood in Chicago, 4, 127; *Class By Itself*, 158; daughters Mary and Martha, 5, 10, 64; death, 10; Evanston Township High School, 4; Fred A. & Jane R. Stindt Photography Award, 201; influence on photography, 3; Interstate Commerce Commission activities, 95; *Little Jewel, The*, 9, 96–97; love of music, 4, 203; marriage to Martha Jewett, 5; at Milwaukee Road, 9, *28–29*; photography, early, 6; railroad summer jobs, 9; at *Railway Age*, 9; at Santa Fe's 21st Street Shop, 9, 127, 158; self-portrait, *25, 27, 30*; at Soo Line, 9, 95–97; "Super Railroad" story, 34, 64; at *Trains* magazine, 5, 7, *31*, 34, 63–64
Algren, Nelson, 128
Akin, Bill, 7
Amtrak: *Empire Builder* at Minneapolis, *17*
Anderson, Willard V., 64

Association of American Railroads: Transportation Technology Center, 10
Association of Western Railways, 9, 64, 172
Atchison, Topeka & Santa Fe Railway: Abbey's favorite railroad, 33; near Albuquerque, *59*; Albuquerque Shops, 34, *37*; Argentine Yard, 34, *167*; Cajon Pass, *57, 58*; Chanute, KS, *38*; Chanute, KS, FT diesels at, *167*; *Chicagoan*, at Kansas City, *12, 49*; *Chicagoan*, at Lawrence, KS, *41*; *Chief* at Joliet, IL, *156*; Corwith Yard, *51*; Dearborn Station, *39, 40, 46*; dining-car worker, *56*; Edelstein Hill, *44*; 18th Street engine house, *141, 153*; *El Capitan*, *8*, 7, 64; Emporia roundhouse, *45*; *Fast Mail Express* at Turner, KS, *165*; FTs at Berwyn, IL, *168*; FT engineer, *163*; *Grand Canyon*, at Chicago, *126*; *Grand Canyon*, Holliday, KS, *61*; *Grand Canyon*, at Joliet, *62*; *Grand Canyon*, at Sibley, MO, *54*; M.154 "doodlebug," *14*; Matfield Green, KS, *55*; *Oil Flyer*, 4, 34; *Oil Flyer*, at Chanute, KS, *42*; *Oil Flyer*, at Cherryvale, *50*; Olathe Hill, *6*, 32, 34; PA diesels at Lemont, IL, *43*; summer job, 9; *Super Chief*, at Dearborn Station, *151*; *Super Chief*, at Newton, KS, *48*; *Super Chief*, at Pasadena, *60*; "Super Railroad" story, 34, 64; Tehachapi Pass, *60*; *Texas Chief* at Oklahoma City, *36*; track worker, *90*; train orders at Ottawa, KS, *52*; Tulsa Subdivision, 4, 33; *Tulsan*, *34*; 2-8-2 at Chillicothe, IL, *35*; Williamsburg, KS, *53*

Baltimore & Ohio Railroad: at Cincinnati Union Terminal, *89*; at Grand Central Station, Chicago, *149*; *Cincinnatian* at Deshler, OH, *72*; EM-1 at Cumberland, MD, *77*; washing diesel at Cumberland, *91*
Bergene, John, 96
Burlington Northern, 9; freight at St. Paul, *22*

Canadian Pacific, 95, 100, 106, 111, 187
Center for Railroad Photography & Art, 201, 207
Central States Dispatch, 64, 69
Chanute, KS, 5, 7, 34, 38, 42, 167
Chanute Daily Tribune, 5, 34
Cherryvale, KS, 4, 5, 11, 14, 15, 33, 34, *50*
Chesapeake & Ohio Railway: E8 at Cincinnati Union Terminal, *90*; GP9s at White Sulphur Springs, W.Va., *16*
Chicago, Burlington & Quincy Railroad, 9, 127; Cicero Yard, *148*; FTs at West Hinsdale, IL, *162*; *Pioneer Zephyr* conductor, *74*; 14th Street coach yards, *135*; *Zephyrs*, *171*
Chicago, Illinois, 4, 5, 9, 10, 33, 34, 39, 40, 46, 51, 112, 127–129, *129–155*, 158, 159, 168, 172, 179, 189, 201

Chicago, Milwaukee, St. Paul & Pacific Railroad. *See* Milwaukee Road
Chicago, Rock Island & Pacific. *See* Rock Island
Chicago & North Western Railway, 4, 9, 128; Canal Street tower, *130*; Chicago Avenue roundhouse, *139*; 400 passenger trains, 128, *171*; Iroquois (S.D.) depot, *20–21*; FTs, at Elburn, IL, *166*; FTs, at Kickapoo Jct., IL, *161*; FTs, at Rochelle, IL, *164*; Mayfair tower, 128; North Western Terminal, 33, *131*, *132*, *140*; *Twin Cities 400*, at Milwaukee, *68*, *83*; *Twin Cities 400*, at Clyman Junction, WI, *82*; *Twin Cities 400*, at Evanston, *143*; *Viking* at Devils Lake, WI, *81*
Chicago & Western Indiana Railroad: State Line Tower, *145*
Chicago Tribune, 4, 5
Chicago Union Station, 127, *144*, *146*, *179*
Cincinnati Union Terminal, 2, 3, 64, *88*, *89*, *90*, 201; rotunda, *200*
Classic Trains, 64, 201, 204
Cole, Ted, *30*

Dearborn Station, Chicago, 33, *39*, *40*, *46*, 127, *137*, *151*, 158
Draney, John, 158
Duluth, South Shore & Atlantic Railroad. *See* Soo Line

Electro-Motive FT, 157–158; C&NW, at Elburn, IL, *166*; C&NW, at Kickapoo Jct., IL, *161*; C&NW, at Rochelle, IL, *164*; CB&Q at West Hinsdale, IL, *162*; *Class By Itself*, 158; Erie at Maybrook, N.Y., *160*; Santa Fe, at 18th Street engine house, *159*; Santa Fe, at Argentine Yard, *169*; Santa Fe, at Berwyn, IL, *168*; Santa Fe, at Chanute, KS, *167*; Santa Fe, at Joliet, *156*; Santa Fe, at Turner, KS, *165*; Santa Fe engineer, *163*
Englewood Union Station, *154*; *155*
Entringer, Rosemary, *31*, 64

Erie Railroad, 64; Hudson River car floats, *65*; Flying Saucer, *66*; Croxton Yard, *67*; FTs at Maybrook, N.Y., *160*
Evanston, IL, 4–7, 128, *143*

Falls City, NE, 4, 10
Frailey, Fred W., 6, 204
Fred Harvey, 34
Frisco Railroad. *See* St. Louis-San Francisco
FT diesel. *See* Electro-Motive FT

Grand Central Station, Chicago, 127, *149*, *150*
Grand Trunk Western: 4-8-4 at Dearborn Station, *137*
Great Northern: crossing Soo at Crystal Tower, *23*; "Mid-Century" *Empire Builder* at Chicago, IL, *135*; Nicollet Island Bridge, Minneapolis, MN, *17*
Griffiths, Henry R., 7
Gruber, John, 64, 201, *203*

Hale, Robert, 7
Harkness, Vint, 5
Harley, Tom, 5
Hastings, Philip R., 7
Hiawathas. *See* Milwaukee Road
Hillman, Stanley E.G., 172

Illinois Central Railroad: 4-8-2 at Madison, IL, *73*; caboose at Forreston, IL, *205*; freight on St. Charles Air Line, *152*; switchers at 21st Street, Chicago, *133*
Interstate Commerce Commission, 95

Jensen, Axel, 6
Jewett, J. M., Dr., 5
Jewett, Martha. *See* Abbey, Martha Jewett
Jewett, Mavis Laizure, 5
Joliet, IL, *62*, *156*

Kalmbach, Albert C., 5, 7, 63
Kansas City Union Station, *12*, *49*, *85*

Kerrigan, Chic, 5, *30*
Kooistra, Blair, 7–8, 204

Lamb, J. Parker, 7
LaSalle Street Station, Chicago, 127, *129*, *136*
LaVake, James A., 7
Lehigh & Hudson River Railroad: at Andover, N.J., *69*
Lothes, Scott, 201, 204, 207
Little Jewel, The, 9, *96*

McElroy, Bob, 5
McGonigal, Robert S., 201, 204
McMullen, Katie, *31*
Middleton, William D., 7
Milwaukee Road, 9, 171–173; 4-4-2 washed at Milwaukee Shops, *174*; 4-8-4, at Elgin, IL, *176*; 4-8-4, at Rondout, IL, *177*, *178*; Baldwin diesels at St. Paul, *180*; bankruptcy, 172; Beer Line (Milwaukee), 172, *173*, *184*; Bicentennial diesel, *189*; Bitterroot Mountains, *198*; caboose at Forreston, IL, *205*; child in full-length dome, *182*; commuter train at Libertyville, IL, *190*; Duplainville (WI) tower, *191*; Donald, MT, *193*; Haugan, MT, *199*; *Hiawathas*, *171*; *Hiawathas*, at Chicago Union Station, *179*; Hillman, Stanley E. G., 172; Grand Crossing tower, La Crosse, WI, *185*, *186*; Medary Tower, La Crosse, *186*; Milwaukee Shops, *187*, *188*; *Morning Hiawatha*, at Grayland Tower, *142*; *Morning Hiawatha*, at Milwaukee, *175*, *183*; Ogilvie, Richard B., 172; Pacific Extension, 172; Pig's Eye Yard (St. Paul), *181*; St. Regis, MT, *194*; SD40-2 diesels at Lanark, IL, *195*; Skytop car, *170*; Smith, Worthington, 172; stored diesels, *197*; switchman at Wheaton, MN, *196*; Tower A-20, *148*; Vendome Loop, MT, *192*
Minneapolis, St. Paul & Sault Ste. Marie Railroad. *See* Soo Line
Morgan, David P., 5, 6, 7, 9, *31*, 34, 61, 64, *103*; 158, 207

New York Central Railroad: Beech Grove Shops, *76*, *93*; E7 at Cincinnati Union Terminal, *90*; Hudson at Cincinnati Union Terminal, *88*; *James Whitcomb Riley*, 2, 3; *New England States* at LaSalle Street Station, *136*; Toledo station, *71*; *20th Century Limited* at Chicago, *129*

North Shore Line: Chicago street scene, *146*

Northwestern University, 4, 5, 172

O'Dell, Grover, UP operator, 24

Ogilvie, Richard B., 172, 199

Omaha Union Station, *86*, *88*

Penn Station (New York), *70*

Pennsylvania Railroad, 4, 64; E8 at Cincinnati Union Terminal, *90*; Englewood Union Station, *154*; GG1 at Secaucus, N.J., *67*; K4 at 21st Street, Chicago, *134*; Penn Station (New York), *70*

Peoria & Eastern Railroad: freight train, *75*

Railroad Magazine, 5, 7

Railway Age magazine, 9, 95, 172

Railway & Locomotive Historical Society, 201

Reid, H., 7

Rock Island: Golden State, at Joliet, IL, *62*; at Chicago, *129*; at St. Paul, *197*

Roosevelt Road (Chicago), 5, 127, 128

Shaughnessy, Jim, 7

Sims, Don, 7

Smith, Worthington, 172

Soo Line, 9, 95–97, 172; Ashland ore dock, *99*; *Atlantic Limited*, *97*; bowling team, *104*; Boyd (WI) depot, *103*; caboose hop, *112*; Crystal Tower, *23*; derailment at Duplainville, WI, *119*; Duplainville tower, *123*; F3 diesel at Prentice, WI, *120*; freight train on Camden Place Bridge, *101*, *107*; freight train on Robert Street Bridge, *116*; *Laker* at Chicago, *150*; Murray, Leonard H., *114*; New Richmond (WI) depot, *110*; North Fond du Lac (WI) yard, *122*; paint scheme, *96*; piggyback train at Shoreham Yard, *100*; RS-27 diesels, *109*, *110*; SD40 diesels at Turtle Lake, WI; *124*; St. Croix River bridge, *113*; Shoreham Yard, *94*, *105*, *106*, *111*, *114*; snow-fighting, *117*, *118*; track workers, *121*; train 7 at Minneapolis, *98*; train orders at Mundelein, IL, *108*; train orders at New Richmond, *102*; U30C on Shoreham turntable, *115*

South Kansas & Oklahoma Railroad, 34

Squier, Samuel Webner, 4, 33

Squier, Luella Russell, 4, 33

State Line Tower, 128, *145*

Steinheimer, Richard, 7

St. Louis-San Francisco Railroad, 4, 34; at Cherryvale, KS, *11*, *15*

Swanson, Joseph A., 172

Trailer Train Company, 10

Trains magazine (including *Trains & Travel*), 3, 5, 7, *31*, 34, 41, 63–64, 128, 171, 201, 204

Transportation Technology Center. *See* Association of American Railroads

Union Pacific, 26, 64; 4-12-2, at Lawrence, KS, *13*; 4-12-2, at North Platte, NE, *80*; Challengers at North Platte, NE, *79*; *City of Portland* at Chicago, *132*, *146*; *City of San Francisco* at Chicago, *132*; *City of St. Louis* at Denver, *84*; Council Bluffs roundhouse, *87*; Green River, WY, *78*; Hermosa Tunnel, *18–19*; operator at East Portland Tower, *24*; Omaha, *88*

University of Kansas, 5, 12, 34, 207

Wabash Railroad: 4-6-4 at Dearborn Station, *138*

Wallace, Dave, 5

Wisconsin Central Railroad. *See* Soo Line

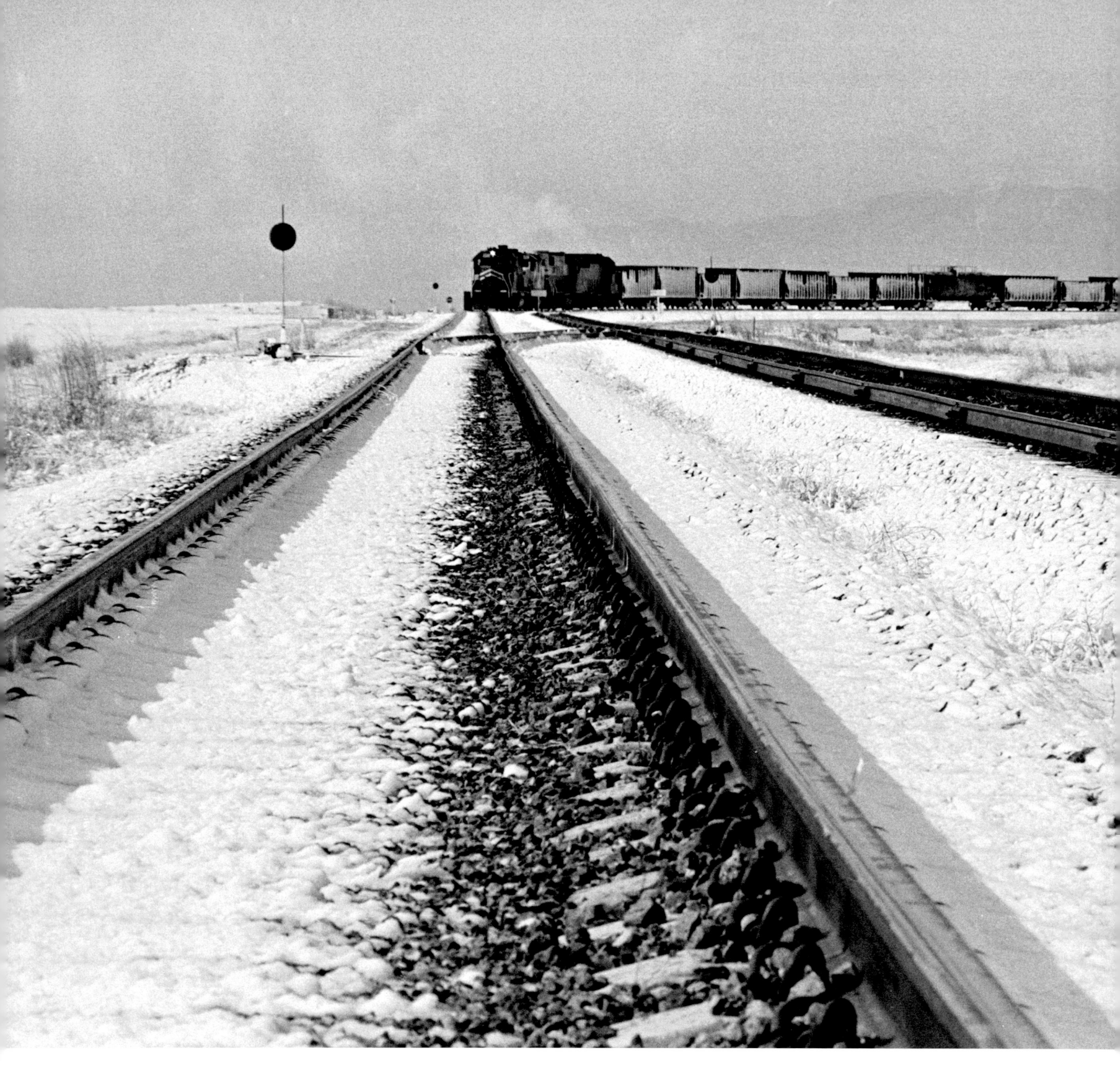

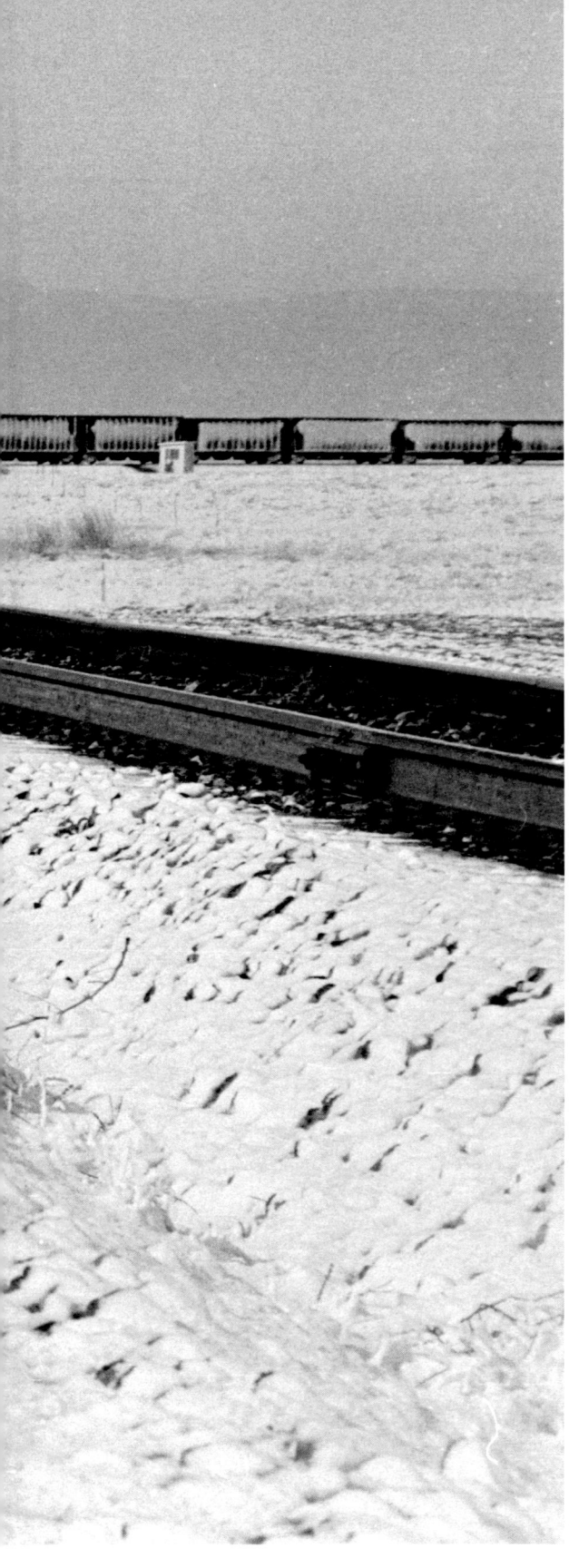

Wallace W. Abbey, 1927–2014, had a long career as a railroad journalist and public relations executive. A native of Chicago and graduate of the journalism program at the University of Kansas, he joined the staff of *Trains* magazine in Milwaukee, Wisconsin, in 1950, where he worked alongside legendary editor David P. Morgan. Transitioning to a railroad industry career in public relations, he held executive positions at the Soo Line in Minneapolis, Minnesota, as well as at the Milwaukee Road in Chicago. The insider access afforded by his career allowed the talented photographer to capture a singular perspective of railroading in the Upper Midwest spanning the dramatic period of the 1940s through the 1970s.

Kevin P. Keefe is a Milwaukee-based journalist. He was the editor of *Trains* magazine from 1992 through 2000 and subsequently served as the magazine's publisher. He was also vice president–editorial at the parent firm of *Trains*, Kalmbach Publishing Co., until he retired in 2016. He is a director of the Center for Railroad Photography & Art. His award-winning book *Twelve Twenty-Five: The Life and Times of a Steam Locomotive* was published in 2016 by Michigan State University Press.

Scott Lothes is president and executive director of the Center for Railroad Photography & Art in Madison, Wisconsin, and editor of its journal, *Railroad Heritage*. He is also a freelance author and award-winning photographer whose work appears frequently in *Trains*, *Railfan & Railroad*, and other national publications. Originally from West Virginia, he was graduated magna cum laude from Case Western Reserve University in Cleveland, Ohio, in 2002. He served as the assistant editor of the engineering magazine *Sound & Vibration* and taught English at a high school in Sapporo, Japan, prior to joining the Center's staff in 2008.

The Center for Railroad Photography & Art, www.railphoto-art.org, is a nonprofit arts and education organization based in Madison, Wisconsin, whose mission is to preserve and present significant images of railroading. Its work includes preserving collections of railroad photography and art (including that of Wallace W. Abbey), preparing and circulating traveling exhibitions, publishing a quarterly journal and books, hosting conferences and other events, and making annual awards for creative photography.